MERGERS AND ACQUISITIONS HANDBOOK FOR SMALL AND MIDSIZE COMPANIES

MERGERS AND ACQUISITIONS HANDBOOK FOR SMALL AND MIDSIZE COMPANIES

EDITED BY THOMAS L. WEST AND JEFFREY D. JONES

JOHN WILEY & SONS, INC.

New York • Chichester • Weinheim • Brisbane • Singapore • Toronto

ISBN 0-471-13330-2

Printed in the United States of America

10 9 8 7 6 5

Editors

THOMAS L. WEST, founder of Business Brokerage Press and creator of many of its publications, has been in business brokerage for over 30 years. He was also the founder of United Business Investments, a California-based business brokerage firm that operated over 50 company-owned offices in 10 states, and co-founder of VR Business Brokers, the nation's largest franchised network of business brokerage offices.

He is the editor and publisher of *The Business Brokers*, the leading industry newsletter, now in its fourteenth year, and publisher of *M&A Today*, a leading newsletter for the mergers and acquisitions industry. In addition to the books published by Business Brokerage Press, his other books include: *Buying Your Own Small Business* and *Buying a Franchise*. He is co-editor of *Handbook of Business Valuation* published by John Wiley & Sons, Inc.

West is nationally recognized as an expert in the field of business brokerage and is widely quoted in newspapers, magazines, and other media. He conducts seminars on business brokerage, small business, and franchising around the country, and frequently serves as a consultant in these areas. He was founder, past president and executive director of the International Business Brokers Association.

JEFFREY D. JONES has been a business broker and appraiser for the past 20 years. As president of Certified Appraisers, Inc., he manages the firm's multidiscipline appraisal practice, which includes valuation of businesses, machinery and equipment, and real estate. As chairman of Certified Business Brokers, he and his staff of 18 agents have been involved in over 1,000 business sales since 1976.

Jones holds a master's degree from Pepperdine University and is licensed by the Texas Real Estate Commission and the Texas Securities Commission. He is a designated senior member of the American Society of Appraisers (ASA), the Institute of Business Appraisers (CBA), Texas Association of Business Brokers (BCB), and the International Business Brokers Association (CBI).

Jones serves as the editor of the *IBBA Journal,* a technical journal for the business brokerage industry, and is the current chairman of the IBBA's Standards Committee. For the past eight years, he has served on ASA's Standards Committee.

During the past 16 years, Jones has served as a business counselor with SCORE, a voluntary group of executives sponsored by the Small Business Administration (SBA). He has taught a variety of topics including buying, selling, financing, and operating small to midsized businesses.

Contributors

Weston Anson is Chairman of Trademark & Licensing Associates, Inc., a licensing/consulting firm specializing in trademark, patent, and copyright licensing, valuations, and expert testimony. The firm is headquartered in La Jolla, California, and has offices on the East Coast, New York City, and London. He served for six years as vice president of the Licensing Industry Merchandisers' Association, and is a current member of its Board of Directors. He also serves as chairman of the Valuation Committee of the Licensing Executives Society, and was chairman of the Trademark Licensing Committee for three years.

Anson was also senior vice president of Hang Ten International, which grew to about 100 licensees in 30 countries under his direction. Since founding Trademark & Licensing Associates, Inc. in 1980, he has developed numerous licensing strategies for major corporations and has performed valuations of hundreds of intellectual property components.

He has published over 75 articles in the United States and overseas, and is active in nearly all international trademark associations as a speaker and officer. He travels extensively, counseling major multinational corporations and small companies in the United States and overseas.

David M. Bishop is a principal with The Bishop Law Firm, Charlotte, North Carolina. Bishop is an attorney, CPA, business appraiser, and intermediary. He has a B.S. in Business Administration and a J.D. from the University of North Carolina, Chapel Hill. His firm provides mergers and acquisitions advisory, valuation, and intermediary services to small and midsize businesses. He has written numerous articles on buying and selling businesses and has participated in the purchase and sale of 75 businesses.

James J. Blaha is principal in BAC, Inc., Chicago, Illinois. It is one of the Midwest's oldest privately held merger-acquisition firms, specializing in middle-market companies. He is a graduate of Northwestern University, B.S. with Honors, CPA/Financial Management; and he holds an M.B.A., G.M.D., from the University of New York at Buffalo. Blaha is a former executive with the Westinghouse Electric Corporation. He serves on the board of directors of several companies.

Ann C. Bonis is a senior associate of O'Connor Broude & Aronson, which is a law firm serving emerging businesses, principally in the high-technology area. It concentrates in business planning and corporate, tax, and securities law. Bonis holds an A.B. from Bowdoin College and a J.D. from Harvard Law School.

Theodore Burbank is president of the Burbank Group, Inc. of Shrewsbury, Massachusetts. Since 1979, he has consulted with and provided valuation, marketing, and sales assistance to more than 2,000 family and private business owners.

Burbank authored *In and Out of Business . . . Happily,* published by Parker & Nelson Publishing; and he was a contributing author of *Handbook of Business Valuations,* published by John Wiley & Sons, Inc. He also has written many articles on business sales and valuations, and conducted seminars and addressed many trade associations in the United States and Canada on family and private business transfers and valuations.

Ramon Carrion is an attorney at law specializing in immigration and international law. He is a frequent lecturer and speaker on the subject of foreign investment in the United States, and is currently president-elect of the Central Florida Chapter of the American Immigration Lawyers' Association. Carrion holds a B.A. from Rutgers University and a J.D. from Rutgers Law School. A member of the New Jersey and Florida bars, he is based in Clearwater, Florida.

George E. Christodoulo is a partner in the Corporate Department and a member of the Intellectual Property Group and the Family Business Group, Burns & Levinson, Boston, Massachusetts. He has spent over 20 years in private practice in Boston, counseling both private and public established and emerging growth companies, as well as individual investors in general corporate, securities, financing and restructuring, mergers and acquisitions, and real estate matters.

In the area of intellectual property, Christodoulo represents clients and speaks and writes on electronic privacy, security, and copyright protection, focusing on the implementation of a comprehensive corporate policy to protect the corporate entity and its officers. He received an A.B. (magna cum laude) from Harvard College, an M.B.A. from Harvard University School of Business Administration, and a J.D. from Harvard Law School. He is a graduate of Northfield Mt. Hermon School.

William H. Dunn, B.S. Engineering, Princeton University, J.D., Stanford Law School, has been in private law practice for 35 years in the San Jose, California area specializing in the sales of businesses and real estate. He has served as an instructor at West Valley College in Saratoga and for the University of California extension, teaching courses in real estate law and sales of businesses. He has served as a panelist for statewide programs of the California Continuing Education of the Bar and the California Escrow Association on the sale of businesses. He has appeared before numerous real estate boards and bar association groups. He currently presents a one-day seminar entitled "The Sale of a Business," approved by the California Department of Real Estate for continuing education credit.

Gayle P. Ehrlich is a partner in Sullivan & Worcester, a Boston-based law firm, where she specializes in corporate restructuring, reorganization, and bankruptcy. The firm, which also maintains offices in New York City and Washington, D.C., provides a broad range of legal services to its business clients.

Ehrlich holds a B.A. from Sarah Lawrence College and a J.D. from Cardozo School of Law. She was law clerk for the Honorable Harold Lavien, United States Bankruptcy Judge, District of Massachusetts. She is a member of Massachusetts, New York, and Rhode Island bars and frequently appears on behalf of clients in court proceedings throughout the country.

Ehrlich is experienced in representing parties to transactions involving the sale of troubled businesses, both in and outside of bankruptcy.

Darrell L. Fouts is the founder and president of Colorado Business Consultants, Inc., Denver, Colorado. This firm, founded in 1978, specializes in the sale of manufacturing and distribution companies with sales of $1 to $20 million.

Fouts received his B.S. in Business Administration from the University of Nebraska, and has done graduate work in management and marketing at the University of Colorado. He has owned and operated 13 businesses in widely diversified industries. Fouts has extensive experience as a consultant, business developer, and chief executive officer. He is a past president and former member of the Board of Directors of the

International Business Brokers Association. Fouts is a nationally recognized lecturer in the area of midsized company sales.

Richard Houlihan is the founder of Houlihan Valuation Advisors, a national firm of financial professionals focusing on business valuation and related financial consulting. He currently is a principal in the Orange County office.

Houlihan has a B.S. in Accounting from Brigham Young University, and has completed coursework on his master's degree in Valuation Sciences at Lindenwood College. Houlihan is a Certified Public Accountant (CPA), and has earned the Accredited Senior Appraiser (ASA) designation from the American Society of Appraisers where he currently serves on the Business Valuation Committee and its Public Relations Committee. In addition, Houlihan serves on the Southern Nevada Estate Planning Council.

Houlihan has authored many articles in local and national publications on subjects such as estate tax freezes, methods of measuring worth, the value of a business, ESOPs, and tax reform.

G. William Hubbard II is a partner in the Chicago office of the law firm of Hinshaw & Culbertson, which has 14 offices located in Wisconsin, Missouri, and Florida. His areas of concentration include corporate and securities transactions, mergers and acquisitions, joint ventures, taxation, and family business and succession planning. He graduated from the United States Military Academy (B.S., 1973) and IIT Chicago-Kent College of Law (J.D., with high honors, 1978) and is a Certified Public Accountant. He thanks his partner, Ed Proctor, and attorney, Patti Mehler, for their comments and editorial suggestions.

Thomas H. Jacoby is president of Mercor, Inc., a Columbus, Ohio, merger and acquisition consulting firm. As both a Certified Public Accountant and a Certified Valuation Analyst, Jacoby has been involved in nearly 1,100 valuation engagements. As a consultant, a merger and acquisition dealmaker for Mercor, and as an affiliate intermediary of the Geneva Companies, he has also participated in the sale of more than 60 midsized private industrial companies.

J. Michael Julius is a vice president of Mercer Capital, Memphis, Tennessee. He has completed over 250 projects in the area of business valuation and financial consulting for client companies operating in a wide variety of industries.

He holds a B.A. from Rhodes College (magna cum laude, Phi Beta Kappa) and was a Fulbright Scholar in Economics. He is an Accredited Senior Appraiser and Chartered Financial Analyst.

Stallworth M. Larson is the founder and president of Corporate Growth Services, which was established in 1986 to provide professional merger and acquisition intermediary services on a national and international basis for clients seeking to sell, buy, or arrange financing for mid-sized businesses.

Prior to starting Corporate Growth Services, from 1981 to 1986, Larson was chairman and chief executive officer of Custom American Furniture, Newtown, Connecticut, a case goods manufacturer.

From 1969 to 1981, Larson was at the Chase Manhattan Bank, New York City where he was a vice president. From 1980 to 1981, he worked in the Project Finance Division of the Merchant Banking Group, where he advised and assisted major multinational corporations and domestic and foreign government entities in structuring, negotiating, and arranging finance for multisponsored international and domestic projects.

Larson has an M.B.A. in Finance from Columbia University, and is a 1963 graduate of Yale University.

Kevin Macdonald is director of Accounting and Audit at Macdonald, Levine, Jenkins & Co., P.C., Boston, Massachusetts. MLJ is a 20-professional CPA firm that specializes in providing accounting, tax, and management consulting services to closely held businesses and their owners.

Robert B. Machiz is the president of Exchange Capital, Inc., a Phoenix-based firm specializing in the sale, purchase, and financing of middle-market companies with sales in the $1 million to $50 million range. Exchange Capital, Inc. was established in 1990. In addition, Machiz is a principal of MoneySoft, Inc., a developer and publisher of software for business valuation, capital development, structuring business transfers (mergers, acquisitions, LBOs, and employee stock ownership plans), and corporate financial planning.

His career as an intermediary started in 1987 when he joined American Business Group, Inc., Dallas, Texas. Previously, Machiz managed the Federal Plastics Division of Federal Chicago Corporation, with business interests in thermoinjection molded plastics, toolmaking, printing, and aluminum die-casting. He has authored numerous articles on the negotiation and structure of business transfers.

Machiz attended Southampton College, and holds an Arizona Real Estate Sales License; his professional affiliations include the International Business Brokers Association, the M&A Source, the Financial Intelligence Network, and the World M&A Network.

John D. Menke is a tax attorney and an experienced professional in the field of employee benefits. Prior to founding Menke & Associates, Inc. in 1974, he was associated with the law firm of Kelso, Cotton, Seligman &

Ray, where he practiced in the fields of tax planning and deferred compensation.

Menke has authored over 20 articles regarding qualified plans and estate planning techniques, as well as a leading book on employee stock ownership plans.

Menke received his B.A. from the University of Texas and his LL.B. from Yale Law School.

Z. Christopher Mercer is the president of Mercer Capital, Memphis, Tennessee, a leading valuation firm. He holds the Accredited Senior Appraiser designation from the American Society of Appraisers, and the Chartered Financial Analyst designation from the Association for Investment Management and Research.

Mercer is a graduate of Stetson University (cum laude) and holds an M.A. from Vanderbilt University in Economics. He has served as the vice-chairman of the American Society of Appraiser's International Board of Examiners, and has been a faculty member of the University of Maryland, Memphis State University, and the Mid-South School of Banking.

Mercer has testified and provided depositions in many business valuation court cases. He is a frequent speaker on business valuation issues; in addition, he has written several books and articles. He serves on the board of directors of several companies and charitable organizations.

Leslie H. Miles, Jr. is chief executive officer of MB Valuation Services, Inc., an international appraisal firm and sales company with offices throughout the world. He is acknowledged as having designed and implemented the most sophisticated and widely accepted, appraisal-oriented, computer technology system for the asset-based lending community.

Miles is a senior member of the American Society of Appraisers, certified in the machinery and equipment, real estate, and technical valuation disciplines. He is also a senior member of several appraisal societies, past chairman of ASA's M&E Committee, and currently serves on the faculty for ASA educational courses. He is a licensed real estate broker, state certified in Texas and Colorado, and holds auctioneer licenses in Texas and many other states.

Miles has appeared as an expert witness in federal and state courts throughout the United States. He is a former director of the American Bankruptcy Institute (ABI) and is the only appraiser who is a fellow of ABI's College of Fellows.

Miles publishes *Market & Valuations,* a newsletter for the lending industry. He is a column writer for the MTS and ABI Journals, and has been published many times in the Commercial Finance Association's *The Secured Lender* magazine. He also has published two books and numerous papers.

Miles has spoken in the United States, Europe, and China, and has been a speaker for colleges, numerous educational seminars and courses throughout the world.

Russell Robb started and sold three small businesses between 1963 and 1983. Since 1985, he has been a mergers and acquisitions intermediary for O'Conor, Wright Wyman, Inc., Boston, Massachusetts. Robb is the author of *Buying Your Own Business* and is the editor of *M&A Today,* a national newsletter.

Robert W. Scarlata is founder and president of The March Group, Nashville, Tennessee, which specializes in the sale of midsized companies and provides acquisition searches and business valuations.

Scarlata has a B.S. in Business Administration from the University of Connecticut and a J.D. from the University of Miami in Florida. He started in business at the age of 21 at the University of Connecticut, renting refrigerators to students; at one time, he owned 500. Scarlata was a sales engineer for over 10 years selling highly sophisticated and expensive machinery to the paper plastics industry.

Scarlata is a member of the International Business Brokers Association and received his Certified Business Intermediary designation (CBI).

John W. Slater, Jr. is the founder and managing partner of Asset Services, L.P. of Memphis, Tennessee. Asset Services provides financial advisory and investment banking services to private business with a focus on mergers and acquisitions. During 1995, Slater served as president of M&A International, a worldwide network of independent investment banking and financial advisory firms. He graduated from Princeton University in 1970 with an A.B. in Economics; he also has a J.D. from the University of Virginia Law School. In 1986, he achieved the professional designation Chartered Financial Analyst. Prior to forming Asset Services in 1985, Slater engaged in the private practice of law for nine years, emphasizing the areas of securities law, corporate financing, and taxation. He also served for three years as a senior professional in the corporate finance department of a New York Stock Exchange member firm.

Professional honors include service as chairman of the program of Publicly Traded Limited Partnerships at the 1983 American Bar Association Annual Meeting. Professional writings include, *Capital Accumulation in an Age of Security; A Requiem for the American Corporation; New Tools to Make Commercial Loan Pricing More Effective; How Bankers Can Prepare for the Coming Recession;* and *Vertical Mergers of For-Profit Home Care Providers.* Slater is a member of the Association for Corporate Growth.

Lawrence E. Stirtz is a founder and the chairman of Stirtz Bernards Boyden Surdel & Larter. He is the company's liaison partner with Moores Rowland International. Prior to forming Stirtz Bernards, he was partner-in-charge of the tax department in the Minneapolis office of an international accounting firm, and the Midwest region representative to its national tax advisory committee. Previous to that he was a partner in a Twin Cities CPA firm.

He has been a lecturer and instructor on taxation and financial planning for the American College, the University of Minnesota, and the Minnesota Society of Certified Public Accountants.

Stirtz co-authored an article and paper on ownership succession presented at the forty-third New York University Institute of Taxation. He has written testimony on tax reform in connection with the Minnesota Society of Certified Public Accountants tax committees.

He received his B.S. in business administration from the University of Nebraska and his master's in business taxation from the University of Minnesota.

Bret Tack is a principal in the Los Angeles office of Houlihan Valuation Advisors, a national firm of financial professionals focusing on business valuation and related financial consulting.

Tack has a B.S. in Business Administration from the University of Southern California with an emphasis in finance. Tack has earned the Accredited Senior Appraiser (ASA) designation from the American Society of Appraisers.

Over the past 11 years, Tack has valued over 500 businesses in a wide variety of industries for purposes including mergers and acquisitions, estate and tax planning, employee stock ownership plans, and litigation support. Tack has also spoken on valuation-related topics to numerous legal and professional organizations.

Maxwell J. "Mac" Taub has been a business broker and business appraiser on Long Island since 1985. He is the president of M.J. Taub Associates, Inc. in Forest Hills, New York. He has been involved in the sale or appraisal of closely held companies, from tiny retail operations to midsized wholesalers and manufacturers in a wide variety of industries. His appraisals have been performed for purposes as diverse as buy-sell, marital dissolution, dissenting shareholder actions, estate planning, partner disputes, and gift and estate taxes.

Taub has spoken numerous times on purchasing and valuing a business. He has published over a dozen articles in various technical journals on selling, buying, and valuing businesses.

Edward C. Telling, Jr. is the founder and president of E.C. Telling, Jr. Associates, Inc., Syracuse, New York. This firm specializes in business brokerage transactions of $500,000 or larger.

Telling has a B.S. in Business Administration from Drexel University and an M.B.A. in Business Corporate Finance from Cornell University. He was also a member of the President's Financial Staff of the General

Motors Corporation. He served as captain in the United States Army. Telling has operated E.C. Telling, Jr. and Associates since 1982.

Telling is a member of the Corporate Acquisitions and Mergers Affiliates (CAMA) and the International Business Brokers Association (IBBA), where he currently serves on the Board of Directors. He is also a member of the Institute of Business Appraisers in the Greater Syracuse Board of Realtors. He is the author of the Professional Packaging System (the most popular brokerage packaging system available), which is a software program that provides business packaging services.

Dennis J. White is a partner in Sullivan & Worcester, a Boston-based law firm, where he is director of the firm's Corporate Law Department. The firm, which also maintains offices in New York City and Washington, D.C., provides a broad range of legal services to its business clients.

White holds a B.A. in English, summa cum laude, from the College of the Holy Cross and a J.D., cum laude, from Harvard Law School. He is listed in *Who's Who in American Law*.

He frequently represents clients involved in business acquisitions and combination, both on the sell and buy side of such transactions. Many of such transactions involve target companies that are troubled businesses.

Contents

Introduction

The sale or acquisition of a business is a complex transaction frequently requiring the expertise of many advisors. It would be difficult, if not impossible, for any one person to have the knowledge in all the related professions to write a book on this topic. Like our previous volume, *Handbook of Business Valuation,* we have asked experts to contribute chapters on issues within their expertise so that this book can cover a broader spectrum of topics than would otherwise be possible. Some subjects called for the expertise of the lawyer or accountant, others required the experience of the deal-maker, while still others needed the knowledge of the business appraiser. Finding the appropriate experts has been a challenge.

We asked our contributors to assume that the reader had no, or very limited, knowledge of the subject that they were writing about. Such a variety of subjects are covered that we doubt any of our readers are familiar with them all. This assumption of absence of knowledge, enabled us to produce a book of benefit to more people.

This book should be of interest to anyone who is even remotely involved in the buying or selling of small or midsized companies. As noted, a myriad of subjects are covered, and several of our contributors were concerned that their chapters would overlap some of the territory of other writers. We were not concerned because we believe one of the advantages of using many contributors is that the reader is offered information from various viewpoints.

We may, however, have left out some topics that our readers feel should have been included; we are aware that there may be some gaps. For example, because the tax laws are everchanging, we elected not to attempt to cover certain tax issues. We also felt that some subjects could not be dealt with adequately in the space that we could afford to give each contributor. For example, originally we wanted to include the subject of family succession, but subsequently felt that enough excellent books are available to address this topic in much more detail than we could. We chose to concentrate on those areas in which we could realistically educate and inform our readers in the space we had available. We think we have accomplished this.

As in our previous book, the format is particularly useful. Each part stands on its own and can be read for the specific information it contains. The reader does not have to start with Chapter 1 and read consecutively through to understand the material in any one part. The reader can choose one of interest or that offers the needed information. This is one of the few books on this subject where the reader can quickly access information in any order desired.

We owe a huge debt of gratitude to our contributors. Many worked hard and long to write their chapters. A few brave authors bailed us out at the last minute when two contributors fell behind in their "real" work and were unable to complete their chapters. We especially thank these last-minute contributors. We feel fortunate to have secured such quality input.

We are especially grateful to Mike Hamilton, Senior Editor, at John Wiley & Sons, Inc., for the idea for this book, and for allowing us the opportunity to do it the way we wanted. We would also like to thank Liza Cormier for preparing the correspondence to our contributors and the "flowcharts" that allowed us to see where we were even when we didn't have a clue. And, last, to our wives and families, who became contributors whether or not they wanted to. Their patience and support helped make this book possible.

TOM WEST
JEFF JONES

THE BASICS

Defining the Midsized Company and the Market

THOMAS L. WEST
BUSINESS BROKERAGE PRESS

WHAT ARE MIDSIZED COMPANIES?

There are probably as many definitions of the midsized company as there are midsized companies. Intermediaries, business appraisers, and others in the field all have their own definitions. Some use the value or the seller's asking price of the company to establish size. Others rely on sales volume to determine whether a company is a midmarket one. Still others use the number of employees as the primary basis for determining size.

There may also be a distinction between midsized companies and the term *midmarket*. It would be very easy to say that the midmarket is composed of midsized companies, but that may not be true. Midmarket, we suspect, is a catchall term used by intermediaries to describe the marketplace they work in. In this section, we will define the term *midsized company*, since that is the term used in the title of this book.

There is an additional definition problem: What is the difference between a company and a business? The answer is most likely one of perception than of semantics. When people think of a company, they tend to visualize a manufacturing, distribution, or wholesale business, as opposed to a large dry-cleaning operation, which may, in fact, be larger, utilizing all three definitions already mentioned. For purposes of this discussion, we will use "business" to mean small, and "company" to mean midsized, although, in most cases, the words company and business are interchangeable. After all, one uses a business card, not a company card!

The point is that size alone may not be the primary distinction between a small business and a midsized business or company. Most intermediaries would not handle the dry-cleaning business, regardless of the size. A real key in determining whether a business is small or midsized may be who the prospective buyers are and what their purpose is in acquiring the company. A second key might lie in the differences between a small and a midsized business. Let's take a look at both of these.

Mac Taub, in an article in the *Journal of the International Business Brokers Association,* writes, "Looking at the characteristics of a midsize firm versus a smaller one, the midsize is more likely to:

- Be longer established. It probably took awhile to become midsize.
- Have more employees. Therefore there is a greater chance that it will be unionized. Also, it may have reached the stage and size where it has a layer of middle management.
- Part of the reason for its greater longevity and size may be that it has carved out a niche in the marketplace; it has attained a strong foothold within a certain market segment. It is doing something better than its competitors. In manufacturing, perhaps it possesses proprietary technology or patents. (With a publicly held firm, it might well possess one or more recognized brand names.) It might be a hi-tech firm, and the broker might be particularly challenged to locate the rare buyer who could handle it.
- The financial statements are likely to be of better quality. Of the three levels of accounting thoroughness—compiled, reviewed, audited—the small firm is most likely to be compiled, while the publicly held firm will be audited. The midsize firm will tend to be compiled or reviewed; but even if compiled, will probably be of higher quality with more detail available, and less skim involved, than a smaller firm. Also, with a midsize firm, it is more likely that there will be financial statements, in addition to income tax returns. Many small firms have only tax returns.
- While occasionally one runs into a midsize firm that is exactly like a smaller firm but with more digits in the financial statement numbers, in almost all instances, the midsize firm is also a more complex operation, both in management and financial structure."

Taub goes on to say, "As a very general rule, the owner of a midsize firm is more likely to be more sophisticated, more educated, more knowledgeable about his industry, business, and about the process of selling a business, even if he has never sold one before. He will probably consult advisors more frequently—accountant, attorney, CFO. . . . He will probably also be more particular about potential buyers, exhibiting greater concern about their financial strength, business background, and knowledge of his industry."

Robert Scarlata, in the *Handbook of Business Valuation,* edited by West and Jones, and published by John Wiley & Sons, Inc., says "The buyer of a small business can become quite successful through a strong desire to succeed, a conservative lifestyle, a strong dose of humility (knowing when to seek outside counsel), a great willingness to expand his or her base of knowledge, a modicum of accounting/business knowledge, and some knowledge of the (low level of sophistication) business involved . . . . Gradually, the skill level is increased, employees are hired, equipment is purchased to increase efficiency and production, and, perhaps, such a business becomes a 'middle market' business."

Scarlata goes on to say, "The larger 'middle market' [as opposed to small businesses] business is generally more complicated to manage, requiring greater business skills, more experience, an ability to manage many more discrete activities involving professionals at many different levels, a larger number of employees, more organizational levels, higher levels of investment in plant and equipment, and a concomitant greater level of capital. The essence of the middle market enterprise is leverage—leverage of the skills of the owner/manager, leverage of capital, leverage of ideas and skills, for no one person can possibly accomplish the production with this form of sophisticated economic organization without the use of other 'tools' to effect such a productive result."

Those who buy businesses, especially small ones, tend to be buying income substitution; or, to put it more bluntly, they are buying jobs. Buying a small business generally entails being the proverbial "chief, cook, and bottle washer." Those who buy small businesses tend to do the work. Those who buy midsize businesses or companies tend to be managers and get the work done by delegating rather than doing it themselves. This is a very "black-and-white" distinction, and one that many company owners will challenge. The owners and managers of midsized companies have to do a lot more "hands-on" work than officers of very large companies.

DETERMINING NUMBERS

So far, we have attempted to distinguish between those who buy small businesses and those who buy midsized businesses. However, we have not discussed the size nor the number of businesses in each size category. Let's first take a look at the three major indicators of size: number of employees, value or asking price of the business, and the total sales volume.

Number of Employees

First, let's examine the size of a business based on its number of employees. Only the Small Business Administration (SBA), a part of the

U.S. Department of Commerce, uses this indicator as a measurement of size. And although the number of employees is only one measurement, the SBA does tend to rely on it.

Interestingly enough, the SBA defines small business ". . . as any concern organized for profit that, including its affiliates, is independently owned and operated, is not dominant in the industry in which the procurement is classified [pertains to government contracts], and can further qualify under the criteria set forth in the SBA's Rules and Regulations. . . . In general, however, a business bidding on a government contract is regarded as small if it has fewer than 500 employees."

Here is the size breakdown used by the SBA:

Very small   Any business with fewer than 20 employees
Small   20 to 100 employees
Medium   100 to 500 employees
Large   500-plus employees

It is interesting to note that using generally accepted figures, over 99 percent of all businesses have fewer than 100 employees. These figures would imply that over 99 percent of all businesses in the United States are either small or very small according to the SBA. The other categories—medium and large—represent less than 1 percent of all businesses.

Value or Asking Price

Intermediaries and many others generally do not use the number of employees as an indicator of size. Especially today with many firms using independent contractors and so-called leased employees, coupled with the downsizing of American businesses, the number of employees is unlikely to be a realistic assessment of size. Most intermediaries—and almost everyone else, with the exception of the SBA—use either value or asking price or sales volume.

Although a discussion of the difference between value and asking price is not warranted in this section, obviously, there is a distinction. There is also a difference, generally, between asking price and the price negotiated between a buyer and a seller, although there are those rare instances when the asking price ultimately ends up to be the final price paid by a buyer. The ultimate selling price in most cases, however, is less than the asking price—and may be more or less than a value determined by a business appraiser.

A breakdown, based on price, is supplied by Business Brokerage Press, in its *1996 Business Reference Guide:*

General business: Businesses priced under $500,000.

The larger business: Businesses priced from $500,000 to $1 million.

The midsized company: Businesses priced from $1 million to $20 million.

The larger company: Businesses priced $20 million and up. (These transactions tend to be called mergers and acquisitions.)

Some intermediaries are comfortable with the asking price of a company as a determinate of size because they are used to dealing with asking price and how the market reacts to it. And while buyers may be interested in the sales volumes, they invariably ask, "What is the price?" Most intermediaries and business brokers will say that a midsized company will sell for between $1 million and $20 million. That is a broad range, but as we will see shortly, the number of businesses that fall into that range is not as big as one might suspect. In fact, as we pointed out in the SBA comments, the bulk of American businesses fall into the small or very small categories. However, the small category contains, in our opinion, many midsized companies.

Sales Volume

The other size standard in general use is the sales volume of the company. Russ Robb, in his book *Buying Your Own Business,* published by Adams Publishing, defines middle-market companies as those that have "$2 million to $50 million in sales." We discussed the issue of sales as determinants of size, and although Russ agrees with this standard, he threw out a "monkey wrench" in using sales as a criteria. "There are tons of 'public' companies with sales of only $10, $20, or $40 million; and the investment community does not discuss employees or sales, but 'market capitalization,' which is the number of shares outstanding: for example, 2,000,000 times the bid price, $5 per share, or $10 million. What about the bio-tech company, Internurion, with no sales, but 10 million shares at $30 per share or a $300 million 'market cap.' Under the definition used in this section, that is a 'small' company, right? No sales!" Robb has a point. Valuing a business is difficult work today. We'll stick with our outline for purposes of this section.

Mac Taub in the article previously quoted says, "There is no 'official' definition of midsized. Different sources propose different dividing lines. Also, one may draw the lines on the basis of sales volume, earnings, assets, net worth, or selling price of the business. I personally am partial to sales volume, and a midsize of $1–20 million in annual sales."

Bob Scarlata, in the book also quoted in this section, defines the "middle-market business as that having a cash flow of between $85,000 and $600,000 per year. Any larger and the company becomes an excellent candidate for a corporate acquirer . . . ."

Others have said that a midsize company has less than $20 million in revenues, or a price between $1 million to $20 million; and still another says $1 million EBIT (earnings before interest and taxes). It would appear that defining the midsize company or the middle market, as some call it, is not as easy as one would think. And, since there does not appear to be an "official" definition, it is difficult to say just which is correct.

Nevertheless, to attempt to discover how many midsized companies there are, we obviously need a definition—or do we? Perhaps, before agreeing on a definition of a midsize company, it might pay to look at some numbers. After all, if we come up with a definition and find that very few businesses and companies fall into it, or that there are more larger companies than midsized ones, we have missed the point.

American Business Lists, a major list company located in Omaha, Nebraska, breaks down the number of businesses by number of employees and by sales volume. We have found their lists to be accurate, and quite frankly, more dependable than information from the SBA, which is usually so dated that it is of very little use. However, the total number of businesses according to American Business Lists is 9,077,347, which includes industry groups that we wouldn't normally include in the types of businesses we are examining in this book, and 316,836 businesses for which the size was unknown. We subtracted this number from the total, but had no way of deleting them by industry group as far as size was concerned. Ultimately, the number we used to arrive at our final numbers and percentages was 8,760,511.

The following table may be as close as anyone can get. If we define small businesses, for our purposes, as those with sales of under $1 million (and fewer than nine employees), we can see that there are approximately 7.1 million businesses, or about 81 percent of the total number of businesses in the United States.

Number of Employees	Sales Volume	Number of Businesses by Percentage	
1–4	Less than $500,000	61.60%	(5,396,923)
5–9	$500,000–$1 million	19.50	(1,708,766)
10–19	$1–$2.5 million	10.00	(876,975)
20–49	$2.5–$5 million	6.50	(576,308)
50–99	$5–$10 million	2.30	(201,539)
100–249	$10–$20 million	.01	(106,472)
250–499	$20–$50 million	*	(25,579)
500–999	$50–$100 million	*	(9,716)
1,000–4,999	$100–$500 million	*	(7,391)
5,000–9,000	$500 million–$1 billion	*	(908)
10,000 +	Over $1 billion	*	(881)

*Less than 1%.

Now, finally, our definition of the midsized company! The midsize company has sales of $1 million to $20 million, has 10 to 249 employees, and represents approximately 18 percent of all businesses. Thus, the number of midsize companies is about 1.7 million.

If we want to go a step further, we could make a case that the price range used by the *1996 Business Reference Guide,* which uses price rather than sales volume as an indicator of size, may also be correct. There, the midsize company was defined as one that would sell for a range of between $1 million to $20 million. A business with sales of only $1 million would almost certainly sell for less than $1 million. However, once you get to $2 million and above in sales, these companies would most likely fall into the over $1 million in price figure. And a company with $20 million in sales would more than likely sell for less than $20 million.

As noted in the Introduction, this book contains contributions from many different and diverse contributors, and our definition of size may not be compatible with all of theirs. We are, however, comfortable in repeating that a midsize company will sell for a little above the threshold of $1 million to about $20 million, and will have a sales volume of generally less than $20 million in total revenues. Despite the SBA employee breakdown, we think that a midsize company will have about 10 to 249 employees.

Needless to say, as the economy changes from one of manufacturing to that of service provider, the old definitions will not be applicable. The number of employees may be irrelevant, since so much work will be done by new technology or outsourced to others. Sales may become irrelevant, because without a cost of goods factored in, a service company may have smaller sales, but much more profit. And Robb's comment quoted previously reinforces these concerns regarding sales. Defining the midsized company is an everchanging process. For the present, however, we will stick with our definition.

Who Owns Midsized Companies and Why Are They for Sale?

MAXWELL TAUB
PRESIDENT
M.J. TAUB ASSOCIATES, INC.

The two questions posed by this chapter's title are very important for buyers and business brokers. At first glance, it would appear that while the second question is extremely important, the first is not. The truth is not just the opposite, but the process of buying and selling a business involves more than just numbers. There is a lot of emotion, ego, human chemistry, and sizing each other up going on, too. Buyers want to know: "Why is this guy selling?" "Does this fellow have the right stuff to run my business?" Purchasing a business is not like buying a pair of shoes. You don't just briefly look over a business, and then pull out your billfold or credit card. It is a slow process, a gradual coming together. The title of one book by James Freund gives an apt description: *The Acquisition Mating Dance*. Those who have been through it are familiar with the flirtation, the mock rejection, the feigned indignation, the fight over the dowry, the aggravation of interfering family members (lawyers and accountants), the advance of one party coupled with the retreat of the other, and then vice versa.

IDENTIFYING THE SELLER

Therefore, who the seller is affects how the buyer and business broker should deal with him.

The Entrepreneur

One type of seller (or owner) is the quintessential entrepreneur. He started the business from scratch and ran it for 30 to 40 years. He's successful, prosperous, autocratic. He's weathered and has adapted to many changes—the economy's peaks and troughs; the industry's restructuring; fierce competitors; labor disputes; and maybe a fire, flood, or earthquake, too. He will probably be very interested in finding a buyer who will take the business to new heights. It may be very important to him that the name of the company remain unchanged, particularly if his name is part of it. Buyer and broker should determine what beyond money this seller wants, and within reason try to accommodate him. For example, he may want to retain some sort of advisory role, as a board member or consultant. With the right nonmonetary factors in place, such a seller might even accept a lower price from a buyer that he likes.

The Heir

He has worked in the business for 30 years, reporting to his father, who founded and ran it. When the father had a major heart attack, he let the son, age 55, take over.

Often, this is too late. The son may be burned out, incapable of making important final decisions. The spark of innovation is barely present, and he is unskilled and untested in adjusting to and profiting from market change. The power and authority are not enjoyable at this stage. Still, he runs it for a few years in a desultory, or perhaps insecure, tyrannical fashion, and then decides he'd like to cash out.

Buyer and broker must often compliment such a person extensively, reassure him, allay his fears, assuage his insecurities.

(*Note:* Obviously, in this chapter, we are dealing to some extent with stereotypes, to make a point. While there are many heirs that fit this description, there are also numerous variations:

- The heir who took over the company at a young age and did a great job running it.

- The heir whose father let him run a division or subsidiary to gain management expertise and responsibility.
- The heir who never worked for the company; his father died suddenly, and he is trying to keep it running temporarily until it can be sold.)

It comes down to the buyer (and to some degree the broker) performing due diligence on the company, and depends on the personality of the seller—what makes him tick, what his interests and desires are, where his "hot buttons" are.

The Family

There may be both active and passive family members to deal with, and perhaps the passive ones own a good chunk of the stock; and—count on it—at least one passive member will be a lawyer or a spouse of a lawyer.

The situation here is that the buyer and broker are dealing with multiple sellers, each with different wants, expectations, and personalities. This can present difficulties. On the bright side, all buyers are facing the same situation. Frequently, it is not until several well-qualified buyers have walked away from the deal that the family as a unit enters the realm of reality as to asking price.

The Reseller

Here is a person who bought a midsized business, ran it for a few years, and then decided, for whatever combination of reasons, to sell it. He may have been a very good or a poor manager; but the odds are, he was very good. He knows what he paid for the business; he knows what has happened to the business and the market since his purchase; and he has a very good feel for the current value of the business. His asking price will be a function of how motivated he is to sell. He will probably deal with buyer and broker in a very efficient, businesslike, no-nonsense manner.

Partners

There could be two, three, or more partners, family or nonfamily. The legal form of ownership may be a partnership, but it is more likely an S- or C-corporation.

The point again is that the buyer and broker must deal with multiple sellers. Hopefully, one is dominant, and the others will go along with whatever deal he agrees to.

Subsidiary

Sometimes, for whatever reason, a company decides to sell a subsidiary or division. In this case, the seller (owner) is the parent corporation. At an early stage, the buyer and broker may be dealing with a designated negotiator. As the deal grows serious, however, the CEO, CFO, and assorted advisers may enter the picture. (For that matter, if the buyer is a corporation, the same thing may happen on the buying side.) This is something a buyer should expect. And, depending on the size of the deal, he should decide on his own advisory team. The buyer should be careful to retain control, and confine his advisers to advising. Some advisers tend to be biased to make a deal; others to kill it. The buyer himself should weigh all the information and make the final decision.

Assorted Other Owners

More rarely, a buyer or broker comes across a midsized business seller that is somewhat different than the preceding:

- A business in bankruptcy. A later chapter is devoted to this topic.
- A business owned by a foreign person or company. Here, the early negotiations would probably be handled by a local representative, with the foreign owner probably becoming personally involved near the end.
- A business owned by an investment company or venture capital group. Probably at an early stage, the plan was to build up the business and take it public. But things didn't work out; they don't see this happening soon, and they'd just as soon sell it and invest the proceeds in what they perceive to be more promising ventures.
- The owner is dead. The buyer and broker are dealing with a widow/widower, or estate. Such a situation has many tricky aspects, from dealing with an unrealistic, unknowledgeable owner or attorney to observing how the business has been operating since the original owner's death to determining who is available to educate and train the new buyer.

WHY ARE MIDSIZED COMPANIES FOR SALE?

A business brokerage consultant once advised me that the most important point on the listing form is Reason for Sale. Then I met a very successful business broker who did not include this item on his lengthy listing agreement. When I asked why, he said: "Why bother? They're all lying anyhow."

These two seemingly irreconcilable points of view are really not that disparate. The answer to the question "Why is this business for sale?" is very important to buyers and business brokers. But finding the answer is not easy, and will take a great deal of due diligence.

I remember one of my first sales as a business broker. During the listing and through many subsequent visits, the seller kept saying that he was retiring, that he had worked long and hard and was ready to pack it in; he had bought a home in Florida, and as soon as the business was sold, he and his wife were moving to Florida. At the closing, just to make conversation, I asked, "When are you planning to move to Florida?" He repeated, "Florida?" and looked at me like I was crazy.

Obviously, there are many reasons why a midsized business is put up for sale, all of them legitimate from the seller's point of view, but only some from the buyer's or broker's. First we should note that of those businesses ostensibly for sale (listed with a broker, advertised in the newspaper), only some are actually for sale; others are not, and some are sort of in the middle.

Those that are not really for sale include the listings by the merely curious owner, who is just interested to know *if* he could sell his business, and if so, how much he could get for it. A variation of this is the owner who has a specific buyer in mind, say his nephew. Everything is already agreed upon between them, except the price. The two decide privately that the nephew will have the right of first refusal; that is, that he will match the highest bona fide offer received. So the business is never really for sale; it is only set up that way so a private-deal selling price can be arrived at (maybe less a broker's commission.)

Another offshoot is the resale of a franchise, which many business brokers refuse to handle. It works this way: A franchisee lists his business with a broker. The broker finds a buyer. But it turns out there is a clause in the franchise agreement that says the buyer must be approved by the franchisor. The buyer visits the franchisor, who switches him to another business. Therefore, there is no commission for the broker and no sale through a broker for the seller. Only buyer and franchisor are happy.

The sort of "halfway for sale" situation is where an owner says to himself, "I don't really care if I sell or not, so I'll set an asking price considerably above what the business is worth. If someone is willing to pay that price, fine, I'll sell. If not, I'll keep it."

In a similar vein, an owner might say, "This is one beautiful, profitable business. Anyone who wants this is going to have to pay a hefty price for it." Or there is the owner whose accountant (who, if the business is sold, loses a client) has told the owner his opinion of what the business is worth; in effect, making it unsalable. (I once sat with the owner of a small retail cosmetics store whose accountant had told him it was worth 10 times earnings [earnings including the owner's salary].)

Some owners are subject to conflicting pressures: He wants to keep the business, but his wife and/or others are pressuring him to sell. I encountered one owner who wanted to sell, but his girlfriend, who worked there, didn't want him to. In situations such as this, at best, you have a lukewarm seller.

Then there is the question of "potential." I once dealt with the owner of a small retail food store, at which a few of the ethnic foods they sold were made. He told me that if a buyer nationally franchised the name of the store and those foods, he'd make a fortune. He was pricing the business accordingly. I would not classify a business like this as actually being for sale.

BUSINESSES THAT ARE FOR SALE

Let us now focus on those businesses that really are for sale, and the reasons why.

Owner Retiring

An owner retiring can certainly be a good, legitimate reason for a business being for sale. The owner decides he doesn't want to die with his boots on; he wants to spend his remaining years fishing, or painting, or gardening. It is a reassuring reason for a buyer.

But some caveats are in order. Beware if the owner is young and he gives this reason. And regardless of the owner's age, due diligence is in order. The owner may be retiring because the business is not doing well. Or he is about to lose his biggest customer. Or a major lawsuit is looming. Or the city is going to replace the sewer pipes in the street in front of the store and construction will take a year. The point is, there are many inquiries to be made, and they are not all financial. Prospective buyers or their advisers should contact the local chamber of commerce, bankers, trade publications, trade associations, suppliers, customers, and competitors for whatever helpful information can be obtained. And this has to be done very discreetly, or the entire deal could fall apart.

Owner Is Sick

From the point of view of the buyer and broker, this is another legitimate reason to sell. The owner's doctor tells him he must retire. Or the owner finds he doesn't have sufficient strength and energy to run the business properly. Again, though, proceed with due diligence. Is this the real reason? How is the business doing?

Owner Bored and/or Tired

This *could* be a legitimate reason. I have met owners who felt they must have a change and/or rest. Sometimes, I've even met them as buyers: "I sold a perfectly good business two years ago. Now I see it was a mistake, and I want to buy another business."

It could also be that, as the old expression goes, maybe the owner is just sick and tired of losing money. Again, a thorough investigation is in order.

Next-Generation Difficulties

An owner would like to keep the business in the family; pass it on to the next generation. But he has two sons, one a doctor, the other a lawyer, and neither has any interest in running the business. So he puts it up for sale. From a buyer's viewpoint, this is an excellent reason to sell.

- Variation 1: The owner has one or more children who would like to take over the business. But the owner feels they aren't competent, and doesn't want to risk their destroying the business.
- Variation 2: Owner wants to sell the business to one of his children, who can't afford to buy it on the owner's terms. So it is put up for general sale.
- Variation 3: Owner wants his son or daughter to take over the business, but the child is not particularly interested. Enter the Stalking Horse ploy: Owner lists business with a broker. Broker brings in a parade of buyers. Child becomes scared, makes deal with owner. Unfortunately, this scenario is a big waste of time for buyers and brokers.

(*Note:* Some not-so-knowledgeable readers may be wondering at this point, if the broker has an exclusive right to sell listing and he brings in a full offer, how can the seller back out of a deal? The answer is twofold: There are very few full offers, and there are many ways for a seller to get around an exclusive listing, such as to simply let it expire, or just be uncooperative.)

Partners

The company is owned by partners, whether or not they are members of the same family, and whether the legal form of the company is a partnership or a corporation.

Let's say there are two partners, and they are fighting. They can't stand to work with each other. One wants out, but the other can't afford to pay him on his terms (assuming they've agreed on a price). The only solution they can agree on is to sell the business.

A potential buyer must examine "personal goodwill" here. How well will the business operate without both partners? Will any major customers be lost? Who will stay to ease the transition?

A variation: Two partners, one active and one silent. The silent one wants to cash out; the active one can't afford to pay him. So the active one is forced to sell.

Or, let's say there is family ownership, with active and silent partners. The active ones receive high salaries and perks; the silent ones get only paltry dividends. The silents rebel, and want to cash out. The actives can't afford to do this, so the company is put up for sale.

I experienced this situation twice: There were three partners, but one was key. The key one wanted to leave. The other two were afraid they couldn't operate with the key one gone. So they all agreed to put the business up for sale. In such a case, a buyer must find out what each of the partners do, why the others won't stay, then calculate how he plans to replace the skills of all of them.

Company Losing Money or Earning Little

There are many variations on this theme, and they are all fraught with danger for the buyer. This is not to say that a buyer should never buy a company that is losing money, but if he does, he should know why they are losing money and believe that he can solve the problems. He should not overpay, and he should either have experience in the same industry, be bringing the company into a synergistic situation, or be a turnaround specialist.

The plain vanilla version is where the company has been losing money for some time; it all shows on the books, and the owner or owners are tired of sinking more money into a situation they have been unable to turn around. A buyer, mindful of the points in the preceding paragraph, should investigate thoroughly before making his decision.

A not uncommon situation is where a company for sale is losing money, but it does *not* show on the books, either because of creative accounting or outright fraud. Again, a potential buyer who suspects that all is not as it should be might want to enlist the services of a forensic accountant, who is like a detective accountant. (A buyer should not automatically assume that an accounting statement or tax return prepared by a CPA is truthful.)

Sometimes, although the owner has been working hard and is not actually losing money, he is making very little. (I knew a fellow who had an established business, worked 60 hours a week, but his salary plus net profit for the year was $5,600.) When examining such a business (or any business), a buyer and his accountant should create a pro forma financial statement of the first year under "his" ownership. This often uncovers vital information, such as the owner drawing a very low salary, or the business paying no rent because the real estate is owned by the seller's mother.

A buyer might come across a company in a cyclical industry in which the owner sees a few lean years coming, and decides to sell at the beginning of the down cycle. A buyer contemplating the purchase of such a company should read up on the industry, particularly its trade publications for the most recent year or so. Phoning a trade publication and arranging to purchase its most recent year's issues is a simple task.

A fairly common situation is the owner who stayed on too long. The ideal time to sell a business is just before its earnings are apparently going to peak. Too many owners stay long after the peak has passed. They do this because they're not ready to retire, or let go, or give up a position of prestige and authority. But the results can be very damaging. They can lose customers, fail to invest in the latest technology, and thus allow the company to get out of balance (my terminology). To elaborate, ideally, a manufacturer with a certain sales volume has a proper-size building, a sufficient amount of the latest machinery and equipment, the appropriate number of employees, amount of working capital, and so on. I once went to take a listing from an owner, age 82. He owned a factory and land worth $2.5 million, machinery and equipment worth $750,000, and inventory worth $600,000. His annual sales were $500,000, and his combined salary and net profit were $50,000. Four years earlier, his sales had been $5,000,000. Clearly, this was an owner who stayed too long, and let the components of the business get out of balance. In such a situation, it is doubtful that the owner would ever agree to a realistic selling price. For my part, I didn't take this listing, and learned three years later that the owner had died: his estate was trying to sell the business.

Sometimes a company's low or negative profits have a financial origin. Maybe it financed an expansion or acquisition with bank debt, but the project isn't going well and the debt burden is oppressive; maybe the bank wants to pull out and is threatening to call the loan. Or the company cannot afford to pay off the bank, and can locate no other source of funds; or other sources of funds charge very high interest rates, and the company would be forced to pledge so much collateral that if everything didn't work out well, a lifetime of effort would soon be wiped out. The owner prudently decides it is safer to sell. A buyer has to do some thorough analysis before he makes an offer on a company like this.

As a company grows substantially in size, concomitant changes in organizational structure and procedures should be made to handle the increased volume. Sometimes, companies don't keep up in this fashion. The organizational structure is ineffective in handling the new growth. The company becomes inefficient, costs get out of line, quality control worsens, customer dissatisfaction grows. A good management consultant could probably correct this, but sometimes as an alternative, the company is put up for sale. The buyer must realistically assess whether he can do what has to be done and whether it will be worth it.

In some industries, the passage of time brings many changes in competition and technology. An owner who successfully adapted when he was younger, in recent years, has fallen behind. Now the company's products are not positioned so well in the marketplace, and the owner puts the business up for sale. A potential buyer must carefully analyze what there is to buy, what it is worth, and what he can hope to do with it.

Multiple Businesses, Subsidiaries, Divisions, or Branches

It is not unusual that a parent company decides to sell a subsidiary or division. It might sell it because the subsidiary doesn't fit in with the rest of the business, or because the parent company needs money or wants money for other purposes. The parent company might believe, rightly or wrongly, that the subsidiary is unprofitable, in which case, it may admit it or try to hide it.

A buyer should know that whenever a subsidiary is involved, the accounting for that subsidiary vis-à-vis the balance of the company may not be scrupulously accurate. If the subsidiary occupies separate premises, the buyer must investigate how much parent overhead is charged to the subsidiary, and how this was arrived at. If the subsidiary occupies the same premises, there is even more to look at. How was rent apportioned? Salaries? Utilities? The phone bill? Top management salaries? Creating a pro forma is all important. How will the subsidiary look financially on a stand-alone basis under the buyer's ownership?

If the seller admits that the subsidiary is losing money, the buyer should attempt to find out why. Is it being neglected? Poorly managed? Underfunded? Is it using obsolete equipment, poor costing procedures, poor pricing practices, poor quality control? Are returns and allowances too high? Is bad debt expense too high? Does the buyer think that he can correct what is wrong? What will it cost him to do so, and is it worth it?

Sometimes the midsized business is a small conglomerate, a collection of, say, four very different businesses. And sometimes the seller, who wants to retire for example, only wants to sell them as a package. This is a particularly tough problem for a business broker or buyer. The buyer must decide if he wants to buy—and run—those particular businesses.

A variation is the seller who owns several businesses, either different or the same. He may want to sell one or two of them, and keep the rest. Or he may want to sell all of them, one at a time. In the latter case, he knows that if he sells the best ones first, he will never sell the others. So he tries to sell the worst ones first. A buyer must judge the one currently for sale on its own merits.

Wherever there are several businesses under one owner, there is the strong possibility of commingling on the financial and tax statements. My dealings with the owner of five furniture stores in contiguous towns, another owner of six bars, and a third owner of two pharmacies come to mind. In all these cases, there was a shifting of sales, purchases, and expenses among stores. The bar owner would have liquor, wine, and beer delivered and invoiced to one bar, and then load it from the back door into the trunk of his car to deliver to another bar. The pharmacist would have prescriptions ordered at one pharmacy, then filled by, delivered by, and credited to the sales of the second pharmacy. Naturally, it was the second pharmacy that was for sale. Woe to the buyer of the second pharmacy, who would experience a rapid falloff of sales as soon as the title changed hands.

Again, I stress the importance of the buyer employing a forensic accountant and creating a realistic pro forma.

Off-the-Books

In my experience, many businesses have sales, purchases, expenses, and profit off the books. Where these sums are small, both buyer and seller should ignore them. But where they are sizable, I tell a seller he has three choices:

1. Sell the business for what is on the books.
2. Delay the sale a year or two, while gradually putting everything on the books.
3. Try to sell the business now for a price based on what is off the books. This involves two problems: proving to a potential buyer that what is off the books exists; and risking that his revelation of off-the-books profit will come to the attention of the IRS.

Strangely enough, in the New York area at least, the third option is often chosen.

I know that the general advice given to buyers is "don't pay for what's not on the books," but in the New York area, this would leave the buyer with a much-reduced pool of businesses available for purchase. If a buyer decides to buy such a business, the use of a good forensic accountant is very important. Being shown the private notebook is one thing; verifying its truthfulness is another problem entirely.

Miscellaneous

There are other situations that surface occasionally, and deserve mention:

A company has considerable off-balance sheet debt; the owner is pushing strongly for a stock sale. One common solution: Many buyers' attorneys will insist on an asset sale. Otherwise, the buyer must rely on his lawyer to protect him in terms of the wording on the various legal documents. *Note:* A buyer should only use an attorney experienced in the buying and selling of businesses.

A company had legal problems. The owner is in jail. He is afraid his employees won't keep the business running until he gets out, so he decides to sell. A buyer should be very wary here, and perform legal *due* diligence in addition to the normal investigations.

The owner is dead. The estate or widow/widower is selling the business. This is particularly tricky for a buyer. He has to see who can brief him, who can answer questions, who can train him. Is there anyone in top management or middle management who can do these things? Otherwise, this probably shouldn't be touched, except by a competitor. Also, what has happened since the owner died? Is the business still operating? Did it lose any customers? Did they close the doors? In the latter case, for a purchase price, we are talking about not much more than liquidation value.

Sometimes there are hidden problems, which are not revealed until late in the game. I once listed a manufacturer whose company owned the real estate. The owner said he'd prefer to sell the business and real estate together. I explained that that would be more difficult, and suggested a listing that would sell the business either with the real estate or without it. In the latter case, the seller would become a landlord for a few years. He agreed. When we got very close to a sale of the business alone, the owner revealed that one of the terms of the company's bank loan agreement was that the business could not be sold apart from the real estate. I don't know if there is any practical defense against a problem of this nature.

The reader of this chapter may have assumed at the beginning that its contents would be a bland recitation of whos and whys. I have tried to emphasize that these simple questions have important, sometimes complex, answers, and I have lightly touched on serious implications and potential problems that will be explored more fully in subsequent chapters.

Preparing a Business for Sale: The Do's and Don'ts

THEODORE BURBANK
PRESIDENT
THE BURBANK GROUP, INC.

Examples are legion of long-established businesses simply closing their doors. Many others are sold under duress because of ill health, divorce, partner disputes, owner burnout, business slowdown, or death. A business sold under adverse conditions does not command much value; many are sold for their liquidation value only. Most such businesses just fade or are given away. Conversely, there are also stories of companies selling for fantastic prices, and sometimes reportedly for cash!

The million-dollar question, (perhaps literally) is "Why?" After much thought, and more than 16 years of experience gained in selling several hundred companies, my answer may seem simple, yet, beneath the surface, complex. My simple answer, in a word, is *preparation*.

THE WINNING STRATEGY

Preparation involves a combination of dynamic and subtle factors, many of which are so obvious they are often overlooked:

Decide that you will sell someday.

Prepare yourself for the sale.

Identify your ideal successor.

Realize the buyer's primary motivations are not financial.

Avoid the "I'll do-it-myself" urge and obtain professional assistance.

Understand the unique rules involved in small and midsize company valuations and sales.

Understand the factors, financial and nonfinancial, that drive the value of your company.

Position your company properly.

To Sell or Not to Sell

Perhaps the most difficult decision you, as a business owner, will ever have to make is the decision to sell. Unfortunately, many business owners agonize over the many variables involved in selling without ever actually making the decision to sell. Others wait too long to sell (businesses are seldom sold too soon), and a significant number feel they cannot afford to sell their only source of income. But nothing stays the same, and over time, a business changes and so does its owner. Eventually, the demands and needs of the business may grow to conflict with an owner's perspective and skills. Something has to give. Will it be the owner's personal life and health, or will it be the business that suffers? Perhaps both? Only two endgame options exist:

The business is sold to family, employees, or outsiders.

The business is closed.

By failing to prepare for eventual sale, the business owner allows the endgame to be determined by external forces. The result? Usually an attempt to sell under conditions of personal or business distress.

Poor health, divorce, slumping sales, creditor demands, poor employee relations, lack of operating or expansion capital very often are the symptoms of an owner who could have sold, but failed to heed "early warning signals." Indecision or lack of proper planning and preparation can prove to be very costly, not only to the business owner, but also to family, employees, vendors, and customers.

To avoid this situation, a business owner should first make the decision that the business will be sold, someday; then begin preparations and, when appropriate, set the process in motion. Once the decision has been made, professional help can be obtained to address the multiple variables, and implement a plan.

Prepare for the Sale

This seemingly obvious step in preparing a business for sale is very often overlooked or given only superficial attention. It seems that no matter how strong a grasp one has of the business, given enough time, that grasp will turn into a stranglehold. This dynamic occurs in large public companies all the time—IBM and Digital, for example. Make sure your business is not in need of change before you are prepared to make the change as well. Remember, in business it is either grow or go— there is no such thing as status quo. When a business owner decides to "coast," in what direction is the business headed?

Decide What You Will Do after the Sale

Most great men and women in history have had more than one career. Most have enjoyed several, and have developed many diverse nonbusiness interests and hobbies. Perhaps you want to devote more time developing other business interests. Maybe you want to change your avocation into your vocation. You might decide to devote six months, or maybe a year, after the sale to choose your next course of action.

Invest Money Outside of Your Business

If retirement is your choice, can you afford to retire? Take advantage of the several retirement plan investment options allowed under IRS rules. Keogh plans and Individual Retirement Accounts (IRAs), Defined Benefit and Defined Contribution Annuities are all examples of financial vehicles, other than your business, in which you should be investing for retirement. Few businesses will command the dollars required to allow for a comfortable retirement from sale proceeds alone.

Develop Outside Interests

Owning a business can be an all-consuming experience. "All work and no play makes Johnny a dull boy." If your business represents your identity and, if you "are the business", you have two problems: First, you probably are unwilling to lose your identity; second, your business will be difficult to sell and probably will not command a premium price.

Identify Your Ideal Successor

Your business is a vehicle. How far and fast you have driven it will not predict its performance in the future. The future of your company depends upon whom you allow behind the wheel. Whether your successor wins the "Indy 500" or runs your "baby" into the ground, depends, in large measure, on how well you choose.

Choose a successor. When you understand where your business is today, you can see what it could be tomorrow. Finding the right buyer starts with a review of where your business is and who you are. Ideally, your successor will have talents and skills that complement yours. Also, it is imperative that your successor appreciate and be able to maintain the strengths of the business you created; in other words, recognize the strengths and build upon them.

Your buyer should regard existing problem areas as opportunity. The right buyer will see that "all the right things are wrong." Only the right buyer will pay the "right price." Only the right buyer will fully capitalize upon the opportunity you have created.

Recognize that the buyer's primary motivations are not financial. Both buy and sell sides are motivated by personal, rather than purely financial, factors. If you are considering the sale of your business, you probably will agree that your primary motivation to sell is to enable you to do something else. The money expected from the sale is important to you but not your chief motivation.

A buyer's primary motivations to buy or own a business revolve around issues of control and self-expression. As just stated, money is important but not the prime motivation. Buyers want to "show their stuff" and "do it themselves." Buyers really do not want *your* business; they want a business they can make *theirs.* That is why, as one of your first steps in preparation for sale, you attempt to identify your ideal successor. Buyers want the opportunity to make your business better and, in the process, make it their business—and, of course, make money doing it.

NUMBERS DON'T SELL A COMPANY—OPPORTUNITIES DO

Financial data alone will not give buyers the complete picture of opportunity your business represents. Actually, financial statements and tax returns for most small and private businesses are more like mystery novels; they certainly are not operating manuals. Tax returns seldom highlight the opportunities a business represents. Why is it then that historic financial data is the first information everyone expects to be exchanged?

Prepare a Profile or Prospectus That Highlights the Opportunities

Financial statements alone may not sell your business, no matter how profitable they indicate your business is or has been. The opportunity your business represents will. Do not assume the "numbers" will accurately reflect this. Remember, money is a secondary motivation, whereas capitalizing upon opportunities is a primary motivation. (Additional information on preparing a prospectus or profile is given later in this chapter, and Chapters 6 and 7 cover this subject in depth.)

Obtain Professional Assistance

Unlike management personnel of larger corporations who can draw upon many resources for support, information, and operational advice, the management of small private companies must wear all the hats. Competition, and the many financial drains challenging small business owners, mandate that they "do it themselves" whenever possible. The luxury of drawing upon outside resources is generally restricted to limited accounting and legal advice.

Most business owners have received unsolicited inquiries from potential buyers. It would seem logical therefore that attracting an appropriate buyer would be easy. To the successful do-it-yourselfer, selling the business might also appear simple, especially to someone who has experience in successfully selling his company's product or service. An owner making this assumption is only partially correct. Finding buyers *is* relatively easy; in fact, everyone "has a buyer." Buyers hire firms to search for companies, and network actively with lawyers, accountants, bankers, and others searching for the right business. The typical aggressive buyer will look at scores of companies, make several offers, and still be looking for a company.

Buyers constantly report that most sellers are unrealistic—they don't know what their business is worth, and often don't know how much they are making or losing. They also report that getting adequate information on a business is usually difficult and frustrating (like pulling teeth).

The problem is that the businesses have not been adequately prepared for sale, and thus are being exposed to the wrong buyers, or are positioned as less than attractive opportunities. Selling a business should not be a do-it-yourself project.

Where to obtain assistance in selling your business.   Finding the right buyer for your business can be time-consuming and frustrating. When your business demands your full time and attention, and its sale is important, professional assistance may be a wise consideration. And such assistance may be a necessity if maintaining confidentiality is important.

Help comes in several forms, and depends upon the type of buyer most appropriate for your company as well as the size of your firm:

Investment bankers: It is unlikely that readers of this book have companies large enough to warrant the use of an investment banker. Company revenues generally have to be in the range of $30 million to meet the minimum size requirements investment bankers set.

Merger and acquisition (M&A) specialists: M&A specialists serve the "middle market"; that is, businesses with revenues ranging from $10 to $100 million.

Business intermediaries: Business intermediaries serve companies whose sales generally are under $20 million. Fees by both the intermediary and M&A specialist include an initial retainer plus commission, or success fee, from which the retainer may or may not be deducted.

Business broker: Business brokers serve businesses whose revenues typically are less than $1 million.

Law and accounting firms: Many law and accounting firms are entering the M&A arena. Typically, they target the same companies served by M&A specialists and intermediaries. Finding a firm or individual with whom you will be comfortable generally means interviewing several and, of course, checking their credentials and references. (See Chapter 27 for more information on obtaining professional assistance.)

Understand the Unique Rules Involved in Small and Midsized Company Valuation and Sale

Public perception of how and to whom you should sell your company comes from several sources: newspapers, movies, television, and hearsay. Unfortunately, these sources often provide information that is misleading, inappropriate, and wrong, particularly when applied to small or midsized companies. They report or depict public company events that tend to be on much too grand a scale for smaller private companies. There is a world of difference between the two.

No one person owns a public company; many shareholders do. Public company accounting focuses on *maximizing* profits to satisfy shareholders demands, and to enable management to retain their jobs. Private company accounting focuses on *minimizing* profits to reduce the owner's tax bill. Private company owners need not be concerned with hostile takeovers, junk bonds, price/earnings (P/E) ratios, or loss of jobs because the company did not show appropriate profits in recent quarters. Most observers agree that major differences in management convention and culture exist between private and public companies. Because virtually no public information is available regarding the sale process and prices of private companies, many business owners and their advisors attempt to apply public company methodology and price/earnings ratios to the sale process of private companies. The following are a few examples of unfortunate results:

Wrong Buyer: Most public company acquisitions occur within their industry or one tangential to it. Therefore, uninitiated private company owners very often approach competitors, major vendors, or customers when attempting a sale. Unfortunately, private sector "industry buyers" pay prices based on selected hard assets, which produce low prices.

Result: Generally unproductive. Confidentiality is destroyed, with its attendant problems (employees, creditors, competition, and so on). If successful, the company is sold for essentially its hard asset value.

Wrong Price: Public company stock prices are published daily and price/earnings (P/E) ratios of 15 times earnings, or more, are common. Assuming that a private company's value can be calculated by applying public company P/E ratios will produce unrealistic prices.

Results:

When priced too high: Possible loss of the best buyer, and the business stays on the market for a lengthy period of time. Exposure to many potential buyers results in loss of confidentiality. If sold, it is done so at shopworn price, usually after several costly attempts (legal and accounting fees) to put a deal together have failed.

When priced too low: The owner obviously fails to receive full value for the company. Not so obvious is the loss to employees, vendors, and customers. Buyers pay prices proportionate to the opportunity they perceive. Hence, buyers paying low prices generally have not recognized the full opportunity the firm represents and therefore cannot capitalize upon it. The firm's full potential is never reached and those it serves are shortchanged.

Chapters 11 through 15 provide an overview of the appropriateness of the many approaches to estimating a firm's value.

Understand the Factors That Drive Your Company's Value

Financial results are surprisingly not the most important factor to drive a company's value. Knowing your customer is! The person, or firm, recognizing the highest value will pay the highest price. To identify your best buyer or customer for your business, you must first understand both objective and subjective elements within your company. How does your firm appear from the outside in? To whom will your problems appear as valuable and exciting opportunities? *The value of a company lies in the buyer's view of its future. Financial results reflect only the past.*

The next three chapters address summarizing your company's past and anticipating its future. Chapter 8 discusses displaying historical financial data, and Chapter 9 deals with future prospects. The impact and importance of this data depends upon its interpretation by the type of buyer you have attracted.

Customer or buyer identification.   This should be the first item on a list of important factors that drive a company's value. Unfortunately, this factor usually does not receive the attention it deserves, which is understandable since few of us are able to objectively view ourselves, our business, or anything else we are very close to. Also, business owners and most advisors, although immersed in the business climate, are not familiar with driving marketplace forces or the various types and categories of buyers operating therein.

Opportunity. Opportunity is an obvious factor that must be on everyone's list. But what is opportunity? It is different from potential. Buyers will pay for opportunity but not for potential. Why? Opportunity is perceived as having been created by the business owner, and potential as that which *will be* created by the acquiror. Buyers will not pay you for what they will do (potential); they will pay for what you have done (opportunity). Perception of opportunity will vary depending on the type of buyer, which emphasizes the critical need to know your customer. (Chapters 19 through 22 discuss the criteria of various buyer types.)

Earnings. Earnings factor high on most observers' list of important factors. Since most private companies' financial statements are driven by the owners' desire to minimize taxes, reported earnings are usually misleading. The numbers alone, even after recasting or normalizing, will not adequately reflect a firm's true value. The value of a company lies in a buyer's view of its future.

Position Your Company Properly

Positioning is similar to attitude, in that proper positioning will produce positive results, just as a positive attitude produces a richer and fuller life. To properly position a company for acquisition, you must first objectively determine the company's strengths and weaknesses. Identify the firm's *uniqueness* and *hidden values*. Understand the subjective environment that surrounds the business. Gather data and research information from outside sources to substantiate and ratify opportunity. Quantify subjective data so as to give credibility to expectations of future profits. Weave the gathered information and data into a comprehensive prospectus on the company, and highlight the opportunity the firm represents.

A properly positioned firm sells for a premium price to a person or entity able to enhance its operation. Everyone wins: The owner receives an optimum price. The buyer acquires an exciting opportunity. Customers, employees, and vendors continue their beneficial relationship with the firm.

SUMMARY

Ultimately, two options exist for every business owner. Either the succession of your business will be a planned event, and controlled by you, or it will be an unplanned occurrence brought about by outside factors. For the good of your business, your employees, customers, vendors, and family, decide! Decide to begin your succession planning now.

- Face the reality that both you and your business are constantly changing. Eventually, the needs and requirements of your business will conflict with your personal lifestyle. No matter how good you are, if you stay around long enough, your grasp of the business will turn into a stranglehold.

- Develop some nonbusiness interests. Find time to develop these outside interests.

- Begin to establish financial resources independent of your business.

- Start sooner, not later. Transition takes time. You have a lot to do before you can let go.

- Identify your ideal replacement. What skills, interests, and resources must succession management possess in order to capitalize upon the opportunities your business represents?

- Prepare the business for transfer. Take stock of those areas where your personality, skills, or influence are the key elements of your firm's success. Begin a program to transfer these activities to others within the company.

- Review the company's financial statements. In most private companies, the need to show bottom-line results is overridden by the owner's desire to minimize taxes. Make sure your accountant has not done this job too well. It is important for wary suitors and advisors to be able to easily identify discretionary and nonrecurring expenses that can be added back to profits.

- Trim or eliminate those activities, expenses, and personnel that exist essentially to satisfy your personal and/or ego needs.

- Seek and use advisors. Succession is a very personal and emotional process. It's not unlike giving your daughter away in marriage or putting a child up for adoption. This is a once-in-a-lifetime decision. You need every advantage you can garner.

- Determine the optimum value of your company. In order to accomplish this, you need to understand the differences between the various types of buyers in the marketplace today. To some, your company may be worthless; to others, it may be worth millions.

Obtaining the best results begins with a timely decision to commence the planning and preparation process. Every good general has a retreat plan. Before you act, have a plan. To formulate the very best plan, you need to know what your business requires of its succession management. You should know what the company is worth and that the timing is right. You must identify the attributes of an ideal successor, the one who will recognize the full opportunity you have created, pay the optimum value, and move the company up to the next level of profitability.

Doing it yourself should be limited to the decision to sell *only*. Thereafter, professional assistance should be obtained in order to maximize value, maintain confidentiality, and avoid costly mistakes. Major corporations engage "pros" to enhance the value of their products in the marketplace. Professional athletes use their promoters, actors their agents, and public companies their investment bankers. An unfortunate fact is that most small to midsized companies are never sold; or, when sold, transact for much less than they should. Perhaps this indicates that owners of family businesses and private companies need professional assistance also.

CHAPTER FOUR

Putting Your Best Foot Forward

EDWARD C. TELLING, JR.
PRESIDENT
E. C. TELLING, JR. ASSOCIATES, INC.

During the mid-1980s, there was no vendor for a standardized business packaging system. Yes, some brokers did package, but most did either custom work (with little organization) or, in most cases, were not up to the task at hand. Out of this frustration, the concept of Professional Packaging System (PPS) was developed.

PPS is no more or less than an orderly systematic approach to gathering, then reporting, information. Its goal is to collect and report all the basic business information a serious and qualified buyer would want to review before a serious offer is made.

PPS is generic by design, so that specific industry questions can be added to the report. Clarity and the intended audience are important. Consider these factors:

- Degree of sophistication in regard to the acquisition, the industry, and so on affect how the report should be tailored.
- Knowledge of the geographic area affect the amount and type of data supplied; for example, if you expect the buyer to be from outside the

area, a detailed discussion of the regional features is important, as are weather, educational opportunity, demographics, economics, and so on.

The report should have two components:

- An executive summary of 20–40 pages.
- A full report of 50–200 pages.

This chapter includes the Executive Summary, plus the information-gathering factbook as examples of what could be done. Putting your best foot forward doesn't mean hiding bad news, but it does mean high-lighting the good, then making suggested adjustments for the less than good news.

EXAMPLE OF AN EXECUTIVE SUMMARY

Confidential Business Review

Two Hardware/Lumber Companies

NOTICE

The information presented in this document is highly sensitive and Confidential and is for use only by those who have signed a Confidentiality Agreement for the purpose of considering the business described herein as an acquisition. This Confidential Business Review and the information presented shall be treated as Secret and Confidential and no part of it shall be disclosed to others, except as provided in the Confidentiality Agreement. Nor shall it be reproduced, duplicated or revealed, in whole or in part, or used in any other manner without the prior written permission. Should there be no interest in the business as an acquisition, the Confidential Business Review and all information shall be promptly returned or destroyed, as directed.

Presented to: _____

For further information Contact: _____

Copy No.: _____

TABLE OF CONTENTS

PURPOSE AND DISCLAIMER

This Confidential Business Review is intended to acquaint a prospective purchaser with preliminary information regarding a Company whose business is currently available for acquisition, sale, or merger. The format of the Confidential Business Review is designed to reflect to a prospective purchaser the factors that create the value within the Client Company.

The information and exhibits contained in the Confidential Business Review have been obtained primarily from the Company. Although the Company believes the data to be a fair representation of the Company's activities, its completeness or accuracy cannot be guaranteed.

Any representations or warranties with respect to the business or the property of the Company shall be contained in a definitive agreement, negotiated in good faith, and mutually agreed upon between the Company and the prospective purchaser.

This Confidential Business Review is to be furnished only to prospective purchasers having signed a Confidentiality Agreement, and having made a specific request for information regarding the Company for the purpose of determining any interest in submitting an offer to acquire the Company or its business. Each prospective purchaser is responsible for the performance and expense of the due diligence review prior to any acquisition.

The information contained in this Confidential Business Review, including but not limited to the executive summary, business description, corporate history, organization, facilities, and financial statements has been supplied by the Company described. This information has not necessarily been audited or independently confirmed, and no representations, expressed or implied, are made as to its accuracy or completeness or the conclusions drawn. The parties providing such information shall in no way be responsible for the content, accuracy, and truthfulness of such information. Any and all representations shall be made solely by the Company as set forth in a signed acquisition agreement or purchase contract, which agreement or contract shall control as to representations and warranties, if any. By requesting this Confidential Business Review, the recipient acknowledges the responsibility to perform a due diligence review prior to any acquisition of or business combination with the Company.

The Pro Forma Income Statements presuppose infusion of any necessary operating capital, adequacy of personnel, expertise at all levels of operations, and a firm dedication to attain growth. Such pro forma financial information and projections cannot anticipate economic, socioeconomic, and political factors which might impact upon the expected growth. Accordingly, no representations, expressed or implied, are made as to the validity of the pro forma projections.

We believe this would be an excellent operation for the following groups:

1. National group with expansion plans.
2. Current hardware/home center owner in a contiguous territory.
3. Investor/owner who desires a solid base upon which to develop.

1.0 EXECUTIVE SUMMARY

Executive summary normally goes here.

2.0 BUSINESS DESCRIPTION

Two Hardware/Lumber Companies since 1960 with locations in:

- Anywhere 1, USA.
- Anywhere 2, USA.

The first Anywhere operation sells more lumber and lumber products as a percentage of gross sales than does the second Anywhere operation. Neither operation has a single customer accounting for more than five (5) percent of its total sales. Both stores have:

- Credit Terms: Most with approved credit are 30 day/net 10 days. Master Card, VISA, Discover, and American Express accepted.
- Market Area:
  Anywhere 1—Greater Syracuse area with some in Rome/Utica.
  Anywhere 2—Approximately thirty (30) county region.
- Customer Base (estimated percent):

	General Public	Commercial	Government
Anywhere 1	15	80	5
Anywhere 2	30	60	10

- New Business: Generated in equal parts by salespeople, word of mouth, and advertising.

ADVERTISING MEDIA USED

- Direct mail.
- Newspapers.
- Yellow pages.
- Brochures by manufacturers.
- Trade shows for contractors.
- Television (limited).
- Radio (infrequent).

COMPETITORS

EMPLOYEE BENEFITS

- Workers' compensation.
- Group medical/life.
- Paid vacations.
- Paid holidays.
- Sick time—6 days per year.
- Profit-sharing plan.

COMPUTERIZATION

In both locations, covers all areas of operation (two separate systems).

3.0 MARKET

OVERVIEW OF REGION

Regional Statistics—1990

Demographics

	Anywhere Country	Anywhere State	Percent
Land Area (in sq. miles)	9,702	47,219	20.5
Total Population	419,374	17,990,455	2.3
Population Density	43	381	11.3
Number of Families	103,605	4,489,312	2.3
Number of Households	144,195	6,639,322	2.1

Income

	1979	1989
Per Capita Income	$ 5,602	$11,160
Median Family Income	$16,295	$29,535
Median Household Income	$13,547	$25,929
Ranges of Household Incomes		
Less than $5,000	n/a	1,756
$5–30,000	n/a	20,191
$30–55,000	n/a	11,338
$55–150,000	n/a	4,424
More than $150,000	n/a	184
Persons Living in Poverty	11,924	12,252

Employment

	1980	1990
Income Sources		
Total Employment	37,317	50,014
Military	446	9,193
Self-Employed	3,031	3,113
Government	6,909	10,040
Unemployed	4,263	5,107
Employment by Sector		
Total Civilian	32,588	40,821
All Manufacturing	7,300	5,514
Wholesale/Retail	6,224	9,057
Services	7,332	18,616
Farming, Forestry	n/a	1,716
Other	11,732	5,918

Education

	1985	1991
K-12 Enrollments	16,509	19,326
Per Capita K-12	$4,305	$8,204

	1990
Expenditures	
Persons over 25 years, (by years of schooling)	
Less Than 9th Grade	$ 4,602
9–12 (no diploma)	10,707
High School Graduate	24,922
Some college through Bachelor's Degree	21,692
Graduate/Professional Degree	3,044

Income/Employment

	Anywhere Country	Anywhere State	Percent
Per Capita Income	$10,819	$16,501	65.6
Median Family Income	$43,793	$46,820	93.5
Median Household Income	$31,465	$44,712	70.4
Persons Living in Poverty	55,072	2,272,629	2.4
Total Civilian Employment	164,953	n/a	
All Manufacturing	22,473	n/a	
Wholesale/Retail	34,588	n/a	
Services	79,064	n/a	
Other	28,838	n/a	

Note: Percent indicates the Anywhere Country as a percentage of Anywhere State.

North Country Economic Development Agencies

Adirondack Economic Development Corporation
Ernest S. Hohmeyer, Executive Director
518-891-5523

Adirondack North Country Association
Terry de Franco, Executive Director
518-891-6200

Ausable Valley Local Development Corporation
Owen Bombard, Chairman

CITTEC Business Assistance Center
Thomas Plastino, Executive Director
315-286-3778

Champlain (town of) IDA & LDA
William Karstens, Executive Director
518-289-3224

Clinton County Area Development Corporation
Gerard E. Kelly, President
518-563-3100

Development Authority of the North Country
Robert Juravich, Director of Project Development
315-785-2593

Essex County IDA
Arthur Norton, Executive Director
518-873-9114

Franklin County IDA
Stephen Dutton, Executive Director
518-483-6767

Friends of the North Country
Ann Holland, Director
518-834-9606

Jefferson County Economic Development Corporation
Donald A. Foster, Executive Director
315-785-3242

Jefferson County IDA
John H. Nichols, Executive Director
315-785-3226

Lewis County IDA
James E. Monroe, Executive Director
315-376-3014

Massena Economic Development Council
Frank Alguire, Executive Director
315-769-8484

New York State Department of Economic Development
North County Region
Richard Weigel, Director
315-393-3980

Niagara Mohawk Power Corporation
Erik Andersson, Economic Development Coordinator
315-785-7164

Ogdensburg Bridge & Port Authority
Daniel L. Duprey, Executive Director
315-393-4080

Plattsburgh (City of) Community Development Office
Rosemarie Schoonmaker, Director
518-563-7642

St. Lawrence County IDA
Edmund J. Russell, Administrative Director
315-379-2283

St. Regis Mohawk Tribe
Patricia Thomas, Director of Planning & Economic Development
518-358-2272

Watertown Local Development Corporation
Roann J. Dermady, Executive Director

North Country Colleges and Universities

Canton College of Technology
Dr. Joseph Kennedy, President
315-386-7300

Clarkson University
Dr. Richard Gallagher, President
315-265-6467

Clinton Community College
Jay Fennell, President
518-562-4200

Jefferson Community College
Dr. John Deans, President
315-786-2236

Mater Dei College
Father Ron Mronzinski, President
315-393-5930

North Country Community College
Dr. Gail R. Rice, President
518-585-4454 ext. 249

Paul Smith's College
H. David Chamberlin, President
518-327-3030

Potsdam College of the State University of New York
Dr. William Merwin, President
315-267-2115

St. Lawrence University
Dr. Patti McGill, President
315-379-5585

SUNY College at Plattsburgh
Dr. Walter von Saal, Interim President
518-564-2090

Wadhams Hall Seminary College
The Reverend Richard Siepka, President
315-393-4231

JEFFERSON COUNTY

Jefferson County is the westernmost county in the North Country. It is bordered by St. Lawrence County to the northeast, Lewis County to the southeast, Oswego County to the south, Lake Ontario to the west, and the St. Lawrence River to the northwest. At Cape Vincent in Jefferson County, Lake Ontario flows into the St. Lawrence River, and from here to just beyond Alexandria Bay are found the Thousand Islands, which are shared with Canada.

Most of Jefferson County's land area is within the Lake Ontario Plain, consisting of flat to rolling terrain which is intensely farmed. The southeastern part of the county is part of the Tug Hill region. The Black River enters the county near Carthage, flowing westerly to Lake Ontario. Watertown, the North Country's largest city, with 29,080 residents in 1990, is located along its banks. Interstate Route 81, which connects Canada with Syracuse and points south, bisects the county.

The total population of Jefferson County increased 21.1 percent between 1980 and 1990, largely an effect of the dramatic expansion of Fort Drum. While some individual communities lost population, the Fort Drum impact was broadly distributed across the county.

The impact of the Fort Drum expansion on the county economy has been substantial. The construction industry alone accounted for 3,300 of the 41,600 employed in 1989. Estimates for December 1990 showed construction employment falling to only 2,000 (of 40,800 total workers). While civilian employment at Fort Drum and spin-off business from the facility will continue to be significant to the economy, the long-run health of the county is determined more by Jefferson's healthy manufacturing sector. Manufacturing employment, however, actually grew from 5,300 in 1989 to an estimated 5,400 in late 1990.

Manufacturing employment in the county is heavily dependent on employment at New York Air Brake (with employment of about 950) and paper mills large and small. Trade employment is also significant and growing. Coinciding with the Fort Drum buildup and associated retail construction (such as the Salmon Run Mall), total retail employment grew from 7,100 in 1985 to an estimated 10,200 in 1990, a 44 percent increase.

Abundant water power from the Black River led in the nineteenth century to the development of industry in Carthage, Watertown, and other points along the river. Wood-related industries were later joined by a more diversified group of mostly durable-goods manufacturers. Leading industrial employers in Jefferson County include Fort Drum; New York Air Brake; Champion International; Sherwood Medical, which produces thermometers; Northland Electric Motors; Bomax, Inc; and Stature Electric. Paper products are manufactured by Champion International in Deferiet, James River Corporation, Climax Manufacturing Corporation in Carthage, Brownville Specialty Paper in Brownville, and the James River Corporation.

The county is also a regional center for retailing and finance with several retail chains and banks also servicing the geographically isolated counties of Lewis, St. Lawrence, and Franklin.

While industry is concentrated in towns along the Black River, much of the county's land area outside of Fort Drum is farmland. Over 45 percent of the county's land area was in farms in 1982, the highest percentage in the North Country. Like most counties in the state, Jefferson County saw total farm acreage decline between 1982 and 1987. In Jefferson, the decrease was almost 13 percent. With products sold of $77 million in 1987, Jefferson County was a significant contributor to the state's agricultural economy, although total sales fell slightly from 1982. Dairy farms predominate in this area. Jefferson County is a close second to St. Lawrence County in milk production in New York State.

Per capita income was $14,276 in Jefferson County in 1988. While the highest in the North Country, it still lagged the state average by almost $5,000. Relatively higher incomes in Jefferson County are the result of the county's larger concentration of higher-paying, durable-goods manufacturing jobs, relative to other North County counties.

Recent Economic Trends

The fact that Jefferson County does have a sizable industrial base made it more susceptible to the recessions of the past 10 years. The Fort Drum expansion has contributed to a spectacular expansion of employment since 1985, however. Employment covered by unemployment insurance grew 30 percent from 29,500 in 1985 to 38,400 in 1988. Much of this employment was temporary, however, as 1988 was one of the peak construction years for Fort Drum. Despite an absolute increase in manufacturing employment, the share of employment by industry actually shrank from 30.3 percent in 1980 to 17.9 percent in 1988.

The Fort Drum expansion and the county's proximity to Canada have boosted the retail sector in Jefferson County, enabling the construction of the Pyramid Corporation's Salmon Run Mall. Since its construction, Salmon Run has become a retail sales magnet for shoppers from Lewis and St. Lawrence Counties plus Canada. Total retail sales in Jefferson County grew 67 percent between 1985 and 1989, substantially more than the 44 percent growth of the remainder of the region.

While the other counties of the North Country experienced their largest postdepression unemployment rates during the mid-1970s, Jefferson County's peak of 13.8 percent in 1983 was the highest in the North Country. During early 1984, the county had the second-highest unemployment rate in New York State, reaching a staggering 20.4 percent in January 1984. The county's jobless rate fell below 10 percent from June through September, but rose to double digits in October. The December rate of 15.6 percent was the highest in the state. The Fort Drum expansion drove down these unemployment statistics, although they have remained at or above the regional average. Annual average unemployment for 1989 was 8.6 percent, equal to the region's average. November 1990 unemployment stood at 7.6 percent.

Major Strengths and Weaknesses

A discussion of strengths and weaknesses in Jefferson County must focus on the substantial impact of the Fort Drum expansion. Along with increased economic opportunities, a severe strain was placed on local facilities, including police and fire protection, roads, sewage, water, schools, and housing. The Development Authority of the North Country (DANC) was formed by the state to help communities plan cooperatively for major infrastructure improvements. By most accounts, local government and DANC have responded very favorably to the changes, adapting well in the face of "boomtown" growth.

The county boasts significant strengths. Interstate 81 gives the county excellent access to both the Syracuse Hancock Airport and Canada's Route 401. With a well-established industrial infrastructure and considerable population base, the county has seen substantial new investment in manufacturing, service, and retail industry over the previous several years. Much of the 1,000 Islands' attractions are located in Jefferson County communities, giving the county high visibility within the state.

CENTRAL NEW YORK AREA

Introduction

Location: Greater Syracuse is a nexus for the movement of goods and people along the north-south and east-west axes of many transportation routes in the Northeast. Located in the center of New York State on the southern shore of Lake Ontario, the Syracuse Metropolitan Statistical Area (MSA) is a 3,400-square-mile land area composed of four counties: Cayuga, Madison, Onondaga, and Oswego.

The City of Syracuse, located in Onondaga County, is the region's major metropolitan center. It has been appropriately called "the Crossroads of New York State," due to its central location and the fact the state's two major interstate routes—the east-west New York State Thruway (Interstate 90) and north-south Interstate 81—intersect here. In addition to Syracuse, the principal population centers of the MSA are cities of Oswego and Fulton in Oswego County, Oneida in Madison County, and Auburn in Cayuga County.

Transportation: A strategic central location and a well-developed transportation network have made Syracuse a major distribution center. The 1993 Rand McNally *Places Rated Almanac* declared Syracuse 11th of the 343 metropolitan areas examined in regard to transportation facilities. The ranking was based on daily commuting time, public transportation availability, interstate highway convenience, air service, and passenger service. This reflects Syracuse's success in regulating traffic flows, maintaining high-quality infrastructure standards, and encouraging facility expansion.

Approximately 60 million people live within a 350-mile radius of Syracuse. This radius includes the populations of Boston, New York City, Philadelphia, Baltimore, Washington, Pittsburgh, Toronto, and Montreal. Within a 750-mile radius of the Greater Syracuse area, companies have access to over 50 percent of all American and Canadian retail sales, American business establishments, American and Canadian manufacturing facilities, and American wholesale sales.

More than 150 motor carriers and small package carriers service the Syracuse area. Air and rail terminals are just 15 minutes from downtown. Six major airlines, along with affiliated commuter service, offer approximately 250 daily arrivals and departures. Over 2 million travelers pass through Hancock International Airport each year. The region is also serviced by seven major air cargo carriers. Conrail's computerized rail yard has the capacity to handle 2,200 cars per day, while Amtrak services rail passenger needs.

The deep water port of Oswego and the New York State Barge Canal System provide access to the Great Lakes and overseas.

Geography: The Greater Syracuse area is a region of rolling hills, flat plains, lakes, and streams. The City of Syracuse is located on a rise at the southern end of Onondaga Lake. The gently rolling terrain stretches north of the city for 30 miles, where it meets Lake Ontario. The Finger Lakes begin 20 miles to the southwest, and Oneida Lake is 8 miles northeast.

City altitude ranges from 364 to 681 feet, while approximately five miles south of Syracuse, the hills mount to about 1,500 feet. Immediately to the west, the terrain is rolling and elevated 500 to 800 feet above mean sea level.

Natural resources in the area include hardwoods, used in furniture making, and abundant water of high quality, used by local corporations such as Anheuser-Busch and Bristol-Myers Company.

Climate: The Syracuse area enjoys a four-season continental climate with marked season changes. Due to geographical location, cyclonic systems that move from the interior of the country through the St. Lawrence Valley affect the Syracuse weather, as do the cold air masses that advance through the Great Lakes region from the Hudson Bay area, making winters cold and snowy.

During the summer and parts of spring and autumn, temperatures customarily rise rapidly during daytime to fall rapidly after sunset, so the nights are relatively cool and comfortable. Excessive warm spells are rare. Temperatures average 24 degrees in January, 46 degrees in April, 71 in July, and 62 degrees in September.

Greater Syracuse generally enjoys sufficient precipitation to comfortably meet the needs of agriculture and water supplies. Rainfall is well distributed, with monthly averages close to three inches. As a rule, wind velocities are moderate, reaching around 11 miles per hour during the colder months.

Population

County of Onondaga   1990   468,973   + 1.09 (over 1980)

F.W. Dodge Construction Report

(Madison, Onondaga, and Oswego Counties)

Housing—Onondaga County

Municipality	1983	1984	1985	1986	1987	1988	1989	1990	1991	1992	1993	Annual Average 1983–1993	No. by Type 1983–1993
Towns Subtotal													
Single	1288	1685	1819	2067	1855	1799	1668	1200	1000	1221	991	1944.0	91.1
Multiple	104	195	571	387	265	50	128	40	90	26	22	188.8	8.8
Total	1392	1880	2390	2454	2120	1849	1796	1240	1090	1247	1212	2132.8	0
Syracuse													
Single	59	24	39	52	50	31	100	47	65	48	56	51.9	32.6
Multiple	45	199	55	59	281	116	199	117	40	26	45	107.5	67.4
Total	104	223	94	111	331	147	299	164	105	74	101	159.4	0
Onondaga County													
Single	1346	1709	1858	2119	1907	1827	1768	1265	1065	1269	1047	1561.8	84.1
Multiple	149	394	626	446	546	166	327	157	130	52	266	296.2	15.9
Total	1495	2103	2484	2565	2451	1987	2095	1422	1195	1321	1313	1858.0	0

Note: Town totals include villages (if available).
Source: Syracuse-Onondaga County Planning Agency 2/94.

	March No. of Projects (Cumulative to Date)		March Value ($000) (Cumulative to Date)	
	1993	1994	1993	1994
Total Construction	301	278	$278,239	$81,854
Total Building·	275	248	65,838	69,486
Nonresidential	61	58	33,387	44,203
Residential	214	190	32,451	25,283
Nonbuilding	26	30	212,401	12,368

New Homes

Year	No. of Building Permits Issued
1983	1,495
1984	2,103
1985	2,484
1986	2,565
1987	2,451
1988	1,987
1989	2,095
1990	1,422
1991	1,195
1992	1,321
1993	1,313

Source: Syracuse-Onondaga County Planning Agency.

Median Selling Price of Homes

Comparative Regions	
Onondaga County	$ 72,320
U.S. Median	106,800
Northeast Median (New England, NY, PA, NJ)	139,500
Midwest	85,200
South	95,100
West	142,500

Source: Greater Syracuse Association of Realtors 1/94.

Effective Buying Income

Syracuse Metropolitan Statistical Area (MSA) (Cayuga, Madison, Onondaga, and Oswego Counties)

Syracuse MSA	10,370,061	32,925	10,833,532	33,677
Madison County	940,353	33,784	986,579	34,949
Oswego County	1,493,823	30,576	1,574,234	31,890
Onondaga County	6,945,587	33,409	7,259,126	34,607
City of Syracuse	1,924,682	23,112	2,008,434	23,795

Source: Sales and Marketing Management Survey of Buying Power 1992 and 1993.

1994 Unemployment Rates (in Percentage Figures)

Month	Syracuse MSA	Onondaga County	New York State	United States
January	6.7%	5.4%	8.2%	7.3%
February	7.6	6.2	8.5	7.1
March	6.8	5.7	8.1	6.8
April	6.4	5.3	7.6	6.2

Source: New York State Department of Labor, Division of Research Statistics.

EXHIBIT—ANYWHERE FACT SHEET

4.0 ORGANIZATION

NORMALLY A CHART OF PERSONNEL

5.0 FACILITIES

A. Anywhere 1, USA

@ 434 Anywhere Boulevard

Leased Facility

Site Development: The subject is located on the southeast corner of Eastern Boulevard and Huntington Street and between Hunt Street on the east and Eastern Boulevard to the west. It contains approximately 8.46 acres according to assessment records, and is irregular in shape. Subject has frontages of 660 feet on the eastern side of Eastern Boulevard, 142.58 feet on the southerly side of Huntington Street, and 149.20 feet on the western side of Hunt Street. It is above grade from just about all frontage except for that portion south from the driveway entrance off Eastern Boulevard, which is nearly level.

The property is encumbered by two waterline easements of 24- and 16-inch mains. They both traverse subject in a southwest-northeast direction and are located along Eastern Boulevard.

All public utilities are available to the site with the exception of sewer.

Site improvements consist of approximately 19,000 square feet of paved tarvia drive and parking, 51,341 square feet of stone and gravel cover, 480 square feet of concrete walk, about 422 linear foot of 6-foot high chain-link fencing with four gates and three strand barbed wire. The underground fuel tank and pump have been removed since our last appraisal, and a new septic system has been installed.

Building Improvements: The subject property is improved with 13 buildings, which contain a total ground floor area of 57,296 square feet.

Building #1 is a 13,600-square foot Quonset building and retail store having 9,200 square feet of finished office and showroom space and 4,000 square feet of warehouse space. The finished office space consists of four private offices, sales counter, two two-fixture lavatories, and employee break room with flooring which is half concrete and half blacktop covered with combination asphalt/tile/carpet, drop acoustical ceiling with indirect lighting, combination paneled/sheetrock/pegboard walls; and oil-fired forced air heat. The rear warehouse and storage area is open space, having an 18-foot ceiling, incandescent lighting, second-story loft on each end, and no plumbing or heating. The 80- x 72-foot retail store area is new and is attached to the existing showroom area via an adjoining 20-foot hallway. This addition is essentially a warehouse-type construction that has steel walls, steel bar joist with steel decking, and built-up roof cover. Floors are vinyl tile over reinforced concrete. Walls and open ceilings are fully insulated. There is incandescent lighting, and it is heated by the existing system. Electric service has been upgraded from 200 to 400 amp entrance.

Building #2 is a 4,320-square foot warehouse structure connected by wood frame roof enclosure consisting of wood trusses and flat built-up roof, having a 16-foot ceiling, floor, incandescent lighting, a 12-foot overhead door; no plumbing or heating.

Building #3 is a 7,200-square foot Quonset warehouse building having an 18-foot ceiling, blacktop floor, incandescent lighting, 12-foot overhead door; no plumbing or heating.

Building #4 is a 4,320 square foot warehouse building connected to Building #3 by a wood frame roof enclosure consisting of wood trusses and flat built-up roof. It is partially connected to Building #5 along its other side, with the remaining wall being frame construction with sheet metal siding. It has a 16-foot ceiling, blacktop floor, incandescent lighting, 12-foot overhead door; no plumbing or heating.

Buildings #1 through #4 appear to be interconnected with subsequent improvements having been done since 1983. A brick façade with mansard has been added to the storefront, and there has been exterior painting of the Quonset sections. These buildings are in fair to average condition with the exception of the retail store addition, which is near new.

Building #5 is a 2,400-square-foot Quonset warehouse having an 18-foot ceiling, blacktop floor, incandescent lighting, sliding doors; no plumbing or heating. The building is old construction and in generally poor condition.

Buildings #6, 7, 8, and 13 are one-story pole construction lumber storage buildings with shed-type roofs, metal roof and siding, and open to one side. The buildings are in average condition, and contain a total gross building area of 5,712 square feet.

Building #9 is a one-story, four-stall garage of pole construction with gable roof having metal covering, metal siding, and four metal 10-foot overhead doors. It is in average condition, and contains a total gross building area of 1,536 square feet.

Building #10 is a one-story combination masonry/frame Quonset loading dock, office, and storage building containing, 4,208 square feet of gross building area. It contains 1,280 square feet of enclosed dock area with four 8-foot overhead doors. This portion of the building is concrete block with frame flat built-up roof and overhang. The remainder of the building consists of Quonset-type storage and finished office area consisting of five private offices, two two-fixture lavatories, storage room, block ceilings, panelled and sheetrock walls, carpet over plywood flooring, neon lighting; oil-fired forced air heat. The frame portion of the building has aluminum siding. The building is in generally fair condition. However, its floor plan is poorly laid out and cut up due to a series of add-on construction over the years.

Building #11 is a one-story 5,000-square foot frame warehouse with office and shop. It is wood frame construction with aluminum clapboard siding, flat built-up roof, aluminum sash windows, wood passdoors, and wood overhead door. The warehouse and shop area has concrete floor, incandescent lighting; no plumbing or heating. The small office space consists of 600 square feet, is of older-type construction having tile-covered floors, sheetrock walls and ceilings, neon lighting, and two two-fixture lavatories. The building is older and in generally only fair to average condition.

Building #12: A major portion of this structure collapsed and has subsequently been rebuilt. Present construction consists of a metal S-type structure with a gable style metal roof. This new section contains about 7,800 square feet, and was built within the same perimeters of the former structure. It has sheetrock walls and ceiling, a 12-foot clear span, incandescent lighting, and a small office area. The remaining 1,200 square feet consist of the former Quonset-type construction, and has an 18-foot clear span. Total building area is 9,000 square feet. There are four overhead doors, two at either end. Building has no heating or plumbing and is generally in average condition.

NOTE: Buildings 10, 11, and 12 are not used by the Company. They are leased to another party.

Neighborhood Data: The subject neighborhood is located in the extreme northeast section of the City of Watertown, some 2 plus/minus miles from the downtown central business district. Eastern Boulevard (NYS Route 3), running north off State Street, is the major highway running through the subject neighborhood carrying local traffic as well as northbound thru-traffic. The neighborhood is generally bounded on the north by Black River, on the south by State Street, on the east by Hunt Street, and on the west by the city line.

Land use in the immediate neighborhood is mixed with light industrial, commercial, institutional, and residential (both single-family and multifamily). The immediate neighborhood is sparsely developed with such uses as the Watertown Racquet Club, Parkside Bible Church, Stebbin's Engineering, City municipal water pumping station, HUD Housing Project, East Hill Apartment complex, and the subject. Commercial uses to the south include the Northland Shopping Strip Center, Watertown Savings Bank, McDonald's fast-food restaurant, Cole and Monro Muffler automotive centers, gasoline service stations, and former residences that have been converted to commercial/office uses, which are located a short distance south along Eastern Boulevard and State Street.

In general, the neighborhood is relatively stable, and will continue to experience moderate demand and growth when the recession wanes.

Economic Trends: The construction boom and fast-paced real property value growth of the mid- to late-1980s has ceased. This growth was a direct result of the Fort Drum expansion. Subsequent completion and the recession has resulted in stabilization at best, and in most instances, a decline in property values.

State equalization rates have declined from 118.15 percent in 1989 to 93.87 percent currently. This is a 20 percent decrease, indicating an approximate increase in property value of 7 percent per year. However, publication of these rates lag research by two to three years and include residential properties. Due to falling interest rates, the housing market has been more active than other property types.

Conversations with local real estate professionals indicate a declining commercial market, with demand slight. Consequently, allocations of minus 3 percent to 5 percent per year are allocated since 1989-1990.

B. Anywhere 2, USA

Leased

- 6,000 plus/minus square foot warehouse.
- 5,000 plus/minus square foot main building, which includes office and showroom.
- Additional pole barn storage units located on property.

RECAST FINANCIAL STATEMENTS

Since privately owned companies tend to keep reported profits and thus taxes as low as possible, financial recasting is an important element to understanding the earning capacity of the business enterprise. Recasting provides an economic view of the Company and allows meaningful comparisons with other investment opportunities. Financial recasting eliminates such items as excessive and discretionary expenses and nonrecurring revenues and expenses from the historical financial presentation, along with debt and interest expense since they reflect the financing decision of the current owner and may not represent financing preferences of a new owner.

Recast and pro forma financial information and schedules are based upon data and information submitted by the Company, and assumptions and estimates of future transactions which might occur with new ownership. The Company's books and records have not necessarily been audited, nor have the statements and assumptions of the Company been independently verified.

Changes involved in recasting are set forth in the footnotes accompanying each financial statement within the available report or document. The reader should recognize that recast and pro forma financial statements and schedules are intended to be used for analytical purposes only and are not suitable for financial statement or financial reporting purposes.

6.0 FINANCIALS

PROFESSIONAL PACKAGING SYSTEM

The purpose of this Material is to:

1. Serve as a workbook that will accurately reflect the Business and answer the questions we know will come up in the sale or transfer of the Business. It will not answer all the questions, unfortunately.
2. Serve as the Model for Package One, which goes to the interested and qualified client after qualification.
3. Serve as a model for Package One Supplement, which typically goes to a client only after a Letter of Intent or Offer to Purchase.

THESE NUMBERS WERE SUPPLIED TO
(INSERT COMPANY INFORMATION)

BY THE SELLER
(INSERT COMPANY INFORMATION)

HAS NEITHER AUDITED
NOR CONFIRMED THE ACCURACY OF SAME
(INSERT COMPANY INFORMATION)

BUSINESS PACKAGE

1. a. Description of business.
   b. History of business.
   c. Reason for sale.
   d. Area in which the business is located—map.
   e. Support material.
2. Marketing considerations.
   a. Price and terms.
   b. Gross sales, gross profit—on accounting spreadsheet.
   c. Fixture and equipment list.
   d. Monthly expenses/sales comparison.
   e. Changes likely to be made by new owner (assumption).
   f. Financial changes to be made, RMA; Dun & Bradstreet, industry numbers (assumption).
   g. Photographs.
   h. Advertising material used by business.
   i. Price list/advertising material, and so on.

3. Property description or lease.
   a. Value/description.
   b. Survey.
   c. Condition of property.
   d. Comparables.
   e. Professional appraisal of real property (recommend, MAI).
4. Competition in market.
5. Market conditions affecting the business (local and industry data).
6. Personnel requirements of business.
7. Bankability analysis.

APPENDIX 1A SUPPLEMENT

8. Financials.
   a. Five years federal and account statements as available.
   b. Three years sales tax reports with checks.
   c. Assumptions/disclaimer.
      Adjusted P&L for last year.
   d. Adjusted pro forma for next year with assumptions and disclaimer.
   e. Key operating detail.
   f. New depreciation schedule.
   g. Cash flow analysis.
9. Computer business evaluation type _____.
   Available: YES _____ NO _____ DATE _____.

INFORMATION NEEDED TO SELL YOUR BUSINESS

1. Lease (current and executed).*
2. Furniture/fixtures/equipment list: signed, dated, and priced.*
3. Financial information:*
   a. Profit and loss statements (5-year period).
   b. Balance sheets (5-year period).
   c. Federal tax (5-year period).
   d. Payroll records (2-year period) and employee names, ages, service length.
4. Sales tax reports (3 years by quarter with a copy of payment check).*
5. Franchise agreement (if applicable).*
6. Advertising material used in business.*
7. Pictures by broker.

*THIS INFORMATION REQUIRED FROM THE OWNER!

8. Economic evaluation.

9. Copy of licenses.*

10. Copy of last month's prime paid invoices.*

11. Court house check UCCI–By (INSERT COMPANY INFORMATION) or closing attorney.

12. Speak with landlord (INSERT COMPANY INFORMATION).

13. Copy of several advertisements on business.

14. Written description of business.*

WHAT BUYERS ARE LOOKING FOR WHEN BUYING A BUSINESS

1. *F, F, & E*

   Estimated value for tax depreciation, state sales tax. In working order and pass inspection.

2. *Copy of Lease*

   Transferability, expiration date, option, C.P.I., and other costs.

3. *Proof of Sales and/or Proof of Purchases*

   Monthly P & Ls plus state sales tax returns, Schedule C for federal income tax return—for debt service. Intraworkings of the business.

4. *Training and Transition Period*

   Ten days to two weeks after the close: 80 percent are first-time buyers, who will pay the highest price closest to the price you want for your business. The Pro buyer won't pay the seller's price.

5. *Covenant Not to Compete*

   Time, distance, and dollar amount (fear and tax implication).

6. *R.O.I.*

   10 percent now—was 15 percent.

7. *Can Buyer Make a Decent Living Wage after Debt Service?*

8. *Leverage*

   VA-O, FHA 5–20 percent D/P, Bus 30 percent D/P or one year's provable net income. Back-up monies by buyers can be $5 and up.

9. *Franchise Agreement*

   Transfer fee?

   Training period/cost?

   Years left?

10. *Reason for Sale?*

11. *Time Is of the Essence*

    When we get the Deposit Receipt signed.

12. *What Else Should We Know about Your Business?*

    We can handle anything if we know, such as landlord problems, state, and IRS taxes, existing notes, and so on, but you must tell us now!!

EXPANDED DOCUMENT CHECKLIST

REVIEW AND USE AS REQUIRED

1. Credit report (Dun & Bradstreet).
2. Aged schedule of accounts receivable.
3. Physical inventory: when; quality of inventory; standard accounting methods followed?
4. Analysis of insurance—get policy and invoice.
5. Schedule of other assets.
6. Schedule of accounts payable.
7. Analysis of long-term debt.
8. Mortgage.
9. Loan agreements.
10. List of contingent liabilities.
11. List of stockholders and stock held.
12. Schedule of earnings and profits.
13. Analysis of lease agreements.
14. Acquisition audit.
15. Internal Revenue Service agent's reports.
16. Executives' resumés.
17. Employment contracts.
18. Union contracts.
19. All other major contracts.
20. All employee benefit plans (profit sharing, pensions, stock options, health, life, and so on).
21. Appraisals (inventory, machinery, equipment, buildings, and so on).
22. Pro forma balance sheet after the purchase.
23. Projected income for five years after acquisition.
24. Memorandum discussing the appraisal rights of the dissenting stockholders.
25. Favorable Internal Revenue Service rulings—ask client's CPA.
26. Covenant not to compete—detail out.
27. Consulting agreements.
28. Attorney's representation letter.
29. Seller's representation and warranties.
30. Letter of intent.
31. Closing agreements.

INTRODUCTION TO PROCESS

When reviewing a proposed listing, resolve the following issues:

1. Is this a business that you can sell? Will it be right for the buyer, and will it be successful after it is acquired?
2. Can you get a "fair" price agreed and with "fair" terms?
3. After acquisition, will the business be properly financed (that is, adequate working capital, good long-term financing and sufficient equity)?
4. Will the business generate sufficient cash flow to service its debt and provide your buyer with a good return on his/her investment?

To answer these questions, the following information must be developed:

1. Past financial history.
2. Management appraisal.
3. Determination of the market value of the assets to be acquired.
4. A knowledge of the competition.
5. Method of acquisition.
6. Projected statements of income and cash flow for five years *after* purchase.

This checklist should help you to acquire the desired and necessary information.

GENERAL INFORMATION

Name of Company:

Address:

Telephone Number:

Chief Executive Officer:

Chief Financial Officer:

Outside Auditors:

Name of Firm:

Name of Contact:

Address:

Telephone:

Appointment Date with CPA:

Attorney:

    Name of Firm:

    Name of Contact:

    Address:

    Telephone:

Appointment Date with Attorney:

Broker: NAME

    Name of Contact: No. _____

    Address: COMPANY ADDRESS

    Telephone Number: PHONE

Other Key Individuals or Consultants:

Name	Relationship	Telephone Number

USE ADDITIONAL SHEETS IF REQUIRED

1-E.   INTRODUCTION TO THE BUSINESS

Business Background: _____

Business Established   Date: _____   City: _____   State: _____

Business Incorporated   Date: _____   City: _____   State: _____

Business Operations: _____

_____

Strengths of Company: _____

_____

Weaknesses of Company: _____

_____

Liabilities or Legal Actions Pending:

1. _____

2. _____

3. _____

4. _____

5. _____

Description of Facilities Owned: _____

_____

Description of Facilities Leased: _____

_____

Terms of Lease: _____

_____

_____

Details of Any Renewal Options:

_____

_____

_____

_____

Equipment Included in Sale

Quantity	Type	Value	Total

_____

_____

_____

Is There a Permit or License Required ( )Yes ( )No Type: _____

Describe Any Required Specialized Skills: _____

_____

_____

_____

Professional Staff Critical to Operations: _____

_____

_____

_____

Describe Customer Base: _____

_____

_____

_____

Number of Active Accts: _____

Indiv. Represent _____ % of Regular Accts. _____

Corp. Represent _____ % of Regular Accts. _____

Gov't. Represent _____ % of Regular Accts. _____

Describe Customers Accounting for More than 10 Percent of Revenues: _____

_____

_____

Days and Hours of Operation: _____ Peak Business Hours: _____

Revenues are Seasonal   (   ) Yes (   ) No   Peak Season: _____

Represents _____ % of Revenues

Major Competitors:

1. _____

2. _____

3. _____

4. _____

5. _____

6. _____

Also Note: Strong, specialty competition.

_____

Marketing Strategy: _____

_____

Advertising and Promotional Expense Last Year

$ _____ Contracts

Media Used: _____

_____

Employees: _____ No. of Employees by Function: _____

Last Name	First Initial	Service Job Function	Wage	Full/Part

Total Numbers: _____

Payroll Service _____ Who _____ # _____ Permission

If not, get one year's records (last year's).

Have there been any major changes in employment in the last year?

ADDITIONAL INFORMATION

	Yes	No	When
1. Training agreement on listing.	_____	_____	_____
2. Signed by all owners (check one).			
Corporation	_____	_____	_____
Partnership	_____	_____	_____
Proprietorship	_____	_____	_____
3. Covenant not to compete on listing.	_____	_____	_____
4. Seller compliance and payments current with:			
Sales tax returns	_____	_____	_____
IRS withholding	_____	_____	_____
Mortgage payments	_____	_____	_____
Chattel Lien	_____	_____	_____
5. Seller compliance with:			
Zoning laws	_____	_____	_____
Health and safety laws	_____	_____	_____
6. Property included:			
In total price	_____	_____	_____
Option to purchase in lease	_____	_____	_____
If yes, are we covered for commission on exercise of option?	_____	_____	_____

1. Introduction to the Business.

    A. Written description of business.

    B. History of business—details: be accurate.

    C. Reason for sale.

    D. Area located on a map (photo $8\frac{1}{2} \times 11$, if possible).

    Mark Competition on the map in a different color.

2. Marketing Considerations.

    A. Price of business.

    Price and terms.

        Total price: _____

        Down payment: _____

        Note: $_____$ Term: _____ % _____

        How secured: _____

    Assets Being Sold   Value

    1. _____   _____

    2. _____   _____

    3. _____   _____

    4. _____   _____

    5. _____   _____

    6. _____   _____

    7. _____   _____

        Total Value: _____

B. We suggest these changes should be made by new owner:

C. Financial changes to be made by new owner by the following adjustments:

D. Photographs (insert).

E. Advertising material used by business—copies.

F. Price List, and so on.

3. Market Conditions Affecting the Business.

   Local/National/Industry.

4. Bankability Analysis

   Total price: _____ Down payment: _____

   Terms: _____ Year: _____ % _____ Monthly

   Adjusted cash flow of $ _____

   Less debt service

   A. Bank: _____

   B. Seller: _____

   Estimated

   Closing costs: _____

   Back-up funds: _____

   Additional funds: _____

   Buyer Needs

   Cash: _____

   Usable collateral of: _____

   Skills of Buyer to Make Bank Comfortable

FINANCIAL INFORMATION

Assets: In determining the value of a company, the book value of its tangible and intangible assets must be adjusted to reflect fair market value.

Items to consider:

Accounts Receivable:

1. Obtain a schedule of accounts receivable.

2. Determine the age of the balances due.

3. Determine the reasons for all overdue accounts.

4. Find out if any amounts are in dispute.

5. Do the delinquent accounts have the ability to pay?

6. Are any of the accounts pledged?

7. Are the reserves for bad debts sufficient?

8. Total adjustment required $ _____ .

Inventory:

1. Make sure the inventory is determined by physical count.

2. Establish the method of valuation (cost, market, retail LIFO, FIFO, other).

3. Determine the age and condition of the inventory.

4. How is damaged or obsolete inventory valued?

5. Is the amount of inventory sufficient to operate efficiently?

6. Should the inventory be reduced?

7. Is the inventory properly insured?

8. Should an appraisal be obtained?

9. Total adjustment required: $ _____ .

Marketing Securities:

1. Obtain a list of marketable securities.

2. How are the securities valued?

3. Determine the fair market value of the securities.

4. Are any securities restricted or pledged?

5. Should the portfolio be sold or exchanged?

6. Total adjustment required $ _____ .

Real Estate (Get Survey—Check Date):

1. Obtain a schedule of real estate owned.

2. Determine the condition and age of the real estate.

3. Establish the fair market value of the buildings and land.

4. Should appraisals be obtained? Absolutely _____ Probably not _____

5. Are repairs or improvements required? Details? Codes?

6. Are maintenance costs reasonable?

7. Is the real estate required to operate the business efficiently?

8. How is the real estate financed?

9. Are the mortgages assumable?

10. Will additional real estate be required within the near future (estimated cost $ _____)?

11. Should the company be moved to a new location?

12. Should any real estate be sold (estimated sales price $ _____)?

13. Is the real estate adequately insured?

14. Total adjustment required $ _____ .

Machinery and Equipment:

1. Obtain a schedule of machinery and equipment owned or leased.

2. Determine the condition and age of the machinery and equipment.

3. Identify the machinery and equipment that is obsolete.

4. Establish the fair market value of the machinery and equipment owned.

5. Should an appraisal be obtained?

6. Will immediate repairs be required? (If yes, estimated cost $ _____).

7. Is the maintenance cost reasonable?

8. Will additional machinery and equipment be needed within the near future (estimated cost ($ _____)?

9. Should some of the machinery be sold (estimated sales price $ _____)?

10. Should any leases be canceled?

11. Is the machinery and equipment adequately insured?

12. Total adjustment required $ _____ .

Other Assets:

1. Review all other assets and determine their fair market value.

Assets	Book Value	Fair Market Value
_____	_____	_____
_____	_____	_____
_____	_____	_____
_____	_____	_____

2. Total adjustment required $ _____ .

Liabilities: All liabilities should be reviewed to determine contingent liabilities and adjustments for undisclosed liabilities and amounts in dispute.

Accounts Payable:

1. Obtain a schedule of accounts payable.

2. Determine the age of amounts due.

3. Identify all amounts in dispute and determine the reason.

4. Determine amounts owed to present owners and related companies.

5. Review transaction to determine undisclosed and contingent liabilities and amounts in dispute.

6. Total adjustment required $ _____ .

Accrued Liabilities:

1. Obtain a schedule of accrued liabilities.

2. Determine the accounting treatment of:
—Unpaid wages at end of the period.
—Accrued vacation pay.
—Accrued sick leave.
—Payroll taxes due and payable.
—Accrued federal income taxes.
—Other accruals.

3. Search for unrecorded accrued liabilities.

4. Total adjustment required $ _____ .

Notes Payable:

1. Obtain a schedule of notes payable.

2. Identify reason for indebtedness.

3. Determine terms and payment schedule.

4. Will the acquisition accelerate the note?

5. Determine if there are any balloon payments to be made, the amounts, and dates due.

Description of Note	Amount of Balloon Payment	Payment Due Date
_____	_____	_____
_____	_____	_____
_____	_____	_____
_____	_____	_____
_____	_____	_____

6. Should the obligations be paid off or reduced?

7. Could interest expense be reduced through refinancing?

Mortgages Payable:

1. Obtain a schedule of mortgages payable.

2. Prepare an amortization schedule.

3. Determine if there are any balloon payments to be made, the amount, and date due.

Description of Mortgage	Amount of Balloon Payment	Payment Due Date
_____	_____	_____
_____	_____	_____
_____	_____	_____
_____	_____	_____
_____	_____	_____

4. Are the mortgages assumable?

5. Will the acquisition accelerate the mortgage?

6. Could interest expense be reduced through refinancing?

Other Long-Term Liabilities:

1. Obtain a schedule of other long-term liabilities.

2. Examine documents to confirm amounts, interest rates.

3. Search for undisclosed liabilities resulting from violation, fines, penalties, disputed amounts, lawsuits, uncapitalized leases, other.

Type of Liability	Amount
_____	_____
_____	_____
_____	_____
_____	_____
_____	_____

4. Total adjustment required $ _____ .

Shareholders' Equity:

1. Determine the number of shares authorized, issued, and held in the treasury.

2. Obtain a list of stockholders.

3. Determine the source of paid-in capital.

4. Obtain an analysis of earnings and profits.

2-A. Income Statement Data

	19x Last Fiscal Year	19x Actual Fiscal Year
Sales Revenue		
Gross Profit		
Income before Taxes		
Owner's Compensation		
Owner's Car and Memberships		
Owner's Travel and Entertainment		
Owner's Insurance and Other		
Depreciation		
Total Owner's Compensation		
Debt Service of Existing Business		

Target Company's Statement of Income and Expense

Five Years Prior to Acquisition

	5th Year	4th Year	3rd Year	2nd Year	Latest Year
Sales	$ _____	_____	_____	_____	_____
Less Cost of Sales	_____	_____	_____	_____	_____
Gross Profit	_____	_____	_____	_____	_____
Less Selling Expense	_____	_____	_____	_____	_____
General and Admin. Expense	_____	_____	_____	_____	_____
Net Income	_____	_____	_____	_____	_____
Less Interest Expense	_____	_____	_____	_____	_____
Net Income before Taxes	_____	_____	_____	_____	_____
Less Federal Income Taxes	_____	_____	_____	_____	_____
Net Income after Taxes	$ _____	_____	_____	_____	_____

2-B. Monthly Expenses/Sales Comparison

Gross Monthly Sales		Basic Cost of Operation
19____ 19____		per Month

JAN $_____	JAN $_____	Rent/taxes	_____
FEB _____	FEB _____	Salary (owner)	_____
MAR _____	MAR _____	Utilities	_____
APR _____	APR _____	Insurance	_____
MAY _____	MAY _____	Accounting	_____
JUN _____	JUN _____	Licenses	_____
JUL _____	JUL _____	Equip. rental	_____
AUG _____	AUG _____	Payroll FT PT _____	
SEP _____	SEP _____	Payroll Taxes	_____
OCT _____	OCT _____	Advertising	_____
NOV _____	NOV _____	Repairs	_____
DEC _____	DEC _____	Maintenance	_____
		Supplies	_____
TOT. _____	TOT. _____	Depreciation	_____
(Mo./Avg._____)	(Mo./Avg._____)	Amortization	_____
		Auto	_____
Less Cost of Goods		Travel	_____
_____ %	_____ %	Entertainment	_____
		Other	_____
Monthly/Gross	Monthly/Gross		
Profit _____	Profit_____	Total $ _____	

Loan Payments

A. _____

B. _____

C. _____

D. _____

Insurance (Does client bid insurance annually? Y/N)

	Type	Amount	Agent/Company
A.	_____	_____	_____
B.	_____	_____	_____
C.	_____	_____	_____
D.	_____	_____	_____

Utilities

Gas _____

Electric _____

Water _____

3. *Property Description*

A. Estimated Value _____

Appraisal Included _____

B. Survey _____

C. Condition of Property:

Unusual conditions/problems:

D. Are Comparables Included?

E. Recommended Professional Appraisal _____

Survey By:

To P & L Summary:

1. Owner(s) (_____)

   Salary, if included in expense. $ _____

2. Discretionary Expense, if indicated

   in expense.

   a. Auto expenses   _____

   b. Travel   _____

   c. Insurance   _____

   d. Interest, if not applicable   _____

   e. Entertainment   _____

   f. _____   _____

   g. _____   _____

3. Noncash Expenses:

   a. Depreciation   _____

   b. Amortization   _____

4. Total Adjustments   _____

5. Net Profit (Loss) from P & L   _____

6. Seller's Discretionary Cash   _____ ×.75
                                                      (Debt Service)

7. Buyer's Discretionary Cash   _____ divided by 1.10
                                                      (Return on Cash)

8. Recommended Down Payment

      Living Wage   _____ divided by .4
                                                        (Industry Standard)

9. Agreement—one-year wage set aside   _____

10. Recommended Selling Price   _____

Note: If you use a stand-alone computer evaluation tool, there is no need to use this sheet.

Confidential

Broker's Pricing Guide

Business Name: _____ Date: _____

The following methods of pricing a business are to be used only as a guideline. It is suggested that you determine the price of a business using various methods; once this is done, you should select a reasonable price and terms that will do the job. The business will not sell if it has an unrealistic price.

1. Avg. Monthly Receipts (Proven)

$ _____ × Factor _____ = $ _____

2. Asset Value Equipment $ _____

   Inventory $ _____

   Proven 1 Yrs Net $ _____ (Include Owner Wage)

   Total $ _____

3. Net Cash Flow: $ _____ × 2.5 = $ _____

4. SDS: Price According to SDS Formula $ _____

5. Seller's Valuation $ _____

6. Other Pricing Method $ _____

Remember, terms will sell a business faster than price. You should obtain the best terms the seller will offer. The seller will get his best price with good terms.

Note: If you use a stand-alone computer evaluation tool, there is no need to use this sheet.

Ratios and Other Financial Analysis:

The following ratios and analyses will set forth the Company's financial strengths and weaknesses. A comparison over the past five years will show financial trends.

Short-Term Liquidity

	5th Year	4th Year	3rd Year	2nd Year	Latest Year
1. Current ratio	_____	_____	_____	_____	_____
Current assets/ Current liabilities					
2. Quick ratio	_____	_____	_____	_____	_____
Cash and market securities and accounts receivable and notes/Current liabilities					
3. Accounts receivable turnover	_____	_____	_____	_____	_____
Net credit sales/Average accounts receivable					
4. Collection period	_____	_____	_____	_____	_____
365 days/Average accounts receivable turnover					
5. Inventory turnover	_____	_____	_____	_____	_____
Cost of goods sold/Average inventory					
6. Days to sell	_____	_____	_____	_____	_____
365 days/Inventory turnover					

Capital Structure and Long-Term Solvency

	5th Year	4th Year	3rd Year	2nd Year	Latest Year
1. Total debt to equity	_____	_____	_____	_____	_____

Current and long-term debt to equity

2. Long-term debt to equity	_____	_____	_____	_____	_____

Return on Investment

	5th Year	4th Year	3rd Year	2nd Year	Latest Year
1. Return on total assets	_____	_____	_____	_____	_____

Net income/Total assets

2. Return on equity	_____	_____	_____	_____	_____

Net income/Total equity

8-A. Operating Performance

	5th Year	4th Year	3rd Year	2nd Year	Latest Year
1. Gross margins	_____	_____	_____	_____	_____

Gross profit/Sales

2. Pretax income to sales	_____	_____	_____	_____	_____

Pretax income/Sales

3. Net income to sales	_____	_____	_____	_____	_____

Net income/Sales

4. Sales to accounts receivable	_____	_____	_____	_____	_____

Sales/Accounts receivable

5. Sales to inventory	_____	_____	_____	_____	_____

Sales/Inventory

Have client sign copy of disclaimer prior to releasing package.

8-B. *Adjusted next year pro forma* _____ *yr*

8-C. *Key Operating Detail*

8-D. *New Depreciation Schedule*

8-E. *Cash Flow Analysis*

8-F. *Projected Income and Cash Flow for Five Years After Purchase*

	1st Year	2nd Year	3rd Year	4th Year	5th Year
Sales	_____	_____	_____	_____	_____
Less Cost of Sales	_____	_____	_____	_____	_____
Gross Profit	_____	_____	_____	_____	_____
Less Expenses	_____	_____	_____	_____	_____
Net Income before Taxes	_____	_____	_____	_____	_____
Less Taxes	_____	_____	_____	_____	_____
Net Income	_____	_____	_____	_____	_____
Plus Depreciation	_____	_____	_____	_____	_____
Plus Other Noncash Expenses	_____	_____	_____	_____	_____
Cash Flow	_____	_____	_____	_____	_____

9-A. Management

Name:

Position:

Summary of duties:

Number of years with the company:

Age:

Resumé obtained?

Shares held:

Shares under option:

Salary and benefit package (total amount):

Employment contract?

Will executive remain with the company after acquisition?

Is a replacement available should the executive leave?

9-B. Personnel Requirements

A. Detail employees as to job description, pay rate, fringe benefits, hours worked, and length of employment.

B. Changes that should (or could) be made.

C. Raises due? To whom? How much?

9-C. (Supplemental)

Should the payroll be increased or (reduced):

Number of Employees   Classification   Total Compensation

Total payroll adjustment $ _____

Are any employees members of a union?

List names of unions:

When are union contracts due for renegotiation?

Have the employees ever gone out on strike?

If the Company is nonunion, what efforts has a union made to organize the Company?

Is there any possibility that the Company will be reorganized within the next two years?

10. Information Regarding Major Competitors

Name:

Owner:

Location:

Distance:

Is this a public company?

Sales volume:

Percentage of market penetration:

Net worth (Check D&B Book):

Other information:

COULD REQUIRE D&B REPORT

CHAPTER FIVE

Who Are the Buyers?

THOMAS L. WEST
BUSINESS BROKERAGE PRESS

Before taking a look at the buyers of small and midsized companies, it might be helpful to first look at the buyers of small businesses; there is indeed, a big difference. Buyers of small businesses are most likely replacing lost jobs. Some may have simply lost their jobs, while others have become so unhappy with their employment situation that buying a business is the best alternative. The American dream of owning one's own business is still alive and well. The American worker is acutely aware that job security is a thing of the past. Owning a business is one way of guaranteeing job security.

The buyer for the small business wants to run his or her own operation. Studies indicate that buyers purchase small businesses for the following reasons (which we have listed in order):

1. To do their own thing, control their own destiny.
2. They don't want to work for someone else.
3. To make better use of their skills and abilities.
4. To make money.

As stated, buyers of small businesses are replacing jobs or, as one writer put it, they are buying income substitution. The purchase of a small business can be an emotional decision based on the prospective buyer's attraction to the type of business. Certainly, the track record of the firm is important, but since the buyer will be working in it, usually a "pride of ownership" is factored into the purchase decision, whether psychologically or emotionally.

There are individuals who purchase companies to manage and operate themselves. There are groups of people who buy companies to either operate themselves or as an investment. There are private companies that purchase other companies as investments or to install their own management team. There are investment companies who buy companies to build and then, hopefully, sell for a profit. And operating companies even buy other companies as investments. There is also the foreign buyer, which, because of the federal immigration laws, presents unique problems and therefore is covered in detail in its own section.

It is informative to break down the buyers of small and midsized companies (and larger ones, too) and group them into larger categories. The major buying groups can be identified as:

Individuals.
Publicly held companies.
Privately owned companies.
Investments groups.
Foreign companies.

Each of these buying groups can be further broken down by the motive or purpose of the acquisition or merger, and to some extent by the size of the acquisition. Following is a breakdown of the buyers of companies based on revenues. The study was prepared by Geneva Business Services, based in Irvine, California.

	Total Revenues		
Buying Group	**Less than $3 Million**	**$3 to $10 Million**	**$10 Million+**
Individuals	44%	26%	4%
Public Companies	28	21	17
Private Companies	11	14	14
Investment Groups	17	29	47
Foreign Companies	—	10	18

Each type of buyer or buying group, has its own reasons for buying a company, and consequently, establishes its own purchasing criteria. Here are some of the questions that buyers ask when considering whether a company is a possible acquisition candidate. For example, Harold Geneen, the legendary former head of ITT, built the company's revenues from $766 million to over $22 billion, largely through acquisitions. He used the following criteria when considering the purchase of a company:

- Is the business in a growing or declining market?
- What is the company's rate of return?
- How easy will financing the transaction be?
- What are the necessary capital investments?
- How much stress on management will there be?
- Is the product or service repeat business?
- Is it bid work or rapidly changing technology?
- Can the buyer add value?
- Can the company fit into the acquiring company's systems?
- Does the company earn money in good and bad times?
- Is the company really available for sale?

The buy-out firm of Clayton, Dubilier, and Rice seek underperforming companies with sales of around $200 million with a negative cash flow. Usually, they will not consider a company if:

- The industry is in a declining market.
- It is technology-driven.
- It has high fixed costs; or
- Is based on a commodity product (oil, paper, etc.).

Warren Buffett, the well-known investor, has some basic questions he asks when considering the purchase of a company. When looking at one company that he subsequently purchased, he wanted to know the following:

- What are the sales?
- What's the annual net increase in sales?
- What's in inventory?
- What's the debt?
- Is the owner willing to stay on?

He would also ask the seller the following:

- What differentiates your company?
- How do you grow the company?
- What would you do if the company received a sizable windfall of cash?

Russ Robb, a Boston intermediary, says in his book, *Buying Your Business* (published by Adams Publishing, Holbrook, Massachusetts),

"Since I am an intermediary working almost exclusively for corporate buyers and sellers, I receive telephone calls daily from individuals seeking to buy a business. While I am cordial and respectful, I too cannot afford to give potential buyers an hour of my valuable time unless they pass my short evaluation test. Admittedly, the following questions are curt and project unfriendliness:

- How much equity are you willing to invest?
- Have you been a CEO of a company and/or have you previously been involved in acquiring a company?
- Would you consider paying a retainer to an intermediary for the acquisition search?"

Russ goes on to say that the answers to these questions provide him with a "quick snapshot" of the buyer. Following is his checklist "for an ideal individual buyer":

- Is capable of investing $250,000 to $500,000 of his or her own cash in the deal.
- Was previously involved with a corporate acquisition, either personally or for an employer.
- Has had CEO experience or has been head of a division of a substantial company.
- Has prepared an acquisition plan for this assignment or printed a condensed version of the plan in brochure form.
- Has narrowed the focus to target industries.
- Has targeted industries similar to his or her business background.
- Is willing to sign a fee agreement with the intermediary.
- Is willing to pay a financial retainer to the intermediary.
- Is likely to have good personal chemistry with a seller.
- Has already spent time looking for an acquisition.
- Is willing to pay a full price for the target company and does not have the characteristic of being a "bottom fisher," that is, one who constantly bids low.
- Is willing to accept a company with some warts (problems).

Here is a look at the major categories of buyers of small to midsized companies.

THE INDIVIDUAL BUYER

Many individuals with the financial resources and the necessary experience purchase small and midsize companies. They generally buy a company that is in the field with which they are familiar. Individual buyers usually purchase a company that is financially sound and promises a sound return for the investment and work involved.

These buyers, if they don't have the financial resources personally, may have access to family funds or venture capital. However, there is a price line for individual buyers. They are generally limited in financial resources and their access to additional capital. For this reason they are usually involved in transactions that require less than $1 million in cash. A few individuals either have access to more, or in fact have it themselves, but they certainly do not represent a major portion of the individual buyers.

THE STRATEGIC BUYER

This type of buyer, usually a company, buys businesses as part of a long-term plan. It is a way of entering new markets, increasing market share, gaining new technology, or in some cases eliminating competition. Strategic buyers can be either in the same business as the company under consideration or a competitor. Simply put, it is part of the acquiring company's strategy to acquire this type business. For example, a bank in one part of the state purchases or merges with one in another part of the same state. The acquiring bank enters a new market that it feels it should be serving.

Ted Burbank, in his book *In & Out of Business . . . Happily* states, "To be attractive to a Strategic Acquiror your firm should fit the following acquisition criteria:

- Sales in excess of $20 million.
- Proprietary process or product.
- Suitable levels of management in place.
- Unique market presence or share.
- Synergistic market presence or share.
- Synergistic fit with acquirer's goals.
- Management willing to stay."

THE SYNERGISTIC BUYER

This buyer, again usually a company, differs from the strategic buyer in that the acquisition or merger makes sense because the two companies complement each other so well. Synergy, by definition, means that the joining of the two companies will produce more or be worth more than just the sum of the parts. A large real estate company purchases a mortgage company. It can use its existing customer base (those who buy homes) and offer them mortgage funds to finance the purchase. The benefits of this type of acquisition help both companies be more competitive and profitable.

THE INDUSTRY BUYER

It has been said that the industry buyer is the buyer of last resort. An industry buyer already knows the industry as well as the seller and usually is not willing to pay for the expertise and knowledge of the seller. This buyer is willing to pay for assets, but probably not what the seller thinks they are worth. The industry buyer wants to buy because there are some economies to be realized; for example, one sales force can sell the products or services of both companies; or perhaps they can utilize the same space or equipment. The industry buyer sees an opportunity to grow or expand at very little cost. An industry buyer will not pay for goodwill, for covenants not to compete, or for consulting agreements with the seller. However, there are some occasions when an industry buyer is also a strategic buyer, and in these cases, the price will be determined by the motivation of the acquiring company.

THE FINANCIAL BUYER

This type of buyer is the most common. They are influenced by the return or profit that can be derived from the business, coupled with their ability to finance as large a portion of the purchase price as possible. They buy a business with the sole purpose of making the maximum amount of money from the business with the least amount of their capital invested. This buyer's thinking is that debt is the lowest cost of capital.

Each of the buyers defined here has his or her own motives for buying a company. The price each buyer would be willing to pay for a company is directly proportional to the motive for buying. In small business, the first-time buyer is willing to pay for the time, effort, and goodwill that the owner has given to the business. On the other hand, in buying the small to midsized company, an industry buyer doesn't need or necessarily want to pay for time, effort, or goodwill, which is why the industry buyer is known as the buyer of last resort.

The financial buyer is interested only in the dollars and cash involved. The lower the price and the lower the cash investment, the better the financial buyer likes the deal. The synergistic buyer may be the best buyer because this type sees the value of the two companies as being larger than just a combination of the two entities. The strategic buyer also sees the value of the acquisition for business reasons and is usually willing to pay a premium for what he or she is acquiring. To paraphrase the old expression, "Value is in the eyes of the acquirer."

CHAPTER SIX

The Foreign Buyer

RAMON CARRION
ATTORNEY AT LAW

U.S. immigration and visa laws no longer favor the entry of unskilled laborers to the United States. Instead, the U.S. immigration system now provides many visa options for highly skilled individuals as well as for businesspersons and entrepreneurs. As a result, foreign prospective buyers of U.S. business enterprises are now among the highest profile of foreigners seeking to enter the United States. This reality presents a special opportunity for the astute and conscientious business intermediary, because the most recommended manner for a foreign businessperson to develop and manage a U.S. business enterprise is by acquiring one.

This fact has long been known to business immigration lawyers, but only recently has been discovered by the business intermediary profession. For foreign buyers, acquiring an existing business enterprise is usually easier and safer than organizing a new business enterprise from the ground up. Purely passive investments do not support long-term visas to the United States.

Foreign persons make good buyer prospects for three very sound reasons:

- First, the immigration laws require the foreign person to capitalize an investment in a business enterprise with a relatively higher percentage than what the market requires of U.S. buyers. For businesses costing more than $100,000, the minimum capital requirement is usually at least 60 percent.

- Second, the foreign buyer is more apt to persevere with an investment than a typical U.S. buyer. The reason for this is simple: The foreign buyer's visa status to the United States is almost always dependent on the continued existence of the business in which the foreign person has invested. This threat of losing his or her visa motivates many foreign buyers to "hang in there" a little longer. Indeed, it makes business sense to forgo a desired return on investment or to sustain moderate business losses for a given period of time rather than to face the prospect of not only losing the investment but of also being forced to return to the home country.

- Third, all the motivations that encourage domestic buyers to acquire a going business enterprise apply with even more persuasion to a foreign person. It just does not make business sense for a person who is essentially a stranger to the local community to attempt to originate a U.S. business enterprise when he or she can acquire an ongoing business and thus advance on the learning curve much more quickly.

I advise my foreign clients that the order of preference is as follows:

1. *Acquire an ongoing business.* Then, if absolutely not feasible,
2. *Acquire a franchised business.* Finally, if neither of these is feasible,
3. *Develop a new business enterprise.*

The distance between preference 2 and 3 is much greater than the distance between preference 1 and 2.

In analyzing this potential market the business intermediary should view the transaction from the perspective of a typical foreign buyer. The characteristics of *opportunity* and *risk* encompass different concepts than they would for a typical U.S. buyer.

U.S. BUSINESSES ARE AFFORDABLE

Foreign buyers are attracted to the United States by many extra-business tangible and intangible factors, but one of the strongest motivations is very understandable—cost. Over the last decade and a half, the value of the United States dollar has dropped precipitously compared to the currency of other developed countries. In short, this has rendered U.S. business investments relatively affordable—at least for persons from hard-currency countries in the European Common Market and in Asian countries such as Japan and Korea.

TROUBLED BUSINESSES ARE NOT ATTRACTIVE

Some brokers feel that foreign buyers are good candidates to buy troubled businesses and are therefore a solution for moving some of the less successful businesses in the broker's inventory. Actually, the reverse is true. A foreign person is ill advised to acquire a U.S. business that requires a major redirection of strategy and marketing for survival. This is due to the foreign person's unfamiliarity with the nuances of the local U.S. market. Where a business merely needs an infusion of cash for new equipment, inventory, or perhaps just working capital, the foreign buyer may not be in any worse of a competitive position than a U.S. buyer. But if the business has other more fundamental problems, most consultants will advise the foreign buyer to avoid the acquisition.

From the intermediary's perspective, it is better to present the best businesses in the inventory within the price reach of the prospect since these businesses usually present the best probability of survival after a takeover.

CAUTION IS IN ORDER

The prospective foreign investor must be regarded as a businessperson first and an immigrant second. The business acquisition must therefore make good business sense. Many U.S. business brokers are struck by the fact that the foreign prospect often asks very poignant questions concerning the target business, and are very often searching for a "guarantee" of profitability. Again, it must be remembered that the foreign person faces many more complications from a business failure than his or her U.S. counterpart. The U.S. investor does not face the prospect of deportation and of uprooting the family in the event of business failure. However, a foreign businessperson who has amassed a considerable amount of capital is probably commercially astute and not disposed to taking unreasonable investment risk.

U.S. VISAS

There are only two categories of visas to the United States. They consist of the nonimmigrant visas, of which there are many, and the permanent residency visas of which there is only one type. The graphic on page 91 is a simple illustration of this concept.

The following are the principal nonimmigrant visas with which a business intermediary should be familiar.

The E-2 Visa

The United States has signed treaties of friendship and commerce with certain countries that provide for the issuance of E-2 visas for

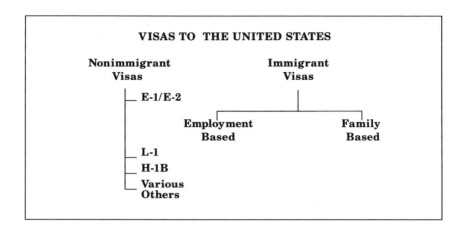

VISAS TO THE UNITED STATES

Nonimmigrant Visas

— E-1/E-2

Immigrant Visas

Employment Based

Family Based

— L-1
— H-1B
— Various Others

their citizens. The current list of countries follows, and the list continues to grow. The visa is issued to a person who seeks to enter the United States to develop and manage a business enterprise into which he or she has invested or is committed to invest a substantial amount of capital, and which investment is not marginal. The key questions in the E-2 category are: What constitutes a substantial investment? How is the capital attributed to the investor? What constitutes a marginal investment? and What do the terms "direct and manage" encompass?

Argentina	Iran	Romania
Australia	Ireland	Senegal
Austria	Italy	Slovakia
Bangladesh	Japan	Spain
Belgium	Kazakhstan	Sri Lanka
Bulgaria	Korea	Suriname
Cameroon	Kyrgyzstan	Sweden
China	Liberia	Switzerland
Colombia	Luxembourg	Thailand
Congo	Morocco	Togo
Costa Rica	The Netherlands	Tunisia
The Czech Republic	Norway	Turkey
Egypt	Oman	The United Kingdom
Ethiopia	Pakistan	Vietnam
France	Panama	Yugoslavia
Germany	Paraguay	Zaire
Grenada	The Philippines	
Honduras	Poland	

These are all technical terms.

Substantiality. There is no mathematical formula or fixed minimum amount for determining "substantial." Substantiality is very often determined by the use of a proportionality or relative test. There are two methods:

In the case of the acquisition of an existing business enterprise, the capital invested must be proportional to the total value or cost of the particular business enterprise. The following generally paraphrases the applicable State Department regulations on this subject:

1. A small business costing below $100,000 will usually require a cash investment of 90–100 percent of the purchase price.
2. A business costing $100,000 might require an investment of 75–100 percent.
3. A small business costing $500,000 would demand generally upward of a 60 percent investment, with a $375,000 investment clearly meeting the test.
4. In the case of a million-dollar business, a lesser percentage might be needed, but a 50–60 percent investment would qualify.
5. A business requiring $10 million to purchase or establish would require a much lower percentage. A $3 million investment might suffice in view of the sheer magnitude of the dollar amount invested.
6. An investment of $10 million in a $100 million business would qualify based on the sheer magnitude of the investment itself.

In the case of the creation of a new business by the foreign person, the capital invested must be an amount normally considered necessary to establish a viable business enterprise of the type contemplated. As a general guideline, the minimum amount of cash that will meet the test of substantiality without special explanations is $100,000 U.S. In certain U.S. consulates abroad, $100,000 would be considered minimal. This figure, therefore, must be considered only as a rule of thumb, and must be analyzed in light of the type of business, the investment, the proportion of capital to acquisition cost, the rate of return, and all of the other factors described in this section. Nonetheless, an investment of less than this sum might be considered as insubstantial, per se, unless the business is a service business in which capital equipment and inventory are not really germane to the success of the business. The cost of acquiring an E-2 visa is often inversely proportional to the cost of the business and the amount of the buyer's cash investment. This is probably true for other areas of the business intermediary field.

If the business enterprise by its nature does not require a high capital cost (such as a service business), then a relatively small amount of capital, say $50,000 might be considered substantial. This would be the case when the investor possesses special and unique skills and talent such as an artist, architect, or other type of designer. As an example, in the case of an architect, engineer, or other designer who heavily utilizes computers, the office headquarters might not require much more than standard office furniture in order to be a complete and properly functioning enterprise.

Investor's own funds. The U.S. Consul abroad will usually require documentary proof that the funds invested are the investor's own. Loans that are guaranteed by the personal credit of the investor will suffice to meet the standard of substantiality as long as the loan is not also collateralized by the acquired assets. An investor may be tempted, for various reasons, to use capital which is not technically owned by the investor but that is controlled by the investor. These devices usually do not succeed. In addition, an investor cannot inherit or receive by gift a title to a U.S. business. Rather the regulations require the investor to come into the funds by way of gift or inheritance and then use those funds to acquire the investment.

The investor is not limited to a capital investment of cash only into the enterprise. Equipment, fixtures, inventory, and other valuable tangible and intangible assets are also valid assets for investment.

Investor to direct and manage. It is imperative that the alien proves that he or she is entering the United States to direct and manage the investment/enterprise. While ordinarily the alien must establish ownership of at least 50 percent of the equity in the enterprise, it may be possible to demonstrate control by contracts or other agreements that essentially place the management and control of the enterprise in the hands of the alien. Passive investments do not qualify for the issuance of the E-2 visas because the investor is not required to direct and manage. In purely passive investments the foreign investor is really nothing more than a lender and is not entitled to the visa. This regulatory term requires evidence that the business acquired requires the active entrepreneurial supervision by the foreign person. This regulation is often not susceptible to a bright line resolution in that some business enterprises and mixtures of passive and active assets such as a case where one of the major components of a business enterprise is real estate.

Note: Very often, the prospective purchaser will question the reasonableness of committing a substantial investment of capital for the acquisition of a business enterprise or commercial property before the visa is issued. While this is a logical question, the U.S. government will not issue a visa until it is convinced that the investor is irrevocably committed to the deal. This problem can be resolved by conducting the closing in escrow and by placing the buyer's funds and the seller's documents of title with an escrow agent. The escrow agent is then empowered to disburse the funds to the seller and the documents of title to the buyer as soon as the visa is issued. In this manner, both parties are protected: The buyer is not at risk of purchasing a business which he or she cannot operate, and the seller is satisfied that the deal will be completed unless the visa is not issued.

Marginality. The investment (business enterprise) cannot be marginal. If the investment would provide only sufficient funds for the person to make a living, the foreign person's investment would fail as being marginal. Unless the business history documents a reasonable profit (above 15 percent return on capital) the investor must document that he or she has an outside source of income.

Another element of the concept of marginality is whether the investment will benefit the United States. This is normally satisfied by providing employment for U.S. citizens and/or residents. If the proposed business investment will provide for employment of other persons, the less it is likely the investment will be found to be marginal. If the business will employ only the investor and one or two other subsidiary employees, an investment may not support an E-2 visa unless the other factors described are present to some degree. The requirement of employment and outside income are intertwined somewhat and the entire E-2 visa application must be considered as a whole. The more U.S. authorized workers that will be employed by the business, the less attention or importance will be placed on the profitability of the business.

Advantages of the E-2 visa.   The E-2 visa may be renewed indefinitely as long as the investment originally supporting the E-visa continues in existence, although the visa is initially granted for up to five years at most U.S. consulates. Additionally, employment by family members is not normally viewed as a violation of status even though the rules do not specifically sanction such employment.

Another advantage of the E-2 visa is its flexibility. There is no requirement for the foreign person to have previously conducted business in a particular legal entity in the home country. Unlike the situation with the L-1 visa (discussed next), individuals (by investing the funds) can qualify for the E-2 visa themselves even if they have operated in the past and intend to operate in the future as a sole proprietor. Additionally, the investors do not need to prove that they are an executive or manager, but merely prove that they are in a position to direct and manage the enterprise.

Employees of E-visa traders or investors.   If the E-visa applicant is not the trader or investor principal, then the applicant's job must be of either managerial or executive in nature or the applicant must be a highly trained or other specially qualified person. In addition, the applicant must have the same nationality as the E-Treaty principal.

The Intra-Company Transferee (L-1 Visa)

This is another important visa for prospective foreign buyers of U.S. business enterprises. The purpose of the L-1 visa is to facilitate the transfer of key employees to the United States from companies that are affiliated or related to United States corporations. This visa is important because it is not limited to specific countries with which the United States may have entered a treaty.

Duration of stay. The L-1 visa has a duration of seven years for "managers" and "executives" and five years for persons of "specialized knowledge." The duration of stay is issued for an initial period of three years and may be extended for additional period of two years. In the case of a new office, the visa is issued for one year and may be extended for two periods of three years.

Requirements

Duration of employment. The corporate employee (who may also be the owner of the foreign business enterprise) who is being transferred must have been continuously employed by the overseas (extra-United States) company for a period of at least one year out of the last three years prior to entry into the United States.

Intra-company relationship. The prior employer/foreign company must be related to the U.S. company, either as a subsidiary, an affiliate, or a division. In order to establish that the foreign-domestic entities are one and the same for immigration purposes, it is necessary that the corporations be controlled by the same person(s) (affiliate) or that one corporation controls the other (subsidiary). In order to document this, it must be shown that the U.S. corporation owns at least 51 percent of the shares of the foreign corporation (or vice versa), or that the same stockholders own 51 percent of each of the corporations. Another alternative is to show that the foreign corporation is a branch or division of the U.S. corporation, or vice versa.

In addition, the petitioning company must continue to function as a viable business entity throughout the employment period of the L-1 visa holder. If the foreign entity ceases to exist or to function as a viable business entity, then the L-visa status of the employee is jeopardized. This is an extremely important point for a small company to bear in mind.

Other qualifying companies. The immigration regulations permit entities other than a corporation to serve as a qualifying company. Partnerships and even sole proprietorships can serve as qualifying companies for L-1 visa purposes. In a noncorporate setting, it is important to establish that the employing company is a separate entity from the employee being transferred.

Employee's qualifications. The law subdivides the L-visa into two categories. The L-1A is issued to managers and executives and the L-1B is issued to a person of specialized knowledge. The regulatory definition of these job titles are as follows.

Manager

- Primarily manages the organization; or a department, subdivision, function, or component of the organization.
- Primarily supervises and controls the work of other supervisory, professional, or managerial employees; or manages an essential function within the organization, or a department or subdivision of the organization.
- Has the authority to hire and fire or recommend those as well as other personnel actions if another employee or other employees are supervised; if no other employees are supervised, functions at a senior level within the organizational hierarchy or with respect to the function managed.
- Exercises discretion over the day-to-day operations of the activity or function for which the employee has authority.

Executive

- Directs the management of the organization or a major component or function. (Note that this is similar to the third point under Manager.)
- Establishes the goals and policies of the organization, component, or function.
- Exercises wide latitude in discretionary decision making.
- Receives only general supervision or direction from higher-level executives, the board of directors or stockholders of the organization.

Person of Specialized Knowledge

- Must have special or unique knowledge of the petitioning organization's product, service, research, equipment, techniques, management, or other interests and its application of international markets; or an advanced level of knowledge or expertise in the organization's processes and procedures.
- "Special Knowledge" is knowledge that is different from or exceeds the ordinary or usual knowledge of an employee in a particular field.
- A specialized knowledge professional is a person who has specialized knowledge and is a member of the professions.

If the L-1 visa employee is a major stockholder of the company, proof must be submitted that the employee will be transferred abroad at the completion of temporary duties in the United States.

All of these points must be minutely documented to the INS. Indeed, the following, among other things, should be provided: copies of the lease for the premises, copies of any business contracts, a cash projection for the business, and copies of accounting and bank records to indicate that both the foreign company and the U.S. parent are viable entities. Proof of economic viability usually requires documentation that establishes that the U.S. entity has the financial ability to cover the transferee's salary for at least the first year of operation.

The small- to medium-sized business enterprise will generally support the existence of an "executive" person, while it may not generally satisfy the existence of a "manager."

Company must be "doing business." Both the foreign and U.S. companies must be "qualifying entities"; that is, they must provide regular, systematic, and continuous goods and/or services. The mere presence of an agent or office with no other of commercial activity will disqualify the company from supporting an L-1 visa.

Ordinarily, a U.S. company that seeks to bestow permanent residency status ("green card") for a foreign worker must obtain a labor certification from the U.S. Department of Labor. This process can take a long time and is fraught with risk. A manager or executive who holds an L-1 visa can qualify for a *first preference employment-based permanent residency visa* as a *multinational manager or executive* without the necessity of a labor certification. This is a highly coveted advantage. Note that a person of specialized knowledge who holds the L-1B visa must still be the beneficiary of a labor certification and is distinguished from a multinational manager or executive.

PRINCIPAL IMMIGRANT VISAS

The following are the principal categories of immigrant visas that are available for foreign investors and executives.

Permanent Residency (Immigrant Visas) for Multinational Executives or Managers

A U.S. company may petition for permanent residency on behalf of an executive or manager who essentially meets the requirements of the L-1 visa as long as the company has been in operation for at least one year. In addition, the U.S. company must also satisfy the L-1 requirements for a qualifying organization.

The ability to "convert" an L-1A (manager or executive) visa to a permanent residency visa is one of the most important and desirable characteristics of the L-1A visa. Of course, it is possible to petition directly for a permanent residency visa if the U.S. company has already been in existence for more than one year and the alien otherwise satisfies the requirements for an "executive" or "manager." This alternative would be viable if the foreign person acquires the shares of stock of an existing U.S. corporation. If the foreign person acquires the assets of an existing business, which are then transferred to a newly formed corporation (as is routinely done), then the permanent residency option will not be available until the U.S. corporation has completed one year of existence.

Immigrant Investors/Employment Creation

A permanent residency visa may be issued to foreign persons who invest a minimum amount of capital in a new enterprise that creates employment. The amount of the required investment ranges from a low of $500,000 for "targeted employment areas" up to a high of $3,000,000 for an enterprise located in a region deemed to be of low unemployment. The alien (the statute and regulations refer to all non-U.S. persons as "aliens" in the context of immigration rhetoric) must have invested the capital after November 29, 1990 or be in the active process of investing the capital.

The standard investment must be of $1,000,000, and must create at least 10 full-time jobs for U.S. citizens, permanent resident aliens, or other immigrants lawfully authorized to be employed in the United States. This group of 10 workers provided for by the law cannot include the investor or the investor's immediate family.

Targeted Employment Areas

The law encourages investment in areas of high unemployment or other areas designated as "targeted employment areas." These are defined as rural areas or areas having an unemployment rate at least one-and-a-half times the national average; the required investment is reduced to $500,000. A total of 3,000 of the 10,000 annual visas in this preference category are reserved for targeted employment areas.

In order to implement the application of the $500,000 amount, it is necessary for the individual states to designate, subject to federal government approval, the state authority that will identify the geographic areas or political subdivisions that are deemed as rural or targeted employment areas.

The administrative regulations published by the Immigration and Naturalization Service provide that a qualified investment includes the purchase of an existing business as long as the enterprise's net worth, after the completion of the sale, is at least 140 percent of the value of the enterprise prior to the date of the acquisition, or that there is a 40 percent increase in the level of employment. This requirement will preclude an investor from merely purchasing an ongoing business without causing any substantive improvement in the capital or employment levels of the enterprise.

In addition, the regulations provide for the purchase and overhaul of a troubled or undercapitalized business enterprise by a foreign person as long as the acquisition will save jobs. A troubled business is defined as one that has been in existence for at least two years and that has experienced a 20 percent diminution of its net worth during the last two years. In any event, a total of $1,000,000 (or $500,000 if applicable) must be invested, and 10 jobs must have been created or preserved.

This immigrant visa category requires that the investor manage the business personally; it does not anticipate that the investor will be merely a passive financier, with one exception: the case of a limited partner of a limited partnership formed in accordance with the requirements of a certain uniform limited partnership law. The provision for the limited partner is contradictory to the requirement that the investor directly manage and/or supervise the investment, because the limited partnership act referred to, by its very terms, defines the limited partner as a passive investor. Since a limited partnership interest is a security and will support an employment creation investor visa, it is curious that the INS regulations do not also permit other types of securities or passive investment arrangements to warrant a permanent visa as long as the requisite level of employment is created.

Conditional Grant of Visa

The law provides a number of measures to discourage fraud by immigrant investors by providing for fines of up to $250,000 and jail for up to five years. In addition, the law also makes the grant of permanent residence to immigrant investors conditional and has established a two-year trial period. During this two-year period, by rule and regulation, the Immigration and Naturalization Service will determine whether the enterprise was in fact established; whether the capital was in fact invested; or whether the alien did not sustain the enterprise. During a 90-day period prior to the end of the two-year period, the investor must file an additional petition with the Immigration and Naturalization Service requesting that the conditional status of residence be removed.

This visa is quite appropriate for the acquisition of hotel/motel properties especially in resort or tourist areas where the real estate can be expected to retain its value. Real estate enterprises, including hotels and motels, and other franchised enterprises are good candidates for this level of investment.

It must be remembered, however, that by becoming permanent residents of the United States, foreign persons become United States taxpayers and, thus, subject their worldwide income to taxation. Proper preinvestment planning is absolutely essential in order to avoid fiscal disasters, and a foreign investor should consult a number of consultants, both abroad as well as in the United States to assist in the various phases of the investment.

MARKETING TIPS

In addition to acquiring more knowledge in this field, the business intermediary who desires to develop this component of the profession needs to
do a few other things to bring the prospects or clients through the door.
These are a few suggestions based upon personal experience as well as
discussion with other business intermediaries who are actively working
with foreign buyers:

- Develop (and distribute) brochures and other "internal" literature
  that briefly explain the visa options for foreign investors, together
  with other salient characteristics of the intermediary's business.
- Notify local chambers of commerce as well as U.S. chambers of
  commerce abroad of the intermediary's ability to market to foreign
  buyers, utilizing the newly prepared brochures and literature. The
  local business development agency is also a good source of leads as
  well as the appropriate state business development office.
- Place advertisements in the local ethnic newspapers or other
  publications.
- Contact the commercial officer of the U.S. consulate in the "origi-
  nating" countries of the intermediary's program for servicing
  prospective foreign investors from that country.
- Attend and participate in foreign trade and property shows.
- Establish networks with residential real estate professionals who
  routinely work with foreign buyers. Real estate brokers who sell
  holiday-type properties such as condominiums are good network
  prospects.
- Establish networks with foreign travel agents who routinely book
  tours of foreign visitors to the nearest local community.
- Establish networks with foreign real estate and other professionals
  who are referral sources.

This list of suggestions is by no means exclusive of other ideas and is only
the starting point for efforts which can be richly rewarded in business.

SUMMARY

The United States generally desires to attract entrepreneurs to the
United States—even though there is no articulated and synchronized policy to this effect. The U.S. immigration system as applicable to investors
and entrepreneurs is often contradictory and confusing. Yet people continue to come to our shores. The typical foreign investor is not typical at
all. As a businessperson, he or she has all of the attributes that U.S. business intermediaries typically see in prospective buyers, that is, the desire

to minimize the cash outlay and to derive a profit as soon as possible. But the foreign person also has strong motivations not present in the typical domestic buyer, to persevere with the acquired business in order to satisfy the governmental conditions for the maintenance of his or her visa. On the other hand, the process of visa acquisition presents additional challenges both to the seller and the intermediary—the need to satisfy the stringent and often extraneous governmental conditions.

For the seller, however, the requirements of liquidity coupled with the foreigner's intense motivation to succeed usually outweigh the inconveniences and delays involved. For the traditional business intermediary, the ability to market listings effectively to foreign persons provides him or her with a considerable advantage in obtaining listings from business owners. Most business owners/sellers will react favorably to the business intermediary who can bring in one more qualified prospect. Furthermore, for those brokers who work as "buyer's agents," the foreign person is the ideal client and provides the opportunity to help the broker build a solid referral business based upon satisfied buyer/clients.

CHAPTER SEVEN

Growth by Acquisition

JEFFREY D. JONES
PRESIDENT
CERTIFIED APPRAISERS, INC.

Every company, big or small, is concerned about growth. It has been said that a company never stands still for very long; it either grows or declines. A major portion of small to midsize business owners' time is devoted to planning and implementing activities that hopefully lead to their companies' growth. The options business owners have for growing their companies include the following:

- Expand in their existing markets by taking business away from competitors.
- Expand in their existing markets by getting a share of new business growth.
- Expand into new product and service lines that are compatible with existing lines.
- Expand into new geographic markets.
- Expand into unrelated business products and services.

All of these methods of growth require planning, time, and resources that include people, inventory, equipment, and money. Because most small to midsized businesses have limited resources, if the wrong decisions are made in the attempts to grow, the results can be disastrous. One of the more successful methods for growth of small to midsized companies is through acquisition of other existing companies.

REASONS TO ACQUIRE

Expanding through acquisition has been a method frequently used by large closely held and publicly held companies. For many of the same reasons large companies buy existing businesses, small to midsized companies can often benefit from this practice. These reasons include:

- *Synergism with your existing business:* Due to synergism of the combined resources of both companies, sales and profits can often be increased. Sales increase due to the combined marketing efforts and costs can often be reduced as a result of greater purchasing power, combined facilities, and additional skilled employees.
- *Open new geographic markets for existing products and services:* The acquisition of existing businesses in new geographic markets enables small to midsize companies to expand into new markets by leapfrogging two to five years over start-up operations. Most companies find it easier to expand from an existing base of business than to try to build from scratch, especially in geographic markets that are not as familiar as the home market.
- *Expansion of related lines of business:* Opening up related lines of products that can be sold to existing customers of the acquiring company can lead to sales growth without adding significant overhead costs.
- *Expansion of new project or service lines in existing markets:* By way of acquisition, a company can obtain new product or service lines within its existing geographic markets. This works especially well if your company has available space, can obtain new products and services not otherwise available, and has the staff, time, and ability to handle the additional lines.

Advantages to Acquiring Existing Businesses

Some of the advatages in acquiring existing businesses include:

- Being able to review a company's existing track record as reflected in P&Ls, tax returns, and other financial records can be very helpful in determining expansion plans. Growth potential can be measured based on actual experience rather than conjecture associated with start-up ventures.

- The need for additional working capital is reduced due to the immediate cash flow being generated by the acquired company.
- Obtaining skilled employees who are familiar with the business operation and market are a major benefit of any acquisition.
- Gaining established customers significantly reduces the time it would otherwise take to attract an adequate number of customers to support the overhead of a new operation.
- Obtaining existing licenses and permits can often reduce the time and cost of making application, gathering information, and conforming to required regulations.
- Sources of capital to purchase existing businesses are more readily available than start-up ventures. It is very common for the owner of an acquired business to finance part of the purchase price. Banks and other financial institutions prefer to loan money to existing operations that have a proven track record.

REASONS OWNERS SELL PROFITABLE BUSINESSES

There is a general misconception that only businesses in trouble are for sale. The truth is that unprofitable businesses are difficult to sell. Most acquisitions involve profitable businesses where the owner is willing to sell due to retirement, ill health, partnership problems, family problems, burnout, desire to go into another profession, or undercapitalization.

Where to Look for Existing Businesses for Sale

Finding profitable businesses for sale at reasonable prices can be difficult. Often, business owners have an inflated idea as to the value of their business due to articles in *The Wall Street Journal* describing the high multiples of earnings obtained by some of the publicly owned companies. The primary resources for finding profitable businesses for sale are varied.

- Each week there are hundreds of businesses advertised in local newspapers, *The Wall Street Journal,* and trade publications. Business owners or brokers representing owners describe their business offerings in these publications. By regularly checking these publications, it may be possible to find a business that meets your criteria; however, owners are often reluctant to openly advertise their businesses for sale, so other methods may need to be employed.
- Suppliers may be good sources of information regarding businesses for sale within the industries that they service. Calling or writing to your suppliers and vendors and making them aware of

your acquisition criteria may surface several prospective sellers that are not actively on the market, but would consider selling.

- Using direct mail to contact business owners whose businesses meet your general acquisition criteria can generate potential seller prospects. This method is frequently used by business brokers to seek out business owners who desire to sell. A shortcoming of this method is that you are contacting owners who may not be actively for sale, and therefore, their motivation to sell may not be very strong, which often results in unacceptable prices and terms of sale.

- Business brokers can be a valuable resource of businesses for sale. Their full-time job is to contact business owners and find those who are motivated to sell. Brokers usually help the business owner to determine a reasonable value for the business, and can often assist in finding financial resources for the buyer acquisition. Further, business brokers will have knowledge of a variety of businesses for sale, and can help eliminate those for which the price does not make any economic sense. The broker's fee is typically paid by the seller based on the market price of the business; it is not additive to the market price. There are a growing number of business brokers who represent only buyers, and for a fee will actively search out businesses that meet your acquisition criteria. If there is an immediate need to make an acquisition, hiring a broker to do a comprehensive search will produce the quickest results.

- Searching the Internet is the newest method for finding businesses for sale. A keyword search will turn up over 200 home pages indicating a listing of businesses for sale. Many business brokers have set up their own home page and provide a list of businesses for sale at their Web sites. Some of these sites are national and international in their scope. One such site is Bizquest, wherein over 200 brokers provide information on businesses for sale. The address is http://www.bizquest.com. Many local business brokers have their own Web sites. In Houston, for example, the Certified Business Brokers' Web site is http://www.mgroup.com/cbb.html. It provides information on how to buy and sell a business, along with a list of businesses for sale in the Houston area. A recent search of the Internet under "business broker" turned up over 200 Web sites.

Success by Example

Each year there are approximately 750,000 new businesses that start up in the United States, yet less than 15 percent survive beyond five years. On the other hand, approximately 200,000 existing businesses are acquired by companies and individuals each year with over 75 percent continuing to be successful after five years.

In 1986, Steve Berdines left his job as an engineer for Schlumberger and acquired a small Houston business known as Bishop Office Supply. This company had been in business four years and was grossing approximately $200,000. Steve was successful in increasing sales; however, he was not satisfied with the rate of growth or his ability to buy at the lowest prices. So in 1987, Steve acquired Snappy Office Products; then in 1989, acquired Davis Office Products. Finally, in 1990, Steve acquired Park Ten Office Products.

About this time, several major discount office supply companies had established multiple stores throughout the Houston area. Many of the smaller office supply companies could not compete with these larger firms and chose to sell or go out of business. Steve felt that he could compete with the larger firms by providing personalized service, but he had to be able to buy in large quantities to effectively compete with the discounters. So in 1992, he acquired Associated Stationers; in 1993, Garden Oaks Office Supply; and in 1994, he was able to structure the acquisition of Automation Accessories and Supplies, a company larger than his own at the time. Steve recently joined a national buying co-op known as Office City, which today operates as Bishop's Office City. His company now has gross sales of $2.5 million. "I could never have grown to my present level of sales merely by trying to take customers away from my competitors," says Mr. Berdines. "By way of acquiring several competitors in my market and acquiring other office supply companies in other geographic markets, we were able to grow much faster than other methods of growth would have allowed."

Growth through acquisition is a proven way to both get into business and to make it grow. While in the past, finding profitable businesses and then getting them financed were major problems, today there are excellent resources to assist in an acquisition search and plentiful sources of debt and equity capital. Public and large private companies frequently used the acquisition method of growth, and now many small to midsize companies are finding that it is often less expensive and more profitable to buy an existing business rather than to start from scratch.

FINANCIAL AND VALUATION ASPECTS

Normalizing Historical Financial Statements: A Picture of Where You Are

THOMAS H. JACOBY
PRESIDENT
MERCOR, INC.

FAIR MARKET VALUE

Most buyers and sellers of businesses know that the common definition of fair market value is "the price at which such property would change hands between a willing buyer and a willing seller, neither being under any compulsion to buy or sell, and both having reasonable knowledge of relevant facts" (Treasury Reg. 25.2512-1). However, in the real world of purchase and sale of companies, such a definition is much too generalized. Though the concept is hypothetical, it is also incomplete because it omits personalities from the valuation equation. For instance, there is no consideration of the needs (compulsions) of the parties, such as illness or burnout of the seller or the ego of the buyer. There is also no contemplation of the likely disparities between the (hypothetical) willing buyer and seller in experience and skills in negotiating and deal-structuring. Nor does such a broad definition contemplate the purpose of the acquisition, the types or classes of buyers or the disproportionate knowledge of the industry, economy, or particular company. These and other factors have a significant impact on the resulting price.

The Foundation for Business Valuations

With so many components of value "neutralized" in the appraisal definition of fair market value, it is crucial that a valuation focus upon the concept of "both parties having reasonable knowledge of the relative facts." Accordingly, *the foundation for business valuations should be suitably adjusted historical financial statements of the company being valued.* The resulting "normalized" or "economic" financial statements should reflect the fair market value of assets on the balance sheet and the true current and/or expected future benefit stream (available to the buyer) on the income statement.

The process of normalizing begins with the seller's historical financial statements that are commonly prepared either in-house or under the control of independent accountants. Greater credibility results from independent audits of the financial statements prior to presenting a company for sale. Even though the historical income statement of a closely held business normally minimizes the company's net income by using tax-saving principles, this conflicts with valuation concepts that use realistic "economic income." Also, the historical balance sheet usually understates shareholder equity, because assets are stated at tax-adjusted historical costs, rather than at current market value. Important intangible assets such as goodwill, which includes items like going-concern, excess earnings, technology, systems, customer base, and trained workforce are also excluded. It is easy to understand why unadjusted historical financial statements are nearly worthless in helping either the buyer or seller make sound business valuation decisions.

In addition to the intentional understating of net income, a study of the historical financial statements frequently discloses significant departures from generally accepted accounting principles (GAAP). These departures include the overstating of accounts receivable (no consideration of collectibility), the understating of inventories (with LIFO cost), the understating of the cost of machinery and equipment (overaggressive capitalization policy), and the improper matching of revenue and expense. GAAP deficiencies also require adjustments to avoid working with misleading normalized financial statements.

The Need for Normalized Financial Statements

A principal requirement of a normalized financial statement is that it be useful for comparison purposes; furthermore, this statement will aid in predicting the future of the subject business.[1] Some multiple of normalized income or the resulting projected income will be a major factor used to estimate value by either the buyer or seller.

Under ideal circumstances, the seller will provide the appropriately recasted financial statement for the business valuation process. The seller, his accountant, and business appraiser, because of their in-depth knowledge of the company to be sold are in the best position to determine the suitable recasting concepts. The recasting adjustments and, in fact, the statement itself, must be able to withstand the research and due diligence examination of the buyer and his advisors. The buyer and seller may not ultimately agree to every adjustment. However, the seller is still in the lead position to initiate and educate the buyer about the future income and benefits from the company or the assets that have been understated in the historic balance sheet. The recast economic financial statement should not be an advocacy document; it is not a sales presentation.[2]

KNOWLEDGE AND TECHNIQUE

For the valuation of a business, a serious attempt must be made to realistically project future cash flow. A cash flow projection should include a complete analysis of the capital expenditures, debt servicing, and acquisition costs.[3] This will more clearly depict the affordability of the proposed acquisition. Sometimes, history, current results (when adjusted for abnormal years), and nonrecurring and nonoperating items are most indicative of the future. Long-term growth trends, if consistent, can reasonably be expected to continue.

Ultimately, normalized earnings should indicate the probable future earnings of the business.[4] The company's financial statement projections or budgets of prior years, when proven by the actual results, are a positive indication of the seller's ability to make appropriate projections. The *IRS Valuation Guide* suggests, "The first step . . . is to project future earnings for some period. Often, the period used is the next five years. These projections are based on the average growth of the prior (five) years."[5] However, there may be unusual circumstances such as changes in machinery, facilities, products, and customers, which will drastically alter the future earnings curve. If growth trends and profits are inconsistent, then averaging of historical results, with the exclusion of significantly abnormal or subnormal years, may be a better proxy for the income to be capitalized in a valuation.

The normalization adjustments made to the balance sheet (subsequent to any GAAP adjustments) should result in a balance sheet that indicates adjusted book value (shareholder equity). This is a basic valuation "approach" that can be a market value indicator where liquidation is imminent or there is asset value in excess of earnings derived value.[6] Regardless of the approach, the seller (and his advisors) should carefully and thoughtfully perform this recasting to avoid the loss of credibility from the onset of negotiations.

The seller and his accountant will normally have a thorough understanding of the mechanics of the company's historical financial statements. This does not suggest that they will also have the combined knowledge or technique to appropriately recast the financial statements for valuation purposes. The recasting is such an important task that it should be undertaken with a broker (or intermediary) and valuation consultant who are thoroughly competent in applicable theory. The valuation of the company may be the prelude to the most important business decision in the career of the seller. Therefore, it is essential that the normalized financial statements be a clear "picture of where you are" and "where you are going."

Although the normalization adjustments are likely to be a departure from GAAP, adjustments made to one account (such as on a balance sheet) also require a corresponding adjustment to another account (such as on an income statement).[7]

In summary, the purpose of the normalization adjustment is to:

- Provide a consistent, reasonable starting point for the valuation decision (GAAP) and adjustments.
- Give insight into:

  What prior operations might have looked like normal conditions.

  What a prospective buyer might reasonably be expected to obtain from the company in the future, using history as a guide (normalization adjustments).[8]

Remember that *complete and fair disclosure* is the standard for normalized financial statements and that the ultimate users are the decision makers (both buyers and sellers) or their advisors.

A SENSIBLE APPROACH TO NORMALIZING

Few of the many excellent books written about business valuation standards and procedures offer more than a clue about how to recast a historical financial statement into one suitable for a business valuation. One excellent source that provides a sample worksheet for normalized net income is the *Guide to Business Valuation.*[9] However, there are no valuation texts with in-depth instruction for this vital valuation procedure that use a "cookbook" approach. The goal of the normalization case study that follows is to identify common problem areas that require adjusting for use with a business valuation and to provide examples of appropriate solution.

A suitable format for the recasting/normalization process utilizes worksheets and statements that simultaneously disclose the details of the historic financial statements and the related normalization adjustments. In addition, each adjustment should be cross-referenced to detailed notes that thoroughly explain the concepts of the normalization. The case study includes recast financial statements that are similar to those used by Geneva Companies in their marketing package for client companies being sold.[10]

Before beginning the case study, it is appropriate to comment about the type of normalized earnings most suitable for valuation analysis. Generally speaking, the more common choices are as follows:

Net operating income.

Net income before taxes.

Net income after taxes.

Net income (earnings) before interest and taxes (EBIT).

Net income (earnings) before depreciation, interest, and taxes (EBDIT).

Net cash flow.

Most valuation consultants agree that if the capitalization or discount rates and guideline company information (for comparison) are appropriate (and consistent) with the type of income chosen, the value result should be the same (within a reasonable range).[11] So the choice of earnings probably depends upon the requirements of the user and the information available. Accordingly, the statements and worksheets in the case study are designed to provide results for most of the common choices of earnings.

THE NORMALIZATION CASE STUDY

The following is a step-by-step (cookbook) approach to the normalization of financial statements for valuation purposes of Example Manufacturing Co., Inc. ("the Company"). This hypothetical Company was founded in 1976 as a machine shop to provide support for small local manufacturers. Company sales reached $1,000,000 in 1980, $2,000,000 in 1986, and $3,000,000 in 1990.

By late 1990, the Company had changed its focus from servicing small manufacturers to producing large precision-machined parts and tools, plus the fabricating of large components for manufacturing automotive assembly machinery. In the five-year period from 1991 to 1995, the Company made investments of more than $500,000 in used heavy machinery, which was extensively overhauled before it could be used for the new endeavor. During the same period, the Company adopted an aggressive tax policy whereby only the acquisition costs of the machinery were capitalized (recorded as an asset on the balance sheet). The related labor and material costs of $480,000 incurred for overhauling, retrofitting, and installing the new machinery were not capitalized. These costs were charged (expensed) to cost of sales as incurred.

With the new focus on manufacturing large precision products, the Company sales grew at a compound annual rate of 18 percent for the years from 1991 through 1995. However, growth had declined slightly by 1995, when sales reached $7,320,000. Manufacturing efficiencies had improved after the acquisition of the heavy machinery; beginning in 1994 and thereafter, the cost of sales had declined by more than 5 percent of revenue.

A Summary of Normalizing/Recasting Procedures

1. Adjust the (five years of) historical income statements for GAAP and normalization, as required for business valuation purposes (Schedule 1).

2. Adjust the balance sheet as of the end of the most current year for GAAP and normalization, as required for business valuation purposes (Schedule 4).

3. Analyze the revenue, cost, and expense ratios and trends of the historical income statements (Schedule 2).

4. Analyze the asset and liability ratios and trends of the historical balance sheets (Schedule 6-B).

5. Discuss and confirm historic income statement and balance sheet ratios, trends, and supportable expectations (with management, accountants, and consultants).

6. Project future revenue, cost, expense, income, asset and liability ratios, and trends, based upon normalized historical results and supportable expectations in worksheet format that shows common choices of valuation income (Schedule 6-A).

7. Prepare projected income statements if trends are clear, until stability is achieved. This is not needed if the base year is a fair proxy for future income (Schedule 3).

8. Prepare projected balance sheets (based upon historical trends and ratios and the normalized balance sheet) as needed to coincide with projected income statements (Schedule 5).

9. Review projected statements carefully to assure fairness and reasonableness.

10. *Always disclaim the projections* by warning buyers of the limited use conditions, and the basis for the assumptions, and clearly state that projections do not constitute seller representations or warranties, but are only (management) estimates.

Schedule 1
Example Manufacturing Co., Inc.
Recast Income Statements Adjustment Summary
Years Ended December 31 ($000)

	1991	1992	1993	1994	1995
Sales	$3,760	$4,570	$5,220	$6,370	$7,320
Adjustments (1)	(20)	(30)	(50)	(60)	(70)
Recast	3,740	4,540	5,170	6,310	7,250
Cost of Sales	2,930	3,540	3,870	4,610	5,400
Adjustments (2)	80	80	90	130	110
Recast	3,010	3,620	3,960	4,740	5,510
Gross Profit					
Per Books	830	1,030	1,350	1,760	1,920
Recast	730	920	1,210	1,570	1,740
Operating Expenses	680	980	1,110	1,230	1,310
Adjustments (3)	(130)	(430)	(410)	(500)	(490)
Recast	550	550	700	730	820
Operating Income					
Per Books	150	50	240	530	610
Recast	180	370	510	840	920
Other Expense (Income)	40	40	200	120	140
Adjustments (4)	(40)	(40)	(200)	(120)	(140)
Recast	0	0	0	0	0
Pretax Income					
Per Books	110	10	40	410	470
Recast	180	370	510	840	920
Income Taxes					
Per Books (5)	0	0	0	0	0
Recast (6)	72	148	204	336	368
Net Income					
Per Books	110	10	40	410	470
Recast	108	222	306	504	552

Facilities: The stand alone value of the business has been separated from the value of the real estate (land and buildings) of Example Manufacturing Co., Inc. Accordingly, the recast net book value these properties of $390,000 has been eliminated on the Recast Balance Sheet-Schedule 4, although it has been recorded separately in the Estimated Fair Market Value column of that statement.

An independent appraisal of the fair market value of the real estate owned and used by the Company is approximately $1,690,000 at December 31, 1995. Theoretical fair market rent has been substituted for historical depreciation of the real estate in the Recast Income Statements and in the Income Statement Projections. Fair market annual rent has been estimated to be $186,000 in 1995 with retroactive annual reductions for inflation with adjustments as follows:

	1991	1992	1993	1994	1995
Estimated Fair Market Rent	$155	$161	$168	$175	$186
Less: Depreciation on Plant Buildings	(15)	(11)	(8)	(5)	(6)
Adjustments to Increase Cost of Sales see Summary (2)(a)	140	150	160	170	180

The owner believes present Company facilities are adequate for the future growth shown in the Projected Income Statements (see Schedules 3 and 6).

Management Compensation: The fair market value ("FMV") of management compensation (salary and benefits) required to replace the owner with a professional manager is estimated to be $90,000 per year in 1995. There are annual retroactive reductions each year for inflation adjustments as shown below. Actual historic management compensation is included in Operating Expenses on the Recast Income Statement (Schedule 1). In the recasting, it is reduced to the FMV estimates of management compensation. The resulting recast adjustments to management compensation are as follows:

(Continued)

Schedule 1 (Continued)

	1991	1992	1993	1994	1995
Owner's Compensation Per Books	$(186)	$(429)	$(402)	$(475)	$(450)
Deduct: FMV Compensation	76	79	82	85	90
Adjustments to Decrease Operating Expenses					
See Summary (3)(a)	(110)	(350)	(320)	(390)	(360)

Recast Adjustments Summary: Following is a summary of the adjustments made to the Recast Income Statements (Schedule 1). Included with the adjustments explained in detail on the following pages are those expenses of labor and material for machinery (capitalization) as well as other adjustments for non-recurring, non-operating and discretionary expenses, as follows:

	1991	1992	1993	1994	1995
(1) Adjustments to Sales					
Reclassify Special Sales					
Discounts from Other Income (Expense)	$(20)	$(30)	$(50)	$(60)	$(70)
(2) Adjustments to Cost of Sales					
(a) Adjust rent per Facilities Note	140	150	160	170	180
(b) Reduce repairs & maintenance for direct labor and material used to install and upgrade machinery (to be capitalized)	(70)	(90)	(100)	(80)	(140)
(c) Adjust depreciation for capitalized costs in (2)(b) above	10	20	30	40	70
Total Adjustments to Cost of Sales	80	80	90	130	110
(3) Adjustments to Operating Expenses					
(a) Adjust owner compensation per Management Compensation Note	(110)	(350)	(320)	(390)	(360)
(b) Eliminate other business expenses which are non-recurring, nonoperating or discretionary:					
(i) Owner's personal life insurance	(20)	(20)	(10)	(10)	(10)
(ii) Intermediary engagement fee					(30)
(iii) Environmental remediation fees	0	0	(110)	(120)	(140)
(iv) Expenses to convert from septic system to sanitary sewer (to be capitalized)	0	(60)	0	0	0
(c) Reclassify bad debt expense from Other Income (Expense)	0	0	30	20	50
Total Adjustments to Operating Expenses	(130)	(430)	(410)	(500)	(490)
(4) Adjustments to Other Expense (Income)					
(a) Eliminate contingency expense for environmental remediation as a non-recurring, non-operating expense	0	0	(100)	(50)	(50)
(b) Eliminate miscellaneous non-recurring or non-operating income	10	10	10	30	40
(c) Eliminate interest expense for debt free presentation	(30)	(20)	(30)	(20)	(30)
(d) Reclassify special sales discounts expense as a reduction of sales	(20)	(30)	(50)	(60)	(70)
(e) Reclassify bad debt expense to Operating Expenses	0	0	(30)	(20)	(30)
Total Adjustments to Other Expense (Income)	(40)	(40)	(200)	(120)	(140)

(5) Income taxes have not been deducted from Company income per books because of elected S Corporation status which provides for stockholder income to be reported on the owner's tax return.

(6) Recast income taxes are calculated as an assumed blended rate of 40% to theoretically show federal and state taxes for a C Corporation.

Schedule 2
Example Manufacturing Co., Inc.
Recast Fixed and Variable Costs/Expense Ratios
Year's Ending December 31 ($000)

	1991	1992	1993	1994	1995
Recast Sales (See Schedule 6-A)	$3,740	$4,540	$5,170	$6,310	$7,250
Recast Cost of Sales (See Schedule 6-A)	3,010	3,620	3,960	4,740	5,510
Less: Depreciation Machinery, Equipment	(90)	(70)	(90)	(100)	(150)
Recast Net Cost of Sales	$2,920	$3,550	$3,870	$4,640	$5,360
Recast Net Cost of Sales as a Percentage of Recast Sales	78.07%	78.19%	74.85%	73.53%	73.93%
Recast Fixed Net Cost of Sales					
Supervisory Salaries / Expenses	$ 20	$ 20	$ 30	$ 30	$ 34
Rent	155	161	168	175	186
General Insurance & Taxes	25	30	30	40	45
Utilities	135	140	145	140	145
Recast Fixed Net Cost of Sales	335	351	373	385	410
Recast Variable Net Cost of Sales	$2,585	$3,199	$3,497	$4,255	$4,950
Recast Variable Net Cost of Sales as a Percentage of Recast Sales	69.12%	70.46%	67.64%	67.43%	68.28%
Recast Operating Expenses	$ 550	$ 550	$ 700	$ 730	$ 820
Less: Depreciation Operating Equipment	(20)	(20)	(30)	(20)	(30)
Recast Net Operating Expenses	530	530	670	710	790
Recast Fixed Net Operating Expenses					
Owners Salaries and Expenses	89	89	90	98	110
Supervisory Salaries and Expenses	120	117	116	120	120
General Insurance	4	4	4	4	4
Telephone	8	9	10	12	12
Recast Fixed Net Operating Expenses	221	219	220	234	246
Recast Variable Net Operating Expenses	309	311	450	476	544
Recast Variable Net Operating Expenses as a Percentage of Recast Sales	0	0	0	0	0
Depreciation Expense Deducted from					
Recast Cost of Sales	90	70	90	100	150
Recast Operating Expenses	20	20	30	20	30
Total Recast Depreciation	110	90	120	120	180

Schedule 3
Example Manufacturing Co., Inc.
Projected Income Statements
Base Year and Five Future Years ($000)

	Base Year	1996	1997	1998	1999	2000
Sales	$7,200	$8,352	$9,605	$10,950	$12,374	$13,859
Cost of Sales						
Variable Costs	4,970	5,763	6,627	7,556	8,538	9,563
Fixed Costs	410	442	478	516	557	602
Total Cost of Sales	5,380	6,205	7,105	8,072	9,095	10,165
Gross Profit	1,820	2,147	2,500	2,878	3,279	3,694
Operating Expenses						
Variable Expenses	569	660	759	865	978	1,095
Fixed Expenses	246	266	287	310	335	362
Total Operating Expenses	815	926	1,046	1,175	1,313	1,457
Depreciation (Note 1)	180	190	202	215	224	236
Pretax Income	825	1,031	1,252	1,488	1,742	2,001
Income Taxes (Note 2)	330	412	501	595	697	800
Net Income	$ 495	$ 619	$ 751	$ 893	$1,045	$1,201

1. Depreciation: Depreciation expense has been deducted from both the Cost of Sales and Operating Expenses in the process of determining fixed and variable costs and expenses, per Schedule 2. Depreciation is shown separately here to allow for calculation of cash flow (see also Schedule 6).
2. Income Taxes: The Company has elected to be treated as an S Corporation for income tax purposes, under which the corporate income is reported on shareholder's income tax returns. For this illustration the corporation's income is taxed as a regular C Corporation using a blended tax rate of 40%.
3. Worksheet: Refer also to Income and Cash Flow analysis on Schedule 6.
4. Warning: Remember to include a disclaimer on this projection.

Schedule 4
Example Manufacturing Co., Inc.
Recast Balance Sheet
December 31, 1995 ($000)

	Per Books	Adjustments	Recast	Estimated Fair Market Value
ASSETS				
Current Assets				
Cash	$ 380		$ 380	$ 380
Accounts Receivable—Net	610		610	610
Inventory	1,250		1,250	1,250
Other Current Assets	30		30	30
Total Current Assets	2,270		2,270	2,270
Fixed Assets—Net				
Machinery & Equipment	250	$ 310[1]	560	700*
Land & Buildings	330	60[2]		
		(390)[3]	0	1,690*
Total Fixed Assets—Net	580	(20)	560	2,390
Other Assets	170	(160)[4]	10	10
Total Assets	$3,020	$(180)	$2,840	$4,670
LIABILITIES & EQUITY				
Current Liabilities				
Accounts Payable	$ 280		$ 280	$ 280
Notes Payable	220	$(220)[5]	—	—
Accrued Expenses	390	(210)[6]	180	180
Total Current Liabilities	890	(430)	460	460
Long Term Liabilities	20	(20)[7]	—	—
Total Liabilities	910	(450)	460	460
Stockholder's Equity				
Paid in Capital	50		50	50
Retained Earnings	2,060		2,060	2,060
Normalizing Adjustments		270[8]	270	2,100**
Total Stockholder's Equity	2,110	270	2,380	4,210
Total Liabilities & Equity	$3,020	$(180)	$2,840	$4,670

[1] Increase Machinery and Equipment by capitalized cost of direct labor and materials (previously expensed as repairs and maintenance) which was used to install and upgrade machinery. See also notes to Recast Income Statements—Schedule 1, Note (2)(b). Adjustment is net of tax basis depreciation.

[2] Capitalize as additional real estate basis the cost of new sanitary sewer connection which was previously expensed in 1992. See also Notes to Recast Income Statements—Schedule 1, Note (3)(b)(iv).

[3] Eliminate net book value of real estate to allow for a "stand alone" valuation of the business. On the Recast Income Statements depreciation expense for real estate has been eliminated, but theoretical fair market rental expense has been deducted. See also Notes to Recast Income Statements—Schedule 1, Note (2)(a) and also details in the related Facilities note.

[4] Eliminate cash value of officer's life insurance which will be distributed to the owner.

[5] Eliminate Note Payable for a debt free analysis of income.

[6] Eliminate Accrued Environmental Remediation expenses which are the responsibility of the owner, will not be assumed by a buyer and is treated as a nonrecurring expense on the Recast Income Statement.

[7] Also eliminate Long Term Notes payable for a debt free analysis of income.

[8] Record the net effect of the combined normalizing adjustments as an increase to Stockholder's Equity.

*Fair market value of Machinery and Equipment and Land and Buildings is based upon 1995 independent appraisal reports.

**The Normalizing Adjustments shown in the Estimated Fair Market Value column represent the net difference between the recast book value and the appraisal of Fixed Assets, plus the net effect of the Normalizing Adjustments in the Recast Balance Sheet.

Schedule 5
Example Manufacturing Co., Inc.
Projected Balance Sheets
for the Base Year and Five Future Years ($000)

	Base Year 1995	1996	1997	1998	1999	2000
ASSETS						
Current Assets						
Cash	$ 380	$ 556	$1,170	$1,553	$2,488	$2,867
Accounts Receivable—Net	610	1,027	1,181	1,347	1,525	1,710
Inventory	1,250	1,378	1,460	1,768	1,876	2,198
Other Current Assets	30	30	30	30	30	30
Total Current Assets	2,270	2,991	3,841	4,698	5,919	6,805
Machinery & Equipment—Cost	1,867	1,972	2,081	2,194	2,312	2,435
Accumulated Depreciation	1,307	1,497	1,699	1,914	2,138	1,874
Net Machinery & Equipment	560	475	382	280	174	561
Other Assets	10	10	15	205	205	205
Total Assets	$2,840	$3,476	$4,238	$5,183	$6,298	$7,571
LIABILITIES AND EQUITY						
Current Liabilities						
Accounts Payable	$ 280	$ 286	$ 290	$ 329	$ 366	$ 409
Accrued Expenses	180	191	198	211	244	273
Total Liabilities	460	477	488	540	610	682
Stockholder's Equity	2,380	2,999	3,750	4,643	5,688	6,889
Total Liabilities and Stockholder's Equity	$2,840	$3,476	$4,238	$5,183	$6,298	$7,571

1. Changes in accounts receivable, inventory and accounts payable result from the turnover assumptions on Schedule 6-B and the sales, cost of sales and purchases assumptions developed on Schedules 2 and 6-A.
2. Excess cash has not been distributed.
3. Warning: Remember to include a disclaimer on this projection.

Schedule 6-A
Example Manufacturing Co., Inc.
Income Statement / Cash Flow Analysis
Years Ending December 31 ($000)

	Recast Years					Base Year	Projected Years				
	1991	1992	1993	1994	1995		1996	1997	1998	1999	2000
Sales	$3,740	$4,540	$5,170	$6,310	$7,250	$7,200	$8,352	$9,605	$10,950	$12,374	$13,859
Growth		21.39%	13.87%	22.05%	14.90%		16.00%	15.00%	14.00%	13.00%	12.00%
Fixed Net Cost of Sales	$ 335	$ 351	$ 373	$ 385	$ 410	$ 410	$ 442	$ 478	$ 516	$ 557	$ 602
Variable Net Cost of Sales	2,585	3,199	3,497	4,255	4,950	4,970	5,763	6,627	7,556	8,538	9,563
Net Cost of Sales	2,920	3,550	3,870	4,640	5,360	5,380	6,205	7,105	8,072	9,095	10,165
Gross Profit Before Deprec.	820	990	1,300	1,670	1,890	1,820	2,147	2,500	2,878	3,279	3,694
Percent of Sales	21.93%	21.81%	25.15%	26.47%	26.07%	25.28%	25.71%	26.03%	26.28%	26.50%	26.65%
Gross Profit after Deprec.	$ 710	$ 900	$1,180	$1,550	$1,710						
Percent of Sales	18.98%	19.82%	22.82%	24.56%	23.59%						
Fixed Net Operating Expenses	$ 221	$ 219	$ 220	$ 234	$ 246	$ 246	$ 266	$ 287	$ 310	$ 335	$ 362
Variable Net Operating Exp.	309	311	450	476	544	569	660	759	865	978	1,095
Total Operating Expenses	530	530	670	710	790	815	926	1,046	1,175	1,313	1,457
Depreciation—Total	110	90	120	120	180	180	190	202	215	224	236
Recast Earnings Before Interest and Taxes (EBIT)	180	370	510	840	920	825	1,031	1,252	1,488	1,742	2,001
Percent of Sales	4.81%	8.15%	9.86%	13.31%	12.69%	11.46%	12.34%	13.03%	13.59%	14.08%	14.44%
Net Income	$ 108	$ 222	$ 306	$ 504	$ 552	$ 495	$ 619	$ 751	$ 893	$ 1,045	$ 1,201
Percent of Sales	2.89%	4.89%	5.92%	7.99%	7.61%	6.88%	7.41%	7.82%	8.16%	8.45%	8.67%
Recast Earnings Before Interest, Depreciation, Taxes (EBDIT)	$ 290	$ 460	$ 630	$ 960	$1,100	$1,005	$1,221	$1,454	$ 1,703	$ 1,966	$ 2,237
Percent of Sales	7.75%	10.13%	12.19%	15.21%	15.17%	13.96%	14.62%	15.14%	15.55%	15.89%	16.14%
Working Capital (Increase)							$ (704)	$ (839)	$ (805)	$(1,151)	$ (814)
Excess Cash in Working Capital							67	533	295	844	782
Recast Capital Expenditures	$ (124)	$ (182)	$ (180)	$ (257)	$ (240)	$ (101)	(105)	(109)	(113)	(118)	(623)
Recast Pretax / predebt Net Cash Flow							479	1,039	1,080	1,541	1,582
Percent of Sales							5.74%	10.82%	9.86%	12.45%	11.41%

121

Schedule 6–B

Example Manufacturing Co., Inc.

Income Statement/Cash Flow Analysis

Years Ending December 31 ($000)

	Recast Years					Base Year	Projected Years				
	1991	1992	1993	1994	1995		1996	1997	1998	1999	2000
Variable Cost of Sales	69.10%	70.50%	67.60%	67.40%	68.70%	69%	69.00%	69.00%	69.00%	69.00%	69.00%
Variable Operating Expenses	8.30	6.90	8.70	7.20	7.50	7.9	7.90	7.90	7.90	7.90	7.90
Total Variable Costs	77.40%	77.40%	76.30%	74.60%	76.20%	76.9%	76.90%	76.90%	76.90%	76.90%	76.90%
Accounts Receivable (days)	37	31	48	35	45	45	45	45	45	45	45
Inventory Turn (times)	4	4	5	4	5	5	5	5	5	5	5
Accounts Payable (days)	15	18	20	22	20	20	20	20	20	20	20
Pretax per Books (before Recasting)	110	10	40	410	470						
Recast Adjustments											
(1) Sales	(20)	(30)	(50)	(60)	(70)						
(2) (a) Rent	(140)	(150)	(160)	(170)	(180)						
(b) Repairs & Maintenance	70	90	100	80	140						
(c) Depreciation—Cap.	(10)	(20)	(30)	(40)	(70)						
(3) (a) Owner's Compensation	110	350	320	390	360						
(b) (i) Owner's Life Insurance	20	20	10	10	10						
(ii) Intermediary Fee	—	—	—	—	30						
(iii) Environmental Fees	—	—	110	120	140						
(iv) Sanitary Sewer	—	60	—	—	—						
(c) Bad Debt—Operating	—	—	(30)	(20)	(50)						
(4) (a) Addit. Environ. Cost Est.	—	—	100	50	50						
(b) Nonoperating Income	(10)	(10)	(10)	(30)	(40)						
(c) Interest Expense	30	20	30	20	30						
(d) Sales Discounts	20	30	50	60	70						
(e) Bad Debts—Nonoper.	—	—	30	20	30						
Total Recast Adjustments	70	360	470	430	450						
Recast EBIT	180	370	510	840	920						

Notes to Schedules 6-A and 6-B

1. *Sales* have grown at an annual rate from a low of 13.9% (1993) to a high of 22.4% (1994). The average compound annual historic sales growth rate was 18.1% from 1991 through 1995. For purposes of these projections the compound annual growth rates of sales begin at 16% for 1996 and decline 1% per year through the year 2000.

2. *Fixed Net Cost of Sales* have grown at a compound annual rate of 5% from 1991 to 1995. For these projections, fixed net cost of sales have grown at a compound annual growth rate of 8% for the years 1996 through 2000.

122

3. *Variable Net Cost of Sales* have historically run from a low of 67.43% of Sales in 1994 to a high of 70.46% in 1992. The simple average percentage of sales for variable net Cost of Sales for the five year period from 1991 through 1995 is 68.59% (see also Schedule 2). For purposes of the projections, an annual rate of 69.0% of sales has been used for variable net cost of sales for the years 1996 through 2000.

4. *Fixed Net Operating Expenses* historically increased at a compound annual rate of slightly above 3.0% from 1991 through 1995. For purposes of the projections of the years 1996 through 2000, an 8.0% compound annual growth rate has been used.

5. *Variable Net Operating Expenses* have run from a low of 6.85% of Sales in 1991 to a high of 8.70% for 1993. The five year simple average was 7.77% (see also Schedule 2). For purposes of the projections, Variable Net Operating expenses have been compounded at 7.90% of sales.

6. *Depreciation* has been netted out (deducted) from both Cost of Sales and Operating Expenses. Hence the terms (Fixed or Variable) "Net" Cost of Sales and (Fixed or Variable) "Net" Operating Expenses. Historic depreciation for machinery and equipment has been based upon a seven year life using the straight line method which approximates the Company's tax depreciation. To the historic depreciation has been added depreciation for the costs charged to repairs and maintenance during the years 1991 through 1995 which were of a capital nature. On the recast balance sheet (Schedule 4) these costs were capitalized as machinery and equipment. There were offsetting reductions to the Cost of Sales in the related Recast Income Statements (see also notes to Schedule 1).

7. *Capital Expenditures* (Machinery and Equipment) were normally capitalized when acquired; however, related costs such as labor and materials to install, rebuild or retrofit acquired machines were expensed as repairs and maintenance. This was the time during which the Company changed its manufacturing focus to upsize its capacity to produce large precision machined parts and production machinery with substantial capital expenditures for the basic components at a cost of $503,000 over the five year period. For these recast financial statements, we have also capitalized the $480,000 originally recorded as repairs and maintenance costs from 1991 through 1995.

For the projected years 1996 through 1999, capital expenditures are expected to be slightly more than $100,000 per year, with adjustments for inflation. However, in the year 2000 the Company expects to purchase major precision CNC machining centers with related material handling equipment at a cost of $500,000, in addition to spending approximately $123,000 for other replacements and upgrading. These amounts are included in the projected balance sheets and included on Schedule 6-A in computing Recast Pretax Predebt net cash flow.

8. Warning: Remember to include your disclaimer on this projection.

123

Some of the Assumptions Used

Future sales growth. As shown on the Income Statement/Cash Flow Analysis Worksheet (Schedule 6-A), projected sales growth was estimated by Company management at 16 percent in 1996, declining 1 percent per year down to a stable 12 percent beginning in the year 2000.

Future cost of sales. Historic cost of sales (Schedule 2) has declined from a high of 78 percent of sales in 1991 and 1992 to below 74 percent in 1994 and 1995. Variable cost of sales (also Schedule 2) has also declined since 1992 to below 68 percent in 1993 and 1994 and below 69 percent in 1995. Based upon these trends and Company management's expectations, projected net cost of sales (Schedule 6-A) will decline from approximately 74.3 percent in 1996 down to 73.3 percent by the year 2000.

Future gross profit. Historic gross profit before depreciation expense (Schedule 6-A) increased from 21.9 percent of sales in 1991 to above 26 percent in both 1994 and 1995. Accordingly, with sales increasing (as previously), fixed cost of sales increasing at a slightly decreasing rate, and variable costs stable (as previously), projected gross profits (before depreciation) are expected to increase from 25.7 percent in 1996 to 26.7 percent in the year 2000.

Depreciation expense. Recast depreciation expense is adjusted in two ways: First, the real estate is theoretically separated from the corporation, (to allow for stand-alone valuation of the business); then a theoretical rent expense is deducted, and the related depreciation of the plant facility is deleted. Recast depreciation is increased due to the additional costs relating to the heavy machinery (capitalized labor and material). Note that the depreciation expense (Schedule 6-A) is deducted from both the cost of goods sold and operating expense and combined as a single line item below total operating expenses. This allows for ease in computing EBDIT and cash flow at the bottom of Schedule 6-A.

SUMMARY

After reading the notes to the statements, carefully follow the key concepts through the schedules. Then the normalized or projected financial statements are ready to be used in conjunction with the appropriate valuation approaches.

NOTES

1. Miles, Raymond C., *Basic Business Appraisal*, 1984, John Wiley & Sons, Inc., p. 132.

2. Bishop, David M., *Analyzing and Recasting Financial Statements,* 1995, text and course of International Business Brokers, p. 10.

3. Davis, F.T., Jr., *Business Acquisitions Desk Book,* Second Edition, 1981, Institute for Business Planning, p. 58.

4. Pratt, Shannon, *Valuing Small Businesses and Professional Practices,* 1991, Business One Irwin, p. 220.

5. *IRS Valuation Guide,* Internal Revenue Service, 1994, Commerce Clearing House, p. 7–17.

6. *Ibid.,* p. 7–5.

7. Black/Green & Co., *Business Valuations Training Systems,* 1994, National Association of Certified Valuation Analysts, p. 24.

8. Fishman, Jay E., *Guide to Business Valuations,* Volume 1, Fifth Edition, 1995, Practitioners Publishing Co., Sec. 420.04.

9. *Ibid.,* Volume 3, VAL-7.

10. Use of the recast statement concepts is authorized by Geneva Companies, an international merger and acquisition firm with headquarters in Irvine, California.

11. Trugman, Gary R., *Conducting a Valuation of a Closely Held Business,* 1993, American Institute of Certified Public Accountants.

Utilizing Forecasts to Maximize Acquisition Success

ROBERT B. MACHIZ
PRESIDENT
EXCHANGE CAPITAL, INC.

The preparation of a credible financial forecast is one of the critical success factors for maximizing acquisition opportunities. A forecast is a good-faith attempt to estimate the passage of time upon a company's financial performance. The forecast provides a foundation to support critical decisions by buyer, seller, and their respective advisors throughout the process of negotiating a transaction. In addition, a credible forecast is a valuable device to communicate a financial blueprint for the transaction to the various parties whose input and approval is necessary for closure.

This chapter provides an overview to the business issues of forecasting with emphasis on acquisition planning. An outline of the steps involved in preparing a credible forecast is included, along with a review of the misunderstandings and myths commonly associated with financial forecasting.

The process of preparing a forecast can be organized into six primary stages:

Determining the purpose of the projection.
Determining the number of years to be forecast.
Gathering the information needed to prepare the forecast.
Analyzing the information.
Identifying underlying assumptions.
Pulling the numbers together into a working model.

DEFINING THE PURPOSE OF THE PROJECTION

The purpose of the forecast is largely determined by whether you are a seller, buyer, or advisor. Each has its own special considerations that come into play when preparing the forecast. The essential questions include: What is the purpose of the forecast? Who is going to review and rely upon the forecast? What are the risks if the forecast proves to be unrealistic? In addition to having different needs, buyer, seller, and advisor each bring unique strengths and weaknesses to the assignment.

The Seller's Forecast

Aside from being an invaluable financial planning and management tool, a forecast should be prepared for every prospective company that is for sale, regardless of its size. The selling firm's objective in preparing a forecast is to estimate the future cash flow and capital requirements, which are important elements in reaching the decision to sell and establishing both asking and bottom-line prices. The forecast may be shared with other shareholders or owners and, in some instances, with a prospective buyer or an intermediary in order to illustrate the future earnings capacity of the business. Care is needed when sharing forecasts with prospective buyers to make certain that a seller's representation or promise about the future earnings of the business is not made to the buyer.

The seller and the firm's management are generally in a position to prepare or commission a reliable forecast because of their awareness of the intimate details of the business. A seller may have unique insights and knowledge about the factors that impact future sales income and expenses, such as the strength of customer relationships and whether any critical relationships are in jeopardy; order backlogs, product or service quality and reliability; the strengths and weaknesses of management and the workforce; and the actual condition of facility and equipment. Such firsthand knowledge of the intimate aspects of the business can place the seller in a superior position to prepare a credible and reliable forecast. Naturally, the reliability of any forecast will be determined by the seller's or management's objectivity, judgment, and analytical skills. If the seller is generally unfamiliar with the process of preparing a forecast, an accountant or consultant may be employed to prepare the forecast.

The Buyer's Forecast

If a seller's forecast helps the seller better understand the income stream, then it follows that a buyer's forecast helps him or her better understand what is being bought. The buyer's forecast provides the foundation for a host of significant business questions: What is the value of the business? How much should be paid to achieve the benchmark rate of return? How should purchase price and terms be structured? How much money will it take to finance the acquisition and future growth? How will different funding scenarios impact the bottom line and return to investors?

The forecast along with the supporting assumptions might be included as part of a presentation to senior management, funding sources, and prospective investors. The buyer has a big stake in the forecast. If it's not credible, the deal may not be approved or funded. And, if forecast income does not materialize, money can be lost and careers ruined. Diligence and care is essential when preparing a buyer's forecast, especially if the buyer is unfamiliar with the industry. In addition, if forecasts are shared with prospective investors, extreme care needs to be exercised to make certain that the investor does not interpret the forecast as a promise that future income will reach those levels.

The Advisors' Forecast

There are a number of different types of advisors to any acquisition, including appraisers, intermediaries, and accountants. Each may be called upon to generate a forecast for his or her client. An appraiser can be retained by either the buyer or the seller to provide an independent estimate of fair market value. The appraiser will prepare a forecast in order to estimate and value the future earning stream of the business. The appraiser may be engaged by a seller to make an independent estimate of value. On the flip side, a buyer may retain an appraiser or other qualified independent party to prepare a fairness opinion. A fairness opinion is a letter from a qualified professional to the board of directors of the buyer that the purchase price is fair and prudent. In such cases, the intent of the directors is to protect themselves from a stockholder claim of a failure to act prudently or breach of fiduciary duty.

An intermediary such as a business broker or merger and acquisition specialist may prepare a forecast or projection as part of the selling document or prospectus presented to potential buyers. Here again, care must be exercised to make certain that the forecast is not presented in a way that creates a promise for future earnings. Some intermediaries may prepare an internal forecast to make a determination of whether the seller's asking price and desired terms are realistic before accepting the engagement.

DETERMINING THE NUMBER OF YEARS TO BE FORECAST

After determining the reason for preparing a forecast, the next step is to determine the appropriate number of years to be included in the forecast. One of the keys to a credible forecast is to select a time frame that is reasonably estimable—bearing in mind that the longer the time line, the higher the degree of uncertainty. Despite one's best efforts, there is practically no way to estimate the impact, for better or worse, of unforeseen events such as the introduction of brand-new technologies, the rise of new players in the market, legislative and regulatory change, demographic shifts, and the general business environment.

Aside from the criterion of "reasonably estimable," there is no established rule for determining the required time frame of a forecast. As a practical matter, select a time frame that is sufficient to allow you to obtain answers to the questions that you wish to ask of the forecast. For instance, if you are preparing the forecast to demonstrate that the business's cash flow can support the acquisition or estimate anticipated return on investment, then the forecast should be long enough to amortize the debt and possibly provide an exit for investors.

GATHERING NEEDED INFORMATION

The next step is to gather the information necessary to prepare the forecast. Your objective is to collect as much information as possible about the internal and external factors that *might* impact the company's revenues, bottom line, and cash flow. Needed information addressed:

The historic performance of the company.

The company's capabilities and capacity.

The future outlook for the market and industry.

The critical success factors for the business.

A review of the company's strengths, weaknesses, opportunities, and threats (SWOT analysis).

Performance of the Company

Sources of performance-related information include financial statements (year-end and interim), tax forms, aging of receivables and payables, order backlog reports, listing of the terms of all notes payable, business plans, and budgets. Information about how similar companies perform is available from sources such as Robert Morris Associates, Dun & Bradstreet Information Services, and the Internal Revenue Service. You want to learn as much as possible about where the company has been, where it is today, and where management thinks the company is going. The past and present form the basis on which you will consider the future.

Capabilities and Capacity

A company's capability and capacity is limited by human resources and productive assets. Human resource data can be found by reviewing the resumés and the work record of key personnel, employment agreements, collective bargaining agreements, hiring requirements, labor availability reports, recruitment practices, and any other information that will help you determine whether the company has access to the future talent it will need. Data on capital assets might be found in asset lists, facility utilization versus capacity studies, a review of maintenance procedures, and capital equipment budgets. It is not enough to assume that human and capital assets will automatically be available to meet future needs: A credible forecast will address capital spending as well as the funding required to meet growth.

Future Outlook for Market and Industry

There are any given number of market factors that impact a company's future. Such factors include the legislative and regulatory climate, growth of the market, trends that impact customer behavior, and competitive factors. You can start by estimating how these factors have affected the historic performance of the company. Market and competitive data may be available from the company. Sources of market and industry data include research reports, S&P outlook reports, Predicasts, and various studies and forecasts prepared by trade associations, publications, and consulting groups. An analysis of the market should include a review of the competition. A list of competitors should be developed including their relative size, strengths, and weaknesses. Sources of competitive information include information and credit reports that have appeared in the press. In today's information society, there are any number of groups that monitor and index horizontal as well as vertical markets. Your objective is to obtain as much information as possible to help you reasonably estimate the impact that market factors will have on the future of the enterprise.

Critical Success Factors

Every enterprise has its own "keys to success." Certain behaviors, if performed diligently, will almost always assure success. Your objective is to identify these critical success factors and form a picture of how well the company is addressing each one. Will the success factors shift in the future? Probably. The best way to assemble data is to talk to as many people with industry knowledge as possible, including key management, suppliers, advisors, and consultants. A credible forecast is much more than a straight-line projection of numbers. To be credible, the forecast must consider the anticipated outcomes of events and actions that you believe the enterprise will take.

SWOT Analysis

SWOT is an acronym for the analysis of strengths, weaknesses, opportunities, and threats. You will most likely need to prepare your own SWOT analysis. Assemble a list for each category. Internal and external factors should be considered. The key questions to be asking constantly (even beyond the closing) are: What are the factors, both inside and outside the company, that favor the future of the enterprise? Similarly, what are the enterprise's weaknesses? What opportunities face the business? What factors, internal and external, threaten the company or might present a significant risk? It's helpful to review the list and then ask: How can we capitalize on strengths? How can we eliminate or minimize weaknesses? How can we take advantage of opportunities? And, how can we minimize threats and risks?

Acquisition Planning Criteria and Transaction Details

The buyer's acquisition criteria as well as the proposed transaction details should also be considered when preparing the forecast. Acquisition criteria include the cost of capital, benchmark return requirements, cash available to invest, and debt capacity. The terms of the transaction include the purchase price, how the price will be structured, and anticipated acquisition costs such as broker, legal, accounting, and other advisor fees. In addition, the forecast should address funding requirements, structure, and terms.

Obtaining Information

For a buyer, most of the information to prepare a forecast is part of the data required to perform due diligence. If key members of the management team are available, interview them to learn about their backgrounds, management philosophy, and anything else you might glean about the company. Obviously, if you are a buyer, management may not be totally accessible or open to your questioning. Moreover, it is not likely that you will gain access to managers whose views differ from the selling control group's, and those managers you do interview may be very reluctant to provide any information that might detract from the "value" of the company or place them in a bad light. When interviewing management and members of the selling group, listen carefully, make notes, and reserve judgment until you can sit down and can sort out the information in a deliberate manner. Stay alert to incongruencies or recurring themes, because they may point toward possible areas of intentional obfuscation or help uncover contentious business issues that may need to be studied further.

In addition to information provided by the company, there is a wealth of outside information available to help you prepare your forecast. Industry studies and research reports are available from industry trade groups and publications, financial information companies, and various purveyors of data. The Internet is an excellent source of on-line information regarding public and private companies.

ANALYZING THE INFORMATION

After you've obtained the necessary information, the next step is to make the information useful by analyzing it. This information is going to provide much of the framework for the forecast. Ironically, a forecast of the future starts with a hard look at the past. How many times have you heard the phrase "We all have 20–20 hindsight"? This implies that we can all see the past clearly. If this were true, jury decisions would always be unanimous and would be made quickly and without contention. In fact, a company's past performance and present situation is often veiled by accounting and timing policies, the reliability of data collection systems, and the hidden agendas of the individuals who organize and present the information.

Your job is to sift through the information and make sense of it. Information is the raw material you will use to form the assumptions that will ultimately become your forecast, and just as raw materials need to be processed to be of any value, you will first need to organize the information. The following four steps will help you analyze the data that you've collected about the company:

1. Classify the information according to area of impact.
2. Assess the reliability of information (sorting fact from fiction and opinion).
3. Estimate the relative weight and importance of the information (the "so what" test).
4. Determine what you still don't know (and may never know).

Classification of Information

Depending upon factors such as the level of cooperation from management, the time you have available, your research skills, and overall diligence, you will have accumulated a pile of data. The first challenge is to make order out of the chaos by organizing the data according to the components from which you will build the forecast: financial performance, capacity and capabilities, market analysis and outlook, critical success factors, and SWOTs. As part of the classification process, cull out information that will not be considered in the forecast.

Reliability of Information

Assess the level of confidence you have in each piece of data. To what extent are you willing to rely upon a given piece of information? Does one piece of information conflict with another? Is the information sufficient, or is more needed? Are the "facts" congruent with your gut-level perceptions of the company and its management? An estimate of the future based upon unreliable information is not a forecast, it's a guess.

Relevance and Importance

Separate significant information from the trivial. One benchmark for determining significant information is whether that bit of information is useful when forming an estimate of the company's future. After all, your forecast is an attempt to quantify the impact of a series of anticipated future events upon the company's financial statements.

Embracing the Unknown

More than likely, there will be some aspects of the business about which you will have little or no information. These missing pieces of the puzzle are important. Even if you are unable to obtain the missing data, it is important that you know where the holes are so that you can factor your limitations into the forecast. A little self-awareness regarding lack of knowledge now can save you from becoming a fool later!

IDENTIFYING UNDERLYING ASSUMPTIONS

At this point in the process, you know why you're preparing the forecast; you've determined its length; and you have gathered and analyzed the needed information. By this time, you should be forming a picture of where the company has been and where it is now. The next step is to identify the underlying assumptions that will shape the future of the company. An assumption is a supposition that something is true, is probably true, or is likely to be true at some point in the future. An assumption is only as reasonable as the facts and logic upon which it is made. A credible forecast should rely upon reasonable assumptions. Assumptions fall into the following four broad categories:

- The present situation of the business and how it got there. This is part of developing a sense of continuity between the past and the forecast future.
- The existing vision of the company's future, why it's going there, and how it plans to get there. This will help provide insight into how the company and management presently define its future.
- The anticipated market and business climate at various intervals throughout the forecast period. These factors are the most difficult to estimate with a high degree of accuracy.
- The buyer's vision for the company in light of the preceding three factors.

These four categories of assumptions determine the decisions and actions of a buyer, whether articulated or not. Once the buyer has established a vision for the future, it is time to begin estimating how that vision will be expressed by the organization. It is then appropriate to begin making nuts-and-bolts assumptions that can be quantified into a line-item forecast. In order to prepare a forecast, specific assumptions regarding revenue growth, expenses, balance sheet turnover rates, productive capacity, and future asset requirements need to be made.

Revenues

Given the historic performance of the company, the outlook for the market, presently known SWOTs, existing plans, and any other relevant data, what is a reasonable rate of growth for each of the years in the forecast? What will be necessary to achieve these sales levels? Does the company have the ability to generate these sales now or will new actions or resources be needed? Will customers be lost or gained as a result of the change in ownership?

There are a number of methods commonly used to forecast revenues. For short-term forecasts, factors such as order backlog, number of bids or proposals outstanding, and customer order patterns can be used to create a fairly reliable forecast. Unfortunately, as the time line is extended, this information becomes less available. There are a number of methods to prepare a longer-term forecast, including:

- An *event-oriented* method would include any assumption that is based upon an actual event or action that the company is likely to make, such as the acquisition of a product line, launching a new marketing campaign, increasing distribution channels, the addition of new or related products, the hiring of additional salespeople, or the addition of new facilities or processes. As the time horizon lengthens, it becomes more difficult to prepare an event-oriented forecast.

- As the name implies, a *statistically-oriented* method is one that attempts to estimate future sales by applying one or more regressions to past sales numbers. One statistical method, trend line analysis, is considered to be one of the most reliable of the common methods for longer-term forecasts. However, for the trend line method to be of value, you need to have a number of historical statements with five or more being desirable.
- A *simple-alternative* to the objective and statistical methods is the application of a set growth rate applied to a historic period. The growth rate can be based upon a historic average, a moving average, or the most recent period's rate of growth. The drawback of a simple percentage forecast is that it does not take causal relationships into account.

Expenses

Given available information and your analysis, what are the factors that determine expenses and costs? Which costs are fixed? Which costs are variable; and if a cost is variable, what determines it? When considering cost structure, it is preferable to review each individual line item on the income statement. Other questions include: What is the company's present capacity? What will the company need to acquire in order to grow, and what are the costs? Are facilities adequate or will they need to be upgraded or replaced if the company grows as expected?

There are four major groups of expenses that need to be addressed in the forecast: cost of goods or services sold, selling expenses, general and administrative, and nonoperating expenses. Sometimes, the selling expenses are combined with the general and administrative costs. Within each group there are certain expenses that are fixed and others that are variable. A fixed expense will tend to remain fairly level regardless of revenues; although with sufficient passage of time most expenses will change due to alterations in contract terms (interest rates, leases, or premiums) or because of inflation. On the other hand, a variable expense will tend to follow the line item on which it is dependent. For instance, labor and materials expenses will generally increase with sales; and payroll tax-related line items will increase with the amount of payroll. So, once an expense is determined to be variable, the next step is to determine the line item or items on which the given variable is dependent.

Balance Sheet Factors

Prior analysis of the company's balance sheet will help stop trends that can pinpoint future "hot spots." Key questions include: Will the company adopt new policies that will affect receivable, payable, and inventory levels? If so, how will turnover rates change? What is the purchase price and how will the terms be structured? Will the transaction be structured as an asset or stock purchase? If assets are purchased, what will be the new basis in acquired assets? Will any liabilities be assumed? What is the net cost of the acquisition, including all fees, and how will the acquisition be funded? What is the anticipated cost for new equipment and facilities that may be needed to meet future production requirements and to remain competitive? How will capital purchases be financed? Will additional working capital be needed? How much equity will be needed?

The balance sheet is divided into asset, liability, and equity sections. At a minimum, there are three general groups of assets to consider: current, fixed, and nonoperating. Other asset groups are possible depending upon the specifics of the company. There are usually three or more liability groups: current, long-term, and other liabilities. Again, more liability sections are possible.

Disclosing Assumptions and Limitations

A credible forecast should include a summary of all the underlying assumptions. This makes it easier to update as your assumptions change and discloses to the prospective reader that your future estimates are contingent upon these assumptions. You do not want to present your forecast in such a way as to create an impression among third parties that you are making a representation about future performance that you may be called to account for in the future if things go awry. When making assumptions, bear in mind that the more unreasonable your assumptions, the less reasonable your forecast. Exponential increases in sales and profits look impressive, but if historic growth has been stagnant, a red flag goes up! If you make such a "hockey stick" forecast, be prepared to offer rock-solid logic to overcome well-deserved skepticism.

Whether in one's vocation or as a one-time event, the art of forecasting is found in the obtaining and analysis of information and the ability to make reasonable assumptions about the future. The creation of the classic "spreadsheet" is usually a matter of simple math. Math is not what undermines a forecast. The real culprit is misunderstanding the enterprise's history and current situation and/or unreasonable assumptions about the future.

PULLING THE NUMBERS TOGETHER

Now it's time to make sense out of all this information, analysis, and supposition. The next step is to quantify the results of the preparation and develop a set of financial forecasts. ideally, your forecast should include an Income Statement, Balance Sheet, and Statement of Cash Flows. A common error is to forecast only the Income Statement. Without the

Balance Sheet and Cash Flow, it is nearly impossible to detrmine whether the company has sufficient capital for the future. Even in a profitable company, capital is needed to fund increases in inventory, accounts receivable growth, added payroll, equipment purchases, and facility upgrades.

An Example of an Acquisition Forecast

To illustrate how the numbers can be pulled together into a financial model, we've prepared the forecast in Exhibits 9.1 to 9.3. This sample case is a buyer's forecast involving a mythical company, Sample Industries, Inc. The forecast includes purchase price, terms, and financing. This forecast was computer-generated using the Buy-Out Plan, an acquisition planning software system that is published by MoneySoft, Inc. The example forecast of the Sample Industries acquisition was prepared for a mythical buyer, XYZ Holdings, a buy-out firm.

Sample Industries will be operated as a stand-alone acquisition. Once approved by XYZ's management, the forecast will be updated to reflect any changes and then included as part of a proposal for acquisition funding.

In order to prepare the forecast, we have to make a number of specific assumptions, as follows:

Revenue and income assumptions. Revenues are divided among three primary sources: Product Sales, Service Sales, and General Sales.

- At the end of the last fiscal year, Product Sales were $1,704,000. Product Sales are forecast to grow to $2,607,307 in FY 2002, based upon the trend line method and resulting in an average annual growth of 6.6 percent.
- Service Sales are forecast to grow to $1,014,472 in FY 2002, based upon the historic average annual growth rate of 2.79 percent. At the end of the most recent fiscal year, Service Sales were $837,000.
- General Sales are forecast to grow to $570,462 in FY 2002, based upon the trend line method and resulting in an average annual growth of 1.9 percent. At the end of the most recent fiscal year, General Sales were $492,000.

For planning purposes, we assume that interest of 4 percent per annum will be earned on cash in the company's bank accounts (including checking).

Expense assumptions. The Cost of Goods Sold is projected to be 45 percent of sales. This is an increase of 5.48 percent over the historic average of 39.52 percent. The increase is due to the anticipated increases that

Exhibit 9.1 Sample Industries, Inc. Pro Forma Projected Income Statements

	Dec 1996	Dec 1997	Dec 1998	Dec 1999	Dec 2000	Dec 2001	Dec 2002
Revenue							
Product Sales	$1,833,044	$1,962,088	$2,091,131	$2,220,175	$2,349,219	$2,478,263	$2,607,307
Service Revenue	860,312	884,274	908,903	934,218	960,238	986,983	1,014,472
General Sales	503,209	514,418	525,627	536,835	548,044	559,253	570,462
Total Revenue	$3,196,565	$3,360,779	$3,525,661	$3,691,228	$3,857,501	$4,024,499	$4,192,241
Cost of Goods Sold							
Product Costs	319,656	336,078	352,566	369,123	385,750	402,450	419,224
Direct Labor	799,141	840,195	881,415	922,807	964,375	1,006,125	1,048,060
Overhead	319,656	336,078	352,566	369,123	385,750	402,450	419,224
Total COGS	$1,438,454	$1,512,351	$1,586,547	$1,661,053	$1,735,876	$1,811,024	$1,886,508
Gross Profit	$1,758,111	$1,848,429	$1,939,113	$2,030,176	$2,121,626	$2,213,474	$2,305,732
Selling Expenses							
Sales Commissions	179,589	188,815	198,079	207,381	216,722	226,104	235,528
Advertising	88,214	92,746	97,296	101,865	106,453	111,062	115,691
Other Promotions	51,853	54,517	57,192	59,877	62,575	65,284	68,005
Total Selling Expenses	$ 319,656	$ 336,078	$ 352,566	$ 369,123	$ 385,750	$ 402,450	$ 419,224
General and Administrative Expenses							
Officer Salaries	159,828	168,039	176,283	184,561	192,875	201,225	209,612
Employee Wages	205,516	216,074	226,675	237,319	248,009	258,746	269,531
Utilities	3,794	3,989	4,185	4,381	4,579	4,777	4,976
Rent	21,079	22,161	23,249	24,340	25,437	26,538	27,644
Shipping & Postage	31,618	33,242	34,873	36,511	38,155	39,807	41,466
Office Supplies	2,319	2,438	2,557	2,677	2,798	2,919	3,041
Travel & Entertainment	7,377	7,756	8,137	8,519	8,903	9,288	9,675
Payroll Taxes	62,445	65,653	68,874	72,109	75,357	78,619	81,896

Depreciation	194,109	172,529	158,586	149,648	151,151	149,061	141,404
Amortization	65,183	65,183	65,183	65,183	65,183	65,183	65,183
Total G&A Expenses	$ 753,268	$ 757,065	$ 768,601	$ 785,249	$ 812,447	$ 836,163	$ 854,428
Operating Income	$ 685,187	$ 755,286	$ 817,947	$ 875,804	$ 923,429	$ 974,861	$1,032,080
Interest Expense:							
Bank Note #2	54,280	46,555	38,021	28,594	18,179	6,675	0
Seller Note	128,460	113,344	96,810	78,724	58,943	37,305	13,638
Work. Cap. Loan	32,099	28,945	21,964	14,252	5,733	66	0
Interest Expense	$ 214,839	$ 188,844	$ 156,795	$ 121,570	$ 82,855	$ 44,045	$ 13,638
Earnings after Interest	470,348	566,442	661,152	754,233	840,574	930,816	1,018,442
Other Revenue / Expense:							
Cash and Equiv. Income	28,081	15,216	13,149	10,633	7,709	5,021	5,642
Income Tax Expense	224,293	261,746	303,435	344,190	381,727	421,126	460,838
NET INCOME	$ 274,136	$ 319,912	$ 370,865	$ 420,677	$ 466,556	$ 514,710	$ 563,246

Exhibit 9.2 Sample Industries, Inc. Pro Forma Projected Balance Sheets

	Dec 1996	Dec 1997	Dec 1998	Dec 1999	Dec 2000	Dec 2001	Dec 2002
Current Assets							
Cash	$ 380,410	$ 328,717	$ 265,837	$ 192,726	$ 125,517	$ 141,046	$ 315,806
Other Receivables	3,130	3,130	3,130	3,130	3,130	3,130	3,130
Accounts Receivable	266,380	280,065	293,805	307,602	321,458	335,375	349,353
(A / R Allowance)	(21,310)	(22,405)	(23,504)	(24,608)	(25,717)	(26,830)	(27,948)
Prepaid Expenses	7,061	7,424	7,788	8,154	8,521	8,890	9,261
Raw Materials Inv.	68,133	71,633	75,147	78,676	82,220	85,780	89,355
Work in Process Inv.	56,777	59,694	62,623	65,564	68,517	71,483	74,463
Finished Goods Inv.	164,654	173,113	181,606	190,134	198,699	207,301	215,941
Other Inventory	30,092	31,638	33,190	34,749	36,314	37,886	39,465
Other Current Asset	2,519	2,648	2,778	2,909	3,040	3,171	3,303
Total Current Assets	$ 957,846	$ 935,657	$ 902,400	$ 859,036	$ 821,700	$ 867,233	$1,072,130
Fixed Assets							
Plant	725,000	800,000	875,000	950,000	1,025,000	1,100,000	1,175,000
(Accum Depreciation)	(46,109)	(94,123)	(143,919)	(195,377)	(248,389)	(302,852)	(358,671)
Vehicles	120,000	145,000	170,000	195,000	220,000	245,000	245,000
(Accum Depreciation)	(48,000)	(86,800)	(120,080)	(150,048)	(178,029)	(201,085)	(214,141)
Furniture & Fixtures	50,000	50,000	50,000	50,000	75,000	100,000	125,000
(Accum Depreciation)	(14,286)	(24,490)	(31,778)	(36,985)	(47,846)	(62,747)	(80,534)
Equipment	300,000	350,000	400,000	450,000	500,000	550,000	600,000
(Accum Depreciation)	(85,714)	(161,224)	(229,446)	(292,461)	(351,758)	(408,399)	(463,142)
Non-Depreciable	25,000	25,000	25,000	25,000	25,000	25,000	25,000
Net Fixed Assets	$1,025,891	$1,003,362	$994,777	$995,129	$1,018,978	$1,044,917	$1,053,513

Other Assets							
Purchase Goodwill	132,741	132,741	132,741	132,741	132,741	132,741	132,741
Other Intangibles	845,000	845,000	845,000	845,000	845,000	845,000	845,000
(Accum Amortization)	(65,183)	(130,365)	(195,548)	(260,731)	(325,914)	(391,096)	(456,279)
Total Other Assets	$ 912,558	$ 847,375	$ 782,193	$ 717,010	$ 651,827	$ 586,644	$ 521,462
Total Assets	$2,896,296	$2,786,395	$2,679,369	$2,571,174	$2,492,505	$2,498,794	$2,647,104
Current Liabilities							
Accounts Payable	35,084	36,887	38,696	40,513	42,338	44,171	46,012
Bank Note 1	502,229	420,733	330,704	231,247	121,376	(0)	0
Cur Portion L.T. Debt	242,926	266,441	292,239	320,540	260,200	275,966	0
Total Current Liabilities	$ 780,239	$ 724,061	$ 661,639	$ 592,301	$ 423,915	$ 320,137	$ 46,012
Long-Term Liabilities							
Seller Note	1,162,598	969,804	758,925	528,264	275,966	0	0
Work. Cap. Loan	252,788	179,140	97,781	7,902	0	0	0
Total L.T. Liabilities	$1,415,386	$1,148,945	$ 856,706	$ 536,166	$ 275,966	$ 0	$ 0
Total Liabilities	$2,195,625	$1,873,006	$1,518,345	$1,128,467	$ 699,881	$ 320,137	$ 46,012
Equity							
Common Stock	519,000	519,000	519,000	519,000	519,000	519,000	519,000
Retained Earnings	181,670	394,389	642,025	923,708	1,273,624	1,659,657	2,082,092
Total Equity	$700,670	$913,389	$1,161,025	$1,442,708	$1,792,624	$2,178,657	$2,601,092
Total Liability and Equity	$2,896,296	$2,786,395	$2,679,369	$2,571,174	$2,492,505	$2,498,794	$2,647,104

Exhbit 9.3 Sample Industries, Inc. Pro Forma Projected Cash Flows

	Dec 1996	Dec 1997	Dec 1998	Dec 1999	Dec 2000	Dec 2001	Dec 2002
Net Income	$ 274,136	$ 319,912	$ 370,865	$ 420,677	$ 466,556	$ 514,710	$ 563,246
Plus: Sources of Cash							
Depreciation and Amortization	259,291	237,712	223,768	214,831	216,334	214,243	206,587
Increase A / P	35,084	1,802	1,810	1,817	1,825	1,833	1,841
Total Sources of Cash	$ 294,376	$ 239,514	$ 225,578	$ 216,648	$ 218,159	$ 216,076	$ 208,428
Less: Uses of Cash							
Increase Equivalent	0	0	0	0	0	0	0
Increase A / R	16,531	12,590	12,641	12,694	12,748	12,803	12,860
Increase Prepaids	361	363	364	366	367	369	371
Increase Inventory	38,156	16,421	16,488	16,557	16,627	16,700	16,774
Increase Other Current	129	129	130	130	131	132	132
Total Uses of Cash	$ 55,178	$ 29,503	$ 29,623	$ 29,746	$ 29,873	$ 30,003	$ 30,137
Cash from Operations	513,334	529,923	566,820	607,578	654,841	700,783	741,537
Capital Expenditures	125,000	150,000	150,000	150,000	175,000	175,000	150,000
Cash after Asset Purchases	$ 388,334	$ 379,923	$ 416,820	$ 457,578	$ 479,841	$ 525,783	$ 591,537
Dividends Common Stock	68,534	79,978	92,716	105,169	116,639	128,678	140,812
Cash after Dividends	$ 319,800	$ 299,945	$ 324,104	$ 352,409	$ 363,202	$ 397,106	$ 450,726
Funding / (Servicing)							
Bank Note 1	(73,771)	(81,496)	(90,029)	(99,457)	(109,871)	(121,376)	0
Seller Note	(161,143)	(176,259)	(192,794)	(210,879)	(230,661)	(252,298)	(275,966)
Working Capital loan	319,455	(66,567)	(73,645)	(81,360)	(89,879)	(7,902)	(0)
Cash after financing	404,341	(24,477)	(32,367)	(39,286)	(67,209)	35,529	174,750
Contingent Earnout	(23,931)	(27,316)	(30,513)	(33,825)	0	0	0
Net Change in Cash	380,410	(51,693)	(62,880)	(73,111)	(67,209)	35,529	174,750
Beginning Cash Balance	0	380,410	328,717	265,837	192,726	125,517	141,046
Ending Cash Balance	$ 380,419	$ 328,717	$ 263,837	$ 192,726	$ 125,517	$ 141,046	$ 315,806

XYZ Holdings will experience in bringing direct labor costs in line with its other facilities, as well as the anticipated loss of certain key purchasing arrangements due to the change in ownership. Details are as follows:

- Product Costs at 10 percent of sales.
- Direct Labor at 25 percent of sales.
- Overhead at 10 percent of sales.

With the exception of Depreciation, Interest, and Officer Salary, all other expenses are assumed at the historic percentage of sales. Officer Salary is assumed at 5 percent of sales to reflect the proposed compensation package to senior management. Depreciation and Interest details are provided elsewhere in this report.

Balance sheet assumptions. Key turnover ratios are detailed as follows:

- Accounts Receivable is expected to turn 12 times. An allowance of 8 percent for uncollectable A/R has been made.
- Inventory is expected to turn 4.5 times.
- Accounts Payable is expected to turn 41 times. The company normally pays its bills in 10 days and takes all available discounts. This practice will be continued under new ownership.

The company is presently operating at 80 percent of its productive capacity. In order to keep pace with technology and sales growth, certain anticipated improvements have been built into the forecast, and these are summarized next:

- $75,000 to be invested in Plant improvements for each year of the forecast. Improvements will be capitalized and depreciated over 31.5 years, using the double declining balance (DDB) method.
- $25,000 to be invested annually for additional Vehicles starting in year 2 of the forecast. Vehicles are depreciated using the DDB method over 5 years.
- $25,000 to be invested annually for additions to Furniture and Fixtures starting in year 5. Furniture and Fixtures are depreciated using the DDB method with an asset life of 7 years.
- $50,000 to be invested for acquisition of new Equipment for each year of the forecast. Equipment is to be depreciated using the DDB method with an asset life of 7 years.

Goodwill and intangibles, including the covenant-not-to-compete agreement with the seller, will be amortized over 15 years. All other balance sheet accounts have been assumed at the historic percentage of sales.

Transaction details.   The terms of the proposed purchase have been built into the forecast. The purchase is to be structured as an asset transaction. The liabilities of Sample Industries are not being assumed. The seller is being paid $2,500,000, with $1,000,000 payable at closing and the balance of $1,500,000 to be paid in 84 monthly installments with interest of 9 percent. The seller is also to receive a contingency payment equal to 2 percent of the annual sales in excess of $2,000,000 for the four years immediately following the closing date.

The purchase price of $2,500,000 is to be allocated as follows: $1,617,259 toward the assets purchased, $750,000 toward the covenant-not-to-compete, and the balance of $132,741 as goodwill.

The seller is responsible for broker commissions. Buyer-related transaction costs have been estimated to be $95,000.

Funding assumptions.   XYZ Holdings will require $2,595,000 to fund the purchase price and related transaction fees. The assets will be acquired by a new entity called NewCo and will be operated as a stand-alone business. Since the company is not assuming liabilities, additional working capital of $375,000 will be required for a total funding of $2,970,000. Proposed sources for this funding are as follows:

- A senior secured note payable with ABC Business Bank in the amount of $576,000 payable in 72 equal monthly installments with an annual interest rate of 10 percent. Proceeds of the loan to be used for acquisition funding.
- A junior note payable to the Seller in the amount of $1,500,000 payable in 84 equal monthly installments with an annual interest rate of 9 percent.
- The purchase of $519,000 of NewCo's common stock by XYZ Holdings. It is anticipated that 25 percent of NewCo's after-tax earnings will be distributed to shareholders as a dividend.
- A second senior secured note payable with ABC Business Bank in the amount of $375,000 payable in 60 equal monthly installments, with an annual interest rate of 10 percent. Proceeds of the loan to be used for working capital.

DYNAMIC PROJECTIONS

It is a myth to think of projections or forecasts as an addendum in the back of a prospectus or deal book. In truth, a forecast should be dynamic, and be updated as negotiations proceed. First you are negotiating with the seller, then with your own internal advisors or management; in addition, you are negotiating with funding sources. Throughout the process of negotiating the transaction, all parties will likely put forth terms. A forecast is a decision-making tool that you can use to evaluate the impact of proposed terms. If you don't run the numbers, how can you be sure that you can live with the terms and fulfill your financial obligations?

Uncertainty is a fact of life when attempting to forecast future performance, but a certain degree of it can be mitigated by identifying the factors that will shape the future of the business and by having a plan to deal with them. An overall plan and forecast, if properly prepared, should tend to sharpen vision and encourage outcome-oriented behaviors which can increase the chances of success and build value through acquisitions.

CHAPTER TEN

The Real Rate of Return on Investment

ROBERT W. SCARLATA
PRESIDENT
THE MARCH GROUP

The focal point of the majority of negotiations between seller and purchaser is either earnings before interest and taxes (EBIT) or earnings before interest, taxes, depreciation, and amortization (EBITDA). This therefore is the most obvious place to begin when calculating the rate of return on investment (ROI). Assuming that the purchaser is willing to pay five times EBIT, and assuming an all-cash transaction, the rate of return would be 20 percent, the inverse of the multiple ($\frac{1}{5} = 20\%$). This is also called the *capitalization rate* or *cap rate* for short. This percentage represents the pretax earnings given an all-cash transaction.

Most transactions, however, are financed through a combination of equity *and* debt. Often, this debt is guaranteed or in some way secured by parties other than the entity making the acquisition/investment (the use of "credit enhancement"). Cash is what remains *after* taxes have been paid, a critical point given that cash is often the equity in a transaction. It is also that which is of greatest significance to the equity holders in evaluating the "real" return associated with their investment. After all, at the end of the day, it's the cash that you spend.

Exhibit 10.1 is an example of a real transaction negotiated in 1995. It reflects the actual terms and conditions agreeable to both a purchaser and a seller after extensive discussion and debate. The purchase price on this transaction was $3,820,205 plus real property. The purchaser put a total cash investment of $1,200,000 into the transaction.

Very few buyers recognize their actual return on investment during the course of negotiations. Instead, they are focusing on their cash flow, their ability to make debt service and their cash flow coverage of these real costs. No matter how high the rate of return, if debt service cannot be covered, all will be lost. A sample of the tools used by the sophisticated purchasers and/or by intermediaries who wish to prove the value of their clients counter offer are as follows:

Pretax Cash-on-Cash Return on Investment.

Pretax Actual Return on Investment.

After-Tax Cash-on-Cash Return on Investment.

Pretax Actual Rate of Return and Growth.

Rate of Return Factored by Guarantees and Credit Enhancements.

Price/Earnings Ratio.

PRETAX CASH-ON-CASH RETURN ON INVESTMENT

This method of determining the ROI is achieved by dividing the spendable dollars available after all expenses (excluding income taxes) have been paid by the total initial cash investment in the business. This method provides an easy reference when comparing rates of return with other readily available fixed return investments such as bonds (assuming retention to maturity, of course). In our example, this rate is 30.82 percent.

PRETAX ACTUAL RETURN ON INVESTMENT

As the acquisition entity pays down its debt, given zero growth and the assumption that the shareholders could sell their business for the same value (based on a multiple of EBIT), equity will have increased as the acquisition debt is amortized. This increase in equity is added to the pretax rate of return. Assuming that the debt is not refinanced, the actual rate of return increases each year as the rate of amortization increases. In our example, this rate is 40 percent.

Exhibit 10.1   ABC Company, Inc. Return on Investment

	1995	1996	1997	1998	1999
Earnings before Interest and Taxes[1]	$730,531	$767,058	$805,411	$845,682	$887,966
Debt Service (Principal and Interest)					
Line of Credit	(27,857)	(27,857)	(27,857)	(27,857)	(27,857)
Seller Financing Note—283,828; 5yr 7.5%	(62,561)	(68,248)	(68,248)	(68,248)	(68,248)
Equipment Note—395,022; 10yr 9.5%	(56,226)	(61,338)	(61,338)	(61,338)	(61,338)
Building Note—280,000; 20yr 9.5%	(28,710)	(31,320)	(31,320)	(31,320)	(31,320)
Purchase Note—1,661,355; 15yr 9%	(185,356)	(202,207)	(202,207)	(202,207)	(202,207)
Total Debt Service	(360,710)	(390,970)	(390,970)	(390,970)	(390,970)
Cash Flow after Debt Service	$369,821	$376,088	$414,441	$454,712	$496,996
Pre Tax Cash-on-Cash ROI (on Downpayment)	*30.82%*	*31.34%*	*34.54%*	*37.89%*	*41.42%*
Principal Amortization[2]					
Seller Financing Note—283,828; 5yr 7.5%	$44,418	$52,058	$56,099	$60,454	$65,147
Equipment Note—395,022; 10yr 9.5%	11,113	13,212	14,451	15,807	17,290
Building Note—280,000; 20yr 9.5%	4,502	5,377	5,911	6,498	7,143
Purchase Note—1,661,355; 15yr 9%	50,147	59,618	65,210	71,327	78,018
Total Principal Amortization	$110,180	$130,265	$141,671	$154,086	$167,598
Total Cash Flow and Principal Amortization	$480,001	$506,353	$556,112	$608,798	$664,594
Pre-Tax Actual Return on Investment[3]	*40.00%*	*42.20%*	*46.34%*	*50.73%*	*55.38%*
Income Taxes (See Schedule Attached)	$147,063	$176,320	$171,588	$176,511	$195,482
After Tax Cash Flow	$332,938	$330,033	$384,524	$432,287	$469,112
After Tax Cash-on-Cash Return on Investment	*27.74%*	*27.50%*	*32.04%*	*36.02%*	*39.09%*

[1] Annual EBIT has a 5% annual growth rate and is based on the 1995 Fiscal Year Financial Statements

[2] Amortization is included in the Cash on Cash ROI + Equity Increase to reflect the company's equity increase occurring subsequent with the decrease in debt

[3] This calculation takes into consideration the initial cash on cash investment, annual earnings, capital expenditures and the paydown of principal effect on equity

AFTER-TAX CASH-ON-CASH RETURN ON INVESTMENT

This method of determining the ROI is achieved by dividing the spendable dollars available after all expenses, including taxes, have been paid by the total initial cash investment in the business. After-tax dollars were invested as equity and the cash-on-cash rate of return provides the investor with an analysis of the actual rate of return. In the example, this rate of return is 27.74 percent, considerably higher than the inverse of the multiple of EBIT would lead one to believe it might be. The reason for this increased ROI is the existence of leverage in the transaction.

PRETAX ACTUAL RATE OF RETURN AND GROWTH

And now the returns really get interesting. Let's assume a rate of growth in earnings, even a nominal one equal to the rate of inflation (no buyer ever acquired a business who didn't think he or she could do better than the seller!). What happens? As we tell those clients who decide not to sell because the current value of their business is too low to meet their personal needs, for every dollar increase in earnings, the equity holders increase their net worth by six [pretax] dollars, the dollar in cash they earned and the five-times multiple increase in the value of the business. (If GAAP required an adjustment of the balance sheet to reflect fair market value every year, goodwill—the present value of future earnings—would increase every year by a multiple of the increase in earnings, thus reflecting the real equity of the business's shareholders.)

THE RATE OF RETURN FACTORED BY
GUARANTEES/CREDIT ENHANCEMENT

Assuming that there are no outside guarantees or any outside collateral and that the extent of risk is the equity investment, then the rates of return are as stated previously. But what if the debt is personally guaranteed by the equity investors? Certainly this guarantee has a cost associated with it. But how does one calculate that cost, and how does this affect the calculation of the rate of return? One must assume that the assets are available to make good the guarantee. We've assumed in the past (given a transaction with two equal purchasers, one of whom invests cash and the other who uses his or her guarantee on debt as a substitute) that the debt portion of the overall financing structure was entitled to the same "return" as the cash portion.

If the company does not have the asset base to make good this debt in a liquidation scenario, then the question concerns the amount that the shareholders are actually guaranteeing in a realistic default scenario.

We've used the following formula to arrive at a "return" associated with this guaranteed debt:

$$\text{Debt Principle} - \text{Value recovered in a liquidation} = \text{Amount at risk}$$

$$\begin{array}{l} \text{Rate of return} \\ \text{attributable to} \\ \text{the guarantee} \end{array} = \left[\left(\begin{array}{c} \text{Cap rate of the} \\ \text{transaction} \end{array} - \begin{array}{c} \text{Risk free rate} \\ \text{of return} \end{array} \right) \times \begin{array}{c} \text{Amount} \\ \text{of risk} \end{array} \right] \times \begin{array}{c} \text{Amount} \\ \text{at risk} \end{array}$$

What does this mean in practice? It effectively provides a way by which the guarantor can be fairly compensated for the risk associated with the "cost" of his or her guarantee. In addition, it places in perspective the cash-on-cash return on investment.

PRICE/EARNINGS RATIO

This, of course, is the ratio that is expressed in the newspaper every day with respect to publicly traded shares. It is the ratio of the price per share × after-tax earnings per share. The after-tax earnings reflect the cash left after all operating expenses, depreciation and amortization, interest, and taxes. This ratio is very rarely used with respect to middle-market transactions. Its closest analogy is the after-tax cash-on-cash rate of return. The difference from our perspective is that in place of depreciation/amortization, we use capital expenditures.

As can be seen, the actual rates of return with respect to successful middle-market transactions are great indeed. That explains why there is so much money chasing so few good transactions (the rates of return on a leveraged basis easily exceed 25 percent). Naturally, such rates do not come without risk. The risks include managerial risk, lack of liquidity, industry, and economic risk, but as Milkin proved with respect to low-grade bonds, the market may indeed impose a risk premium exceeding the risk in fact. For those willing and prepared to accept those risks, the returns can far exceed those attributable to the wide variety of other available investments.

CHAPTER ELEVEN

Valuation Methods for Midsize Companies: Taking Out the Guesswork

RICHARD HOULIHAN
PRINCIPAL
HOULIHAN VALUATION ADVISORS

BRET TACK
PRINCIPAL
HOULIHAN VALUATION ADVISORS

A common problem in many negotiations involving the sale of midsize companies is that neither the prospective buyer nor the seller has a clear idea of the value of the business. In more situations than not, the seller has an unrealistically high impression of what the business is worth, often based more on emotion than logic. Generally, neither party has undertaken any significant fundamental analysis as to the value of the company. Further, most transactions of this size do not have the input of sophisticated valuation advisors (business appraisers, investment bankers, and so on). Therefore, the purpose of this chapter is to familiarize both the prospective buyer and seller of a midsize company as to the fundamental components of value and methods of valuation for such businesses.

Typically, the value of a business enterprise is a derivative of the earning power of that company and the ability to convert this earning power into value. The fundamental premise of valuation is that value today is the present worth of expected future benefits. Any realistic estimate of value must ultimately be reconciled with this relatively simple, though often ignored, concept. The value implied by the amount of time and money that have been invested to bring a business to a particular point are generally irrelevant if the expected future returns from the business do not justify that value.

INADEQUATE BENCHMARKS OF VALUE

Before entertaining a discussion of the appropriate methodologies upon which to value a business enterprise, it is worth discussing some commonly used benchmarks of value that are generally inadequate. The most common reference point for the value of a business is *book value,* or shareholders' equity on the balance sheet. Except for a few types of companies (financial institutions, for example), book value is generally a poor indicator of market value. Consider that book value is based on the historical cost of the company's assets rather than their market value. Also, book value is representative of past earnings, and may not be indicative of future earnings prospects. Finally, the book value of two otherwise identical companies can vary significantly based upon different accounting practices.

In many industries, there are also various "rules of thumb" as to the value of a business. While widely used, these rules of thumb tend to be poor indicators of the value of a company and should not be used as anything more than a cross-check to a more thorough fundamental analysis. The primary reason is that rules of thumb are based on industry averages, while each situation is different and deserves careful individual consideration.

OVERVIEW OF VALUATION APPROACHES

The value of a business is generally determined based upon consideration of three distinct categories of valuation methodologies, each of which has multiple subsets of derivative methods. These are the net asset value approach (sometimes referred to as the cost approach), the market multiple approach (sometimes referred to as the market or comparative sales approach), and the income approach (sometimes referred to as the discounted cash flow approach).

The net asset value approach considers the underlying value of the company's individual assets net of its liabilities. In this approach, the book value is adjusted by substituting the market value of individual assets and liabilities for their carrying value on the balance sheet, with consideration given to so-called off-balance sheet assets and liabilities, including contingent liabilities. This approach is generally most applicable in the context of an asset holding company, where the current return on the assets may significantly understate their underlying value. Real estate holding companies, investment companies, and natural resource companies are often analyzed on a net asset basis.

Market multiple approaches consider the market value of business enterprises similar to the subject company being valued, as observed either in the trading price of publicly traded companies or the purchase price in business sales, relative to the earnings and/or cash flow of those businesses. The market multiples thus derived are applied to the subject company's normalized level of expected earnings and cash flow after being adjusted for the riskiness of the subject company relative to the comparative companies. The normalization of earnings for the subject company involves analyzing financial results over a time frame that takes into consideration fluctuations in the subject company's business cycle and is representative of future prospects, adjusting historical results for any income or expense items of an extraordinary or nonrecurring nature. The riskiness of the subject company relative to the comparative companies is based on consideration of a wide range of qualitative and quantitative factors, including size, leverage, profitability, growth prospects, quality and depth of management, and others.

Income, or discounted cash flow, methodologies involve determining the net present value of expected future returns to investors to be generated by the business utilizing a discount rate that reflects the risks inherent in receiving those returns. The discount rate is generally determined through an analysis of observable required rates of return in the marketplace for investments of similar risk.

SELECTION OF APPROPRIATE METHODOLOGY

It is generally best to consider all types of valuation approaches and apply as many as are relevant to the particular case. This is because each approach has biases, and the best way to determine overall value is to use a number of relevant approaches and find the central tendency. As previously mentioned, each of the three basic valuations methlogies has multiple subsets of derivative methods, and it is normally advisable to use more than one approach within the three broad categories, particularly within the market multiple approach category.

In spite of the relevance of net asset value to certain valuation situations (such as asset holding companies), the value of most operating companies is not based upon individual asset values, but upon the return that the assets generate collectively, as employed in the business. Thus, most businesses are valued based upon capitalization of earnings and/or cash flow. The two valuation approaches that utilize capitalization of earnings and/or cash flow are the market multiple and income approaches.

The relevance of the market multiple approach to any given situation is based in large part on the ability to locate transactions involving companies similar to the subject company and the availability of information on those comparative transactions. Public company comparatives are most often used because of the wealth of information available on such companies. Most public companies trade every day, and their trading prices can be located in the newspaper. Further, the public filings of such companies (which can generally be requested by calling the company) contain detailed financial as well as narrative information about the company. Information services such as Standard & Poor's, Moody's, Disclosure, Value Line, and others (which are available in most business school libraries) allow the user to screen the universe of 12,000 or so public companies by line of business using the standard industrial classification (SIC) code of a given industry, as well as other relevant factors.

The explosion of so-called small cap public offerings over the last several years has substantially increased the likelihood of finding good comparatives in the public market for midsize companies. However, even a thorough search often turns up no public companies that are directly comparable to the midsize, closely held business being valued. Public companies tend to be larger, better capitalized, and more diversified (both in terms of product lines and geography) than the typical midsize private company. Nonetheless, the multiples of such public companies may still be very relevant to the valuation of a midsize private company as long as appropriate adjustments for risk and growth are made in the application of market multiples to the subject company.

Information on private transactions is much more difficult to locate. Even when these transactions can be found, there may not be sufficient information available to calculate market multiples and form a reasonable basis for the determination of relative investment risk between the comparative company and the subject company. But when reliable information can be found for such transactions, the market multiples may represent the best indicators of value for the subject company.

The discounted cash flow approach is the most theoretically sound approach because it directly bases value on the present value of future benefits. However, in practice, the determination of both expected future returns and an appropriate required rate of return can be difficult to calculate with accuracy. Nonetheless, this is generally the desired approach either when no comparative transactions can be found or when the revenues and earnings of the business are highly predictable, making a determination of expected future cash flows an easier task.

APPLICATION OF NET ASSET APPROACH

The net asset approach is the easiest to apply. It involves adjusting the most recent balance sheet of the subject company by substituting the market value for the book value of individual assets and liabilities where appropriate. The net asset value is the adjusted book value obtained by using shareholders' equity as a plug figure to balance the adjusted balance sheet.

There are two ways of performing a net asset value calculation. The first method values each of the assets based on the value at which they could be sold separately, without respect to their value as part of the enterprise as a whole. Under this method, liquidation costs and taxes are often subtracted as well. This approach is most applicable in a liquidation scenario. If the business is likely to continue as a going concern, the assets are usually valued as "in use," based upon their value as part of the enterprise.

Under the going concern concept, current assets are generally valued at close to their book value. However, adjustments should be made to accounts receivable to include any questionable receivables that have not already been reserved for on the balance sheet. Similarly, any obsolete or slow-moving inventory should be adjusted to the extent not already reserved for.

Fixed assets should be shown at their estimated fair market value. When possible, it is advantageous to obtain appraisals on the major items (generally real property, machinery, and equipment).

While liabilities are normally subtracted from the gross asset value at their stated value on the balance sheet, sometimes adjustments are appropriate. For example, if there is any interest-bearing debt whose stated interest rate is either well above or well below a market rate of return, the market value of the debt should be used. Also, any off-balance sheet assets should be added and any off-balance sheet liabilities should be subtracted from shareholders' equity. This includes contingent liabilities for such things as litigation or environmental remediation.

The following example shows a net asset value calculation for a hypothetical manufacturing company, Precision Components Manufacturing Corp., a manufacturer of precision components for a variety of industries, including the aerospace and medical devices industries: In this case, the following adjustments were made to the balance sheet to determine net asset value:

Inventory was reduced by $1,500,000 to reflect obsolete inventory.

Real estate and equipment were adjusted to reflect their current fair market values (per appraisals) of $2,500,000 and $4,000,000, respectively.

The resulting net asset value was $9,754,000.

APPLICATION OF THE MARKET MULTIPLE APPROACH

As stated previously, there are several versions of the market multiple approach, the differentiating factor being the specific earnings or cash flow measure used in each case to calculate the market multiple. These versions can be classified into two categories: *equity value* approaches and *debt-free* approaches. In the equity value approaches, market multiples for the comparative companies are calculated by dividing the purchase price for common stock by measures of earnings and cash flow, which represent returns to common shareholders. Examples of such approaches are the price to earnings (P/E) and price to cash flow (P/CF) approaches. When P/E and P/CF multiples are applied to the subject company's normalized representative earnings and/or cash flow, the resulting product is an indication of the subject company's common equity value.

The debt-free approaches attempt to adjust for the distortions that can occur by comparing companies with significantly different levels of debt in their capital structures. This is done by calculating market multiples for all of the comparative companies assuming that they have no interest-bearing debt in their capital structure. Market multiples are calculated by dividing the purchase price for common stock plus the value of interest-bearing debt (sometimes referred to as total invested capital) by measures of earnings cash flow, which represent returns to both shareholders and debtholders (the returns to debtholders being in the form of interest and principal payments). Examples of such approaches are the total invested capital to earnings before interest and taxes (TIC/EBIT) and total invested capital to earnings before depreciation interest and taxes (TIC/EBDIT) approaches. When TIC/EBIT and TIC/EBDIT multiples are applied to the subject company's normalized representative EBIT and/or EBDIT, the resulting product is an indication of that company's total invested capital, or the value of its common equity assuming the company had no interest-bearing debt. In order to determine the subject company's actual common equity value, the current level of interest-bearing debt must be subtracted from the total invested capital value.

In most situations, a combination of the equity value and debt-free approaches should be used. The equity value approaches are easier to understand and apply, but when there are significant differences in capital structure, the debt-free approaches are probably more reliable.

Another factor that differentiates the P/E and TIC/EBIT approaches from the P/CF and P/EBDIT approaches is that, in the former approaches, multiples are calculated using income figures that are after depreciation expense. The theory is that even though depreciation is a noncash charge, it nonetheless represents an estimate of the ongoing capital expenditure requirements of the business; therefore, earnings and EBIT are more representative of the net return to investors. Conversely, the P/CF and P/EBDIT multiples are calculated using income figures that are before depreciation expense (cash flow is defined as net income plus depreciation). These approaches adjust for different depreciation practices among companies being compared. They are particularly relevant when valuing a capital intensive business.

Many institutional investors focus primarily on EBDIT because they can compare companies based on an income measure, which is unaffected by differences in both the debt levels of the various companies and different depreciation practices of the companies, as well as differences in income taxes. However, again, it is generally advisable to use a combination of approaches.

There are other market approaches, including price to net book value (P/NBV) and total invested capital to revenues (TIC/R), which are useful in certain situations but are not nearly as relevant in most situations as the approaches already mentioned.

Determination of Representative Levels of Earnings, Cash Flow, EBIT, and EBDIT

The market multiples derived from an analysis of comparative transactions should be applied to the subject company's representative level of earnings, cash flow, EBIT and EBDIT, respectively. The goal is to derive income levels that are indicative of expected future income and that would form the basis upon which a prospective investor in the company would base his or her investment decision.

Determination of representative income levels involves two steps:

Identifying the appropriate time frame, historical or projected, over which to base the determination of representative earnings.

Adjusting reported results for extraordinary items that impacted the firm's financial results in the past but that are not expected to repeat or persist.

In addition, certain discretionary expenses, such as above market management compensation, may be identified and adjusted for in determining the earning capacity of a company.

Generally, representative levels are based on historical financial results, as opposed to projected results. This is because projections are inherently speculative, whereas historical results are an actual indication of the income that the company has been capable of generating in the past. Projected results may be more relevant, however, if there is reason to believe that recent or anticipated changes in the business—loss of a key customer, new products, acquisitions, or other—would make historical results largely irrelevant.

The selected historical time over which to calculate representative levels depends on the nature of the business. Highly cyclical businesses, such as the aerospace and automotive industries, are generally evaluated over a longer historical time frame because results in any one year may not be representative; three-year and five-year averages are typical. Conversely, businesses that are growing or declining steadily, will generally be evaluated based upon some measure of current results (latest fiscal year or latest 12 months if the latest fiscal year-end is more than a few months old). Sometimes, it is difficult to differentiate fluctuations in historical operating results that are part of the company's normal business cycle (for which a historical average would be more appropriate) from those that result from fundamental changes in the business (for which near-term results or projections would be more appropriate).

The following is a comparative summary of financial results for Precision Components, our fictional company, over the last five years. In this case, because the business is inherently cyclical, we used an average of historical years. And, due to the loss of a key customer in the middle of 19x2, results for 19x1 and 19x2 were not considered to be representative of current operations. Therefore, a three-year average of 19x3, 19x4, and 19x5 was used.

In terms of adjustments to historical financial results, any nonrecurring or extraordinary expenses should be added back to reported results. Similarly, nonrecurring income should be subtracted. A certain amount of judgment is required to determine whether an income or expense item is nonrecurring; for example, whether items such as write-offs of inventory, gains or losses on the sale of equipment, or start-up expenses associated with a new product would be considered extraordinary depends on the nature of the business. When valuing a controlling interest in the company (as opposed to a minority interest), certain discretionary expenses may be added back to reported income. The most significant of these is usually above-market compensation for the owner. The proper method of adjusting for this is to add the entire amount of actual owner's compensation to reported income and then subtract an estimated amount of market compensation commensurate with the amount that would be paid to a nonowner to perform the same function. In addition, other discretionary expenses that do not in some way increase revenues or benefit the company may be added back. The most common are personal expenses of the owner for such things as travel, automobile, meals, and entertainment. Exhibit 11.1 shows the representative level of calculation for Precision Components.

Exhibit 11.1   Representative Level Determination (in Thousands)

	19X5	19X4	19X3
Reported Pretax Income	$1,509	$ 752	$ 695
Reported Interest Expense	309	320	330
Reported Depreciation Expense	881	901	1,058
Reported EBDIT	$2,698	$1,973	$2,083
Adjustments			
Extraordinary Bad Debt Expense			$ 300
Litigation Settlement	$ 260		
Market Compensation Adjustment	350	$ 350	350
Adjusted EBDIT	$3,308	$2,323	$2,733
Adjusted EBDIT Margin	26.1%	22.2%	27.4%
Representative EBDIT (3 Year Average, Rounded)			$2,800
Less: Depreciation (3 Year Average, Rounded)			(950)
Representative EBIT			1,850
Less: Interest Expense (Latest Year, Rounded)			310
Adjusted Pretax Income			2,160
Less: Income Taxes at 40%			(860)
Representative Earnings			1,300
Add: Depreciation			950
Representative Cash Flow			$2,250

In this case, adjusted EBDIT for the three years was determined by making the following adjustments to reported EBDIT:

An extraordinary litigation settlement expense was added back in 19x5.

An extraordinary bad debt expense was added back in 19x3.

Above-market compensation was added back for each of the years.

The representative EBDIT was based on an approximate three-year average of adjusted EBDIT. Representative EBIT was determined by subtracting average depreciation from representative EBDIT. Representative earnings was calculated by subtracting interest expense (which should be based on current interest expense, not an average) and estimated income taxes at 40 percent from representative EBIT. Finally, representative cash flow was based on adding average depreciation to representative earnings.

Selection of Comparative Companies

When searching for comparative transactions, the goal should be to select those companies that are most similar to the subject company from an investment standpoint. Factors to consider include: line of business, geographic location, size, financial and operating similarities, as well as other relevant items. Generally, the first criterion is to find companies in the same line of business. However, companies may be engaged in somewhat different lines of business but be affected by the same macro-economic factors in similar ways. The relative importance of other factors depends on the industry. For example, finding comparatives in the same geographic region may be extremely important for a construction company, but may not be as important for an aerospace company.

Risk Comparison with Comparative Companies and Multiple Selection

It is important to note that the market multiples observed for the selected comparative companies are just a guideline for the determination of the appropriate multiple to apply to the subject company's representative income levels. A common mistake is to apply the median or average multiples from the comparative companies observed without performing a detailed risk analysis to determine whether the subject company warrants a premium or a discount to the multiples observed. When the comparatives are public companies, the multiple selection for the midsize private company usually involves a discount to the multiples observed in the market, but this is not necessarily the case. A subject company with excellent growth prospects, for example, may command a significantly greater multiple than more mature public companies.

A proper evaluation of relative investment risk will consider a wide range of quantitative and qualitative factors. The quantitative risk analysis usually involves comparing various financial ratios and statistics of the subject company to those of the comparative companies. The ratios and statistics compare the companies on the basis of size, liquidity, leverage, profitability, turnover of assets, and growth. Of all the quantitative factors, size and growth tend to be the most significant. Investors normally pay higher multiples for larger companies when compared with smaller ones in the same industry. Also, strong growth prospects will have a very significant upward influence on the multiple (although good historical growth is not necessarily indicative of strong growth in the future).

The qualitative risk analysis is just as, if not more, important than the quantitative analysis. The major qualitative factors are key-person risk (particularly if the key person is the owner who is leaving the business), reliance on key customers, breadth of product line and proprietary nature of products, diversification of geographic risk, quality and depth of management, access to capital, and more.

Once a determination of relative investment risk is made, this information forms the basis for the multiple selection of the subject company. In addition to looking at the comparative companies' median, particular attention should be paid to the multiples of any comparative companies that are especially comparable to the subject company. Also, it is usually appropriate to look at market multiples for the public companies using earnings and cash flow levels that are calculated over the same time frame as the subject company's representative levels. In other words, if the representative levels were based on a five-year average of earnings for the subject company, then the market multiples for the comparative companies should be calculated using a five-year average of earnings in the denominator (although the price in the numerator is always based on the price closest to the valuation date, regardless of the time frame used for earnings).

For Precision Components, our relative risk analysis indicated that the company was a greater investment risk than the comparative companies, based primarily on its smaller size and greater degree of key-person and key-customer risk. Further, since none of the comparatives was significantly more or less comparable to the subject company than the others, our selection was determined from the comparative companies median multiples. This is summarized next.

Market Multiple Approach Summary

Once the representative levels of income and the selected market multiplies are determined, the value indication for each approach is obtained by multiplying the representative level by the corresponding selected market multiple. Remember to subtract interest-bearing debt from the total invested capital conclusions derived in the debt-free approaches. This is done for Precision Components in Exhibit 11.2.

APPLICATION OF INCOME APPROACH

As with the market multiple approaches, there are many versions of the income or discounted cash flow approach, but all of them are based on discounting or capitalizing some measure of investor return by an appropriate required rate of return. The most common measure of investor return is net cash flow (which can be stated on an equity as well as a

Exhibit 11.2 Market Approach Summary (in Thousands)

Approach	Representative Level	Market Multiple		Total Capital		Debt		Equity Value
Price/Earnings	$1,300	×	9.0	=	—	–	—	= $11,700
Price/Cash Flow	$2,250	×	5.5	=	—	–	—	= $12,375
TIC/EBIT	$1,850	×	8.0	=	$14,800	–	$3,113	= $11,687
TIC/EBDIT	$2,800	×	5.5	=	$15,400	–	$3,113	= $12,287

debt-free basis). In this case we will focus on the equity value method, which is based on net cash flow to common shareholders.

When long-term financial projections are available, it is usually best to perform a net present value (NPV) calculation on the projected net cash flows during the projection period. The present value of net cash flows through the projection period are then added to the present value of the business at the end of the projection period, the so-called terminal value, which is usually determined by applying some capitalization rate to the final year's net cash flow. However, since detailed financial forecasts are normally not available for midsize companies, the Gordon Growth Model can be used to calculate the present value of expected future cash flows without the necessity of using long-term forecasts.

The Gordon Growth Model is a perpetual growth model that capitalizes current expectations of net cash flow for the business by the required rate of return (discount rate) minus the expected growth rate into perpetuity of those net cash flows. Specifically, the formula is stated as follows:

$$\frac{NCF}{r - g}$$

where: NCF = expected net cash flow,
      r = required rate of return, and
      g = perpetual growth rate.

If the expected net cash flow is based upon historical results, sometimes the numerator is expressed as $NCF \times (1 + g)$.

Determination of Net Cash Flow

The net cash flow (or free cash flow) to be capitalized in the model should be reflective of the subject company's current or near-term expected net cash flow level. Often, the representative earnings level selected in the market approach is a starting point. Net cash flow is usually determined by adding depreciation and other noncash charges to net income and subtracting expected capital expenditures and increases in net working capital. While this is an oversimplification of the determination of the true net cash flow of a company, it is a reasonable estimate for valuation purposes.

The amount that is subtracted for capital expenditures should be based on an average expected annual rate, adjusting for abnormally high or low capital expenditures in a given year. Net working capital increases are represented by increases in working capital assets, such as accounts receivable, inventory, prepaid assets, and so on, less increases in working capital liabilities, such as accounts payable, accrued expenses, and others, on an annual basis. A historical analysis should be undertaken to determine the level of net working capital required to support a given revenue level.

For Precision Components, expected net cash flow was determined as follows:

Representative Earnings	$1,300,000
Add: Depreciation	950,000
Less: Capital Expenditures	(600,000)
Less: Working Capital Increases	(400,000)
Net Cash Flow	$1,250,000

Determination of Discount Rate
(or Required Rate of Return)

The required return on an investment is directly related to the risk of that investment. The required rate of return increases with risk. Most models for determining required return are based upon observable returns for other investments in the market. There are many different financial models for required return on a common stock investment, including the widely used Capital Asset Pricing Model (CAPM). However, an easier and more direct method is the build-up method.

The build-up method measures an investor's total required rate of return on an equity investment by sequentially adding various components of that required return, each component being based on observed returns found in the public market. The first component is the *risk-free rate,* usually represented by the rate of return on intermediate-term or long-term government bonds. Because investors require a greater expected return than the risk-free rate to compensate for the inherent risks of an equity investment versus an investment in U.S. Treasury Bonds, the build-up method applies a premium or premiums to the risk-free rate in order to determine the appropriate required return to apply to the subject equity investment. A *market risk premium* is typically added to the risk-free rate to reflect the additional return that investors in the stock market as a whole would require over and above the risk-free rate. The most recent studies compiled by Ibbotson Associates show that, over time, returns associated with common stocks, as a whole, have averaged 7.2 percent above the 20-year Treasury Bond rate. This rate of return is for those companies comprising the upper eight deciles of the New York Stock Exchange (NYSE).

Because of the importance of size in evaluating investment risk and therefore required rates of return, an additional premium is often added to reflect the fact that the subject company being valued may be considerably smaller than the public companies from which the market risk premium was derived. The most recent studies compiled by Ibbotson Associates indicate that, over time, the historical return on the smallest 20 percent of publicly traded stocks has been 5.3 percent above that of the overall market. This is sometimes referred to as the small company premium.

The final component of the build-up rate is a premium for company-specific risk. This premium, based largely on qualitative considerations, measures the premium that an investor would require over and above an investment in the average small public company because of risk factors specific to the subject company. Such factors include the risks of the specific industry in which the subject company operates, financial condition, and operating history and access to capital limitations, among other things. For Precision Components, we selected a relatively small company specific risk premium of 2.5 percent, based on the company's long history of profitable operations (notwithstanding the loss in 19x2, which was the company's only unprofitable year in 40 years of operation).

An important point to remember is that the selected discount rate must consider the attainability of the net cash flows that are expected. Optimistic forecasts should receive correspondingly high required rates of return, and vice versa for more conservative forecasts.

The following summarizes the determination of the discount rate for Precision Components:

Risk-Free Rate (20-Year T-Bond Rate at Valuation Date)	7.0%
Market Risk Premium	7.2
Small-Company Premium	5.3
Company-Specific Risk Premium	2.5
Required Rate of Return	22.0%

Determination of Perpetual Growth Rate

The perpetual growth rate is the expected annual growth of the base net cash flow into perpetuity. Growth may be more rapid in the initial years and then taper off as the company becomes more mature. The selected perpetual growth rate should weigh near-term versus long-term growth expectations. An analysis of historical growth for the subject company as well as expected growth in the industry should be undertaken. For Precision Components, based on all of the evidence analyzed and the future prospects for the company, we used an assumed perpetual growth rate of 9 percent.

Income Approach Summary

Applying the selected net cash flow, discount rate, and perpetual growth rate for Precision Components to the Gordon Growth Model yields the following common equity value:

$$\frac{\$1,250,000 \times (1.09)}{.22 - .09} = \$10,481,000$$

VALUATION SUMMARY

When valuation indications have been derived for each of the individual approaches, an overall value must be selected. As stated previously, more weight should be given to approaches deemed most reliable under the circumstances. Sometimes, the final valuation is determined by applying a specific weighting factor to each approach. Other times, the final value determination is more subjective. Exhibit 11.3 is the valuation summary for Precision Components as of December 31, 19x5.

In this case, no weight was given to the net asset approach. The four market approaches averaged approximately $12,000,000. However, the $12,000,000 figure was not supported by the discounted cash flow approach. As a result, our overall value conclusion for operations was $11,500,000.

OTHER CONSIDERATIONS

The focus of this chapter has been on the value of an entire business enterprise, without regard to fractional ownership interests within the company or different classes of stock (including preferred stock). The treatment of fractional ownership interests and the application of discounts and premiums is the subject of another chapter in this book.

Valuation indications derived from the application of the net asset value approach are generally considered to represent controlling interest level values. Therefore, no further adjustments are required to determine the value of a controlling interest in the subject company under this approach. When using public company comparatives under the market multiple approach, it is important to note the differences between the stock

Exhibit 11.3   Valuation Summary

Net Asset Value	$ 9,754,000
Price/Earnings	11,700,000
Price/Cash Flow	12,375,000
TIC/EBIT	11,687,000
TIC/EBDIT	12,287,000
Discounted Cash Flow	10,481,000
Conclusion	$11,500,000

prices of public companies, which represent noncontrolling yet readily marketable interests, and the value of a controlling interest in the closely held subject company. Often, the value of control in the subject company is adequately considered by making adjustments to the subject company's income levels to reflect the ability of a controlling shareholder to eliminate discretionary expenses and thereby enhance investment returns (which was done in the Precision Components example). The same is true for the income approach when such adjustments are made.

With respect to marketability, some practitioners do not apply a discount for lack of marketability to a controlling interest in a private company because the owner has the ability to sell or liquidate the company. Other practitioners do apply a small discount, but nowhere near that which would be applied to a closely held minority interest.

It is also important to consider whether the subject company has any nonoperating assets, assets that are not being used by the business to generate revenues or assist in the ongoing operations of the company. Nonoperating land is common, although the value of land owned by the company but used in the business should not be added. Other examples include excess machinery and equipment, excess cash, potential legal settlements, and notes receivable. Income from any assets deemed nonoperating must be excluded from the representative level determination to avoid double counting. The value of nonoperating assets should be added to the overall value conclusion for operations, typically on an after-tax basis. Similarly, contingent liabilities such as litigation or environmental problems should be subtracted. Finally, the impact of any above- or below-market interest-bearing debt or leases should be considered.

In the case of Precision Components, it was determined that the company had approximately $500,000 in cash beyond that which was necessary for normal operational requirements. Therefore, this figure was added to the concluded value of operations for a total valuation of $12,000,000.

SUMMARY

It is not expected that the average prospective buyer or seller of a mid-size business would be able to prepare a proper business valuation simply on the basis of reading this chapter. There are many nuances to a business valuation, and substantial judgment is required that can be acquired only through experience. Nevertheless, this chapter can provide a basis for understanding the basic components of business value and reconciling the buyer's or seller's preconceived notions of value with the fundamentals and realities of business valuation.

Selling Partial Ownership Interests: Levels of Value

Z. CHRISTOPHER MERCER
PRESIDENT
MERCER CAPITAL

J. MICHAEL JULIUS
VICE PRESIDENT
MERCER CAPITAL

THE CONCEPT

A key concept in the proper use and interpretation of "the Value" of a business is the concept of *levels of value*. All business appraisals have a context within which they are prepared and within which they are used. The levels of value concept is an essential means for conveying the full context of a business valuation between the business appraisers and the business owner. The concept allows business appraisers to explain clearly the important assumptions behind an appraisal to business owners while allowing business owners to communicate to appraisers precisely the context in which an appraisal is to be used.

Valuations of equity interests tend to fall into three broad categories, based on control of the business and marketability of the interest, as summarized in the following table:

• Controlling interest.	Value of the enterprise as a whole.
• As if freely tradable minority interest.	Value of a minority interest, lacking control, but enjoying the benefit of market liquidity.
• Nonmarketable minority interest.	Value of a minority interest, lacking both control and market liquidity.

An investor is generally thought to have a *controlling interest* in a corporation when he or she holds a majority (more than 50 percent) of the voting stock and is in a position to control the operations of the business and to force a sale or liquidation of the business.[1] A controlling interest is thus valued as a pro rata interest in the enterprise as a whole.

When the *premise of value* (that is, the relevant concept of value in a specific situation) is that of a controlling interest, the appraiser seeks to answer the questions:

What is the value of the enterprise as a whole?

What is the subject interest's appropriate share of that value?

An investor holding less than 50 percent of the voting stock of a corporation is generally considered to have a *minority interest.* A minority shareholder typically cannot force a sale or liquidation of the business and has limited to very limited influence over its operations and management.

Minority interests fall into two categories: marketable and nonmarketable interests. A *marketable minority interest* is freely tradable, as is the case for minority blocks of the common stocks of public companies listed on and actively traded on major exchanges such as the New York Stock Exchange, the American Stock Exchange, and NASDAQ. A *nonmarketable minority interest* is best exemplified by a minority block of stock in a closely held company where an active, public market for its shares is lacking, rendering the subject interest illiquid.[2]

In valuing a minority interest, the appraiser seeks to answer two key questions:

At what price would the market value this interest if it were a freely tradable minority block in a public company?

What is the impact on value of the specific circumstances affecting the marketability of the interest?

VALUATION PREMIUMS AND DISCOUNTS

The relationship among the three levels of value is illustrated in the following chart:

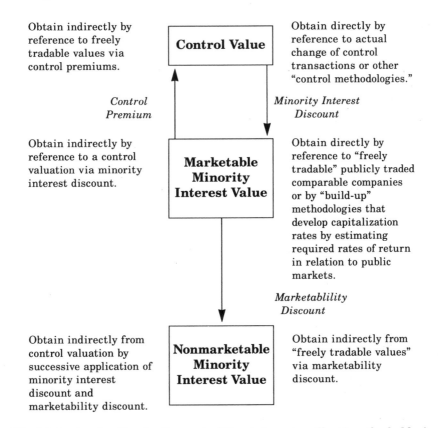

Obtain indirectly by reference to freely tradable values via control premiums.

Control Value

Obtain directly by reference to actual change of control transactions or other "control methodologies."

Control Premium

Minority Interest Discount

Obtain indirectly by reference to a control valuation via minority interest discount.

Marketable Minority Interest Value

Obtain directly by reference to "freely tradable" publicly traded comparable companies or by "build-up" methodologies that develop capitalization rates by estimating required rates of return in relation to public markets.

Marketablility Discount

Obtain indirectly from control valuation by successive application of minority interest discount and marketability discount.

Nonmarketable Minority Interest Value

Obtain indirectly from "freely tradable values" via marketability discount.

The highest value lies in the controlling interest, reflecting the holder's ability to direct the operations of the company or to initiate a sale or liquidation of the business. In order to move to the middle level of the chart, the marketable minority interest value, a *minority interest discount* is applied to controlling interest value to account for the lack of control exercised by the minority investor. To move to the bottom level of the chart, nonmarketable minority interest value, a further discount, a *marketability discount* is applied to reflect the illiquidity of the asset.

Nearly all appraisers would agree that the most complete, consistent, and useful comparative price and investment return information is available at the marketable minority interest level of value, since such information is readily derived from the pricing of the actively traded shares of public companies. Many appraisers therefore begin valuing an enterprise at the marketable minority interest level and then adjust to the controlling interest level by applying an appropriate *control premium,* or to the nonmarketable minority interest level by applying an appropriate *marketability discount.*

Control premiums and marketability discounts are observed in real-life transactions involving public company stocks. The payment of a control premium (over the preannouncement market price of the stock) is frequently observed in buyouts and mergers of public companies. Similarly, sales of illiquid, restricted shares (that is, shares not registered under the U.S. Securities Act of 1933 and therefore subject to extensive restrictions on resale under Securities and Exchange Commission Rule 144) are frequently observed to occur at significant discounts to the market price of the registered shares of the issuing public company.

Each level of value can be approached in two ways. A controlling interest can be valued by reference to the pricing of change-of-control transactions (involving whole companies or majority interests in companies). In the alternative, an appropriate control premium is added to the value implied by the market pricing ratios or historical return on investment statistics of minority blocks of similar publicly traded companies. Both approaches use "guideline" companies to provide relevant market comparisons to the appraiser.

A marketable minority interest can be valued by reference to the market pricing multiples or historical return statistics of minority blocks of the stocks of guideline public companies, or alternatively, by applying a minority interest discount to a controlling interest valuation. A nonmarketable minority interest can be valued either by applying a marketability discount to the "as if freely tradable" indication of value or by applying successive minority interest and marketability discounts to a controlling interest indication of value.

It should be clear that there is no such thing as "the value" of a business. Value is a function of purpose and time. The purpose of an appraisal sets the stage, implying an appropriate set of valuation assumptions and methodologies. Value is also a function of time. It is clear that values of publicly traded securities fluctuate greatly based on market trends and the performance of the issuing companies. The same is true for closely held companies. Further discussion of these factors would be beyond the scope of this chapter.

But value is also a function of the size of the block being valued. A grasp of the levels of value concept is important for business owners as they attempt to understand "the value" of their businesses for different purposes at different times.

ECONOMIC/FINANCIAL MODELS

The levels of value concept is, quite simply, an economic or financial model that is used to describe the observed behavior of many buyers and sellers of business interests in the so-called real world.

During the 1960s and 1970s, when many of today's business owners were in college, the two leading economics texts were written by Paul Samuelson and Campbell McConnell. McConnell writes:

A conglomeration of facts is relatively useless; mere description is not enough. To be meaningful, facts must be systematically arranged, interpreted, and generalized upon. This is the task of economic [or financial] theory or analysis. Principles and theories—the end result of economic analysis—bring order and meaning to a number of facts by tying these facts together, putting them in correct relationship to one another, and generalizing upon them . . . .

Economists talk about "laws," "principles," "theories," and "models." These terms all mean essentially the same thing: generalizations or statements of regularity, concerning the economic behavior of individuals and institutions . . . . *The term "model" has much to commend it. A model is a simplified picture of reality, an abstract generalization of how the relevant data actually behave.* (emphasis added)

. . . [E]conomic theories are practical for the simple reason that they are abstractions. The level of reality is too complex to be very meaningful. Economists theorize in order to give meaning to a maze of facts, which would otherwise be confusing and useless, and to put facts into a more usable, practical form . . . . An economic theory is a model—a simplified picture or map—of some segment of the economy. This model enables us to understand reality better because it avoids the details of reality. Finally, theories—good theories—are grounded on facts and therefore are realistic. *Theories which do not fit the facts are simply not good theories.*[3] (emphasis added)

The levels of value chart presented previously is an economic or financial model used by appraisers to describe the complexities of behavior of individuals and businesses in the process of buying and selling businesses and business interests. It attempts to cut through the detailed maze of facts that give rise to each individual transaction involving a particular business interest, and to describe, generally, the valuation relationships that seem to emerge from observing thousands upon thousands of individual transactions.

THE GENERAL VALUATION MODEL

There are several implicit assumptions in the general valuation model as depicted in the levels of value chart that should be stated clearly:

- Valuation is an imperfect science, and there may be more than a small element of art involved.
- The public stock markets provide a highly visible and ongoing flow of data relating to corporate valuation, which investors and appraisers must investigate to create decision-making information.
- At a point in time, the public stock markets reflect the prevailing consensus pricing for particular securities (and for the market) of a worldwide group consisting of literally millions of investors.

- The market may be "right" and it may be "wrong" with respect to its pricing decisions at a moment in time; however, the market is what it is at each moment in time.
- Based upon financial theory, custom, government regulation, and common sense, business appraisers use information from the public markets to help develop capitalization rates (or factors; that is, price/earnings ratios) with which to capitalize the earnings streams of closely held companies.[4]

The development of capitalization rates is the subject for another discussion. We state these implicit assumptions here, however, as necessary background to understand:

How the markets (and current valuation theory) distinguish between minority and controlling interests.

The general valuation relationships between minority and controlling interest appraisals.

MINORITY VERSUS CONTROLLING INTERESTS

The important difference between minority and controlling interest valuations is that, all other things being equal, a controlling interest is worth more than a minority interest. A holder of a minority interest generally has a passive investment in a company and, in most cases, must consider the company's capital structure and operations to be "given." The minority shareholder cannot initiate the sale of appreciated assets, force a cut in compensation levels, or require a higher dividend payout. In many, if not most, cases, the statements are probably true even if the minority shareholder is an employee of the company.

In determining the earnings value of a minority interest, normalization of earning power generally involves the elimination of nonrecurring items and the possible discounting of high-risk elements of the earnings stream. In a control situation, normalization logically can go much further, since the holder of the interest can influence corporate policy substantially.

In addition to having potentially different sets of normalizing adjustments to reported book value, earnings, and cash flows, controlling interest and minority interest appraisals also involve different sets of public market comparisons. Clearly, applying valuation multiples derived from buyouts of comparable companies (where control changed hands) to a minority interest in a subject company without considering an "appropriate valuation discount" for the lack of control would be unreasonable.

Similarly, applying a price/earnings ratio derived from public market transactions of comparable companies (representing minority interest transactions) to a controlling interest in a subject company would be inappropriate without considering some "appropriate valuation premium" for the presence of control.[5]

Confusion over an appraiser's premise of valuation (minority versus control), either by appraisers or by users of appraisal reports (ESOP trustees, for example), can lead to the placing of inappropriately high or low values on a subject equity interest. The unfortunate result of such errors can include the overpayment of estate taxes, contested estate tax returns, and ESOP transactions that prove uneconomical or unlawful.

It is essential that both business appraisers and the business and other parties using appraisals be aware of the correct premise of valuation, and that appropriate methodologies be followed in deriving the conclusion of value for any interest being appraised.

CRITICAL VALUATION TERMINOLOGY

Levels of Value

The chart shown earlier places minority and controlling interest values in perspective on a conceptual level. Three key levels of value are provided in the chart and discussed further here:

Controlling interest value.
"As if freely tradable" minority interest value.
Nonmarketable minority interest value.

The *controlling interest value* represents the value of the enterprise as a whole. The controlling interest appraisal should therefore encompass the rights, risks, and rewards of having controlling power in a business. In the context of this discussion, controlling interests in enterprises are considered to be marketable, and a marketability discount is not used. Some appraisers, however, do apply a small marketability discount, which may reflect the costs of brokerage or transactions costs, to control values.[6]

"As if freely tradable" minority interest value represents the value of a minority interest that is freely tradable in the public marketplace.[7] This level of value is also referred to as the marketable minority interest level of value. Stated another way, the valuation does not include any of the valuation elements associated with control, yet the conclusion is not penalized by the absence of liquidity inherent in shares that are not traded in the public markets.

A shareholder's total return from an investment in a security is typically divided into dividend yield and capital gains or appreciation (or capital losses). A holder of a publicly traded equity security can choose to liquidate his or her investment at will, thereby realizing the capital portion of his or her return. This may not be possible with a closely held security because of the absence of a market for the shares.

The *nonmarketable minority interest value* considers the lower degree of marketability (or liquidity), which is almost always present in closely held securities (in comparison with publicly traded securities). Reduced levels of liquidity can be due to financial issues, absence of registration for sale on the public stock exchanges, absence of contractual rights to require the purchase or sale of the shares at the holder's will, or other factors. Taken as a whole, however, the illiquidity of closely held shares represents one of the primary reasons their value is generally below that of freely tradable securities, even if all other factors are similar.

STRENGTHS OF THE MODEL

Although the levels of value chart shows three distinct value levels for purposes of discussion and illustration, an alternate depiction is of two extremes of value, with the "controlling interest" block representing the value of 100 percent of an enterprise (the highest value), and the "non-marketable minority interest" block representing the value of a very small minority interest (the lowest value). Between the highest and lowest values are gradations of value.

For example, appraisers must often deal with "control blocks" representing less than 100 percent ownership and with minority interest with differing characteristics that affect marketability and value. The use of appraiser judgment is always necessary in real-life situations. Illustrations like the chart simply provide a framework for the exercise of that judgment consistent with valid financial and valuation theory, objective market evidence, and experience.

The levels of value concept is a model used to explain economic and financial reality. The model is a simplified picture or map of the normal valuation relationships that exist in the real world. To reiterate McConnell, "Theories which do not fit the facts are simply not good theories." The alternative statement would be that theories that do fit the facts (all or nearly all the facts!) are probably pretty good theories. The levels of value model generally fits the facts, therefore it is a good theory or model.

PRACTICAL APPLICATIONS OF LEVELS OF VALUE

Control Premiums and Minority Interest Discounts

The levels of value concept is not only key to the proper preparation and use of appraisals of interests in closely held companies, but is also key to understanding how equity ownership in a closely held business works. Given the relatively large average control premiums and marketability discounts observed in the various studies, fair market value can imply significantly different dollar values for different interests of the same business (at the same time) depending on the relevant *premise of value.*

According to *Mergerstat Review,* the average and median control premiums observed in 1994 were 41.9 percent and 35 percent, respectively.[8] The minority interest discount corresponding to a given control premium can be derived using the following formula:

Minority discount percent = 100% – [100%/(100% + Control premium %)]

The 41.9 percent average control premium therefore implies a minority interest discount of 29.5 percent [100% – (100%/(100% + 41.9%))] while the 35 percent median control premium implies a minority interest discount of 25.9 percent [100% – (100%/(100% + 35%))].

It is important to note that the average and median premiums cited in the preceding paragraph are derived from data that cover a wide range of discounts and target companies exhibiting a wide range of business characteristics. Hence, the simple application of the average control premium from the most recent study may often lead to an inappropriate result. A control premium of 40 percent or more may be appropriate for a large company with specialized, highly differentiated products in an industry with stiff barriers to entry, while a premium of only 10 percent to 20 percent may be suitable for a relatively small firm in a commodity business. A rational willing buyer is likely to offer only a premium commensurate with the realizable benefits of acquiring a controlling interest in a business enterprise. The smaller the universe of likely acquirors and the lower the benefits of acquiring the target company, the lower the probable control premium.

It is also important to correlate control premiums with *control adjustments.* If the appraiser adjusts historical or projected earnings and cash flows to reflect reductions in overhead, higher product prices, distributions of excess assets, and other results of changes in corporate policy or financial position stemming from a contemplated change of control, with most such changes having a beneficial impact upon the calculated value of the subject interest, he or she must also consider a reduction in any control premium to be applied. The capacity and motivation of a willing buyer of a controlling interest to pay a control premium lies substantially in the acquiror's ability to benefit from changes in current corporate policy. To the extent the financial benefits of such changes are explicitly recognized in an appraisal, any control premium should be adjusted downward.

Marketability Discounts

The numerous marketability studies of restricted stock transactions and of studies of companies' stock prices preceding and following initial public offerings tend to indicate average marketability discounts of 30 percent to 40 percent or more for minority blocks of the common stocks of closely held companies and for similarly illiquid equity securities.[9]

Assuming that "average" discounts for minority interest (30 percent) and lack of marketability (35 percent) apply, a closely held company with an aggregate control or total enterprise value of $10 million would have an aggregate marketable minority interest value of $7 million and an aggregate nonmarketable interest value of $4.55 million. Depending on the appropriate premise of value, a 5 percent interest in the subject company would have a fair market value of $500,000 (on a controlling interest basis), $350,000 (on a marketable minority interest basis), or $227,500 (on a nonmarketable minority interest basis). The calculations are shown here.

Control		Minority Interests	
Aggregate Value		Aggregate Value	Value of 5%
$10,000,000	**Control**	$10,000,000	$500,000
none		− 3,000,000	− 150,000
	− 30% Minority Interest Discount		
$10,000,000	**As If Freely Tradable**	$ 7,000,000	$350,000
none		− 2,450,000	− 122,500
	− 35% Marketability Discount		
$10,000,000	**Nonmarketable Minority Interest**	$ 4,550,000	$227,500
×51%		×49%	
$ 5,100,000		$ 2,229,500	

The concept of potentially different values for shares of the same company at the same time can be particularly difficult for controlling shareholders in closely held businesses. Business owners usually think of value in terms of the entire business or at the controlling interest level of value. As the remaining discussion shows, however, the concepts are critical for all shareholders in the context of normal operations of a business and their personal tax-planning strategies.

Minority Interest Shareholders

Minority equity investors in closely held businesses often expect that an appraiser's opinion of fair market value should reflect the total value of the enterprise. That is, they expect their minority interests to be valued on a controlling interest basis whether or not a change of control transaction or some other liquidity event is pending. They may be quite disappointed to see minority interest and marketability discounts applied in deriving the conclusion of value. It is important for appraisers to explain the levels of value concept to their clients and to base their appraisals at the appropriate level of value.

Estate Tax Planning

The levels of value concept is of great significance in estate tax planning. A 51 percent controlling interest in a closely held company valued at $10 million on a total enterprise basis would have a fair market value of $5.1 million. A 49 percent interest in the same company would have a fair market value of $2.230 million, assuming a 30 percent minority interest discount and a 35 percent marketability discount are appropriate.[10]

Assuming the validity of the assumed discounts in the calculations, the taxable estate of the owner of the $10 million (value) company in our example would be substantially lower if gifts were made to reduce his or her ownership position to less than control. The point of the illustration is that there are strong economic incentives under existing tax law to avoid owning a controlling interest in a closely held business at the time of one's death.

To minimize gift and estate taxes, it is important to gift minority interests and to avoid holding a controlling interest at death. Controlling interests can be converted to minority interests over time through regular gifting of shares or by company repurchases of shares from the controlling shareholder. Alternately, a charitable gift of a controlling interest generates the largest possible income tax deduction.[11]

Employee Stock Ownership Plans (ESOPs)

By law, employee stock ownership plans grant participants the right to put distributed shares in a closely held company back to the ESOP at appraised fair market value. Most appraisers interpret this provision to substantially mitigate the normal illiquidity features of a minority block of stock in a closely held company and thus apply no or a nominal marketability discount (0%–10%).[12] It is important for an ESOP trustee to recognize that the put-right attaches to shares distributed to plan participants only and that the trustee is free to negotiate prices below the participants' appraised value for shares tendered by non-ESOP shareholders.

In cases where an ESOP holds a controlling interest, it is important for the appraiser to discuss the levels of value concept with the plan trustee. Since the plan participants do not individually hold controlling interests in the subject company, but rather are beneficiaries of a trust that holds a controlling interest, there is an ambiguity as to whether departing ESOP participants should be cashed out on a controlling interest or minority interest basis. In addition, it is arguable whether it is appropriate for a controlling ESOP to pay a controlling interest price for shares tendered by non-ESOP shareholders. In these circumstances, the appraiser should seek direction from the ESOP trustee regarding the appropriate level of value to reference in determining fair market value.

Buy-Sell Agreements

Absent directions to the contrary, most appraisers will value a minority interest in a closely held business at the nonmarketable minority interest level of value. In drafting shareholder buy-sell agreements, it is important that the parties state precisely the level of value that represents the true intentions of the parties to the agreement. Simply including a provision that the repurchase price shall be at fair market value as determined by one, two, or three independent business appraisers may not provide sufficient instruction. The level of value to be reflected in the appraiser's determination of fair market value should also be specified in order to avoid controversy at an inopportune time.

Participants in buy-sell agreements usually want the right to exit on the most favorable terms, that is, on a controlling interest or marketable minority interest basis. This desire must be balanced against the potential strain on the company's or other shareholders' financial resources when repurchase is demanded. Additionally, the existence of a buy-sell agreement specifying one of the two higher levels of value could prevent the application of minority and/or marketability discounts in valuing shares for gift and estate tax purposes, significantly increasing the shareholders' estate tax liability.

Management Stock Options

As with buy-sell agreements, it is important to apply the levels of value concept in structuring management stock options and phantom stock plans. A stock option would be most unattractive to the recipient if the option exercise price were based on a control or marketable minority interest basis, but the option shares could be sold to third parties or tendered back to the company only on a nonmarketable minority interest basis.[13]

If the exercise price is set based on a nonmarketable minority interest valuation, it would be inappropriate to cash out the beneficiary on a controlling interest basis or on a marketable minority interest basis, unless a change of control transaction or public offering were actually in progress. The upside potential inherent in issuing options in a closely held company at strike prices reflecting nonmarketable minority interest values provides additional incentives for management personnel to grow the company and enhance its performance to make it an attractive candidate for an acquisition or for an initial public stock offering.

Raising New Equity

In raising new equity in a closely held company it is important for existing shareholders to understand the potential impact on their shareholdings of sales of stock at prices reflecting the various levels of value. Other things being equal, sale of new stock at a controlling interest value is likely to be *antidilutive* of (that is, increases) earnings per share and book value per share while the sale of new stock at a nonmarketable minority interest value is likely to be *dilutive* of (that is, decreases) earnings per share and book value per share for the existing shareholders. The sale of new stock at a marketable minority interest value is likely to be *nondilutive* of earnings per share and book value per share. In addition, the higher the price paid for new shares, the lesser the dilution of the voting power of existing shareholders.

It is important for shareholders in a closely held company to understand that new investors are unlikely to purchase new shares at prices exceeding the nonmarketable minority interest level of value without some put-right or other feature providing for an exit value at the same or higher level of value. In raising new equity, existing shareholders have the choice of accepting dilution today, by selling shares at discounted prices, or of trying to minimize dilution by granting put-rights to new shareholders to induce them to buy new shares at "as if freely tradable" minority interest values or controlling interest values.

Providing for a favorable exit is the key to successful investing in closely held companies. Participating in a group that pays a controlling interest value to acquire a company and then shortly thereafter selling out at a price reflecting a fully discounted nonmarketable minority interest value is not a wealth enhancement strategy. An informed investor in closely held companies looks for a favorable buy-sell agreement or a business whose shareholder/management team is focused on building, within a reasonable time horizon, either a "cash cow" that will pay substantial shareholder dividends or a growth company that will be an attractive acquisition target or public offering candidate.

Dissenting Shareholders and Fair Value

Many states' fair value statutes and court precedents would appear to equate fair value with the marketable minority interest level of value, although courts in some states have found fair value to be at the controlling interest level of value.

Every state has implemented statutes providing for the rights of minority shareholders in the event of certain mergers or recapitalizations. These statutes are generally referred to as the dissenting minority shareholder statutes. They provide minority shareholders with the right to dissent from qualifying transactions (following prescribed procedures) and to receive the *fair value* of their shares.

The various definitions of fair value differ somewhat. However, they generally define fair value as:

> The value of the shares immediately before the effectuation of the corporate action giving rise to the right to dissent, excluding any appreciation or depreciation in anticipation of the corporate action.

Fair value has been interpreted by the courts in numerous states to be a *marketable minority interest level of value* concept. A few states have interpreted fair value at the *controlling interest level of value*. Thus, fair value is state-specific. Appraisers should be familiar with the statutory law and judicial precedent before rendering a fair value opinion in any state, and render their opinions in good faith, in light of these precedents. If there are no precedent cases, appraisers should specify their valuation assumptions clearly for their clients and the courts.

The issue of fair value can be important to business owners engaging in transactions giving rise to dissenters' rights. They need competent legal advice in order to understand the implications of these rights in achieving desired corporate objectives.

SUMMARY

Levels of value is an essential concept for business appraisers in specifying what they are valuing and how they are valuing it. The concept is an important means of explaining the implications of various assumptions regarding control and marketability to appraisal users. The concept is similarly important for business owners as well since it is key to understanding the investment characteristics of an equity interest in a closely held company. Levels of value is an important tool in ensuring that business appraisals play a proper role in facilitating (rather than hindering) real-world transactions.

NOTES

1. There is a further concept at *degree of control.* In some states, it takes a supermajority of the vote (two-thirds or more) to effectuate certain corporate

reorganizations or to liquidate a corporation. This is a further refinement of the discussion.

2. Certain minority blocks of shares may have what is referred to as *swing vote* potential. Such stocks may be more liquid (and valuable) than blocks that, when aggregated with another block of stock, have no ability to influence the voting control of a corporation. The existence of swing vote value is a matter deserving the exercise at appraiser judgment.

3. McConnell, Campbell R., *Economics: Principles, Problems, and Policies,* Ninth Edition (New York: McGraw-Hill Book Company, 1984), pp. 4–7. The quotes are excerpted from Campbell's introductory comments about the nature and method of economics.

4. Mercer, Z. Christopher, *"Do Public Company (Minority) Transactions Yield Controlling Interest or Minority Interest Pricing Data?" Business Valuation Review,* December 1990, p. 123.

5. The "appropriate" premiums and discounts are referred to, respectively, as "control premiums" and "minority interest discounts." These concepts, together with another "appropriate valuation discount" called the "marketability discount," are defined and discussed in the chart. On the other hand, if there are *fundamental differences* between the subject private company and the guideline companies (size, expectations regarding future growth management or other risks), an "appropriate valuation adjustment" must also be considered. Based upon our experience reviewing hundreds of appraisal reports, the failure to account for fundamental difference between private companies and publicly traded guideline companies is the source of many valuation errors, usually in the direction of overvaluation.

6. See the further development of this issue in Z. Christopher Mercer, *"Should 'Marketability Discounts' be Applied to Controlling Interests of Private Companies?" Business Valuation Review,* June 1994, p. 55.

7. "Freely tradable" can be defined for the purpose of this article as the ability to acquire or sell minority interest blocks of stock at will. In other words, the shares are fully marketable. The standard against which the tradeability or marketability of shares is gauged is that of a relatively large capitalization, publicly traded corporation on one of the major stock exchanges or over the counter. Significant minority interest blocks of stock of such corporations (e.g., Citicorp or IBM) can be acquired "at the market," or at or very close to the price at which the shares are currently being quoted on the New York Stock Exchange. Similarly, they can be sold "at the market," and the cash proceeds of the sale, net of brokers' commissions, and other transaction costs will be deposited in the seller's brokerage account in three business days.

8. *Mergerstat Review: 1994,* (Schaumberg, Illinois: Merrill Lynch Business Advisory Services, 1995), p. 98. *Mergerstat* defines the control premium as the premium to a publicly traded selling company's closing price five days prior to the announcement of a merger or acquisition transaction. The average and median premiums calculated for 1994 reflect 260 transactions in which there was sufficient public information to impute a premium. The range of these observations, however, is quite wide. We are making no statement that the average control premium applicable to *private businesses* should be 41.9 percent. That is a matter of appraiser judgment exercised in light of all the available facts and circumstances.

9. As with control premiums and minority interest discounts, selection of an appropriate marketability discount is a matter of appraiser judgment exercised in light of all the available facts and circumstances.

10. Discounts at this magnitude may not be appropriate for a 49 percent interest for reasons of inherent control or because of swing vote considerations.

11. Business owners should consult competent legal and tax advice regarding these matters.

12. In cases where the plan lacks cash assets to fund repurchases or where the sponsoring company lacks the financial capacity to make sufficient cash contributions to support repurchases, rendering the put-right ineffective, application of a substantial marketability discount may be appropriate.

13. "Buy high, sell low" is seldom a formula for winning investments!

Valuing Intangible Assets: The Big Pot of Goodwill

WESTON ANSON
CHAIRMAN,
TLA, INC.

We are all aware of the importance of valuing assets for business purposes, such as mergers, acquisitions, sales, and bankruptcies. Confusion arises when we move from tangible assets, such as the machinery in the factory or the desks at corporate headquarters, to the intangible assets, which will be the focus of this chapter. Accurate brand-name, trademark, and technology valuations represent a vast pool of untapped assets. By adding these valuations to financial statements, companies are able to more accurately reflect the real market value of the assets at hand. In fact, intangible assets and intellectual capital can be worth more than the other corporate assets.

There is a broad range of intangible assets that can have measurable value. These intangibles range from the obvious ones, such as trademarks, patents, software, and copyrights, to the less obvious ones such as slogans, formulas, characters, packaging, and graphics. Some of the less obvious intangibles include training programs, customer mailing lists, and specialty libraries. Intangibles generally fall into three broad groups, or "bundles": the technical bundle, the marketing bundle, and the knowledge/skills bundle. When setting royalty rates, or placing a value on a corporate name or logo, it is often better to look at the entire bundle of intangibles, rather than the more narrow view of looking at one intangible at a time.

TECHNICAL BUNDLE

Although the technical bundle of rights encompasses mostly patents, it includes a broader range of intangibles such as trade secrets, blending, instructions, technical know-how, and quality control systems. When setting values for a patent or technology, it is important to determine what other technical intangibles are traveling with the patent that add to its importance. The technical bundle of intangibles includes:

- Trade secrets.
- Packaging technology and sources.
- Proprietary processes.
- Process technology.
- Design technology.
- Product consistency.
- Secondary research.
- Plant production design.
- Formulas.
- Shapes and sizes.
- Key patents.
- Technical training.
- Secret blending techniques.
- Evaluation data.
- Product specifications.

MARKETING BUNDLE

A company's trademark is accompanied by other marketing intangibles that may have taken many years to build, and may have great value to the name. If a department store has outstanding customer service or return policies, or a product has an exceptional reputation and a warranty to back up that reputation, this has value. As a consumer, when you think of that store or product name, there is strong recognition, and thus, the confidence to do business with that particular store, or purchase products made by a specific manufacturer. This goodwill most certainly has a value separate from the recognized hard goods (such as the buildings and their contents). If the store burned down and all was lost, there would still be great value in the name.

Included in the marketing bundle of intangibles are:

- Corporate name and logo.
- Marketing umbrella and brand name.
- Subbrand names and trade dress.
- Worldwide trademark registrations.
- Copyrights.
- Secondary trademarks.
- Consumer advertising concepts.
- Marketing strategy.
- Product warranties.
- Customer service.
- Graphics.
- Promotional concepts.
- Public relations efforts.
- Labeling design and copyrights.
- Package design and copyrights.

KNOWLEDGE/SKILLS BUNDLE

The knowledge-based, or skills-based, intangible asset bundle includes items such as customer lists, employee relations, training programs, on-site management, and quality control. Most of a major insurance company's intangibles will be in training and agency networking, rather than in trademarks or copyrights. The knowledge/skills bundle of intangible assets includes:

- Noncompete clauses.
- Mailing lists.
- Sales knowledge.
- Proprietary management information systems.
- Databases.
- Sales leads.
- Employee education.
- Customer surveys.
- Processing methods.
- Quality control standards.
- Marketing training.
- Customer relations.
- Manuals, instructions, and codes.

VALUATION OF INTANGIBLES

The intellectual property being valued has to be viewed in the context of the associated intangibles traveling with it. The next step is to ask these questions: "Which intangibles have value and meaning in the marketplace? Does the intangible differentiate the company and its products or services from others in the marketplace? Would it have value to someone else? Would someone else want to buy the intangibles or "rent" them by means of a licensing agreement?" If the answer to these basic questions is "yes," then the intangible has measurable value and can command more money in a merger or liquidation, or can be "rented" in a licensing agreement.

Once it has been determined whether the intangible has value in the marketplace, the next step is to determine how broad the application might be. How unique is the technology or the concept? Will it bring the client profit margins? Is the product or concept already saturated in the marketplace, or does it give the company a competitive edge? Is it well protected so as to be a barrier to competition? Where is it in its life cycle?

If the answers indicate that there is indeed value, the next step is to select the most appropriate valuation method. We believe that the marketplace comparable approach is the only reliable way to establish royalty rates or values.

OVERVIEW OF VALUATION METHODS

The formalization of brand name and trademark valuations began in the United Kingdom, and has only been accepted in Europe and the United States for the past 20 years. Because valuation of intangible assets is still in its infancy, a great deal of debate continues about how to value trademarks and patents, and how to acknowledge them on a balance sheet.

Basically, there are five different methodologies utilized to value intellectual property: the cost approach, the income approach, the allocation of goodwill, the marketplace comparables approach, and the replacement approach. Each is briefly discussed here.

Cost Approach

The cost approach puts a value on all the money spent to advertise a trademark or to register a patent. We believe this method is the least useful because it excludes important factors, such as internal development costs, the cost of corporate capital, and market-driven influences on value, therefore, it is not reflective of a true value. It is important to remember that cost does not necessarily represent value. A purchaser of the asset will pay only an amount that will enable him to make a reasonable return based on expected revenue and expenses from utilizing the asset. Similarly, the seller seeks a return on his investment, not simply recoupment of costs. This method is useful where comparable market values are difficult to determine.

Income Approach

The income approach is theoretically the present worth of projected future benefits. This method necessitates three essential factors: an income stream attributable to the asset, the economic remaining life of that income stream, and a rate of return or discount rate commensurate with the risk of realizing the income. Specific calculations of value can be made with this information.

Allocation of Goodwill

Allocation of goodwill provides a rough figure for that portion of a company's goodwill that is attributable to a trademark or trade name in an acquisition or other transaction. It can use historical trends, purchase price allocations, or multiples of book value formulas. It is not advisable to use this calculation alone, but rather as a backup for one of the previously discussed methods.

Replacement Approach

Replacement, or conversion, value can be a useful method when looking for a minimum value, such as in a bankruptcy environment. It reflects what the minimum investment would be to replace the current logo, signage, advertising recognition, and so on. If a well-known company had to change its name tomorrow, what would the conversion costs be? This valuation is based on the cost of converting the company's physical facilities, subsidiaries, internal operations, and more, to another name or associated trade names. We often utilize this method in our reports in addition to a valuation based on the marketplace potential of the intellectual property so that clients can see a minimum and a maximum value for their assets.

Marketplace Approach

Based on 20 years of experience in this field, we believe that the only valuation method that encompasses all of the necessary elements is the marketplace approach, which is based on what a third party would pay to buy or "rent" the intellectual property. This approach is based on market conditions and driven by marketplace royalties. It is practical, simple, and logical; it is also adjustable over time. Just as tangible assets change in value over time, so do intangibles.

The market-based technique starts by finding comparable royalty rates from comparable transactions. Specific royalty rates are then determined or imputed with reference to those comparables being assessed, looking to the intangible's potential expansion and its life cycle to set an appropriate discount rate and growth rate, and then establish a comparable range of value.

There is no such thing as an exact comparable when it comes to intangibles. Some comparables are certainly more comparable than others. One can look for comparables in the same industry or look at similar comparables in similar technologies. It is important to include the marketing intangibles when looking for a match.

Intangibles have to be adjusted over time as they change in strength to reflect a higher or lower royalty, and thus a higher or lower value. It is useful to adjust value and royalty rates every three years to reflect the changes that may have taken place, either with the evolution of the product, service, or technology, or to reflect current marketplace situations.

As industry and commerce transcend borders and become more global, companies are finding the need to professionally manage key intangibles and intellectual property as strategic assets. The potential for disputes between countries with respect to valuation of intangibles creates a need for a globally acceptable approach that can be applied with some certainty. As the world becomes smaller through technological advances, the scope of the marketplace broadens. "Think global, act local" is an important concept to understand, because in order to be successful in today's marketplace, one must have a broader vision than in the past. However, individual nuances and cultures cannot be overlooked or forgotten if one is truly examining marketplace factors and influences.

We believe the future holds an increased awareness of intellectual property and intangible assets. Based on the acceptance and recognition of the value of these intangibles, there is, and will continue to be, an increasing trend toward the professional management of these assets.

Business Risk Characteristics and Their Impact on Valuation Issues

JEFFREY D. JONES
PRESIDENT
CERTIFIED APPRAISERS, INC.

Acquiring an existing business is one of the more successful methods for getting into business or expanding an existing business. Public and large private companies have used acquisitions to grow for many years. Based on information provided by business brokers and research by the Small Business Administration (SBA), the continued success of people who buy existing businesses is over 75 percent compared to only 10 percent to 15 percent of those who start from scratch. Determining the value of small and midsize businesses is a challenging assignment in light of the fact that very little information regarding actual transactions is publicly available, which has led many appraisers to look for alternative sources of guideline transactions and investment criteria from which they can derive applicable valuation ratios and/or investment factors that can be used to convert future benefits into indications of value. Guideline data obtained from public market investments usually require substantial adjustments to account for the additional risk characteristics associated with closely held businesses. Because many appraisers lack specific knowledge of the risk characteristics associated with small and midsize businesses, their final opinions of value are often poorly supported and/or erroneously too high. Based on my involvement with more than 1,000 business acquisitions over the past 20 years and my experience as a small business advisor through the SBA's SCORE consulting program, the following information is intended to provide some insight regarding the primary business risk characteristics that impact small and midsize businesses, and their effect on valuation issues.

THE MARKET

As reported in *The State of Small Business: A Report of the President 1993,*[1] there were 19.6 million business tax returns filed in the United States in 1990. Fewer than 90,000 employ more than 100 workers. The remaining 19.5 million are considered to be small or very small businesses. However, many of these tax returns are filed by either part-time businesses or independent contractors such as real estate and insurance agents. The two procedures used by the SBA to classify the number of full-time businesses are employment and gross sales. Based on studies conducted by the Small Business Administration, there are 5.1 million businesses with one or more employees. Businesses with under 20 employees account for 89.4 percent of the total, while midsize businesses with more than 100 but fewer than 500 employees account for fewer than 75,000 of the total. There are fewer than 15,000 businesses in the United States that have 500 or more employees.

Another measure of firm size is annual gross receipts. Approximately 69.3 percent of all business tax returns report gross sales of less than $50,000 per year. Most of these businesses are considered to be hobby or part-time businesses. Businesses with gross receipts of at least $50,000 but less than $500,000 account for 76.8 percent of all businesses. These businesses are considered to be very small. Those firms with gross receipts of $1 million or more represent only 3.9 percent of all business tax returns.

Businesses by Ownership Structure

Corporations represent only 18.6 percent of all business tax returns filed; however, corporations represent 42 percent of all businesses grossing at least $50,000. According to the SBA, corporations represent nearly 80 percent of those full-time businesses with employees, and account for nearly 90 percent of the nation's sales and employment. Partnerships represent 11.7 percent of businesses grossing over $50,000. Proprietorships represent 73.1 percent of the total business tax returns, but only 46.3 percent of full-time businesses.

Business Start-Ups and Acquisitions

Each year there are approximately 750,000 new businesses that start up in the United States.[2] The number of new firms grows by about 15 percent annually. According to the SBA's studies, annually, 2 to 3 percent of the total businesses in the United States survive as successor firms through merger, buyout, or similar change. In the January 1995 edition of *The Business Broker,* a newsletter for the business brokerage industry published by Business Brokerage Press, Tom West reports on several recent studies that estimate the number of businesses sold in the United States each year at somewhere between 120,000 to 300,000.[3] According to Mr. West, these numbers are substantially smaller than estimates made by others.

BUSINESS RISK CHARACTERISTICS

The two primary needs that influence the decision to buy small and mid-size businesses are lifestyle considerations and expectations of future benefits. They are so intertwined that it is difficult to separate them from each other. In evaluating businesses to buy that will meet these needs, entrepreneurs look at various business risk characteristics that impact business value. Based on interviews with more than 10,000 buyer prospects, the following 10 business risk characteristics are the primary factors that influence the decision to buy and the price to be paid.

Stability of Historical Earnings

The stability of historical earnings and the expectation of their continuance into the near future is one of the most important business risk characteristics considered by most buyers. If earnings are marginal, erratic, and/or have a short history, there is a perception of risk regarding the expectation of future earnings. There are three time plateaus that tend to influence the stability of a company's earnings. Those companies with one year or less of historical earnings have the greatest degree of risk, as they have not yet established a track record of stable earnings. Data from the U.S. Department of Labor[4] show that there is an annual 15 percent growth in new firms. Another 2 or 3 percent of firms survive as successor firms through merger, buyout, or similar change. This gain of about

17 percent is typically offset by about 15 percent of firms that terminate each year. The net gain of about 2 percent a year is the result, indicating the high risk of new start-up businesses. It appears that entrepreneurs tend to underestimate the costs and time required to start a new business and reach the point of profitability.

The second time plateau seems to occur at about three years. At this point, a business has begun to establish a track record sufficient to indicate stability and direction of future earnings. The third time plateau occurs when a company has a track record of five or more years. At this point, companies have weathered most of the major problems of operating a business and have a high likelihood of continued success. In general, given the same amount of future benefits, businesses with a long and stable history of earnings will be valued higher than those with shorter histories and/or erratic benefits.

Business and Industry Growth Prospects

Research of the history, background, and future trends of a subject business and its industry provide insight into the future prospects for growth in revenue and earnings. Businesses in growth industries will be more marketable and will sell at higher values than businesses in declining industries, even when they have similar profitability. Based on the *State of Small Business: Report of the President 1993,* the fastest-growing industries are:

- Health and allied service industries.
- Child care.
- Business services.
- Amusement and recreation services.

The industries showing the greatest job losses are:

- Machinery and equipment manufacturing.
- Building and heavy construction contractors.

Stability of Employees

Experienced and skilled employees are an important asset of any business, especially for a new owner who frequently may have little or no experience in managing a business. It is expensive and time consuming to find, hire, and train employees. A major benefit of buying an existing business is the workforce already in place. While sellers of businesses are usually paranoid about their employees finding out that the business is for sale, buyers are equally concerned that employees might leave. Companies with high turnover and unskilled workers create a negative perception with regard to the future of the business and its future outlook of earnings. Companies with low turnover and skilled employees tend to have good track records of business success and will produce market values greater than businesses with short-term unskilled employees.

Depth of Management

One of the distinguishing characteristics between small and larger businesses is the depth of management. Larger companies usually have multiple layers of management, which tends to strengthen their ability to survive because they can replace key management without significant cost or loss of business. Small and midsize businesses have few, if any, levels of management below the owner/manager. They therefore have greater risk of earnings loss in the event of illness, death, or poor management decisions of the owner/manager. The more reliant a business is on its owner, the less valuable it is to buyers.

Diversification of Products, Services, and Geographic Markets

Another distinguishing characteristic between small and larger businesses is the diversification of products, services, and geographic markets. Typically, small businesses have very narrow lines of products and/or services, and are restricted to limited geographic markets. Expansion of the lines of products, services and/or markets may be restricted by supplier requirements, customer limitations, and/or the owner's inability to raise additional capital required to expand.

Many small businesses are in niche markets that enable an owner to make a good living, but do not provide significant growth potential. As a result, these businesses are not going to be attractive to financial buyers or investors who look for opportunities to take companies public. Larger businesses usually have diversification of products, services, and geographic markets, thus insulating them from significant loss of revenue and earnings in the event of a specific product line or geographic market is lost or severely impacted. Businesses that can diversify are better able to reduce risk and, therefore, increase their market value.

Availability of Capital and/or Terms of Sale

The availability of debt and/or equity capital greatly influences the market value of a company. An axiom that is certainly true in business states, "With unlimited resources of time and money, most any problem can be overcome." Many businesses suffer from a lack of both money and time. According to the Small Business Administration, approximately 45 percent of all new businesses are funded by equity capital because sources of debt capital are severely limited. Public companies can attract equity capital through the sale of stock. The size of a company tends to have a significant impact on the entrepreneur's ability to raise debt and/or equity capital to start, expand, or buy a business. Although buying an existing business is certainly less risky than starting a new business, raising capital is still a very difficult chore. There is a tendency on the part of financial institutions to view small and midsize business acquisitions with a jaundiced eye, given the high failure rate of these businesses in general and the perception that if a business is for sale there must be something wrong with it.

While buyers for larger businesses do have more options available to raise capital, a majority of the reported transactions with values in excess of $1 million are consummated using forms of payment other than all cash. *Mergerstat Review* reports that only 46 percent of the announced transactions in 1994 were done for all cash. Another 13 percent were done for stock, and 40 percent of the transactions were done for a combination of cash and stock. According to *Mergerstat,* only 28 percent of the deals valued at $25 million or less were done for cash, whereas 36 percent of the deals valued over $100 million were done for cash.[5]

Desirability and Marketability for Type of Business

Emulating the mind-set of buyers for small and midsize businesses is a very difficult task. Certainly they are interested in returns on their investments, but other characteristics such as lifestyle, pride, nationality, and past experience play an important role in determining what buyers are willing to pay. Some businesses are much more desirable than others and tend to sell fast. In any case, businesses take six months to a year to sell, and some never sell despite the fact that they are profitable and the owners are willing to sell on reasonable terms. Characteristics that make one business more or less desirable and/or marketable than others include:

- *The general acceptance of the business in society.* Some businesses can be very profitable, but have limited appeal due to the nature of the business. For example, businesses dealing with adult entertainment generally have a limited acquisition market because entrepreneurs tend to start up new businesses rather than acquire existing ones. Adult entertainment businesses can be highly profitable, but they tend to sell at low values due to the low esteem in which they are held by the general public.
- *The degree of technical or specialized training needed to operate the business.* Businesses that require technical training or knowledge are more difficult to sell due to the limited number of buyer prospects that have the prerequisite training and/or experience.

- *The general condition of business equipment and inventory.* Equipment in need of repair and/or inventory that is outdated or nonsalable will have a negative influence on value.
- *The size of the business.* Often, midsize businesses are easier to sell than small businesses, because benefit streams are larger, financing resources are more readily available, and the pool of buyers is expanded to include both private and institutional investors who hire professional management to operate the businesses. Businesses with proven track records of low earnings are extremely difficult to sell, except when the assets can be acquired near liquidation value and the business then utilized for another business concept. For instance, restaurants are frequently sold for their tangible asset value and reopened under a new name and menu concept.

Quality of Location and Facilities

The physical appearance of the neighborhood and facilities where a business is located can have an influence on value. Every town has neighborhoods that are considered good and bad. Given a choice, buyer prospects do not want to buy a business located in an area of town considered high risk due to poor appearance, crime, and/or poor quality of life. Generally, businesses located in bad areas of town or having poor appearances will suffer from reduced market values despite other positive aspects.

Competition

Companies in highly competitive industries are often less valuable than those with similar characteristics, but in more moderate competitive industries. Unstable markets due to newness of products or services or a poor economy can generate hungry competitors who cut prices in order to survive. As a result, sales volume and profits are reduced for everyone in the industry. Industry characteristics that tend to have a positive influence on value include:

- Industries that have a strong trade or professional association.
- Industries that have stable products, services, and pricing.
- Industries with low company failure rates.
- Industries that are regulated by government through licensing, permits, or zoning, which tend to restrict the number of companies.

In some industries, competition is very friendly and actually stimulates business for everyone. Examples include: clusters of restaurants; shopping malls with multiple tenants competing for the consumer dollar, yet jointly advertising to promote business; and auto dealerships jointly advertising and clustering together.

Type of Business

The type of business has an impact on value due to buyers' perceptions of risk relating to the operational nature of the business and the underlying assets required to operate it. In general, businesses that are easy to start and require minimal capital investment will be valued less than businesses that require specialized knowledge, licensing, and/or heavy capital investment.

Service businesses represent the largest growing category of businesses in the United States, and currently account for approximately 38 percent of all businesses (excluding finance, insurance, and real estate). Service businesses usually require minimal investment in tangible assets and can often be easily started, but they also have a reputation for going out of business quickly due to heavy reliance on people skills, competition, and changes in technology. The value of service businesses will often be less than businesses in other categories with similar profitability but more tangible assets.

Retail businesses account for approximately 21.7 percent of all business types. Two major trends in the retail business are franchising and "killer category" stores. Due to the high costs to compete in the industry, retailers are joining networks and franchise to gain recognition and obtain purchasing power. Large specialty stores in excess of 10,000 square feet are now competing with products that previously had been in general line stores. The office supply business is a good example. A few years ago, office supplies were sold either through department stores or many small office supply stores. Today, many businesses buy their office supplies from large specialty stores such as Office Depot and Office Max. Consequently, many of the small office supply stores are now out of business. Small, independent, retail businesses that have to compete with "killer category" stores run a high risk of failing, and thus are often difficult to sell due to the changes occurring in the marketplace.

Manufacturing accounts for approximately 6.4 percent of the total businesses, yet there is a large market of buyers, especially for businesses that manufacture a proprietary product. The interest level in manufacturing businesses is high due to the following:

- A large number of engineers and corporate managers in the United States tend to be entrepreneurial.
- A substantial amount of tangible assets can be financed.
- The perception that manufacturing businesses are more stable than other types of businesses and have the potential for significant growth.

In general, buyers and sellers must be aware of the market of buyers for small and midsize businesses. When there is a large market, the businesses will usually sell quickly and at values significantly higher than those that are difficult to sell and/or the market of buyers is limited.

BUYER CHARACTERISTICS

There is no lack of buyer prospects for small and midsize companies. Our brokerage company, Certified Business Brokers, receives approximately 300 inquiries every month from people who desire to acquire a business. Some of these inquires are from first- and second-generation immigrants who have recently moved to the United States. Because immigrants often have problems with the English language and are unfamiliar with U.S. business methods, they tend to acquire existing businesses rather than start up new ones. Immigrants will often work for a family member for a year or two and then strike out on their own with the help of family to acquire their own business.

White-collar buyers, such as corporate executives, bankers, accountants, and engineers make up a large segment of buyers for small and midsize businesses. They typically want manufacturing or service-related businesses that deal with other businesses.

Investment bankers, private investment groups, and wealthy individuals are considered to be financial buyers, who are usually looking for businesses that can be taken public within five years. Most small businesses are not likely candidates for going public, and many midsize businesses are considered large for the industry that they serve, thus they too are unlikely candidates for being taken public. Financial buyers are interested in acquiring companies with gross sales of over $10 million, and are in industries where significant growth is possible.

Competitors and business owners in similar lines of business represent a smaller segment of the buyer market than many people think. Other than specialty businesses such as bowling centers and automobile dealerships, existing business owners tend to buy only when they can obtain a bargain price. This category of buyer often objects to paying any goodwill value as they believe they already have the skills necessary to obtain a business without having to buy someone else's. While acquisition is a successful means of business growth, many small and midsize business owners are shortsighted when it comes to acquiring other similar companies.

SUMMARY

A fundamental principle in valuing small and midsize businesses is that a determination of value is a question of fact that depends upon the circumstances in each case. A proper valuation should include a dispassionate analysis of company-specific risks, systematic risks of the market in which a business operates, and the acquisition market wherein that has taken into consideration the size of a business, buyer characteristics, and normal terms of sale.

NOTES

1. *The State of Small Business: A Report of the President 1993.* United States Printing Office, Washington, D.C., 1993.
2. Adapted by the U.S. Small Business Administration, Office of Advocacy, from data provided by the U.S. Department of Labor, Employment, and Training Administration, and based upon state employment security agencies' quarterly reports, 1992.
3. *The Business Broker.* Published by Business Brokerage Press, Concord, MA., January 1995.
4. *Ibid.* p. 2.
5. *Mergerstat Review 1994.* Published by Merrill Lynch Business Advisory Services, Schaumburg, IL.

PART THREE

LEGAL ASPECTS

CHAPTER FIFTEEN

Disclosure Requirements and Limitations: Who Has a Need to Know

DAVID M. BISHOP
PRINCIPAL
THE BISHOP LAW FIRM

Proper disclosure is seldom discussed but critically important in the purchase or sale of a business. A seller's improper or inadequate disclosure can result in damages to the buyer, civil or criminal liability to the seller, and a costly legal battle for both. In today's marketplace, "telling no lies" is no longer an acceptable standard. To avoid liability, a seller generally must, in addition to making truthful statements, disclose information that a buyer reasonably needs to make an informed decision to buy. Of course, a buyer should never assume a seller will disclose everything he needs to know. It is the buyer's responsibility to ask the right questions and insist on the seller's full compliance. Battles won prior to closing, as difficult as they may be, are generally less costly and more satisfying to the buyer than those won after the sale.

Disclosure, in the parlance of buying and selling small to medium-sized businesses, is a term used to describe the seller's responsibility to reveal to the buyer information regarding the business. Actually, a seller has twin duties: the duty to disclose and the duty to make truthful representations. Unless indicated otherwise, the term disclosure will be used in its broadest sense to indicate fulfillment of both duties.

To truly understand the value of a business, a buyer must gain an understanding of not only its historical performance, but also all the other factors that bear on the ability of the business to perform. Generally, however, a buyer will not be able to gather this critical information unless the seller discloses it to him or her. Ideally, a seller will disclose *all* information pertinent to the sale of a business; in the real world, however, proper disclosure is determined by whether the seller has met his legal duty to disclose. This legal duty depends upon the nature of the cause of action (common law fraud, federal and state securities laws, contract law, or other state laws) and the facts and circumstances of the particular case.

With the sale of so many businesses in this country, one might think it a simple matter to determine what constitutes proper disclosure. Many buyers and sellers, in fact, assume that there is a checklist of items that must be disclosed. Unfortunately, no such checklist exists.

Deciding what constitutes proper disclosure is a two-step process. First, one must determine the nature of the cause of action (common law fraud, federal and state securities laws, contract law, or other state laws) and the elements necessary to prove a prima facie case. Second, one must apply the law to the facts and circumstances of one's case.

The first step—determining the nature of the cause of action—is absolutely essential in deciding whether a seller has met the duty of disclosure. For example, under a common law fraud claim, the buyer must be able to prove that he was justified in relying on a misrepresentation. If the same buyer is pursuing a breach of contract claim, he need not prove justifiable reliance.

The second step—applying the law to the facts—is more problematic. The courts have considered all kinds of factors in determining whether proper disclosure has been made: the relationship between the parties, the superior knowledge of the seller, the materiality of the information, the intent of the seller, and the carelessness of the buyer. Moreover, courts in different states often take opposite views on nearly identical facts and circumstances. In some states, those facts and circumstances support the particular cause of action; in others, they don't.

This chapter reviews the causes of action related to a business seller's failure to disclose, noting some of the specific circumstances that have been considered in applying the law in actual cases. One should remember, however, two important points. First, the case law discussed represents a particular state's decision with respect to a particular set of facts. In deciding disclosure questions, one must apply the appropriate state law to the facts at hand. Second, case law generally sets minimum standards of disclosure. Buyers and sellers should strive for disclosure that exceeds minimum standards. Accordingly, this chapter concludes with some practical advice for buyers and sellers in achieving a higher standard of disclosure.

COMMON LAW FRAUD

Traditionally, the right of the buyer to sue for fraud has protected a buyer against improper or inadequate disclosure. Most such fraud claims are based on common law fraud. A common law cause of action is one that has been developed by state courts based on prior decisions. By contrast, statutory fraud is a cause of action based upon a state statute.

In a common law fraud action against the seller of a business, a buyer generally must be able to prove seven essential elements:

1. The seller *misrepresented* or failed to disclose, a *matter of past or present fact.*
2. The seller's misrepresentation or nondisclosure was *material.*
3. The seller made the misrepresentation *with knowledge of its falsity* or *without knowing* whether it was true or false; or the *seller had a duty to disclose* the undisclosed fact.
4. The seller *intended to defraud* the buyer.
5. The buyer *actually relied* on the seller's misrepresentation or nondisclosure.
6. The buyer *justifiably relied* on the misrepresentation or nondisclosure.
7. The buyer incurred *damages as a proximate result* of relying on the seller's misrepresentation or nondisclosure.

Misrepresentation or Nondisclosure

To prove this element, a buyer must be able to establish that the seller misrepresented, or failed to disclose, a matter of past or present fact. Expressions of opinion, promises, or statements regarding the future are generally not grounds for fraud. For example, a statement that a business is capable of producing a certain amount of income was not considered fraudulent even though the business did not, in fact, actually produce such income, *Beierle v. Taylor,* 164 Mont. 436, 524 P.2d 783 (1974), but a false statement as to expenses incurred and income earned over several years in the past was actionable, *Butts v. Dragstrem,* 349 S. 2d 1205 (Fla. App. 1977) cert. denied 361 S.2d 831 (Fla. 1978).

If the buyer is asserting that the seller failed to disclose, the buyer will need to prove that the undisclosed information was not, in fact, communicated. Courts have occasionally held that a disclosure was communicated although not in the form or manner that the buyer anticipated or preferred. For example, a seller's failure to include bonuses in a profit and loss column of an automobile dealership's financial statements did not constitute fraudulent nondisclosures because the bonuses were reflected in the net worth section of the statements, *Colonial Lincoln Mercury, Inc. v. Musgrave,* 749 F.2d 1092 (4th Cir. N.C. 1984).

Misrepresentation or Nondisclosure Must Be Material

Not every misrepresentation is grounds for common law fraud. The misrepresentations or nondisclosures must be material. Materiality is generally determined by whether the misrepresentation or nondisclosure was likely to affect a reasonable buyer's decision to purchase the business.

In the sale of a business, misrepresentations or nondisclosures concerning the profits of a business or the physical size or condition of assets are generally considered material. All of the following were considered material misstatements: a statement that an unprofitable business is profitable, *Gilbert v. Mid-South Machinery Co.,* 267 S.C. 211, 227 S.E. 2d 189 (1976); a statement that profits were at least six times greater than actual profits, *Starky v. Bell,* 281 S.C. 308, 315 S.E.2d 153 (App. 1984); a false statement as to the business's gross sales, *Selvidge v. McBeen,* 230 Mont. 237, 750 P.2d 429 (1988); and a false statement as to the condition of floor, foundation, and electrical systems where estimated repairs costs exceeded one-third of the purchase price, *Moschelle v. Hulse,* 622 P.2d 155 (Mont. 1980). Other misrepresentations and nondisclosures have been deemed to be material when they would affect a reasonable buyer's decision to purchase a business. For example, a seller's misrepresentation regarding business's good standing with suppliers, *Lumby v. Doetch,* 183 Mont. 427, 600 P.2d 200 (1970); a supplier's misrepresentation regarding pricing policies, *Enserch Exploration, Inc. v. Star Tex Propane, Inc.,* 608 S.W.2d 791 (Tex. Civ. App. 1980); *Morris v. International Yogurt Co.,* 107 Wash. 2d 314, 729 P.2d 33 (1986), and a franchiser's failure to disclose that its yogurt mix was available to nonfranchisees were all considered to be material misstatements.

Knowledge of Falsity

If the action is based on misrepresentation, the buyer must show that the seller made the misrepresentation with knowledge of its falsity or without knowing whether it was true or false. Knowledge may generally be proved by showing that the seller knew or should have known the actual facts.

Duty to Disclose

If the action is based on failure to disclose, the buyer will need to show that the seller had a duty to disclose the undisclosed fact. While some courts have embraced the doctrine of caveat emptor, "let the buyer beware," other courts have been inclined to find special circumstances that warrant a duty of disclosure. Among the circumstances that have been considered in imposing a common law duty of disclosure are:

The existence of a fiduciary or confidential relationship.

A contractual duty (seller had a duty to disclose under provision in contract stating that sellers . . . have made a full and complete disclosure of all relevant factors concerning the financial status of the corporation), *Nicmoth v. Kohls,* 171 Ill. App. 3d 54, 121 Ill. Dec 37, 524 N.E.2d 1085, appeal denied.

Superior knowledge or means of knowledge on the part of one party.

Knowledge acquired after original statement is made.

Partial disclosures (seller who made positive assertions concerning financial condition of a business incurred a duty to make a full disclosure of any extenuating financial circumstances that counteracted those assertions, recognizing the rule that the speaker has a duty of saying nothing or telling the whole truth), *Ragsdale v. Kennedy,* 286 N.C. 130, 209 S.E.2d 494 (1974).

Request for information.

In essence, the courts have been gradually eroding the doctrine of caveat emptor. According to one court, "The trend is toward finding or imposing a duty to disclose material impediments to a transaction even though there is an absence of a fiduciary relationship between the parties in the classic sense . . . . It is now recognized generally that those facts must be disclosed which are so critical and material to a transaction that if known by one party and not the other, the agreement would be voidable." *Kaas v. Privette,* 12 Wash. App. 142, 529 P.2d 23 (1974).

One should not assume, however, that all courts have a penchant for finding a duty to disclose. In *RNH, Inc. v. Beatty,* 571 S.2d 1039 (Ala. 1990), the court found that a seller of stock of a particular drug company, who was owner of a competing drugstore, had no duty to disclose to buyers that he intended to move and expand his drugstore where parties to agreement were businessmen dealing at arm's length and acting upon advice of attorneys; *RNH, Inc. v. Beatty,* 571 So. 2d 1039 (Ala. 1990). Similarly in *Greenwood Mills, Inc. v. Russel Corp. 981 F.2d 148* (4th Cir. S.C. 1992), the court found that the owner of a textile plant had no duty to disclose extensive environmental problems to the holder of a purchase option on the plant. The court said that while a seller has a duty to disclose any artificially created, and concealed, unstable condition, this duty exists only as to material facts that cannot be discovered through the diligent attention, observation, and judgment of the option holder. The court pointed out that the option holder was a textile manufacturer who should have known of the potential environmental problems and that a reasonable investigation would have revealed the problem.

Intent to Defraud

The buyer must establish that the seller's misrepresentation or failure to disclose was intended to defraud the buyer. Generally, this means that the buyer must show that the seller intended to induce the buyer to act in reliance on the misrepresentation or nondisclosure. Intent can usually be inferred from evidence showing that the misrepresentation or nondisclosure was material and the seller knew or had reason to know it was material.

Actual Reliance

Unless the buyer actually relied on the seller's misrepresentation or nondisclosure, there are no grounds for common law fraud. Proving actual reliance is generally a simple matter of the buyer testifying that he would not have bought the business on the terms that were agreed upon had it not been for the misrepresentation or nondisclosure.

Justifiable Reliance

Proving that the buyer was justified in relying on the misrepresentation or nondisclosure is generally more difficult than proving actual reliance. Whether the buyer's reliance was reasonable is determined by the circumstances including: the buyer's knowledge and experience; the buyer's ability to acquire pertinent information; the relationship of the parties; and the nature of the misrepresentation or nondisclosure. If the seller actively prevents the buyer from discovering the truth, such as when seller refused to turn over the business books to a buyer, *Fitzgerald v. Edelen,* 623 P.2d 418 (Col. App. 1980), the buyer's reliance will be considered reasonable. If the seller's misrepresentation or nondisclosure concerns a condition that is, by its nature, undiscoverable, such as seasonal flooding that was not discoverable at the time buyer examined the premises, *Moschelle v. Hulse,* 622 P.2d 155 (Mont. 1980), the buyer's reliance will be considered reasonable. Reliance may be considered reasonable even if the buyer could have discovered the misrepresentation or nondisclosure with minor investigation; but reliance on the misrepresentation may not be considered reasonable if its falsity is obvious.

For example, the purchasers of a campground could not have justifiably relied on the seller's representation that the gross revenue from the campground "had to be" $50,000, where the purchasers were experienced campground operators who knew that they had received no documentation corroborating the seller's claim regarding the campground's revenue; and they knew that a party that had previously purchased the campground had defaulted on its mortgage, with the sellers reacquiring title to the campground as a result. Since the purchasers acknowledged that they viewed the $50,000 figure as an "honest guess," the court said they could not actually have relied upon it, *Shephard v. Whispering Pines, Inc.* 188 A.D.2d 786, 591 N.Y.S.2d 246 (1992).

Causation and Damages

The final element of common law fraud is actual damages incurred as a proximate result of the seller's misrepresentation or nondisclosure. Damages for fraud are determined differently in different jurisdictions. Under the "benefit of the bargain rule," actual damages are incurred to the extent that the actual value of the business is less than represented value. Under the "out-of-pocket rule," actual damages are incurred to the extent that the actual value of the business is less than the price paid. Approximate cause can be established by showing that the buyer actually relied on the misrepresentation or nondisclosure and that the damages incurred could reasonably be an expected result from such reliance.

DISCLOSURE REQUIREMENTS IMPOSED BY CONTRACT

The vast majority of sales of businesses are governed by either an asset purchase agreement or a stock purchase agreement. Normally included in the contract is a section entitled "Representations and Warranties," which imposes upon the seller a duty to make certain disclosures and representations regarding the business. This provides an opportunity for the buyer to ask and the seller to answer all the important questions concerning the business and its operations.

Most of the disastrous results discussed in the section on common law fraud could have been avoided with proper contract provisions. The purchaser of the textile plant plagued with environmental problems could have imposed a duty to disclose upon the seller by including an environmental provision in the contract between the parties. The purchasers of the campground could have protected themselves by requiring accurate financial disclosures or provisions tying their payments to achieving the expected level of revenue.

Tragically, buyers and sellers often view representations and warranties as needless boilerplate. Consequently, they neglect to examine the language of each representation and to consider whether it accurately states all that should be stated.

A seller should understand that each representation in a contract represents a potential cause of action. He should carefully examine each sentence and agree to its inclusion only if he is prepared to stand by it in the event of a dispute. Exceptions to a particular representation are common and should be noted in the contract itself or on an attached schedule or disclosure letter.

A buyer should make sure that all important representations and disclosures are included in the contract. This can be accomplished by answering these questions:

Have I included all of the representations and warranties that are standard in the purchase of a business?

What special representation should be included to cover all oral representations and other matters that are vitally important in this business and in its future performance?

A lawyer who is well versed in buying and selling businesses should prepare the contract including but not limited to representations and warranties that address the following areas:

- Organization and good standing.
- Authority; no conflict.
- Capitalization.
- Financial statements.
- Books and records.
- Title to properties; encumbrances.
- Condition and sufficiency of assets.
- Accounts receivable.
- Inventory.
- No undisclosed liabilities.
- Taxes.
- No material adverse change.
- Employee benefits.
- Compliance with legal requirements; governmental authorizations.
- Legal proceedings; orders.
- Absence of certain changes and events.
- Contracts; no defaults.
- Insurance.
- Environmental matters.
- Employees.
- Labor relations; compliance.
- Intellectual property.
- Brokers or finders.

These representations and warranties are considered "standard" because they are likely to be included in a contract for the sale of a business, not because the language of the representation or warranty is identical in every contract. The actual language of a particular representation and warranty varies, a product of negotiation between the parties. Accordingly, it is not sufficient to simply "cover" a particular representation and warranty; the actual language of the representation and warranty must adequately and unambiguously address the subject matter of concern.

By now, it should be clear that what is included in the contract can define a seller's duty of disclosure. What is not so apparent is that what is excluded from the contract can also define a seller's duty of disclosure. If the contract contains an "integration" or "merger" clause (a clause indicating that the contract contains the entire agreement between the parties and that any representation made outside the contract is of no force or effect), the seller may be able to assert that he had no duty of disclosure with respect to a matter, and the buyer is precluded from making a breach of contract claim as to matters not addressed in the contract. Furthermore, the buyer may be unable to establish a common law fraud claim because the seller will be able to defend on the basis that the buyer was not justified in relying on the misrepresentation or nondisclosure. Although some courts ignore merger clauses under certain circumstances, it is prudent, nevertheless, for the buyer to assume that unless a representation is included in the contract, the buyer is not justified in relying upon it.

In sum, a well-crafted contract will enable buyers and sellers to define proper disclosure. To be effective, however, the contract must:

Include all the necessary representations, warranties and disclosures.

Be in clear and unambiguous language.

Be tailored to the particular business being sold.

Federal and State Securities Laws

A seller's duty of disclosure is often determined by federal and state securities laws. A discussion of federal and state securities laws is beyond the scope of this article, but it is worth noting for those who think they are exempt from these laws the Rule 10-b5, the broad antifraud provision of the 1934 Securities and Exchange Act applies to all sales of securities, regardless of the size or the private nature of the sale. The complexity of the securities law make it a trap for the unwary. One should consult a securities attorney for questions in this area.

A Higher Standard of Disclosure

At a minimum, a seller should fully and accurately disclose information necessary to avoid liability. Ideally, seller and buyer will agree upon standards that exceed this minimum, thereby minimizing the possibility of a claim for inadequate or improper disclosure. Set forth here is a checklist of disclosure do's and don'ts to achieve this higher standard:

DISCLOSURE DO'S AND DON'TS

Seller Do's

1. Give accurate financial information and financial statements.
2. Read every word of representations and answer them truthfully and accurately.
3. When in doubt, disclose more than may be necessary. To the extent you have disclosed a problem, the buyer will not be able to claim nondisclosure.
4. Update any representations and correct any half truths.
5. Recognize that a stock sale may impose a higher duty to disclose than an asset sale.
6. Correct any misrepresentations or half truths made by agents if you are aware of them.

Seller Don'ts

1. Give opinions without clearly setting forth that they are opinions, not facts.
2. Make projections without disclosing that future performance is not guaranteed.
3. Ignore important facts or likely scenarios when making projections. For example, if new competitors have entered the market, projections may need to be modified.

Buyer Do's

1. Insist on a contract.
2. Insist on receiving financial information and financial statements and making them a part of the contract.
3. Insist that all material representations be included in the agreement, and require seller to update representations up to the closing date.
4. Require that representations survive the closing, and require right of offset to the extent that there is a misrepresentation.
5. Confirm information during due diligence.

Buyer Don'ts

1. Permit disclosures in one part of the contract to address another part of the contract.
2. Sign the document before disclosure schedules have been attached.
3. Assume that the seller has read and completed the agreement. (Sellers are notorious for failing to read purchase agreements.)

Due Diligence of Legal Issues: Don't Buy Problems

GEORGE E. CHRISTODOULO
PARTNER
BURNS AND LEVINSON

This chapter explores legal issues that most frequently arise in the context of the due diligence investigations in the buying and selling of small and midsized companies. This is not a comprehensive description of the buyer's due diligence process, since that discussion is set forth in a later chapter. Rather, the chapter focuses on several primary legal matters that an experienced transaction attorney has found can be most troublesome if not fully explored and resolved during the transaction process. The thrust of this chapter, thus, will be to look beyond the basic information compiled during due diligence for an understanding of issues that may have legal implications after the closing.

CORPORATE QUALIFICATION

The buyer is naturally concerned whether the seller is in corporate good standing (having filed all necessary annual reports) and in tax good standing (having filed all necessary tax returns and paid the amounts shown as due therein) in the seller's state of incorporation and in all states where the seller is qualified to do business.

But the inquiry does not end here. All activities of the seller in other states must be reviewed. Does the seller do business through subsidiaries? Is the seller a member of a joint venture? When a corporation is doing business outside of the state of incorporation, it may be required to qualify to do business in such jurisdictions. What constitutes "doing business" is not definitively answered in one place. Some states list activities in which the corporation may engage without being deemed to do business while other states describe activities, either generally or specifically, which are deemed to be doing business.

The act of qualification involves obtaining a certificate of authority to conduct business and to appoint a resident agent upon whom service of process may be made. Qualification usually subjects the corporation to taxation in such state.

Failure to qualify subjects the corporation to several risks. The corporation cannot bring an action in state court if it should be qualified and is not. In some states, subsequent qualification does not remedy the situation. Officers and directors, as well as the corporation, may be subject to fines. Finally, the corporation may be liable for unpaid state income taxes.

Thus, in the due diligence process, the inquiry of the location of the seller's business activities must be fully explored and understood. Thereafter, a reasonable analysis of whether the seller must qualify in certain states must be made. Ultimately, the risks of failure to qualify must be weighed against the costs to do so.

CAPITALIZATION

The review of the seller's stockholdings and capitalization will result in an understanding of the equity structure of the seller. More important, the buyer will know who controls the voting power of the stock and whose consent is needed to complete the transaction. This review may be a minefield for the uneducated. Among the issues to be analyzed in a review of the articles of incorporation, voting agreements, bylaws, stock restriction and repurchase agreements, and other corporate documentation are the following:

1. Can stockholders sell stock without offering the shares back to the corporation? Can this right of first refusal be waived? By whom?

2. Are there outstanding warrants or options to purchase stock? Does the vesting of such rights accelerate upon a sale of the business?

3. Are there existing buy-out agreements with former shareholders that entitle that person to a share of the proceeds from a sale subsequent to the buyout of such shareholders?

4. Are there voting trust agreements or irrevocable proxies that grant certain persons the right to vote or control a large block of stock?

5. Do the corporate documents contain a requirement for a supermajority vote to act in a sale?

6. Does the state of incorporation of the seller grant a dissident stockholder so-called appraisal rights, requiring an independent valuation of the purchase price?

7. Do holders of nonvoting common or preferred stock have any special right to vote with respect to significant corporate transactions?

8. Are accrued dividends on preferred stock payable upon the closing of the sale of the corporation?

9. Do holders of preferred stock have any "put-rights" (ability to force the corporation to buy out their stock)?

The answers to these inquiries often dictate whether the sale will be structured as an asset sale or a sale of stock. The sale of assets generally requires less than a unanimous vote of stockholders, subject to any appraisal rights. The sale of stock most frequently requires a unanimous or near unanimous action by stockholders, again subject to any appraisal rights. The buyer must decide its level of comfort as to whether the needed consents can and will be obtained, and how to deal with any dissident stockholders.

The experienced buyer explores these issues early in the transaction and determines who must be in agreement to ensure that the necessary consents to complete the transaction will be obtained. Failure to do so can lead to an agreement negotiated with a group of representatives of management that cannot receive the support of stockholders. Finally, most buyers do not wish to consummate a transaction and face the prospect of a claim by a dissident stockholder.

EMPLOYEE AGREEMENTS

The existence of all written and oral agreements of any type with employees and former employees must be ascertained. Generally, these agreements either apply to all employees or are special agreements with key personnel.

It has become more common in recent years to have all employees sign some form of employment/confidentiality/restriction agreement upon hiring. These agreements generally include all or some of the following topics:

Acknowledgment that the employee may resign or be terminated at any time.

Agreement not to compete while employed.

Agreement not to compete after termination of employment.

Agreement not to hire or solicit to hire employees.

Agreement not to disclose or use confidential information.

Acknowledgment that all discoveries, inventions, processes, methods, and improvements conceived of by the employee are the property of the corporation.

Identification of which agreements survive termination of employment, and if so, for what length of time.

The buyer, particularly in transactions where expertise and people are a key asset of the seller, must understand what restrictions and protections are in place in favor of the corporation. Thereafter, a review of the current status of the enforcement of such agreements in the state courts where the seller is located must be completed. In many states, the clear trend in the courts is to not recognize restrictions (as to scope, geographical area and/or duration) that are not necessary to protect the corporation or unduly restrict the ability of the employee to earn a living. Thus, the experienced buyer must have the legal analysis completed in order to understand the enforceability of the restrictive covenants.

Special agreements with key employees may contain provisions that result in substantial cost to either or both the buyer or the seller. Employment agreements often contain change-of-control provisions that allow the employee to terminate the agreement if the corporation is sold. A change of control may also result in the payment of a substantial severance payment to the employee. Employment agreements may also have other provisions that protect the employee and allow him to terminate, including antirelocation of offices, diminishment or change in duties, and others. In a stock transaction, failure to identify such triggering covenants can result in the buyer not being able to retain the services of the employee and, worse, having to make a severance or special payment to the employee.

CONSENTS RELATED TO THE TRANSACTION

Every seller is a party to several types of contracts, whether they be real property leases, operating agreements, purchase orders, loan and financing agreements, or personal property leases. Such agreements are generally assignable to a buyer of assets if there is no prohibition to the contrary. On the other hand, such agreements normally require a consent to the assignment by the other party. Depending upon the nature of the assignment clause, the consent may not be unreasonably withheld or delayed; the consent may be withheld at the sole discretion of the other party; or the seller may have to remain liable on the obligation.

These clauses have implications for both the buyer and the seller. If the seller is to remain liable on the obligations, then some form of security or indemnification from the buyer is appropriate to protect the seller. If the consent can be unilaterally withheld by the other party, then such other party has the opportunity to renegotiate the agreement. For instance, if the agreement is a lease and the rent is below market, the lessor may seek to increase the rent. If the lease expires within a short period of time, the lessor may seek an extension. Well-drafted agreements may also require that a consent of the transaction is a sale of stock. Often, agreements state that a change of control (more than a certain percentage of the stock ownership is sold) will be deemed to require a consent.

Depending upon the nature of the seller's business, the failure to obtain consents may be a deal-breaker. If the buyer is purchasing certain locations and wishes to assume favorable financing or have certain contracts for goods and/or services remain in place, consents become a critical path to the seller being able to deliver and transfer the assets. The buyer and the seller must determine early which agreements require consents, which consents are deal-breakers, which third parties have reason not to consent, what inducements might be necessary to obtain such consents, and who will bear the cost of such inducements.

In addition, there are a number of governmental consents that may be required in a sale transaction. The Hart-Scott-Rodino Antitrust Improvements Act of 1976 and the rules thereunder establish several standards that define mergers and acquisitions that must be reported prior to consummation. Securities laws, both state and federal, may require filings. With certain exceptions, the transfer of a substantial portion of the assets of a business will trigger the so-called bulk sales law of the Uniform Commercial Code. In addition, in regulated industries, permits and/or licenses must be issued or transferred.

EMPLOYEE MATTERS

Perhaps no other subject causes as much concern for a buyer than the issue of general employee matters. This concern is heightened if, in connection with the transaction or after the transaction is closed, some employees of the seller will be terminated.

If terminations are planned, a close look at the seller's severance policy and the policies enunciated in its employee manual must be understood. In addition, the buyer must explore what termination packages have been previously given to former employees of the seller. If these packages exceed the stated severance policies of the seller, then these packages, and not the stated policies, become the applicable policies. Will the seller terminate its employees, pay accrued vacation and sick time and accrued renumeration, and then have the buyer rehire the employees? Or will the buyer assume the employment obligations of all of the seller's employees (as is the case in a stock transaction)? The party assuming the obligations must have a clear understanding of the extent of such liabilities.

The history of claims against the seller for discrimination (age, gender) or sexual harassment should be carefully reviewed. Are all these claims resolved? Who will bear the risk of such claims from recently terminated employees of the seller? Will employees who are terminated after the transaction is consummated bring such claims against the buyer? Is there a company-wide program in place that allows the reporting of sexual harassment claims in a protected manner?

Another issue that should be of concern is the job classifications of the seller's employees. Are employees who should be classified as hourly (and therefore entitled to overtime pay) improperly classified as salaried employees? In recent years, the U.S. Department of Labor has targeted several companies that have improperly docked salaried employees for absence from the office, thereby classifying the entire group of employees in that job description as hourly. In such a case, the company then retroactively owes overtime wages as well as fines to such employees.

Some companies have several people on their payroll who are compensated as independent contractors (without benefits and withholding deductions). The buyer should independently assess whether those people are truly independent contractors or should be treated as employees. If the buyer is not careful and raises this issue, it may be liable for assessments that are made after the closing.

Another concern of a buyer is that the employees of the seller not be engaged in any form of illegal payment scheme. Does the seller have a stated corporate code of ethics in place prohibiting the making or acceptance of payments? Is there an annual questionnaire and reporting system in place requiring key employees to affirm that no such payments are being made? Is there a mechanism in place for employees to report their knowledge of violations in a manner that does not threaten their employment?

Compliance with the Worker Adjustment Restraining Notification Act, which prohibits an employer from a plant closing or mass layoff before giving 60 days written notice to employees, must be addressed. Employers subject to the act are those employing 100 or more people who, in the aggregate, work 4,000 hours per week, exclusive of overtime. The law requires the seller to give notice until a sale is completed, and the buyer bears the responsibility of closing and layoffs thereafter. If the employer fails to afford employees the notice, they may bring a suit to recover lost wages and benefits for the notice period.

A final concern is when a buyer is purchasing a unionized company. The buyer must decide whether:

1. To recognize and bargain with the union, but not agree to assume the Seller's Collective Bargaining Agreement (CBA);
2. Recognize the union and assume the Seller's CBA; or
3. Refuse to assume any obligations under the Seller's CBA and not recognize or bargain with the union.

As you have seen, these employee issues can be thorny and costly to the buyer if not explored and dealt with prior to the closing.

ENVIRONMENTAL ISSUES

Federal, state, and local environmental laws and regulations can have a material adverse impact on a business and its owner. Such costs include potential hazardous waste liability to third parties, assessment and cleanup requirements, or compliance with permits or orders. These risks must be identified and evaluated during the due diligence investigation.

The buyer must investigate current and past operations, as well as the real estate, to assess existing or potential liabilities and their costs, then allocate the risk and determine a value of the business in light of the environmental matters.

The environmental statutes include "superfund" laws, hazardous waste management laws, and laws regulating air and water emissions. Other acts governing the protection of wetlands and storage tanks should be reviewed. Liability under such statutes and regulations is expansive. Several liabilities are strictly enforced, without regard to fault. In addition, liability is often joint and several, meaning that each entity that may be liable for cleanup can be held liable for the entire cost.

It is the task of the buyer to make certain that the transaction documents provide that the buyer will assume only those environmental liabilities specifically identified. In certain circumstances, successor corporations have been held liable even in the context of an asset sale under the theory that the buyer's operations were a mere continuation of the seller's business. Additionally, the parent corporation and, in some cases stockholders, have also been held liable.

The buyer must also evaluate the impact of hazardous waste management statutes on the seller's business. These statutes govern the handling, storage, treatment, and disposal of hazardous waste. Permits and licenses are required for such activities. The buyer must be sure that permits can be transferred and whether notices of violation or noncompliance have been issued in the past. The seller's operation must also comply with air and water quality laws, which govern the emission or discharge of contaminants.

The due diligence investigation evaluates the environmental risks and liabilities. The buyer will surely require that the seller either take necessary corrective action or pay for such remediation. While the seller may indemnify the buyer, the buyer may insist on security or an escrow to fund the action. In the end, the buyer must make an overall determination of the environmental risks, and provide for the payment of all necessary and foreseeable corrective actions.

EMPLOYEE BENEFITS

Because not all employee benefits liabilities are shown on the financial statements of a seller, the employee benefit plans merit special scrutiny. There are three basic types of plans: tax-qualified retirement, welfare benefit, and nonqualified deferred compensation.

Tax-Qualified Retirement Plans

Tax-qualified retirement benefit plans generally provide retirement benefits to a broad group of employees. These plans are heavily regulated and may entail substantial liabilities. Types of such plans include defined benefit pension plans and defined contribution retirement plans. A deferred benefit plan promises a specific level of income to employees upon retirement. The sponsor must comply with a myriad of complicated legal requirements, including specific funding requirements of past and future benefit plans. The failure to meet these requirements can result in significant liabilities to the business, which can become a potential source of liability for the buyer.

Specifically, the buyer must determine the existence, type and size of any liability. Such liabilities include:

The current year's minimum funding liabilities.

Past-due plan funding liabilities for prior year.

Excise taxes for past due funding liabilities.

Premiums due to the Pension Benefit Guaranty Corporation, a federally chartered corporation that insures some benefits.

Funding liabilities for terminating the defined benefit plan.

A defined contribution retirement plan provides benefits based on the amounts that accumulate for participants in their accounts. Participants in such plans bear the risk of the plan investments. Therefore, the manner of assessing liabilities in such a plan is simpler than that of defined benefit plans. Often the business is not bound to make future contributions, but the seller may have accrued a liability for current or past-due amounts.

In the case of both defined benefit and defined contribution plans, the sponsor must take special care to preserve a retirement plan's tax qualification. Failure to comply with applicable tax laws can result in a tax disqualification that has the risk of producing liability of the plan sponsor, both to the IRS or to the employees. An examination of the plan's assets can reveal issues of actual or potential liabilities. In particular, the liquidity of assets should be examined. In addition, speculative plan investments or investments heavily weighted toward one type of security may give rise to employee claims of breach of the fiduciary duties of prudence and diversification.

Welfare Benefit Plans

Welfare benefit plans provide fringe benefits to employees, including group life insurance, medical benefits, group accident and disability insurance, and severance. These plans are funded either by a third-party insurer, the sponsor under a self-insurance program, or a combination thereof. In particular, the application of COBRA, for example, can result in liability to the employee if the group medical insurance coverage has lapsed during the employee's COBRA period. Failure to comply can result in tax exposure to the employer, and the employer may be liable for the payment of medical benefits. Of particular concern are retiree medical and other benefits, which now must be accounted for by current and future liabilities.

Nonqualified Deferred Benefit Plans

Such plans include a number of different contracts and arrangements designed primarily for senior executives. Often a company will grant stock options, phantom stock, stock appreciation rights, or deferred compensation agreements to management. Often, such benefits must be funded and/or paid upon the sale of the company.

In deciding which benefits to provide seller's employees, the buyer must decide whether to assume seller's plans or establish its own. In either case, care must be taken to retain the tax qualification of any qualified retirement plan.

REAL ESTATE

An acquisition that involves the purchase or long-term lease of real estate raises a number of questions that will impact the future use of the facility by the buyer. Specifically, the title to the property must be reviewed to determine any defects. Is title insurance available to protect the buyer from any issues? What easements or land use restrictions or other encumbrances are in the chain of title that may impact the type and extent of the use of the property?

In addition to title matters, the applicability of local zoning ordinances must be analyzed. The property may not comply with the current regulations, but be grandfathered and be a so-called prior existing, nonconforming use. This generally means that as long as the property is continuously used for such purpose, there is no problem. However, if the use lapses and such use is currently prohibited, the use cannot be reinstated. Simultaneously, the property may not conform to current height, dimensional and/or parking requests, but did so when built. Usually, the property may continue in its present state, as long as there is no further nonconformity (additions cannot be made, parking spaces cannot be eliminated, and so on) and the property remains in its current state. It is not uncommon for such regulation to provide that in the case of fire or other casualty, the grandfather status is lost and any rebuilding must be done in conformance with current bylaws. Finally, the local political environment must be checked to determine whether there is a building moratorium in place or threatened, or downzoning (more restrictive zoning) is on the agenda. Last, the environmental status of the property must be assessed.

In short, an experienced buyer determines any current restrictions, environmental, or legal issues with the property, and focuses on the flexibility it has to expand the facility or change its use, or both.

INTELLECTUAL PROPERTY

Many companies have significant intangible assets that comprise valuable intellectual property. These assets consist of patentable or copyrightable technology, trade secrets, trademarks, service marks, or trade names. Companies often are parties to agreements granting or receiving exclusive or nonexclusive rights to intellectual property, such as licensing, franchising, or distribution rights. A buyer must determine the scope and value of such rights. These rights can be determined only through a careful examination of the development history of the technology, the trail of legal ownership, the nature of the intellectual property, and an examination of the steps taken by the seller, if any, to preserve his property rights.

Trademarks and trade names are valuable for market goodwill. While registration is available under both state and federal statutes, registration is optional to achieving protection. Since trademark rights are created by its adoption and use, lack of registration is not a bar to enforcement. Where registration has been obtained, significant procedural and substantive advantages are gained. Federal registration carries with it presumptions of ownership and validity. Such registration also provides constructive nationwide notice to all later users of trademark. Federal law permits the recording of documents of transfer.

The buyer should review alleged dates of adoption of trademarks and the facts supporting the allegations. The buyer should also assure that the issued and pending registrations are in order. Special consideration should be given to trademark rights claimed under an exclusive license. Finally, if the seller is a licensor of a trademark, the buyer must determine whether the seller has undertaken a review of the goods and services sold under the trademark.

Copyright law provides the author of a copyrightable work with certain exclusive rights as to use, distribution, modification, display, and performance of the work. The buyer must determine whether the assets are the subject matter of the copyright law. The work must be examined to determine who owns the rights to the work and whether steps have been taken to preserve the rights. The buyer must determine who is the author of the original version of each work and the terms pursuant to which such contributions were made. The buyer then is ready to determine the original copyright owner of the work.

Patents are often a primary asset of the seller. They may cover key technology of the seller, or they may be licensed to third parties as a source of revenue. Patents are issued federally. The value of the patent is determined by its scope and possible challenges to its validity. The buyer should also review patents covering related technology and the status of pending application.

Trade secret protection is based on the notion of secrecy and breach of a confidential relationship. Trade secret law protects the owner from unauthorized use or disclosure. This protection extends to a very broad range of information. The major disadvantage to trade secret law is that, absent a breach, it does not protect against independent development or reverse engineering, nor does it provide the owner with a claim against a person who learned of the secret through accidental disclosure or someone else's wrongdoing.

The buyer should analyze carefully the safeguards practiced by the seller in regard to its trade secrets. Trade secret protection requires extensive and affirmative steps to maintain secrecy, including internal security measures; maintaining sensitive documents under lock and key; requiring key employees to sign secrecy and confidentiality agreements; and restricted access areas.

The buyer, in embarking on its review of intellectual property, should interview all key employees; obtain a listing of all of seller's files relating to intellectual property; conduct patent, trademark, and copyright searches of the registered property to verify ownership; and review all licenses. As noted earlier, agreements with employees as to the confidential information of the seller must also be reviewed. Finally, all claims made against or by the seller should be analyzed. Only then can a buyer understand these assets and the protections in place with respect to their use.

LITIGATION

The review of the seller's pending and past litigation log is a necessity. The buyer must determine which suits are covered by insurance and the amount of the deductible payable in each case.

The buyer must also review any judgments or decrees that apply to the future operations of the seller. Finally, all pending or threatened claims must be explored. Of particular focus for the buyer is whether there is any pattern to the suits or claims that raise questions about any aspect of the seller's business.

TAXES

The final topic to be explored is taxes. The buyer should have all recent tax returns reviewed to ascertain whether the seller is aggressively deducting certain expenditures that may be questionable. When were the last federal or state audits completed? What were the results? Did the seller take corrective action to eliminate any issues going forward? Are tax returns filed in all required jurisdictions? What previous years remain open for audit? The buyer must reach some level of comfort regarding these issues since tax treatment going forward is of primary concern to the buyer.

As you have seen, a multitude of legal issues may be identified as a result of the due diligence review. The buyer, working closely with his internal acquisition team and legal advisors, accountants, and insurance providers, must fully explore all identified issues. The goal of the buyer is to determine the financial cost to remedy any problems, which issues may be problematic to the future operations of the seller, and the extent of the risk in each case. Only then can the buyer determine the true value of the seller's assets and what measures must be taken to minimize any concerns.

CHAPTER
SEVENTEEN

Advisor
Engagement Letters

G. WILLIAM HUBBARD II
PARTNER
HINSHAW AND CULBERTSON

A buyer's or seller's advisors (business counsel, CPA, intermediary, financial advisor, valuation consultant, appraiser, environmental consultant, and others) help structure, negotiate, and close a deal. They usually do a great job and fully warrant their compensation. Most of these advisors should, generally, be retained by the buyer or seller through the use of an *engagement letter*. The following discussion may prove helpful in locating, retaining, and working with any advisor, particularly with regard to buying or selling a business.

Caution: Please seek specific advice from legal counsel; actual resolution of legal issues depends upon many factors including variations of facts and state, federal, and other laws. This chapter is not intended to provide legal advice but rather to provide insight into the issues involved, which may prove useful to the reader.

What is an advisor engagement letter?
A written agreement, usually in letter form, with someone outside of your business to provide you with specified services.

Is it necessary that the engagement be in writing?
Usually, although the longer you have worked with your advisor and the more you trust your advisor, the less necessary such a document becomes—until a problem develops.

When should I enter into an engagement letter?
Preferably at the outset of any engagement; it is important to know and agree upon the terms of the engagement before the services begin. Equally important is the process to be followed by each advisor and a clear understanding of how these processes may affect the timing and outcome of the deal. If the process is not specified in the engagement letter, and frequently it is not, it should be discussed and agreed upon.

For example, you, a seller, retain an intermediary to help sell your business. Suppose you have a bare-bones agreement that simply provides that the intermediary will be retained for a 12-month period, be paid an initial retainer of, say, $30,000 plus expenses against a commission based upon a modified Lehman formula; both parties will cooperate with one another in providing necessary information, and that the intermediary shall advise, and secure the approval of, the seller prior to contacting or negotiating with potential buyers. This would be a poor agreement. Among other major deficiencies, it neither provides a timetable for the intermediary's actions nor specifies what constitutes the selling price upon which a commission is to be based.

Comment: The Lehman formula for compensation of an intermediary is 5 percent of the first $1 million, 4 percent of the next $1 million, 3 percent of the next $1 million, 2 percent of the next $1 million, and 1 percent of all sums in excess of $4 million. Because this formula was developed many years ago, intermediaries now usually use some modified version resulting in a higher fee than a straight Lehman formula would provide.

In deciding to retain an advisor, or potential advisor, what information should be disclosed and when? And should there be a confidentiality agreement in place prior to disclosing any confidential information to the advisor?
When deciding to buy or sell a business, confidentiality is always important. Confidentiality agreements with prospective or existing advisors should be considered.

Attorneys are bound by the attorney-client privilege and, generally, cannot disclose confidences, therefore no confidentiality agreement is usually necessary (although from time to time, attorneys or their employees either slip and disclose information about a prospective deal that should have remained confidential or, unfortunately, use such information for their own benefit in violation of their duty to their clients and in violation of the law—for which they can be held liable).

Intermediaries depend, for the most part, upon referrals from others. To improperly disclose confidential information would quickly prove their undoing. This does not mean that intermediaries will necessarily keep all information confidential, even with a signed confidentiality agreement. If they frequently work in a particular industry and know many of the players, it may be unrealistic to expect that the existence of a prospective seller or purchaser will be kept confidential, particularly where the company or intermediary firm has a high profile (and particularly if the intermediary fails to land the assignment). If a seller or buyer feels that the disclosure of information by the intermediary or other advisor would be harmful to his or her interests, then a confidentiality agreement with such advisor should be used.

Other advisors. Similar considerations should be given to agreements with other advisors.

What does a confidentiality agreement contain, and when should it be entered into?

Generally, a confidential information agreement should provide:

- A definition of what constitutes confidential information;
- That no confidential information or trade secret provided by the seller (or buyer) may be disclosed to a third party unless it is already in the public domain through no fault of the advisor; and
- For enforcement through the remedy of specific performance (and damages); and
- For return of all such confidential information (written, computer data, and all other forms in which it is stored) upon termination of the relationship or completion of the project.

A confidentiality agreement could require that the intermediary cause all of his, her, or its employees prior to obtaining such information to execute a similar confidentiality agreement obligating themselves, personally, to such confidentiality.

A confidentiality agreement should be entered into at the outset of the relationship or as soon thereafter as practicable. In lieu of a separate confidentiality agreement, a confidentiality provision contained in the engagement letter could suffice.

Comment: While many states have a statute that defines a trade secret and provides penalties for improper disclosure of trade secrets, the parties will want to define for themselves what constitutes confidential information. When providing confidential documents to a third party, such documents should be stamped CONFIDENTIAL.

Should I have counsel review or draft each agreement?

Maybe. It is a question of cost and benefits balanced against time involved and risks. The more dollars involved and the more a particular advisor could help or hurt you, and the less trust there is in the person or company, the more it makes sense to use a written agreement reviewed by counsel. If your advisor presents an agreement, you can be assured that it was written with that advisor's interests in mind.

What, then, should be included in an advisor engagement agreement?

While the content of an advisor engagement agreement depends upon the particular advisor, the length and scope of the relationship, and many other factors, it should, at least, address the following points:

- The services to be performed: What, specifically, is going to be done.
- Who is going to perform the services: Regardless of the size of the advisory firm, you should specify which persons are going to perform the services. While most advisory firms are sensitive to their client's expressed wishes as to who will handle an engagement, it can certainly become a problem if, say, Advisory Partner A is retained, but not specified in the agreement. Suddenly, you may find yourself dealing with Associate B whom you have never met, talked to, or been advised of, and Associate B now becomes the principal contact at the advisory firm. Partner A no longer appears to be involved, and you are not happy about it; what do you do? And what happens if Partner A leaves the firm and your agreement does not permit you to terminate the advisory firm? You may not be happy, or even comfortable with, any other person who may be assigned to your deal; should you and can you terminate the relationship? At what cost?
- When the services are to be performed: Be it a detailed time line or a simple written description with a clear understanding between the parties, each party needs to know when the services are to commence and terminate. Suppose a Phase I environmental audit of the seller's property is needed, and a Phase II is required if the Phase I shows environmental problems (or the seller knows it is going to need one). The valuation, and therefore pricing of the company, is dependent upon such audits and their results (and possible remediation). Therefore, a clearly written agreement that includes performance and completion dates is appropriate. In contrast, such written detail might not be necessary if the seller's CPA firm has just completed its annual audit report, the seller and CPA have a close business and personal relationship, and each is aware of and responsive to the

other's needs and wishes. This failure to provide a specific written time line does not eliminate the need for initial and continued dialogue among the CPA, principal, and any other advisor who may be affected by, or affect, the CPA and his or her various functions.

- With whom, and under what conditions, should the principal and advisor communicate with each other: Because of the sensitivity of disclosures about a potential purchase or sale, it should be clearly understood, and put in writing if desired, how communications are going to be handled. Some sellers may, at least in the initial stages, want no employee, regardless of her or his position, to be aware of the possibility that the company may be sold. If this is the case, such details as to what messages or names of companies may be left with a receptionist, whether any documents are to be mailed to the seller and how they are to be addressed, and what may be discussed with other employees of the seller may all be critical. Even disclosure of the decision to buy or sell a company can have profound effects on the company's future: Key employees may fear for their jobs or look for others; customers may be concerned about the continued viability of the company and be ripe for moving their accounts to competitors; competitors, when they learn of the prospective sale, will use that fact as an additional reason for customers to change their relationship; suppliers may change their credit, pricing, delivery, or other terms; and a lender, particularly if the company has had problems, may alter its position on credit lines to the seller.

- Where and under what conditions are the services to be performed: If the intermediary is to properly perform his or her services, he or she is going to need a thorough understanding of a seller's business. He or she will want to visit the seller's business, probably on several occasions during operating hours, and have an opportunity to talk with some of the key employees. An appraiser will need to view any property being appraised, probably during business hours; and, eventually, a prospective buyer will need to inspect the business and its records. Both the advisor and principal must consider where, and under what conditions, such services may and should be performed; this will affect the timing of the deal. If a prospective buyer is told that he or she may not visit the seller's business until there is a letter of intent agreed upon, the intermediary may determine that this fact will severely limit its pool of potential buyers at a price acceptable to the seller. If so, the intermediary may not be able to satisfactorily perform his or her services and may conclude that he or she does not want the engagement.

- What coordination and discussions are there to be with other advisors: Who the advisor communicates with, and when, is important. Likewise, what coordination and discussion there is among advisors, what authority such advisors have, and what instructions such advisors should take from one or more of the other advisors are significant as well. In some situations, (although I would say infrequently) the seller may want to handle, at least in the early stages, all discussions him- or herself, and not have his or her attorney, CPA, or intermediary talking with the appraisers, financial consultants, or each other, particularly if the seller is unsure as to whether the company is really to be sold. No seller should adopt this strategy without preliminary discussions with his or her primary advisors; the benefits to be gained from such consultations far exceed the fees one will pay.

- How are the services going to be performed: All other special directions or agreements about how the services are to be performed should be specified.
- Right to terminate the services: The terms under which a seller can terminate the advisor's services should be agreed upon.

Should all, or most of, the advisors talk to, or be made aware of, the other advisors?

Yes, in my judgment. A buyer or seller of a company should ensure that appropriate coordinations among its advisors are made at the outset of the process and continue through the close of a deal and thereafter. Frequently, particularly where there is a first-time buyer or seller, a team approach is either not adopted or adopted too late. Sellers and buyers should *insist* that a team approach be followed from the outset of an engagement, and be embodied in both the agreement and the actions of all concerned with a transaction; the leader of this team needs to be specified.

Comment: Intermediaries usually will want to control most dealings with the seller or buyer until there is a letter of intent (or sometimes draft of a contract). Buyers and sellers will want to keep their counsel, CPA, and others (appraisers) from taking actions that would run up fees until it is known there is a deal—unless they feel such involvement is necessary. CPAs and attorneys will frequently limit their roles to their perceived roles (by the buyer, seller, or intermediary), instead of being part of an interactive process through which their general and specific knowledge and experience can provide more meaningful assistance to their client. *None of these approaches should be adopted unless it is as a result of the buyer's or seller's strategic decision, recognizing that a team approach is likely to be most effective and well worth the money.*

In my estimation, the client's principal advisor(s) should play an integral part in the selection of the intermediary. There should be one meeting prior to the engagement of the intermediary (to cover the specific terms of the engagement and those topics addressed previously). Subsequently, a meeting should be held after the engagement to develop a general time line, reach agreement upon and delegate various specific responsibilities, and determine the scheme by which to make the appropriate coordinations. Sometimes, because business intermediaries are concerned (many times rightly so) that involvement of anyone other than their prospective client may hurt their own interests or "screw up" a prospective deal, counsel and CPAs are brought in too late in the process of buying or selling. They should be brought in at the outset.

If the seller or buyer's business counsel or CPA is not involved in the screening of an intermediary, the intermediary may want to suggest that a joint meeting with the seller's or buyer's counsel be arranged to finalize the agreement. If it is the intermediary who is arranging the meeting with the principal and counsel, it is likely that the personal interaction at the meeting is going to result in both an engagement letter for the intermediary and the beginning of a team approach, which will assist the deal. Experienced advisors, intermediaries, attorneys, CPAs, financial advisors, appraisers, and others will be sensitive to most of these issues and will usually adopt some variation on the team approach based upon their own personal styles and judgments.

What other points, in general, do I need to be concerned about when dealing with engagement letters?
Consciously recognize, and then remember throughout the course of the negotiations to buy or sell a company, the various interests of all of your advisors apart from your own.

> *CPA:* Wants you as an ongoing client; and if you are a seller, will not want to lose your business; or, if you have decided to sell, may want to be the CPA for the buyer (which frequently happens). As a result, even though this person or firm may have been your friend and advisor for many years, divided loyalties, and as a result, impaired judgment as to your interests, may result.
>
> *Intermediary:* In midsized deals, the typical intermediary does not average much above two transactions per year. Thus, he or she wants to see the deal close, works toward that end, does not want protracted negotiations, and wants to keep the momentum of a deal until closing. While you may have employed the intermediary, the ultimate results (such as who takes a hit on an increase or decrease in price, who bears responsibility for various liabilities post closing, and the like) can lose their significance to the intermediary provided that such points are unlikely to bring the intermediary into litigation, affect his or her reputation, or crater the deal. Most variations on the Lehman formula (5 percent on the first $1 million, 4 percent on the next $1 million, 3 percent on the next $1 million, 2 percent on the next $1 million, and 1 percent on all sales proceeds in excess of $4 million) affect the intermediary the least for the last dollar obtained through negotiations. In some situations, the intermediary will suggest picking a benchmark price (generally based upon the intermediary's valuation) and then

use some sort of reverse Lehman (1 percent, 2 percent, 3 percent, 4 percent, 5 percent or some other variation) for a sales price in excess of the benchmark price.

FINAL DUE DILIGENCE BEFORE SIGNING AN ENGAGEMENT LETTER

Buyers and sellers should check the references of the advisor, be familiar and comfortable with the advisor and his or her abilities, style, and willingness to work with other advisors, and ensure that any advisor is properly licensed in the states in which he or she is doing business that may affect the transaction. For example, on January 1, 1996, a statute went into effect in Illinois requiring that any intermediary involved in a transaction where it, the buyer or seller is located in Illinois, be licensed under the Illinois Business Broker Act unless an exemption from the act applies. In general, banks and those licensed to sell securities are exempted. This act requires certain disclosures about the broker, filing with the Illinois Securities Department (which administers the act), and, most significantly, provides that any contract with any intermediary who violates any part of the act or the rules thereunder is void; felony criminal penalties apply for violations of the act. Since this statute, and others like it, will limit the activities of intermediaries not licensed in Illinois in their ability to deal with Illinois buyers or sellers, and may encourage other states to enact similarly stringent litigation, licensure in the various states should be discussed and a representation as to such licenses made in the agreement.

If the advisor's abilities, integrity, or likely performance are a concern to the buyer or seller, counsel should investigate whether there is outstanding litigation that involves the advisor. A woman, said to be the wealthiest (mostly self-made) in the United States in the mid-1800s, was reported not to have done business with someone until she had spoken to that person's enemies. Consider it.

What specifics should I know about engagement letters?
They can range from one paragraph to many pages depending upon the principal, advisor, services to be performed, style of the parties, and counsel involved. A review by and input received from counsel, prior to signing, is preferable. Sellers and buyers should establish general budgets for their various advisors. These can and do vary substantially, because each deal is unique.

What additional comments about particular advisor engagement letters do you have?

Intermediaries.   A typical agreement (generally provided by the intermediary for negotiation and revision) may include the following:

1. Agreement to render services as corporate finance consultant, advisor, and investment banker; develop a target list of buyers; dissemination of agreed materials; preparation of book (placement memorandum) on seller (business, financial statements, and so on); screen and prioritize buyers; develop negotiating strategies; coordinate actions with seller's other advisors; approach buyers; arrange and coordinate meetings; negotiate agreement with counsel's assistance; coordinate due diligence; coordinate closing; and obtain the return of documents distributed to prospective buyers.

   Comment: This paragraph may preclude you from retaining your CPA for similar purposes because it may give sole responsibility to the intermediary.

2. Agreement to pay nonrefundable retainer (lump sum or monthly) plus expenses as preapproved above a certain dollar level.

   Comment: The total retainer may be up to 10 percent of the expected compensation, with a floor, dependent upon the intermediary and size of deal, between $7,500 and $35,000. You need to determine what expenses are reasonable and will be approved above a predetermined dollar amount.

3. One-year term on an exclusive basis.

   Comment: You need to determine an appropriate term; one year is generally reasonable with a reputable intermediary. While each intermediary is likely to want, and many require, an exclusive basis, it may be possible to negotiate an agreement for purposes of sale to one or more specific buyers with whom such intermediary has existing relationships.

4. Compensation formula as follows: A Lehman formula, with a minimum selling or buying commission, or some variation (such as a double Lehman—5 percent on the first $2 million of sales price, 4 percent on the next $2 million, and so on; or 5 percent on the first $2 million, 4 percent on the next million, and so on) usually appears. Other sample formulas are: 5 percent on the first $5 million, 2.5 percent on the next $5 million and 1 percent in excess of $10 million; 2.5 percent on the first $10 million and 1 percent thereafter; and 5 percent on the first $2 million, 4 percent on the next $1 million, 3 percent on the next, and so on.

   Comment: The fee established should fairly compensate the intermediary for his or her services. While the fees may, for the first-timer, appear large, the services provided by a good intermediary are worth every penny. The focus by the party paying the commission should be upon what constitutes the sales price—the basis for the compensation to be paid. This may include all proceeds received by the company (and stockholders—including all contingent and installment payments and moneys loaned or guaranteed), fair value of leased interests, stock, notes, cash, and agreements not to compete. It will also include the value of liabilities assumed, including long-term debt other than capital leases, short-term debt not related to seasonal working capital financing, tax liabilities associated with operations prior to closing, and balance sheet deferral income tax liability to be assumed or paid by buyer. The definition of sales price will usually be negotiated. The seller (or buyer), or his or her CPA, should work through a sample calculation of the sales price and compensation payable before the intermediary agreement is signed based upon the seller's existing balance sheet and likely terms of sale; a surprise and possible problem at closing between the seller and intermediary should be prevented.

Frequently the seller, if an individual, stays on as a consultant or otherwise for one or more years for additional compensation. The engagement letter should specify whether any part of this compensation is included in the definition of sales price.

5. Indemnification provision. Typically, there will be a provision indemnifying the intermediary from any untrue statement of material fact (or failure to provide material facts) for information provided by the seller or any agent thereof and addressing how any related suit(s) will be defended and who will bear the related costs.

   Comment: Such a provision is reasonable provided that the indemnification is attributable to solely the acts of the seller, or prorated based upon fault.

6. Confidentiality provision. Usually, there is no provision in an engagement letter about what can or cannot be said about a deal (whether by principal or intermediary) after it is done or if it falls apart. As a minimum, there should be a provision requiring the intermediary to obtain a signed confidentiality agreement (in form suitable to seller) from prospective buyers if this issue is important to seller.

   Comment: The parties may wish to include a provision about what the advisor can disclose, and to whom, after a deal closes or if it falls apart. Tombstone announcements are important to intermediaries as a record of their achievements and for their use in obtaining new clients. These frequently include a disclosure of the price at which a company was bought or sold. Buyers and sellers, however, may not want disclosure of the sale or the price unless it is legally mandated (for example, will be disclosed anyway in SEC filings or annual reports) or they otherwise feel that it would serve their strategic interests. The appropriateness and timing of any such disclosures should be agreed upon.

7. Tail provision. There will frequently be a provision that requires payment of the intermediary in the event of a sale to any party identified by the intermediary within a period of one to two years after termination of the agreement.

Comment: Such a provision, if reasonable in length, seems fair and appropriate. Thought needs to be given whether to limit the compensation to potential purchasers specifically identified in writing to seller prior to the expiration of the term.

8. Boilerplate language. Provisions dealing with what constitutes the entire agreement, the choice of law to apply, mediation, arbitration, or litigation (if a dispute occurs), and the location thereof, will be added.

Comment: While these paragraphs in the agreement may seem perfunctory and not worth hassling over, they can make an important difference in the event of a dispute and should be thought through. Recommendation: mediation.

9. Other possible provisions. Standards, procedures, management representations, client assistance, billing and timing.

Attorney

1. Scope of work. Most attorney engagement letters are broad in scope.

Comment: If the counsel is new, or newly engaged to handle the particular transaction, the specific nature of the representation should be defined. Coordination among all advisors is important even if not part of any engagement letter.

2. Compensation. Most attorneys charge on an hourly basis for their services in connection with the purchase or sale of a business.

Comment: The attorney's hourly compensation should not be the deciding factor as to whether to retain a specific counsel; rather, the ability of the counsel to effectively handle the particular transaction is paramount. Consider monthly, or more frequent, statements with detailed time entries if there is concern over the total fees. If a flat fee is agreed upon, how much can this be in the buyer's or seller's best interest? The less time and thought counsel spends on the deal, the more money he or she receives per hour worked.

Environmental Consultants.

Most engagement letters will provide for a fixed rate for a Phase I audit. A Phase II audit will frequently result in further testing where environmental problems are known to exist or are discovered. The integrity of the consultant is important; check references. The consultant's recognition as qualified by any lenders (or prospective buyers) is important; if not prequalified, a lender or buyer may later require that another expert be used.

Cautions

1. Both buyer and seller should contract with the environmental consultant. If the seller has contracted with an environmental consultant and provides the results to the buyer, the buyer should

contract as well with such consultant for the same results in order to ensure privity of contract. This becomes important if the environmental consultant's conclusions are wrong.

2. Prior to the environmental consultant examining the property, the seller's attorney should advise the consultant of exactly what language needs to be used in the consultant's conclusions in his or her report, which will be based upon the applicable state statutes. Prior to the environmental consultant's issuance of a report, a draft should be submitted to seller for review. Seller's counsel will then have an opportunity to deal with any problems, and perhaps resolve them, prior to issuance of a report, which would be discoverable in any litigation.

Comment: Sellers, if they know or strongly suspect that their property is contaminated, should consider having their attorneys contract for an environmental analysis of the property so that any results may be cloaked in the attorney-client privilege. I am not suggesting that sellers ever not disclose to buyers environmental problems (in fact, disclosure is mandatory); rather, if one parcel is contaminated, and therefore may not be part of any sale (or the seller retains title to that parcel, leases it to the buyer and agrees to remediate, defend, and hold buyer harmless if the government or any contiguous property owner obtains an order requiring remediation or damages), a report obtained through counsel may help to disclose to the seller the extent of a problem, without jeopardizing immediate governmental action.

3. Both buyer and seller should be added as additional insureds to the environmental consultant's malpractice insurance policy. Most malpractice policies expire within one year and are issued on a claims-made basis. If the consultant goes out of business, there will be no insurance. A reliable and financially stable consultant should be used, and, if there is any question about the results, a second consultant may be appropriate.

Appraisers.   As with environmental experts, any buyer, financial institution, or investor who may be called upon to rely on any appraisal, will need to know that the appraiser is qualified; local banks should be queried to determined whether the particular appraiser is on its approved list.

The standard for the appraisal (dependent upon type) should be determined, and the report should state whether it is on a going concern, ordinary course of business, liquidation, or other basis.

Financial Advisors.   A financial advisor should be considered by a seller for the purpose of enabling the seller to help determine an appropriate selling price. In the case of a buyer, a financial advisor can be invaluable to ensure that the buyer is not overpaying for the business. These agreements are likely to be either on a flat-fee or hourly basis, depending upon who is retained to perform the services. Business valuations may provide a range of the value of the business based upon whether the buyer is an entrepreneur, financial buyer, or strategic buyer. Fairness opinions as to price may be required to help the seller or buyer make its decision and to help insulate the board of directors from liability.

Technical Appraisers. Technical appraisers usually are retained to perform special valuations and, accordingly, special expertise is needed. Their qualifications must be established, and the assumptions to be used must be specified and agreed upon.

Bankers. While generally not part of the team involved in the sale (although they may well be part of the purchase), experienced bankers with a commercial lending background can prove invaluable as advisors. Use them as an informal resource.

Investment Bankers. Most investment banking firms act as intermediaries and may provide valuation and financial advisory services. In addition, investment banking firms may also help an owner decide whether to cash out by taking a company public, serve as a source for venture capital financing or recapitalizations, or be able to arrange a merger.

General. Have all materials returned, and specify in the engagement letter who owns all of the advisors' work product. Advisors will want to retain ownership. Sellers and buyers, because they are footing the bill, will want, if not demand, ownership.

Final Note. Engagement letters, like all other agreements, are simply a memorial in writing of the terms to which each party has agreed. Things change; assumptions as to how much time is required, what complexity and skill are involved, and the scope of what is or needs to be done prove wrong. What the engagement letter calls for can be interpreted differently by each party regardless of the labor expended in attempting to reach a comprehensive engagement letter. Each of these can, and occasionally does, result in a disagreement as to the payment of fees. As with most other disputes, the earlier a potential problem is recognized, brought to the attention of the other side, discussed and a solution reached, the more likely it is that the interpersonal relationships will be kept intact; no litigation will ensue, and the deal will successfully close. Should a dispute arise, and prior to seriously contemplating mediation, arbitration, or litigation, I suggest sitting down face to face. Consider addressing what went right, the areas of agreement and satisfaction, and then address, with due regard to each other's frame of reference, the concerns or problems of each and make an honest attempt to resolve the differences. Unless there was outright fraud, or conduct was clearly willful, the two principals involved should first make every effort to resolve any differences that exist. To leave the matter to others to work out—be they subordinates, attorneys, arbitrators, a judge, or a jury—will usually not be worth either the time, emotional capital, opportunity cost, or dollars that are involved. Trust needs to be an important part of the relationship between each of the various advisors and the principal.

Although you may have built a business or are the principal buying a business and believe yourself to be objective with others, this is usually not the case with regard to your own business. Listen to your advisors' counsel concerning appropriate courses of action and give serious consideration *prior* to a decision and action.

Letters of Intent and Purchase and Sale Agreements

G. WILLIAM HUBBARD II
PARTNER
HINSHAW AND CULBERTSON

For the seller, the company has now been shown for sale to one or more buyers; for the buyer, there is sufficient interest to warrant serious negotiations to acquire the company. A letter of intent now may be appropriate, but maybe not; it depends upon the deal. However, prior to negotiating a letter of intent, and prior to disclosure of any significant information to a proposed buyer, there should be, most of the time, a signed confidentiality agreement between the parties (refer to the preceding chapter for a brief discussion of the various points to be covered).

Caution: Please seek specific advice from legal counsel; actual resolution of legal issues depends upon many factors including variations of facts, and state, federal, and other laws. This chapter is not intended to provide legal advice but rather to provide insight into the issues involved, which may prove useful to the reader.

What are letters of intent?

Letters of intent (sometimes referred to as agreements in principle) are letters, signed by prospective buyers and sellers, containing an expression of intent to consummate a purchase and sale of a business under certain terms and conditions. While letters of intent are generally nonbinding, pending a formal written agreement of sale, they can be binding. If so, numerous problems may arise in the event that one or both parties are unwilling to proceed on the terms contained within such letter.

Comment—International Agreements: In common law countries, while each party's good faith is deemed part of the agreement, negotiations leading up to an agreement rarely create significant legal obligations. In most of the rest of the world ("civil code" countries), the parties' negotiations must be done in good faith, and litigation can, and frequently does, ensue for breach of good faith during the negotiation stage and prior to any signed agreement.

How are letters of intent used?

The seller (either orally or in the term sheet or book provided to one or more prospective buyers) will usually state the basic terms under which the business may be purchased: all cash or cash and earn-out, asset deal or stock deal, and so on. The buyer, having considered the seller's preferences, must then decide under what terms an offer should be made and how the offer is presented.

What points need to be considered before determining whether to use a letter of intent?

- Should the proposed terms be determined independent of the intermediary, and then presented verbally to the intermediary, who will then present the terms verbally to the seller?
- Should the buyer develop a written list of deal points, give these to the intermediary, and let the intermediary negotiate the deal?
- Should the buyer and seller meet directly? If so, should this be after the buyer meets with the intermediary to discuss, in depth, what thoughts the intermediary has about terms that the seller may find acceptable? If so, who should be present? Buyer and seller? Buyer, seller, and intermediary? Buyer, seller, and counsel? Buyer, seller, counsel, and intermediary? Any other financial advisors?
- Most intermediaries are likely to counsel that the ball be left in their court to structure meetings and determine how the negotiations will be conducted and how the various points are raised—that is what they get paid to do. While this approach frequently is, and should be, followed, the dynamics must be assessed by the buyer and seller, because each decision may affect the ultimate outcome.

- Intermediaries may have a particular reputation and be very effective generally, but the personality of one or more of the players may suggest face-to-face meetings and negotiations.
- There may be one or more sensitive business or legal issues that should be addressed at the outset (or at the conclusion) by the principals directly, or the deal is likely to be jeopardized.
- Amount to be paid, form, and timing of payment, and whether there will be a noncompete, consulting, or employment agreements, while among the most important terms, do not mean that a deal will close if these points are tentatively agreed upon. Labor issues, tax structure, environmental problems, pension concerns, intellectual property rights and their relative strengths are but a few of the areas that can torpedo a deal. Thus, a deal term sheet containing all the material terms that a buyer or seller is looking for (his or her "dream" sheet) is a useful starting point. This list will then go back and forth (be it directly, through counsel, or through intermediary) until each side feels that all the important terms have been covered.

Remember that letters going each way, regardless of whether they are direct or through an intermediary or verbal understandings, can be a basis for one side alleging that an agreement has been reached (recall the Pennzoil case and the billions of dollars at stake over whether there had been a binding agreement).

Though the list may appear endless for the various concerns, which may lend themselves to different processes for negotiating the deal, eventually there must be an agreement in principle. Letters of intent can be most useful. (See Appendix 18.1 for various points to be considered prior to determining the structure of a deal.)

What is the next step after the basics of a deal appear favorable to determine whether a letter of intent might be appropriate?
Consider the following alternative courses of action and the likely effect of each on the momentum of the deal:

- A short deal sheet signed by no one—or a longer one signed by no one?
- A short letter of intent covering price, assets to be sold, and the basics of the deal?
- Should there be a document that negotiates the parties safely through most of the mines that will be encountered when counsel are drafting and negotiating the purchase and sale agreement?
- Should the parties have their counsel go directly to the purchase and sale agreement and forgo any other document?

There is no one right answer or process that will fit most deals. If the parties want to try to nail down most of the points prior to negotiating the specifics of a draft contract, then a somewhat lengthy letter of intent—say five to eight pages—may be the right approach. With a good intermediary, an educated buyer and seller, experienced business counsel, and thorough coordination with any financial advisors and CPAs, the list of deal points, variations on structure, tax implications, and sensitive business and legal issues should be summarized, quantified as to their economic effects on the deal, laid on the table, and negotiated. To intentionally piecemeal various deal points—adding or changing as the process winds along—is sometimes economically advantageous for one side or the other, but it often smacks of incompetence or deceit, and frequently can and does crater a deal. (This is not to say that terms do not often change, even after a letter of intent. But to get as many points on the table and address them candidly increases the likelihood that the deal will close.)

Why use letters of intent/agreements/lawyers/CPAs? Why not just shake hands and let the deal be done?

You may have done, read about, or heard about handshake deals, but they depend upon one critical factor—trust. Trust, or lack of it, and its cultural effects upon each deal, have a profound effect upon how and why each deal either closes or blows up, as well as the relative success of the company for the period following closing. To paraphrase Francis Fukuyama in his recent significant work entitled, *TRUST* (Free Press, 1995),

> Trust depends upon one's culture, which in turn is dependent upon the shared ethical norms of communities by whom one is influenced. ". . . [P]eople who do not trust one another will end up cooperating only under a system of formal rules and regulations, which have to be negotiated, agreed to, litigated, and enforced, sometimes by coercive means." This legal apparatus, serving as a substitute for trust, entails what economists call "transaction costs". . . . Those who pay attention to community may indeed become the most efficient of all.

Comment: What buyers and sellers should remember above all else, is that after the sale, they remain the principals. Intermediaries, counsel, CPAs and financial advisors can all walk away after closing with comparatively little likelihood of being brought back into the deal if there are problems. The principals frequently still have to deal with each other postclosing; this fact should be recalled during the negotiations, however long and difficult. They should, even at the risk of some loss of face, try to develop and retain a good, if not close, personal rapport with their counterpart. Sun Tzu pointed out in *The Art of War*, ". . . if you know others and know yourself, you will not be imperiled in a hundred battles." Unless you are prepared to do battle (and at what cost?), establishing rapport increases your knowledge, and may be the basis for future alliances—or ammunition if war occurs. As pointed out in the classic *I Ching*, "Leaders plan in the beginning when they do things . . . leaders consider problems and prevent them."

What should a good letter of intent accomplish?

A number of things. It should cover not only the basics of the deal—price, form of payment and closing—but also the structure (cash or stock), take into account the tax (and therefore economic) considerations for both sides, and deal with most, if not all, of the major issues. Infrequently, can these issues be addressed without the principals involving all of the people on their team. The terms in a letter of intent should form the basis for a comprehensive agreement without extensive subsequent negotiation by the principals about the terms—except where counsel cannot agree.

What specific terms should be included in a letter of intent?

All of the basics of what will later appear in the purchase and sale agreement (see Appendix 18.2), plus whether the seller will negotiate with any other prospective buyers while negotiations remain ongoing.

Need the letter of intent contain a discussion of each of these terms?

No; however, for each term that is not discussed, the attorneys involved in the deal will have to deal with both the purchase and sale agreement language and any business issues involved. So you must balance the need to attempt to comprehensively address the various issues with the style and approaches of the parties. A good letter of intent will do much to lubricate the dealings between counsel for the buyer and seller.

What are some reasons why a letter of intent would not be used?

- Basic deal points are agreed upon and the parties do not want to get bogged down in two sets of negotiations (letter of intent terms and sale agreement terms) and parties elect to go directly to contract.
- Complex issues are better addressed in purchase agreement immediately.
- Momentum of deal.
- Timing of deal.
- Style of buyer, seller, counsel, or intermediaries.
- Size of transaction.

What then, are some advantages and disadvantages of a letter of intent?

Advantages: Shows how serious each side is; provides a moral, if not legal, commitment to get the deal done; highlights (by inclusion or exclusion) matters or differences that need further negotiation; may prevent (morally and/or legally) buyer or seller from continuing to look at other buyers or sellers; establishes a written record of the main deal points (helpful given the delays frequently experienced prior to completion of a draft purchase and sale agreement); and may be very helpful in assisting the buyer's financing efforts (or reducing the time required to obtain the financing).

Disadvantages: If the parties are not careful, it could be considered to be a binding agreement (it is critical to state whether the agreement, or any parts of it, are binding on the parties). If the letter of intent is not legally binding, it may morally lock both parties into positions that they later wish they had dealt with differently. Depending upon the type of firm (public or private) and knowledge of others and the marketplace, a signed letter of intent may require, or necessitate, a public announcement prior to executing a purchase and sale agreement. (Frequently a confidentiality agreement may accompany or precede such letter of intent.) Using a letter of intent can result in two sets of lengthy negotiations.

If a comprehensive letter of intent dealing with most of the points covered has been signed, how is it best to proceed to a signed purchase and sale agreement and closing?
As quickly as possible. Momentum has been established, both sides are in accord—so they believe—with the terms of an acceptable deal. The longer the period between a signed letter of intent and a signed agreement, the greater the likelihood that there will never be a signed agreement. It is extremely important to have communication among all team members, and, after a letter of intent has been signed, to circulate the draft of an agreement as soon as possible. The initial draft will usually be prepared by counsel for buyer, although bargaining power may require a buyer to use a draft prepared by seller with opportunity for few changes to the agreement.

Once a letter of intent has been signed, should counsel begin drafting an agreement of sale?
No, unless all—I repeat *all*—of your homework has been done prior to or concurrent with entering into the letter of intent. Here's why: In their negotiations to buy and sell a business, both buyers and sellers are usually focusing upon the other's paramount concern—price. Much time has probably been spent talking about possible forms of transaction (stock sale or asset sale), and various financial models (containing a comparative analysis of the results, including tax effects) may have been generated and discussed, but it is the unusual situation where the deal has been thoroughly thought through. Usually this occurs only when there is a sophisticated buyer or seller or one who has spent the time and money to think through the transaction with her or his advisors. (Even then, however, the analysis may be limited to a comparison of a stock sale with an asset sale based upon various possible prices.)

This result usually flows from the dynamics of each particular deal. Given the numbers of players and variables involved, a thorough analysis cannot usually be made until after deal terms have been tentatively reached or a letter of intent has been signed.

Even when a letter of intent is negotiated in good faith and represents each party's intention as to both the substance and the form of the deal and is intended to serve as the basis for what the contract should contain, it is not, and should not be looked at as, a binding contract. Both before and after a letter of intent has been entered into, it would be worthwhile for each principal to discuss the following topics in a meeting with each of his or her advisors present—either by phone or in person: All the points listed in Appendixes 18.1 and 18.2. This meeting should occur immediately after the letter of intent is signed, after advisors have had an opportunity to digest those terms addressed and those omitted. Counsel should begin drafting an agreement immediately after such meeting provided that no other course of action (such as further negotiations based upon suggested changes in structure) makes more sense.

If a letter of intent has been signed by both principals, when should they next get directly involved with each other?

Again, it depends. The intermediary and counsel will proffer their advice, and buyers and sellers should listen and frequently follow such counsel; but there are times when they must follow their own instincts as to their involvement. Usually, their personal involvement with each other will be on the major points after counsel or intermediaries have reached an impasse.

What happens if there is a major problem that could be a deal breaker?

Frequently, the intermediary and counsel can deal with such issues, but if a problem appears insurmountable, both principals are usually well advised to meet—or talk over the phone—whether with or without their advisors. That said, they should be fully briefed on the various issues and possible outcomes prior to such a meeting and generally refrain from making a legally binding commitment.

Suppose there is a signed purchase and sale agreement, but one or both parties desire to make certain changes to it. What should be done?

As with many other points, negotiate with the other side. Both buyers and sellers may make bad deals or parts of deals. There may have been mistakes or misrepresentations as to certain facts—hopefully innocent—concerning even key matters. The more each side has invested into getting a deal done—time, money, opportunity costs—the greater the willingness, usually, to try to reach some accommodation with which all can live.

Comment: Be aware that financial buyers may be less flexible to deal with than strategic buyers, because the projected returns of financial

buyers are paramount; thus, economic terms affecting their rates of return are much more crucial than those of strategic buyers.

Additional Comment: Sellers, in particular, especially if they founded
or built the business, are apt to let their emotions cloud their judgment.
Advisors who are candid in their feelings about the various deal points
are most effective.

Assuming there is a signed agreement, and some minor modifications, does that mean the deal will close?

No; each party needs to realize and focus its efforts upon taking all actions called for by the agreement and be prepared to change the terms
up until the time money has changed hands at the closing table, and
perhaps thereafter.

What happens when, after closing, one side feels that it has been wronged? Should litigation immediately ensue?

No. As with the steps leading up to closing, both parties should attempt
to negotiate their differences. Neither buyer nor seller wants to be involved in litigation; it takes too long, it costs too much, and, to paraphrase the late Harvey Firestone, a court will only hear what each side
wants it to hear. Emotions should not govern whether to litigate; rather,
a cost benefit analysis should be done by each side; their legal positions
should be analyzed with a rough quantitative analysis; and they should
determine whether there was bad faith by the other party. Generally,
parties must live with the terms of a deal that is cut, be they good or
bad, but mistakes do happen, and each side should be willing to listen to
the other's position before turning to its litigators and "shooting." If a
person develops a reputation for shooting first and asking questions
later, many deals may never come to that person's table.

What are some key areas on the buyer's side that are frequently overlooked?

- *Key person insurance:* If the buyer is relying upon the seller (an individual) to stay on for some time to move key accounts or operate
  the business, frequently the buyer does not take the time to insure
  its interest adequately. Likewise, if the buyer is an individual, he or
  she does not ensure that, as of closing, there is sufficient insurance
  on his or her life to provide adequate cash (without otherwise affecting cash flow or profitability) to hire a replacement.
- *Buy-sell agreement:* If the buyer is composed of more than one person (a management team doing a leveraged buyout, a family acquiring a business with participation by various family members,
  or other configuration) there should be a buy-sell (cross-purchase
  or stock redemption) agreement in place at or very shortly after
  closing. Frequently, buyers will ignore this for some period of time

(given all the time, money, and energy expended to get the deal closed, this is easy to understand). A firm date to sign such an agreement should be agreed upon.

Comment: Even when these agreements are entered into, too frequently a counsel's boilerplate language will be used without a significant amount of thought given to either establishing the purchase price, funding of the purchase price, tax effects, or dealing with all the other relevant issues. Counsel fees to negotiate and draft such agreement should be of small concern given the import of this agreement. If the arithmetic is worked, and a competent independent advisor asked, such agreement should usually be funded, in whole or in large part, by life insurance and disability buy-out insurance. Too often, management feels the funding should be out of operating cash flow instead of obtained from life insurance. Too often such agreements inadequately deal with disability and its effects upon a business. The use of a formula buyout should never be employed without making the calculations of a purchase price based upon historical and various assumed financial results. In one situation about two years after closing, when representing a new shareholder buying into an existing business, I worked through the existing formula agreed to by the two existing shareholders and discovered that if either of them had died, the purchase price for the other's interest would have, contrary to both of their desires and expectations, been close to nothing for a business that cost them millions and on which they, and their estates, were liable to the bank as guarantors.

- *Bank financing:* Both the seller and buyer should ensure that the buyer's bank (if one is used) and any other necessary financing sources are kept apprised of the economic terms of the deal, and, where appropriate, provided copies of the agreement along the way. A seller who knows that a buyer is depending upon outside financing to get a deal closed does not want a surprise at the last minute that the buyer's financing source soured on the deal and that the buyer now lacks the funds to close.

- *Bust-up fees:* Frequently, both parties are well advised to include a provision in their agreement of each to pay the other some fee, either a set amount or a formula, if the deal fails to close. Frequently the deal, while signed, may be subject to boards of directors whose duty may require them to shop the deal prior to ratifying the agreement. Both the buyer and seller will have spent a great deal of time and money pursuing the deal, and therefore it is most appropriate for the parties to consider a provision for a fee to be paid if the deal subsequently falls apart.

- *Conditions:* To the extent that either party inserts certain conditions to closing, which is usually the case, the time period in which to satisfy the conditions should be carefully thought through and agreed upon. Likewise, consideration of what happens if a condition cannot be satisfied within the determined time period. For example, suppose that a purchase of a business was subject to the land being environmentally clean. A Phase II examination shows that remediation is required; remediation is required by a specific date. Suppose the Phase II results require additional testing (and remediation), but insufficient time to test and remediate remains prior to closing. The contract conditions should take into account, if possible, such situations. (However, there is a limit to the number of possibilities that could, or should be, addressed in the contract.)

Should an employee benefits expert be retained?

Frequently, the buyer will want to determine the effects of the business employee compensation structure on the business, its profitability, growth potential, and motivation of employees, both before and after closing. Likewise, if a seller knows that employees may need to be terminated, an appropriate termination package may be in order, in which case, retention of employee benefits experts should be considered.

What nontraditional options are available to the seller or buyer if no deal to sell or buy all of a company can be reached?

Joint ventures, alliances, or sale or purchase of some assets or divisions should be explored. For example, if a seller cannot get the right price from a particular strategic buyer, the seller should consider his, her, or its range of other options, among which are whether it makes sense for the seller to establish a new company with the unsuccessful buyer to promote a line of products, manufacture a new product, or serve as a, or the, distribution channel for the seller. Do not be limited by an all-or-nothing result unless such result is deliberately chosen after an analysis of the relative strategic effects. The consulting firm of Booz, Allen & Hamilton concluded, based upon analyzing joint ventures in its database over a period of 15-plus years, that, where strengths of one joint venturer complemented strengths of the other, average return on equity approximated 17 percent per year—50 percent above the 11 percent average return on equity for U.S. industry, excluding the joint ventures or alliances (Source: Peter Pikar, Jr., Booz, Allen & Hamilton). Many U.S. companies until of late have lagged behind their European and Far East Asia counterparts in forming such joint ventures or alliances. Of course, each situation needs to be analyzed based upon assumptions, strategies, and possible and likely outcomes that make sense to the principals involved.

If the seller intends to sell assets, should he or she plan on distributing all assets immediately after the closing?

No; and this point may well affect both the purchase price and any escrow of funds. Delaware remains the choice for state of incorporation for many companies and practitioners, for a variety of reasons, not the least of which is the very strong reluctance of Delaware courts to pierce the veil of a corporation to hold its shareholders personally liable for reasons other than fraud or failure to act like a corporation. (In one study, many other states pierced corporate veils to hold controlling shareholders personally liable in about 40 percent of the reported cases; Delaware was close to 0 percent.)

When a company sells its assets, it remains liable to third parties for obligations for periods prior to closing. This liability remains for years, regardless whether the company has been voluntarily or involuntarily liquidated under the relevant state statute. If the company's assets have been distributed to shareholders, the shareholders are liable, generally, to the extent of assets received (plus, perhaps, interest thereon). If the assets have been distributed without following the applicable statutory procedures, and making appropriate provisions for actual and contingent liabilities in accordance with the statute, the directors can be jointly and severally liable for the full amount of any judgment to the extent corporate assets have been depleted. This is an important point to keep in mind where there are several or more shareholders, even within the same family.

To be safe, if enough money is involved and the corporation is a Delaware corporation, the following procedure should be used. Adopt a plan of dissolution, give appropriate notices, and retain one or more experts to determine the amount of actual and contingent liabilities. Then ask for a court hearing; an amount will be held in reserve in the corporation for a period of seven years prior to distribution. The corporation could then be dissolved and any earnings either retained or distributed to the shareholders. (This is a relatively new provision under the Delaware code, and, though cumbersome and costly, provides a mechanism to permit discharge of directors and to help fix the amount of claims that may be made against a seller after closing.)

What about successor liability; if I acquire all the stock of a company, am I liable for its liabilities?

The general rule in most states is that a buyer of all of the stock of a company is liable for its obligations, including in many cases, punitive tort and criminal liabilities. (Example: Seller, or any of his or her personnel, know, prior to closing, that some products have a defective design that can cause serious injury or death, but has taken no action to warn consumers or recall products. Company remains liable, postclosing, for all torts, such as failure to warn, and can have punitive damages assessed against it.) These factors must be kept in mind when determining the purchase price, drafting the provisions for liabilities (actual and contingent) for actions prior to date of closing, and deciding whether to escrow or hold back a portion of the purchase price for one or more years pending either an expiration of a reasonable period of time or various statutes of limitations periods. For an excellent analysis of the underlying economic analysis that buyers, sellers, and financial advisors should use when buying or selling a company, see *Mergers & Acquisitions: A Valuation Handbook,* Joseph H. Marren (Business One Irwin, 1993).

If I, as a buyer, want to shield myself from liability, am I safe if I structure the transaction as an asset purchase?

No, even though you might think that compliance with applicable bulk sales laws may eliminate such liabilities. While you reduce the scope and amount of liabilities through use of an asset purchase, a buyer of assets remains liable for many obligations of seller.

Traditionally, with an asset sale, the buyer was liable for liabilities of the seller, in four situations:

1. Where there was an express or implied agreement to assume seller's liabilities.
2. Where the transaction was, for all practical purposes, a merger or consolidation of the selling and purchasing corporations. (Can a C Reorganization [stock for assets] where sole shareholder sells assets in return for stock in acquirer result in successor liability to acquirer? Possibly.)
3. Where the purchaser was merely a continuation of the selling corporation.
4. Where the transaction constituted an attempt to defraud the creditors of the selling corporation.

(If there is any question as to whether any of these four apply to a particular transaction, counsel should be sought.) Recent years have seen the proliferation of federal and state statutes imposing additional liabilities upon buyers of assets, including, among others:

- Employment and labor obligations for employees of the seller where buyers of assets are found to employ seller's employees under the same terms and conditions—including union contracts.
- Liability for environmental damage caused by the seller.
- Tax liability.
- Tort liability (both compensatory and punitive). See, for example, *Punitive Damages Awards against Successor Corporations: Deterrent of Malicious Torts or Legitimate Acquisitions?* Levenstam and Lynch, *Tort & Insurance Law Journal:* 27–44 (Fall 1990).

In particular, asset purchase agreements should be drafted, from a buyer's standpoint, to disclaim all liability for punitive damages. (Although the "product line" reasoning for holding successor corporations liable for products manufactured or actions taken by their predecessor is a minority position, it makes sense to ensure that all customers of the former seller are aware that it [the acquired corporation] is a new or different corporation from its predecessor, especially where the same name is used by the successor.) Even with such language, however, if old management remains after closing, and any wrongful conduct is not remedied by the successor company, the successor company may well be liable in some jurisdictions for both compensatory and punitive damages. This may result from the theory that, since old management continues, it is charged with the knowledge of its predecessor, it is trading on the name identification of such predecessor, or it knew of wrongful conduct and did not make it known to its customers, and thus it should be held to the same standard as its predecessors.

Because many midsized companies are family-owned, what overview of family businesses would be helpful before discussing particular related concerns?
The following information was obtained from the results of the *American Family Business Survey: 1995* sponsored by the Arthur Andersen Center for Family Business and conducted with the Loyola University Chicago Family Business Center and the Family Enterprise Center at Kennesaw State College (Arthur Andersen & Co., SC. 1995).

- In every category except those corporations with sales in excess of $500 million per year, there are substantially more privately held businesses than publicly held companies.
- For those companies whose sales exceed $500 million per year, there are approximately 15 percent more publicly held companies than privately held companies. Of the privately held companies, many would be considered family businesses. Of these, the founder, or CEO, is one of or the sole shareholder.
- In roughly two-thirds of existing privately held businesses, the principal shareholder/CEO is planning to retire or semiretire within the next 10 years. (*Note:* This appears to be due primarily to the volume of existing businesses that were established between 1945 and 1955 and whose founders are now ready to sell their companies or pass the baton to the next generation.)
- Two-thirds of all privately held companies wish their heirs to succeed to the business.
- Roughly 30 percent of all privately held businesses will actually pass to the next generation (based upon anecdotal evidence and other estimates, not from survey).
- It appears that in excess of 55 percent of privately held companies are C corporations, which means that when such companies are

sold (unless structured as a nontaxable transaction or sale of stock), there will be two levels of taxation.

What conclusions can be drawn?

In short, between 1996 and 2005, of the roughly 45,000 privately held businesses in the United States with sales in excess of $25 million, about 30,000 will have their CEO retire or semiretire. Of these, it is reasonable to assume that 10,000 to 15,000 will be sold to third parties. Under sales of $25 million it is reasonable to think that like numbers (by percentage) or more will be sold. Of the 45,000 privately held businesses in the study, about two-thirds desire that their businesses pass to their heirs. However, of these, 40 percent say they do not have a good understanding of what estate taxes may have to be paid at their death. In only 37 percent of the companies do the significant shareholders have significant life insurance; however, it is questionable as to whether many of these have enough insurance to pay the estate taxes due upon their deaths.

Comment: While it is possible to pass an unlimited amount of property to your spouse tax free, any portion of the estate in excess of $600,000 that is to be passed to others is taxed at a rate beginning about 40 percent and increasing to 55 percent at $3 million. If more than 35 percent of the estate is composed of shares of stock in a closely held company, then the estate tax can be paid in installments (with interest) over a period of 10 years subject to a number of conditions. However, payments over this period are likely to significantly affect the cash flow of the company.

To put it differently, 20 percent of the significant shareholders in privately held companies do not have life insurance. Of these, more than half will have successor management within the next 10 years, and many may well need to be sold within the same time period. It is estimated that 70 percent of all businesses do not make it to the second generation and 87 to 90 percent fail to make it to the third.

Given the money pouring into the numerous venture capital funds, and the number of buy-out funds extant, it is likely that strategic and financial buyers will be well financed for the foreseeable future. Both a buyer and seller should keep in mind, however, that when a market goes through a transition from nonhostile to hostile (defined as 40 to 70 percent of market share being divided among three companies) that 60 to 70 percent of the companies that were in the market when it was nonhostile go out of business, are sold or merged, or go into a Chapter 11. Further, when a nonhostile market becomes hostile, profit margins frequently shrink significantly. These observations should be kept in mind by both seller and buyer when negotiating a sales price (Source: Don Potter, Windemere Associates, San Francisco, CA). If the market is turning hostile, a seller is better advised to sell at a lower price than he or she may otherwise think justified, and a buyer to buy at a lower price due to both the fallout of companies and lower prospective profit margins.

What points should family business owners keep in mind when deciding to buy or sell a business?

Several cultures share the saying "shirtsleeves to shirtsleeves in three generations." The founder establishes and grows the business. The next generation minds or oversees the business and reaps its rewards. The third generation watches or causes its demise (or sometimes reaps the benefits of its sale). There have always been, and always will be, exceptions to this generalization, but the actual numbers of family businesses successfully making it to or past the third generation are few. Even then, the question remains how content the family members are whose minority stock pays little or no dividends and whose stock is illiquid. Did the founding shareholder really achieve the result he or she desired?

Owners of businesses should consider whether, in assessing your family members, any one or more of them has that combination of skills, motivation, and drive necessary to give your company the ability to survive and prosper. If not, resist the temptation to pass management on to your children (providing minority shares to nonparticipating family members without a reasonable way for them to dispose of their shares at fair value), and either bring in outside management (providing them enough vested interest to achieve your goals) or sell the company.

Buyers should consider structuring their ownership and financing of the business in such a way as to reduce the effects of family disagreements (if more than one family member is or could be involved), any subordinated indebtedness and other financial leverage other than working capital loans, customary mortgage financing, and standard equipment loans or leases. While a leveraged deal may be the only way to buy a company, it may be advisable to pay off most of this leverage as quickly as possible, especially in light of the ever-increasing speed with which businesses must change and new international and domestic competition appears. If a buyer does want the business to prosper for generations, much thought and planning must be focused in that direction; even then, the odds are not favorable. Serious life planning should be undertaken prior to selling or buying a business.

While sellers wish to maximize and buyers wish to minimize the selling price, both should keep in mind that to close a deal usually takes a fair price. If a seller asks too much for the business, how will that affect the employees thereafter if a fair return cannot be had? Likewise, if a buyer is known as a "shark," over the long term how will that enhance the quality of deals that are brought to him or her? If the buyer is known for dealing fairly, and a fair price is either asked or offered, it is more likely that buyer, seller, and the others affected by the deal they strike (employees, suppliers, partners) will be better off. It is possible to buy low or sell high without compromising integrity and still have the transaction be fundamentally fair to both sides.

SUMMARY

From a buyer's perspective, usually an asset purchase will provide the lowest net present tax cost. For the seller, usually a stock acquisition or tax-free reorganization will provide the best net present proceeds. Each of the methodologies for selling and buying a business and likely tax, economic, and noneconomic reasons should be considered when determining the choice of structures for any particular deal. Advisors, operating as a team, should be an integral part of the transaction.

APPENDIX 18.1

Points to Consider Prior to Letter of Intent or Sale/Purchase Agreement

The comments or definitions given here are provided so that the reader who is unfamiliar with such concepts can become familiar with them. Serious consideration of such techniques should be done in conjunction with knowledgeable advisors.

Comment: The more money that is at stake, the more time and money should be spent (provided that its effect on the likelihood of disrupting the momentum of closing the deal is considered) analyzing the following points prior to a letter of intent, purchase or sale agreement, or agreement of merger.

What forms of transaction would be the most beneficial taking into account tax, economic, and noneconomic considerations?

- Ordinary income problems: Regardless of the form of a sale, will the seller recognize ordinary income (recapture of depreciation, tax credits, deductions for previously expensed items, and others)? These amounts need to be quantified.
- Compliance with governmental requirements: Various acts and governmental action may be required, including, among others: Hart-Scott-Rodino, Securities & Exchange Commission, Federal Trade Commission, Internal Revenue Service, Environmental Protection Agency, Federal Communication Commission, Federal Reserve Comptroller of the Currency, and other federal agencies and corresponding state agencies.

Is there a better strategic or financial buyer or seller? The buyer or seller should reconcile whether there is a more advantageous seller or buyer.

Are the underlying assumptions for the sale or purchase still correct? Frequently market conditions and other assumptions affecting the deal and parties may change during the negotiation process. These things should be thought through again prior to signing a binding agreement.

If a bust-up fee is to be used, how will it affect the transaction? One should consider whether having to pay a bust-up fee will help or hinder getting a deal done, and in what way.

Should the deal be structured as an asset sale or acquisition? An analysis of the short- and long-term effects of this structure including economic and noneconomic factors needs to be made. This analysis should then be compared with a stock acquisition, merger, and other possible structures (e.g., joint venture).

Should the deal be structured as a stock sale or acquisition? The same issues apply here as in considering an asset sale or acquisition.

Should the deal be structured as a taxable or tax-free acquisition or sale? This analysis will be based on the respective motivations of the buyer or seller and will be integral to the structure of the deal.

Will there be an installment sale or purchase? Sellers usually desire all cash up front and buyers often opt for a part of the price being paid over time or on an all out basis.

Is a reorganization or merger worthwhile? Frequently mergers may better serve the ends of either or both the buyer and the seller, among which are the following types:

- Type A Reorganization (Statutory Merger—IRC368(a)(1)(A)): Requires two entities to merge in accordance with applicable state statutes; the acquired corporation, whose assets and liabilities become those of the acquiring corporation, ceases to exist; payment to the acquired corporation's shareholders can be in the form of one or more classes of stock in the acquiring corporation, cash, and/or other securities and property (commonly referred to as "boot"), provided that 50 percent or more of the consideration received by the acquired corporation's shareholders is in stock of the acquiring corporation. Tax basis of the acquired corporation's assets continues; nontaxable to seller except as to boot received.
- Type B Reorganization (Stock for Stock Exchange—IRC368(a)(1)(B): Stock of acquired corporation is exchanged solely for stock of acquiring corporation; nontaxable to seller.

- Type C Reorganization (Stock for Assets Merger—IRC368(a)(1)(C): The acquiring corporation issues its stock to the seller in return for the assets being acquired; nontaxable to seller.
- Type D Reorganization (Parent into Subsidiary—IRC368(a)(1)(D): Can be used to effectuate a spin-off, split-off or split-up; however, cannot be used as a device to extract earnings (transfer of assets in return for shares).

    Spin-off: The distribution of a subsidiary's stock to the parent's shareholders. If the subsidiary is newly formed, this may constitute a 368(a)(1)(D) reorganization.

    Split-off: The distribution of a subsidiary's stock to some of the parent's shareholders in return for the shares in the parent by way of an exchange offer. If the subsidiary is newly formed, this may constitute a 368(a)(1)(D) reorganization.

    Split-up: The distribution, in the liquidation of a parent, of the shares of at least two subsidiaries to the parent's shareholders. If the subsidiary is newly formed, this may constitute a 368(a)(1)(D) reorganization.

- Type E Reorganization (Recapitalization—IRC368(a)(1)(E): The changing or reshuffling of a capital structure within the framework of an existing corporation, with a valid business purpose. Examples: Seller exchanging some common for preferred stock; lender exchanging debt for stock. Tax effects (for instance, reduction of indebtedness versus fair market value of stock received) need to be analyzed.
- Type F Merger (Change Form, Identity, or Place—IRC368(a)(1)(F): Used, for example, to change the state of incorporation.
- Type G Bankruptcy Reorganization: Tax-free-provided shares of the acquiring corporation are distributed to acquirer.
- Triangular Merger, Reverse Triangular Merger, Reverse Subsidiary Merger: Different types of mergers that can be accomplished on a tax-free basis using some of the previously listed reorganizations.

The following points should also be considered by a buyer or seller:

- Deferred stock arrangement, and the use of phantom stock or stock appreciation rights: These can be used to provide incentives to both a seller and management team to reward future efforts.
- Charitable Remainder Trust (with use of Irrevocable Life Insurance Trust): This device can be used by sellers to make donations of property in the future to charities, receive a current income tax deduction for the fair market present value of the property that will eventually go to the charities (using certain IRS-accepted interest assumptions), provide an income stream from the assets for

the seller (and spouse or other person) for either a term of years of life, and replace the assets that otherwise would have been the seller's and likely would have been included in his or her estate and taxed at 55 percent. This can be a very effective device for accomplishing a social good (and perhaps business good as well, because the seller can be recognized as a substantial donor long before his or her death and reap certain intangible and tangible business benefits as well), while not hurting the family's economic interests.

- Deductibility of debt on acquisition: If the interest on the debt to acquire the assets exceeds $5 million per year, any excess may not be deductible for tax purposes.

- IRC § 338 transaction: A buyer of the stock of a company may step up the basis in the corporation's assets if it qualifies for and elects to treat the stock purchase as if it were an asset purchase. However, the buyer (the company purchased) is responsible for payment of all taxes that the seller would have paid had it been an asset sale. In other words, the purchase price a buyer would be willing to pay for assets of a company must be reduced by the amount of taxes the seller would have paid (plus other liabilities assumed); however, the buyer gets a step up in basis to the total of the purchase price.

- IRC § 338(h)(10) transaction: The flip side of a standard 338, in which the seller treats the sale of his or her stock as if it were an asset sale and pays the resulting liabilities; the buyer gets a step up in basis of the assets to equal the purchase price. This requires that the seller be a member of a consolidated group.

- IRC § 351 transaction (stock of a company is issued tax-free in return for assets): Used when seller wants a nontaxable sale and buyer is willing to issue voting for nonvoting shares (usually more flexible than a 368 Reorganization).

- IRC § 303 redemption: Provides for the redemption, without such a redemption being treated as a dividend for the purpose of paying death costs (taxes, funeral expenses, and so on).

- Advance IRS ruling: Should be considered where permitted by the IRS, if critical or important tax matters are involved, and counsel or CPA so recommends; because such early submission is suggested, a ruling usually takes some months to obtain.

- Pooling of interests versus purchase: Unless all 16 requirements of the Accounting Principles Board (APB) are satisfied, the acquisition for accounting purposes will be treated as a purchase. (Used, in part, to avoid goodwill being purchased as an independent asset, although perhaps less critical than pre-1991, tax rules concerning amortization given that amortization of intangibles, is now, usually over a 15-year period.)

- Allocation of purchase price among the various assets in accordance with the Internal Revenue Code. It is critical in an asset purchase (and IRC § 338 transaction) to agree on and have an appraisal support the allocation of purchase price among the various assets. The IRS may reallocate (among the various assets) the purchase price notwithstanding the buyer's and seller's agreement.

- Distribution of assets of company and sale by shareholders: Usually upon the distribution of assets (assuming a C corporation) the gain (fair market value less basis) is recognized by the shareholders upon receipt and may be either capital or treated as ordinary income.

- ESOP (Employee Stock Ownership Plan): Useful in helping seller get money out on tax-deferred basis and in providing benefits to employees. Frequently used in management buyouts.

- Problem with step transaction rule: Sellers and buyers need to be aware that the IRS will not usually respect the tax treatment of individual and permissible steps that, when viewed as a series, achieve a tax result not otherwise permitted under the IRS code.

- Problem with sham transaction rule: The IRS will not respect any transaction which is not a legitimate transaction.

- Personal holding company problem: A company may be an inadvertent personal holding company (and be subject to a 39.6 percent tax on its undistributed income) where more than 50 percent of its value is owned by less than 6 shareholders and 60 percent of its adjusted gross income is personal holding company income (dividends, royalties, annuities, rents, and the like). Whether any exemptions preclude such treatment should be considered prior to the end of any tax year for companies who may be affected by such tax.

- Collapsible corporation problem.

- IRC § 355(d): A spin-off or split-up that constitutes a disqualified distribution results in the distributing company recognizing gain on the distribution of the distributed stock in an amount equal to the difference between the fair market value of the stock less its basis in the hands of the distributing company. A disqualified distribution is one in which a person, since October 9, 1990, has acquired 50 percent or more of the stock of the distributing company within five years preceding the distribution; or, after the distribution, owns 50 percent or more of the stock (by voting power or value) of the subsidiary whose stock was distributed; attribution rules need to be considered.

- Tax free incorporation: Receipt of stock in return for a contribution of property does not usually result in taxable gain if done in accordance with IRC § 355.

- Timing of sale: Tax and economic effects based on the tax year a deal is to close and payments made should always be considered.

- IRC § 269: Gives the IRS the authority to deny all benefit of carry-forwards, credits, deductions, and the like where tax avoidance is the principal purpose of the transaction.

- IRC § 382: Limits loss carryovers when there is a change of 50 percent or more over a three-year period; the limit is determined by application of a specific interest rate times the value of the corporation at the time of change of ownership.

- Use of employment and noncompete agreements to affect stock price: Amounts to be allocated to employment (or consulting) and noncompete agreements for management personnel for periods after closing must be reasonable or the IRS may reallocate such amounts to the original stock purchase price.

- Use of licensing fees, royalty arrangements, or rental agreements: If such fees are to be used, both the tax and economic effects should be thought through, particularly (for the seller) where such amounts may be tied to net profits; such profits frequently never materialize.

- Use of options: Options in an acquirer's stock may prove useful, particularly where selling shareholders are to remain as officers after the deal has closed. Option recipient should consider both the current (and future) tax effects of such options in addition to their likely value based on future stock prices.

- Use of retirement plan assets in purchase or sale: An acquirer (and seller) may wish to consider the use of retirement plan assets by a management team buyout. The standards for such use are very exact and the potential adverse economic effect to affected employees should be considered.

- Use of S corporations and limited liability companies: Both of these types of entities should be seriously considered as entities of choice for qualified buyers and sellers alike in order to avoid taxation on eventual sale.

- Seller as investment company after sale: If a seller of assets is to continue after sale, counsel should be sought as to whether such company may be deemed an inadvertent investment company subject to SEC regulations.

- Installment sale: Where the stock or assets are to be sold over time, the tax effects and security to be used to help ensure payment should be considered.

- Use of life insurance: Life insurance should be used by sellers where payment is on an installment basis and by buyers for many middle market companies where management is the buyer.

These questions should be answered by both the buyer and the seller before a deal is struck: How should probable postclosing changes by buyer to his or her or the acquired corporation's business affect the sales price?

- Will there be economies of scale?
- Will there be combined operations?
- What changes of personnel will there be and at what cost?
- Will there be an elimination or consolidation of business lines or products?

What postclosing operational plan underlies the assumptions used to determine price and other key terms?

Do I feel comfortable that the price is fair?

Are there any points my advisors can suggest that will, without changing the price, make the transaction more advantageous?

How collectible are receivables?

How do the corporation's contracts with its customers, employees, and suppliers affect the likely purchase price?

What are the employee benefits including economic and tax effects of qualified and nonqualified plans?

How do environmental concerns affect the price?

What effects do shareholder agreements and articles of incorporation and bylaws have on the transaction?

Are there potential antitrust or trade regulations and approvals necessary?

What impact do foreign laws or international treaties have on the transaction?

What product liability problems are there, and how do they affect the deal pre- and postclosing?

What tax, income, use, ROI, or other tax matters need addressing?

What stock exchange considerations are there?

Are there any other postclosing liabilities which have not been considered?

What goals, objectives, and plans for action are there for after the closing? This is particularly important for buyers and companies who are to merge. Frequently too little time, effort, and other resources are employed to help ensure the economic prospects past closing.

APPENDIX 18.2

Sample Purchase Agreement Points and
Terms for Consideration

What property will and will not be part of agreement?

What will be the purchase price, and when and how is it to be paid?

Will there be any employment or consulting agreements for key employees; and are there conditions of closing?

When will the closing be?

What will be the seller's obligations at closing? Do they include the following:

- Instruments that will be sufficient to vest good title, free of all liens and encumbrances in buyer (UCC tax, judgment, and lien searches paid by whom).
- Bill of sale.
- Assignment of books and records.
- Corporate resolutions.
- Assignment of copyrights, licenses, trademarks, patents, and trade secrets.
- Employment agreements, consulting agreements, noncompetition, and continuity of business-undertaking agreements.
- Opinions of counsel.

Obligations at closing?

- Cash or collected funds.
- Promissory notes.
- Security agreements.
- Corporate resolutions.

Will the following representations and warranties be made?

- Organization standing and qualification of seller.
- Representation that neither the execution, delivery, nor performance of the agreement would violate anything to which seller is a party.
- That there is no contemplated, pending, or threatened litigation, except as disclosed.
- That the seller has good and marketable title for all his, her, or its assets.

- That all taxes, including income, property, sales, use, franchise, added value, employees' withholding and social security, and real estate have been paid; all returns have been timely filed; and there is no audit pending or threatened by federal, state, or local authorities.
- That nothing in the agreement or any statement or certificate provided by seller will contain any untrue statement or omit to state any material fact required to make the statement not misleading.
- That there have been no material adverse changes to financial condition of the company since the date of financial statements and reports provided.
- That any particular assets, such as inventory, will be maintained at certain levels through the date of closing.

Representations and warranties by buyer?

- That the buyer has been duly organized and may lawfully conduct its business.
- That all proceedings have been taken that were required to close on the purchase.
- That nothing will conflict with the agreement or the closing thereof.
- That there is no legal action, arbitration, or governmental investigation against the buyer.

Access to information?

- Will seller give buyer's representatives full and complete access to seller's personnel properties, documents, contracts, books, records, and such other information as may be reasonably requested?

Seller's debts and liabilities?

- Specifically identify debts, liabilities, or obligations of seller (for example, vacation or other benefits to employees, leasehold obligations, trade payables, environmental liabilities, and trade debt) for which buyer will be responsible.

Bulk sales compliance?

- Note that Illinois and some other states no longer have a Bulk Sales Law requirement; however, notices are still required to Department of Revenue, Department of Employment Security, and Internal Revenue Service. This does not mean that any sale by the seller can be used to defraud creditors of seller. To the contrary, state statutes and the Bankruptcy Code have fraudulent conveyance provisions.

Will seller hold harmless and indemnify purchaser from any cost, expenses, or damages that may result from failure to give any bulk sales notice or any other required notice?

Conditions precedent to buyer's obligations?

- That all representations made by the seller and contained in all documents shall be deemed to have been made again at closing.
- That environmental audit proves negative.
- That all covenants, agreements, and obligations shall have been performed prior to closing.
- That buyer has obtained necessary financing.
- That all documents shall have been delivered prior to closing.
- That all employment agreements have been entered into.

Break-up fee?

- Will a break-up fee be paid, and if so how much; and will it vary, based upon not closing and the reasons therefore?

Conditions precedent to company to sell?

- That all representations and warranties of the purchaser are true and correct as of closing.
- That all obligations have been duly and properly performed.

Indemnification?

- Will the seller be liable to indemnify purchaser for:
  Any untrue representation or breach of warranty?
  All debts that exist as of the date of closing, unless excluded?
  All debts or causes that arise after closing, which are based upon or arise from any act or sale prior to closing?
  Any claims for compensation, severance, or benefits incurred for any period prior to closing?
  Legal expenses incurred by purchaser enforcing this provision?
  Any rent prior to closing?
- Purchaser's indemnification:
  Any loss from broken agreement and legal fees relating thereto?

Offset?

- If there are additional payments provided to the seller, either under employment agreement, consulting agreement, or balance of purchase price, will there be a right of offset?

Cure period?

- If either party defaults, will there be time for other party to cure?

Legal fees?

- Who pays cost and fees; will it be the defaulting party for both sides?
- If there is a default, is the nondefaulting party entitled to interest?

Controlling law: What state or county or international agreement?

Dispute: Will there be a mediation provision? Arbitration? Litigation? One or more alternative dispute resolution provisions will usually prove more helpful and cost effective to both the buyer and the seller.

CHAPTER NINETEEN

Closing Documentation

WILLIAM H. DUNN
ATTORNEY AT LAW

The term *closing* a business sale derives from the concept of closing a business sale escrow. The purpose of a business sale closing is to complete the terms of the sales agreement that the parties have made. An escrow is frequently, although not always, used to accomplish a closing. Legally, the term *close of escrow* means the point in time when the buyer receives the ownership of the business and seller receives the sales price. In this chapter, it will be assumed that the transaction is handled through a formal escrow. The same result may be achieved at a closing meeting, without the participation of a third-party escrow holder, at which the various steps described in this chapter are accomplished.

DEFINITION AND PURPOSE OF AN ESCROW

An escrow is an arrangement for the delivery of a document such as a bill of sale, representing the ownership of property to a third party, the escrow holder, to hold and deliver upon the occurrence of stated conditions. Until the conditions are satisfied, the document is "in escrow" and its effectiveness is suspended. This escrow status ends and the document becomes effective when the conditions have been satisfied. At that time, the "close" or "completion" of the escrow occurs, as does the "consummation" of the transaction. This is true even though there may be further activity required on the part of the escrow holder and the parties to completely close the file on the transaction. An escrow assures the buyer that his money will not be disbursed until the conditions of the sale have been met. An escrow assures the seller that the funds and notes for the purchase are placed beyond the buyer's unilateral control, before the seller proceeds further with the transaction, such as opening up his books for inspection and notifying creditors, employees, and tax agencies of the sale.

Need for an Escrow

The need for an escrow may be influenced by the type of transaction. An escrow may be required by applicable law, such as a sale including the transfer of an alcoholic beverage license. As discussed later, in a sale of assets transaction subject to the bulk sales law, an escrow is almost a necessity in order to comply with the bulk sale requirements, particularly if there are many creditor claims. In a sale of assets, generally, an escrow is very useful because there may be numerous documents of title to be transferred and claims to be paid. In a sale of stock, the actual property transferred is only the stock certificates, so an escrow may not be as essential. In a statutory merger, the filing of the merger documents with the Secretary of State completes the transaction, and an escrow may not be necessary.

Parties to the Escrow

An escrow is essentially a contractual arrangement between the buyer, seller, and escrow holder, although there may be other parties, if the contract so provides, such as brokers and lenders. The terms of the arrangement are set forth in escrow instructions. The escrow instructions may have the effect of superseding and perhaps modifying the sales agreement, so they must be carefully drawn so as not to produce conflicts. Escrows are typically handled by escrow companies, title companies, banks, and attorneys. Many states have regulations regarding escrows.

BULK SALES LAW

The bulk sales law is contained in Article 6 of the Uniform Commercial Code (UCC). This code has been enacted in all states, with local variations. The definition of a bulk sale varies from state to state but, in general, a bulk sale is a consentual sale (not a lien foreclosure, bankruptcy, or other court-supervised sale), not in the ordinary course of business of the seller, of a substantial part of the inventory and equipment of a seller whose principal business is selling merchandise from stock (including manufacturers) or operating a restaurant. Under the usual definition, a bulk sale is of the tangible assets of a business, not of corporate stock or a sale only of intangibles, such as leasehold interests. A bulk sale does not include the sale of a business whose main activity is the delivery of services rather than sale of merchandise.

The steps necessary to comply with the bulk sales law vary according to the jurisdiction. Usually, there is a requirement that the seller provide a list of creditors and that these creditors be notified by the escrow holder. In some states, merely recording and publishing notice of the sale is sufficient. The purpose of the bulk sales law is to notify the seller's creditors of the sale, so that they may submit claims and receive payment prior to the seller obtaining the sales proceeds. To comply with the bulk sales law, the entire purchase price of the business must be available to the creditors before payment to the seller. Although an escrow is not usually required by law, it is a very useful device to facilitate compliance with these rules.

If the bulk sales law is applicable and there is no compliance, then the sale is classified as a "fraudulent transfer." This means that under the Uniform Fraudulent Transfer Act, enacted in most states, the seller's creditors can either set aside the sale or pursue their claim directly against the buyer. If the seller files bankruptcy, these same rights pass to the seller's trustee in bankruptcy. Therefore, if the bulk sales law is applicable, it is very important to the buyer that there be compliance. Otherwise, the buyer may pay twice, once to the seller, and once to seller's creditors who are not paid by the seller. The bulk sales law represents an additional statutory protection for the seller's creditors. If a creditor does not file a claim or its claim is not paid, the creditor retains its claim against the seller.

SALE OF ASSETS

In a sale of assets, the ownership of each asset is transferred from the seller to the buyer. For tangible assets, this is usually accomplished by the delivery of a bill of sale, which is equivalent to a deed in a real estate transaction. The bill of sale typically provides that the seller transfers ownership of the assets to the buyer and usually contains warranties of good title and indemnities against defects in title and perhaps defects in physical condition.

TRANSFER OF CONTRACT RIGHTS

In addition to the assets transferred by the bill of sale, the typical business will include various contract rights and other intangibles. There are usually leases for the business premises and other assets that must be assigned. There may be franchise agreements, existing covenants not to compete, consulting and employment agreements, supplier and customer agreements, and other contractual rights to be assigned. Certain types of assets are registered in some manner, and the registrations must be transferred and changed into the buyer's name. Examples are vehicles, boats, aircraft, trademarks, copyrights, governmental licenses such as public utility and liquor licenses, and many others. The transfer of a governmental license normally requires the approval of the governmental agency issuing the license, in which case this approval must be made a condition to the closing. The same is true regarding assets and contract rights, such as leases and financing arrangements, the transfer of which require the approval of third parties.

LIEN SEARCH

In any type of business sale, it is important that a lien search be done on behalf of the buyer. The buyer will require that the seller pay off these liens prior to closing, or assume them with an appropriate credit on the purchase price. Secured transactions in personal property are covered in Article 9 of the UCC, which provides that there is only one kind of voluntary security interest in personal property, which is created by a security agreement. A security agreement is a written grant by the debtor (owner of the collateral) to the secured party of a security interest in the collateral to secure the performance of an obligation to the secured party. Usually, the obligation secured is a promissory note.

Article 9 contains important definitions. A "security interest" is an interest in personal property securing payment or performance of an obligation. A "debtor" is a person who owes a secured obligation or owns the collateral or both as the context requires. A "secured party" is the holder of a security interest. The "collateral" is any property subject to a security interest. As stated, a "security agreement" creates a security interest.

A security interest "attaches" when the debtor (owner of the collateral) has signed a security agreement describing the collateral; or the secured party has possession of the collateral, value has been given, and the debtor has rights in the collateral. Attachment determines the basic enforceability of the security interest against the debtor. A security interest is "perfected" when it has attached, and appropriate further steps have been taken as prescribed in Article 9 for different types of collateral, such as filing a financing statement, usually in the Secretary of State's office, or taking possession of the collateral. The Uniform Federal Lien Registration Act, enacted in all states, provides for the filing of federal tax liens. Generally, liens against corporation or partnership taxpayers are filed in the Secretary of State's UCC records, provided for by various laws. These tax liens take priority from the time they are perfected by filing. The time of perfecting a security interest in business assets determines its priority and validity against competing ownership and security interests. Article 9 gives the results of various matchups between claimants having competing interests in the collateral. Article 9 also describes the procedure for foreclosing on security interests. The UCC records may be searched to determine whether there are any perfected security interests. This should always be done by the buyer either directly or through the escrow holder.

SUCCESSOR TAX LIABILITY

Many states have statutes providing that the buyer of substantially all the assets of a business must hold out-of-purchase price any amounts the seller owes to various state tax agencies such as those collecting sales taxes and unemployment taxes. These statutes provide that if the seller fails to do this, the buyer becomes subject to successor liability for these taxes, if the seller fails to pay them. If such a statute applies, it is important as part of the escrow to obtain a release of this successor liability from the tax agencies, as part of the closing. Also, many states impose a sales tax on the sale of tangible business assets. This tax is usually payable by the seller, but the seller can be reimbursed by the buyer if the sales agreement or escrow instructions so provide. Most business sales agreements will contain such a provision.

SALE OF STOCK

If the property being transferred is shares of stock, then proper procedures must be followed. If there are restrictions to transferring the stock, those must be satisfied. Usually, these conditions are referenced on the stock certificate itself. The transfer of stock may be subject to a stockholder's agreement or a governmental restriction. For example, some state blue sky laws require an approval from the state corporation commissioner before stock is transferred. There may also be federal restrictions to the transfer. It may be necessary to obtain certain agreements from the buyer as a condition of making a transfer, such as an investment representation.

TRANSFER OF STOCK

The typical stock certificate has an assignment provision on the reverse of the certificate. This should be completed and signed in escrow to be delivered to the buyer at closing. The buyer would then normally surrender this transferred certificate at closing to the corporation and obtain a replacement certificate issued in the buyer's name. For a larger corporation, there may be a corporate transfer agent, through which the stock transfer is accomplished.

PROCEDURE AT CLOSING

As part of the closing, the seller will be entitled to receive the purchase price as provided in the sales agreement. This will usually consist of cash and notes, and perhaps other property. At the time of closing, the escrow holder should have the notes and any security documents in the file and already signed by the seller and buyer. These are then ready to deliver to the seller at the closing. Likewise, all funds required to be paid by the buyer should have been collected in the escrow holder's bank, so that the escrow holder can write out a valid escrow check for the cash due to the seller, and can also pay other parties such as creditors and brokers. The agreement may provide that certified funds are to be delivered directly from the buyer to the seller at closing. Alternatively, the funds could be wired directly to the buyer. It is the delivery of the bill of sale that transfers ownership of the business, in the same way that the delivery of a grant deed transfers ownership of real property.

Closing Statement

One important function of an escrow is the generation of a closing statement or settlement sheet setting forth all of the money adjustments. This must be approved by both buyer and seller before the escrow holder will complete the closing. The closing statement gives the parties a last opportunity to review the numbers and verify that all conditions of the sale have been met. It is common to require the buyer and seller to execute a "bring down" certificate warranting that all conditions and covenants on their part have been performed. It is also common to require the attorneys for buyer and seller each to submit an opinion regarding various matters within the attorneys' purview, such as the proper formation of the selling and buying entities and other matters with which the attorneys should be familiar. The closing statement can serve as a checklist as to items that need to be delivered to the parties or to others. If there are many documents involved, it is advisable to have a closing memorandum agreed to by the parties, listing all documents and payments and how they are to be delivered. Upon completion of the closing, the parties should sign off on this closing memorandum, confirming that all the steps outlined have in fact been taken. If any steps remain to be done, the responsibility for doing those should be assigned.

SUMMARY

As stated, the most important function of the escrow is to protect the buyer and the seller. The seller does not want to part with the ownership of the business until he has received the purchase price. The buyer does not want to part with the purchase price until he has received the legal ownership of the business. The primary purpose of the escrow is to facilitate this exchange. As alluded to, there are usually various conditions that must be satisfied before the closing can occur. Examples are the need for satisfactory government inspections, such as health and fire department approvals. There may be tax audits required prior to closing. The number and types of conditions vary greatly with the transaction. It may be that tax rulings are required. These should be set forth clearly in the escrow instructions. The closing statement should recite that all conditions to the sale have been satisfied, or waived, or are to occur outside of the escrow.

PART FOUR

THE OUTSIDE PROFESSIONALS

The Role of the Intermediary

THOMAS L. WEST
BUSINESS BROKERAGE PRESS

Before we explore the role of the intermediary in the sale or purchase of small and midsized companies, it might be helpful to clarify exactly what an intermediary is. While we're at it, we'll also define all those who may be involved in such transactions.

THE BUSINESS BROKER

There is very little difference between business brokers and intermediaries, and that is basically psychological. Those who handle the larger transactions tend to call themselves intermediaries, while business brokers generally handle the sale of transactions under $1 million. One business broker we know, however, reported that his firm's smallest transaction was $40,000, while the largest was $23 million. Generally, business brokers represent the seller, although buyer representation is occurring more often. Business brokers are not finders; they represent the seller or the buyer, as the case may be. They have an agency relationship with the party that retained them.

In approximately 20 states, business brokers must have a real estate license to handle the sale of a business. The size of the business is not a factor. In fact, in South Carolina, in order to sell a business that is incorporated, where the stock is being transferred (as opposed to strictly a sale of assets), the business broker must have a South Carolina real estate license. It should be pointed out that a real estate license would not be necessary if the business were transferred as an asset sale. Almost every state requires that real estate licensees disclose, in writing, to both the prospective buyer and seller, just whom they represent.

THE INTERMEDIARY

As stated, intermediaries tend to handle the larger transaction, although they are really brokers of businesses. The main distinctions, aside from the size of the transactions, are that many intermediaries represent buyers and usually receive retainers prior to starting an assignment. Business brokers normally take a listing from an owner who wants to sell his or her business, and the broker gets paid on a contingent basis when the sale is consummated. Intermediaries may do a search for a buyer, and receive either a retainer for the search or a monthly fee for as long as the prospective buyer wants the intermediary to search. In doing a search, the intermediary represents the buyer, and, if a satisfactory business is found, the buyer is responsible for the success fee. (Fees will be discussed later in this chapter.) Intermediaries may also represent sellers of companies and, in this capacity, work to find a buyer for the firm. Another distinction between intermediaries and business brokers is that intermediaries generally represent companies not individuals.

Intermediaries and business brokers should not be confused with finders. Finders are just that—they find; essentially they introduce two parties and walk away. If the parties make a deal, the finder receives a predetermined finder's fee. Intermediaries and business brokers negotiate; finders do not. In states where a real estate license is required to sell a business, only California recognizes the role of a finder. The Securities and Exchange Commission (SEC) does recognize the role of finders, but does not require them to hold a securities license as long as their role is only that of finder.

FEES

Intermediaries provide valuable services to both parties in a transaction. When performing searches for buyers, they can approach target companies without identifying the prospective purchaser; and, incidentally, they can tell the selling company that the fee is being paid by the buyer. Intermediaries can also represent sellers, in which case the seller pays the success fee. It should also be noted that assignments are generally accepted only on an exclusive basis, which means that the fee is earned on any disposition of the business, in the case of the seller, and on the purchase of any business by the buyer—during the time frame of the agreement.

A survey in the newsletter *M&A Today* revealed that 86 percent of the intermediaries polled charge retainers. The amount of the retainer ranges from 10 percent to 20 percent of the total estimated success fee, while still others construct an estimate of the amount of work involved coupled with the salability and motivation of the seller. In most cases, the retainer is subtracted from the success fee when the business is sold. Obviously, if the business does not sell, the retainer is forfeited by the seller. In surveying fees, most intermediaries use what is termed the Lehman formula. Apparently, this "formula" grew out of the investment banking work done by the firm of Lehman Brothers many years ago. The formula stuck and has become a fixture in the M & A world. Lehman is simply 5 percent of the first $1 million; 4 percent of the second $1 million; 3 percent of the third, 2 percent of the fourth and 1 percent of everything over $4 million. Since the formula dates back many years, many intermediaries now use what is called double Lehman, which is exactly what it says. Others use what is called "stuttering" Lehman, which is simply 5 percent–5 percent; 4 percent–4 percent and so forth. Obviously, these are methods that increase the amounts of the fees charged by the intermediaries.

THE AGREEMENT

The agreement between the intermediary and the principal may also resolve queries such as the following:

- Will the retainer be deducted from the fee if a sale is consummated?
- Is the agreement exclusive?
- Is there a minimum commission or a cap on the upside of the fee?
- Is there a safety clause? (In other words, does the agreement provide for a period of time, say three years from the expiration, in which the intermediary's fee is protected for procuring a buyer or seller, as the case may be?)
- Is there a fee due the intermediary if a buyer becomes employed by the seller, or is in any way affiliated with the seller?

THE ADVANTAGES OF USING AN INTERMEDIARY

There are many advantages of using an intermediary whether you are a buyer or a seller. From a seller's viewpoint, here are just a few of the things that an intermediary can do:

- Assist the seller in arriving at a fair price and help in the proper structure of the deal itself.
- Gather the necessary information, prepare it in a format convenient for a prospective purchaser, and develop a market strategy.
- Maintain confidentiality and screen the possible buying candidates.
- Arrange visits to the selling company and meetings with company officials, and supply preliminary information.
- Negotiate the sale price and deal structure.
- Work with all of the outside advisors and follow the sale to a satisfactory conclusion.

The intermediary, by performing the aforementioned services for the seller, will also be assisting the buyer. One big plus for buyers using intermediaries is that they will be able to learn about companies for sale that they would not otherwise. Also, as previously stated, intermediaries do represent buyers, as you will note in the next section outlining the various duties and responsibilities of the intermediary.

Regardless of whether the intermediary represents the buyer or the seller, he or she is a deal-maker and is a catalyst for the sale itself. Note, though, that neither an intermediary nor a business broker can represent both the buyer and the seller without disclosing this to both sides. Representing both the buyer and the seller is called dual agency and is discouraged by many state real estate departments and the law of agency itself. Thus, full disclosure is required, otherwise the intermediary may not have a legal claim to the fee.

WHAT TO EXPECT FROM AN INTERMEDIARY

If you are a prospective buyer of a business not being represented by an intermediary involved in the transaction, you should nevertheless expect the following:

- Fairness.
- Honesty.
- Reasonable skill and care.
- Disclosure of any defects or negative conditions.
- An understanding of your criteria for purchasing a company.
- Presentation of all the information regarding the company.
- Information on only those companies with serious sellers.
- A handle on the value of the company.
- Access to the seller.

- Knowledge of deal structuring and the specifics of the business in question.

If the intermediary is representing you, either as a seller or a buyer, you should expect him or her to do the following:

- To act primarily for your benefit with utmost good faith and loyalty.
- To maintain appropriate confidentiality.
- To fully disclose all material facts.
- To use skill, care, and diligence.
- To obey all of your lawful directions.
- To account for all money or property received.

All parties must deal openly and honestly. It is the intermediary's responsibility to know and understand his or her principal's reason for sale, as well as what is expected from the transaction. By reviewing all of the items listed, you should be able to piece together what to expect, whether you are a buyer or a seller and represented by the intermediary or not. If the intermediary is representing you, you are the client. If you are just working with an intermediary, you are the customer. Make sure you understand what your relationship with the intermediary is.

A word of caution to buyers: The responsibility of due diligence always falls on you and your advisors, unless the intermediary is specifically asked to perform due diligence. If the intermediary is not representing you, he or she cannot perform due diligence and still represent the seller. Too many buyers assume that the intermediary will perform this duty or already has performed it, when, in fact, that responsibility falls directly on the purchaser instead.

WHERE TO FIND INTERMEDIARIES

Your lawyer, accountant, or banker may be able to assist you in locating a competent intermediary. In the front of this book are biographies of all of the contributors, which might be another source of assistance. There is no multiple listing type of service for businesses, although some associations or networks might have knowledge and information of businesses offered by members, but it is generally not a condition of membership. The main reason for this lack of a listing service is that most sellers are very concerned with confidentiality.

There are associations of intermediaries who may also be able to refer you to a professional intermediary. The following lists those we are aware of, but the list might be incomplete, though any omissions are inadvertent. Also, addresses and telephone numbers change, and organizations go out of business. But as a starting point, this list of resources is important.

ASSOCIATIONS OF INTERMEDIARIES

International Association of Business Brokers (There is an M&A group
within this association.)
11250 Roger Bacon Drive, Suite 8
Festoon, VA 22090-5202
(703) 437-4377

The Institute of Certified Business Councilors
PO Box 70326
Eugene, OR 70326
(503) 345-8064

International Merger and Acquisition Professionals
60 Revere Drive, Suite 500
Northbrook, IL 60062
(708) 480-9037

M&A International
530 Oak Court Drive, Suite 155
Memphis, TN 38117-3722
(901) 684-1274

Other resources that might be helpful in locating an intermediary are:

Nation-List International
1660 S. Albion St., Suite 407
Denver, CO 80222
(800) 525-9559

Financial Intelligence Network
4555 Lake Forest Drive, Suite 650
Cincinnati, OH 45242
(513) 933-9759

CHAPTER
TWENTY-ONE

The Role of the Lawyer

ANN C. BONIS
SENIOR ASSOCIATE
O'CONNOR BROUDE & ARONSON

The world of mergers and acquisitions (M&A) is not the exclusive domain of corporate giants such as RJR/Nabisco, nor is it marked solely by predatory takeovers of smaller companies by larger businesses. The real world of M&A is actually well populated by smaller companies that engage in transactions that tend to be smaller and considerably less hostile than the ones that make headlines on the business pages.

But business owners would do well to avoid the dangerous trap of thinking that these smaller transactions are by definition smaller transactions. While the average $70 million deal will certainly be more complicated than the average $70,000 deal, the same basic documentation needs to be completed regardless of the size of the transaction.

One of our main goals in handling mergers and acquisitions—regardless of their size—is reducing the costs associated with bringing a deal to closure. With smaller transactions, costs can best be kept under control if the prospective buyers and sellers are willing to observe the following guidelines:

1. *Let your lawyer know what you are up to.* You don't necessarily want your lawyer doing all of your negotiating, but you do want him or her to be aware of where you are headed, to keep you from encountering unforeseen problems. For example, the participants may structure a deal as a cash transaction when in fact such an approach could lead to significant tax consequences. When the attorney then informs the parties of the tax implications, it can bring them back to square one—or worse. One party may have become so attached to the original deal that any proposed changes, such as making it a partial stock deal, will meet with severe opposition.

Sometimes, the most difficult deals to complete are the ones initiated between parties who are friends. These are often presented to attorneys as "done deals," with the attorneys being asked merely to "dot the i's and cross the t's." These types of deals frequently unravel when the attorneys start to probe and learn that each party has a very different view of the deal, and distinctly different recollections of the discussions that have taken place. In the rush to make such deals, many issues are overlooked, such as who assumes debts, what happens to any cash on hand in the company, or who gets the company cars.

2. *Focus on what you really want in structuring the deal.* One common negotiation tactic is for both parties to begin with disparate positions that essentially are competing wish lists. In this scenario, the seller sets an unrealistically high price with ridiculous conditions, the buyer responds with an absurdly low offer with equally impossible conditions, and the game is afoot.

In smaller-dollar value transactions, such an approach is a monumental waste of time. Both the buyer and the seller would be well-advised to inform their attorneys of what they really want out of the deal and instruct them to come up with an appropriate structure.

For the buyer, the key to the deal may involve having the seller stay on with the company in a consulting role, as a way to reassure employees and customers of the company's stability. Or, the buyer may want the seller out of the company, and may need to negotiate some noncompete language to ensure that the seller does not turn around and take the proceeds of the sale to launch a competing company.

The seller may have a different set of interests; for example, to use the proceeds of the sales as the capital needed to start another company. Or the seller may want to sell the business, but retain the real estate to ensure retirement income from the rent.

All of these issues should be negotiable, and all may take some time to settle, so it makes sense to clear the plate of unnecessary clutter as soon as possible so that parties to the deal can concentrate on issues of greatest importance.

3. *Determine what's for sale.* To avoid confusion, the seller should compile a complete inventory of exactly what is being sold. This list should be complete, with the exceptions noted. It is common for larger

companies to buy smaller companies just to get access to one aspect of that company, such as a particular technology, a distribution channel, its research and development team, or a customer list. In such cases, it is imperative that the seller and buyer are in accord on exactly what is being sold.

Also, all parties to the deal should be on the lookout for "seller's remorse," that very common malady of sellers who decide somewhere along the line that they do not really want to sell the company after all. Many deals crumble because the seller simply can't let go of a company that he or she has built from scratch with a heavy personal investment of time, money, and effort.

4. *Establish ground rules.* As mentioned earlier, when talking about the futility of wish lists, anything that cuts down on game-playing or opportunities for grandstanding is worth considering. In smaller transactions, it makes no sense to pay attorneys for posturing, and consequently making deals more complicated than they have to be.

One way to avoid such posturing is to set ground rules about how the deal will proceed. For example, agree at the outset that the party that is acquiring the business will draft all the documents, and the selling party then reviews and makes comments. This helps provide an orderly sequence to the deal.

5. *Use lawyers selectively.* Clients can do a number of things themselves to move a deal along rather than leave everything to their attorneys. Lawyers should handle elements that are clearly "legal" issues, the details for which the attorney's expertise is most needed. But clients can often do a better job of clearing up purely "business" issues by staying involved.

Lawyers are often good and trusted business advisors, but clients may be best served by planning with their attorneys and then resolving open issues with their business counterparts. This is particularly helpful where the lawyer stakes out an initial position, and the client can offer "concessions" that help preserve a good working relationship among the businesspeople.

6. *Maintain complete records.* Another way to smooth a transaction is to have on hand accurate and up-to-date corporate records, especially when stock is involved. It is vital to have a clear record of who owns stock. There have been cases where people listed as shareholders actually were deceased.

Insurance documents are also important, ranging from life insurance to business insurance. If the business owns a life insurance policy on the owner and/or key employees, the sale of the company may affect those policies.

7. *Read all the documents.* Anyone who is buying or selling a company is faced with a considerable amount of paperwork. It sounds basic, but it is imperative that clients really read all the documents prepared by their attorneys. Everyone's worst nightmare is to get to the closing and

have one of the parties look at a document and say, "You know, this isn't correct." At that point, it may not matter that you have a deal that is creatively structured, that your ground rules have moved things along quickly, that your corporate records are immaculate, or that you did a great job overcoming seller's remorse.

8. *Set a realistic time frame.* Once the buyer and seller have agreed to the basic terms of the deal, their natural inclination is to want the transaction to close as soon as possible. It is important, however, to be realistic about the amount of work that must be completed prior to closing and to plan the time frame accordingly. It is a disservice to all parties involved to be working against a false deadline.

9. *Fully understand seller financing.* Often a seller is so pleased with the purchase price being offered for the business that he or she does not examine until later in the transaction how this purchase price is being financed. Many letters of intent are subject to financing contingencies, discharging the buyer of any obligation to proceed with the acquisition if financing is not obtained, on terms acceptable to the buyer, by a specified date.

In the current economic climate, sellers are increasingly being asked to finance the buyer, especially if the buyer is not an established corporation. The means by which the purchase price is being secured should be established early in the negotiations, in order to avoid surprises once buyer and seller are farther along in the process.

10. *Determine what other agreements need to be obtained.* While the majority of negotiations take place between the buyer and seller and their respective counsel, it is likely that other parties will need to consent to the transaction. For example, the acquisition documents may contemplate transferring a particular contract, such as a supply agreement, to the buyer. However, such a transfer may not be able to be effected without the prior written consent of the supplier itself. Whatever documentation is needed from third parties should be identified and obtained as early on in the process as possible.

Following these 10 guidelines will help ensure that the legal bills for your small transaction, no matter how complex it turns out to be, will not match those of the corporate giants.

CHAPTER
TWENTY-TWO

The Role of the Accountant

KEVIN MACDONALD
DIRECTOR OF ACCOUNTING AND AUDIT
MACDONALD, LEVINE, JENKINS & CO., P.C.

In a perfect world, buying a business would be as easy as shopping at a supermarket. The company would come neatly labeled, with all the ingredients listed; directions for use would be succinctly presented, it would be sold at a fair price, and be guaranteed to work. If you were not satisfied with the product, you could return it for a full refund. In the real world, of course, this is not the case, where buying a company can be a time-consuming and expensive proposition filled with risk at every turn. In the real world, the watchword is caveat emptor—let the buyer beware!

Buyers need experienced advisors to help ensure that their interests are clearly presented, any conflicts are resolved fairly, the transaction is properly priced, they have been advised of potential problems attached to the deal, and these positions are appropriately represented in a contract. Using advisors experienced in buying and selling businesses can increase the likelihood that your transaction comes as close to being event-free as shopping at the supermarket.

CHOOSING ADVISORS

The advisors you select to work on an acquisition will depend on how active you plan to be in acquisitions and how complicated each deal will become. The team of advisors will usually include an attorney, investment banker or business broker, and a CPA. Other experts may be needed depending on the circumstances; and, if the deal requires financing, an understanding banker is a must.

It is critical that the team work well together, agree on their respective roles, keep you informed of the progress and status of negotiations, and answer to you. The best advisors provide a balance of strong technical skills and broad business background. The need for advisors with strong technical skills in their respective disciplines is obvious; broad business experience enables them to give consideration to the many varied aspects of any transaction. You should seek out seasoned advisors who will provide clear, honest, objective advice. Remember, the objective is for both the buyer and seller to successfully realize their goals in the transaction.

CHOOSING A CPA

CPAs can be valued advisors in acquisitions because of the breadth of business situations and organizations to which they are exposed. Although there are CPAs experienced in assisting clients in acquisitions in Big 6 and national accounting firms, this is not the only source of skilled professionals. Many regional and local firms are excellent sources of acquisition advisors. If you do not already have a CPA that is experienced in acquisition transactions, your attorney or banker is a good source of referrals to help you find one.

In selecting a CPA firm, you should ask for answers to the following questions:

Does the firm have experience in acquisitions?
Has the firm done deals this size before?
Who in the firm will be working on the deal?
Will experienced staff be assigned to your transaction?
How available will you be?
How does the firm charge for work? Fees can range all over the map.

Keep in mind as you make your selection that most likely you will continue to work with your CPA firm long after the deal is done.

Compensation

When selecting an accounting firm to assist you in an acquisition, review with them the role that you expect them to play. Satisfy yourself that they have the experience that you need, and can and will respond in a reasonable manner to your need for assistance.

Accounting firms charge for services at hourly rates set to reflect the knowledge, skills, and experience of the professionals providing the advice. Be aware that consulting on acquisition is typically done by very experienced professionals, often with the highest billing rates in the firm; thus, the work can be expensive. The good news is that experienced professionals can also provide efficiencies resulting from exposure to past transactions.

Certainly every deal is different, and unexpected or time-consuming issues often arise; nevertheless, your CPA should be able to give you an estimate of the fees required to complete his or her part of the transaction. Depending on the services requested, accounting firms may, and frequently will, provide an engagement letter outlining the services they will perform. You can request fee estimates in writing at any time.

GETTING STARTED

There are four areas that are pivotal to the CPA's role in a business acquisition: giving general business advice regarding the feasibility of the deal; providing tax advice regarding its structure; consulting on accounting matters existing in the target company, and ways to assimilate its operations going forward; and offering financial advice about the acquisition. CPA firms that are experienced in advising clients in the area of business acquisition must have the ability to provide advice on all of these.

Some CPA firms can also offer expertise in a wide range of services including valuation and appraisal, employee benefits and retirement plans, insurance, environmental liability, bankruptcy and dealing with troubled business, as well as other areas that may prove to be valuable because of the circumstances existing in a particular acquisition. If such conditions exist or you suspect that they do, ensure that your accountant has experience in dealing with those special areas. A detailed description of the accountant's role in each area follows.

General Business Advice

Whether you are considering buying a company for the first time or an experienced business owner seeking expansion opportunities, the process is the same. Your CPA can help prepare a strategy to grow your company. Accountants in the role of strategic advisors can help you frame the conversation about strategy for growth. Your CPA can help identify the industry or geographic growth direction or opportunities for consolidation of competitors. Once you have identified the opportunities, your CPA can help you decide if it is more cost- and time-efficient to start from scratch and invest in your own operation, or acquire an existing company with the cost of acquisition and integration and assimilate it into your organization. Your CPA can help answer the build or buy question by exploring alternatives; and, if a decision is made to buy, help develop an outline of the qualities that should be present in order for an acquisition to go forward.

Once the parameters have been established for types of acquisition candidates, your CPA can refer you to investment bankers or brokers to search for target companies. Your CPA can also be used as an intermediary if you have identified an acquisition candidate through your own efforts.

The CPA's role becomes more active when an acquisition candidate has been identified. If you have not already done so, your accountant will meet with you to gain an understanding of what you expect from or want to accomplish through the acquisition. Armed with this knowledge of your goals and objectives for the acquisition, your CPA can assess the target company against established parameters.

Tax Advice

A primary consideration of the buyer in any potential acquisition is understanding the alternatives available in the tax structure of the purchase. At its most basic level, an acquisition will be treated either as a deal in which you buy the assets of a company or a deal in which you buy the shares of stock of a company.

The starting point is a review of the income tax returns, generally for the last five years, for any jurisdictions within which the company operates. Included should be a review of all correspondence from tax authorities. The tax returns and correspondence will provide a good starting point in assessing the tax attributes of the target company.

For reasons that will be explained, from a buyer's position, an asset purchase is usually preferable to a stock purchase; conversely, the seller usually benefits more from a stock sale than an asset sale.

Purchase of assets.   In reviewing the tax returns, your CPA will look for benefits to the buyer of an asset purchase transaction, which include:

- *Basis adjustment:* All assets purchased are recorded at fair market value. The adjustment frequently results in assets with a low basis being increased (stepped up) to a higher value, reflecting the current worth of each asset. The adjustment to fair value applies to both long-term fixed assets and trading assets such as inventory. In a purchase transaction, the entire purchase price is allocated to the fair market value of the assets. Any amount of the purchase price that is greater than the fair market value of the purchased assets is allocated to goodwill. Over time, the value assigned to inventories will be expensed as the inventory is sold; the value placed on fixed assets will be depreciated over future periods. Under current IRS regulations, the value attributed to intangible assets, including goodwill, is amortized over a 15-year period, thus allowing the buyer to expense the purchase price of the company.

- *Elections:* By starting a new company, a buyer is able to make elections about type of organization (C Corporation, S Corporation, LLC), that could not be done as easily in a stock purchase; further, elections about year-end, basis of accounting, inventory treatment, and asset lives can be made when a company is newly organized, and, in most cases, cannot be easily changed at a later date.
- *Avoidance of contingent liabilities:* The outright purchase of assets, or purchase of asset with assumption of liabilities, frees the acquiring company from the hidden obligations of the old company. Contingent liabilities can include undisclosed tax obligations or lawsuits.
- *Minority shareholders:* Purchasing assets eliminates the need to negotiate the purchase of shares from minority or dissident shareholders.

When assets of a company are sold, the seller is faced with the prospect of winding down the company affairs, filing final tax returns, and distributing the proceeds from the sale. This can be a time-consuming and costly process, and, depending on how the assets were sold, may take several years to complete. In addition, liabilities, actual or contingent, will remain with the old company and survive the sale of assets and even liquidation of the company. Sellers of assets are usually faced with two levels of taxation: the transaction first at the company level and second at the individual level when proceeds from the sale are distributed to the shareholders. Asset sales are more complicated for the seller, and cleaner for the buyer.

Stock purchase. In a stock sale, the acquired corporation continues as the operating entity with all the attributes and assets and liabilities remaining in place. If you buy the stock of a company, there is no change within a company as a result of the purchase. Asset values and asset lives remain unchanged; there is no opportunity to write off the purchase price as there is in an asset purchase. Any liability, actual or contingent, resulting from the acquisition of the corporation remains with the company. Because of the transfer of all liabilities both known and unknown in a stock purchase, it is less likely that this option will be recommended in the purchase of a privately held company. However, there are instances when the purchase of stock makes sense, including:

- *Favorable tax treatments:* Favorable tax treatments may exist in a company. You should be aware, however, that limitations on the use of tax attributes may be set off by the change in ownership.
- *Favorable leases, loans, and other contracts:* Long-term contracts and arrangements may contain favorable terms that would not be transferable if the assets were sold.
- *Franchise agreements and contracts:* Favorable contracts or franchise arrangements may expire in an asset sale.

From a seller's perspective, the sale of stock is a very clean transaction. After the stock sale, all corporate liability is transferred to the new owners, although personal liability may remain with the seller. There is only a single level of tax on a stock sale occurring at the shareholder level.

CPAs experienced in acquisition consulting will attempt to understand your goals as the buyer; they will review the attributes of the target company, and advise on the structure of a deal and how to provide the tax treatment that best meets your needs.

Accounting Advice

It is logical that a CPA can assist in the accounting aspects of an acquisition, *but what are the aspects that need review?* The primary areas where accounting assistance is needed are:

Due diligence.   Initially, upon signing a letter of intent to buy a company, accountants will perform due diligence procedures, which will vary depending on the size of the deal and the anticipated timing of its close. The objective of due diligence is to assure buyers that what they think they are buying is what they are actually buying.

As a first step, your accountant will request copies of financial statements, generally for the last five fiscal years and including up to the most recent month-end. Using the statements, your accountant will perform analytical procedures and develop financial ratios and trends, compare these ratios to published industry information, and explore negative trends or discrepancies from the norm, which may be positive or negative. Understanding why there is such a variance will help you to understand how the company works.

When the deal is scheduled to go forward, the accountants can expand the scope of the due diligence to include a more in-depth review of certain assets and liabilities including the following:

- *Accounts receivable:* Reviewing accounts receivable balances to assure that receivables are being collected and that there are no unusual aging or payment terms or disputes that would impact future profits or cash flow.
- *Inventory valuation:* Reviewing inventory records to assure that inventory is turning over and that all of it is good and salable. In a closely held business, inventory balances may be understated as a tax avoidance measure; the implications of this can be explored as well.
- *Inventory observation:* Reviewing inventory balances to ensure that raw material balances are being used in production; work in process is being completed in a reasonable manner; in-process items are scheduled for completion in a reasonable time frame; and finished goods are moving. Any resulting adjustments for obsolescence and lower of cost or market must be made to inventory.
- *Fixed assets:* Observing fixed assets to ensure that the assets exist, and are in service and good repair and will continue to meet the needs of the company.
- *Other assets:* The target company may contain other assets or rights for which it is critical to determine the future value. Your accountants can help locate an expert to perform a valuation.
- *Accounts payable:* Reviewing accounts payable to determine that all payables are properly recorded or accrued.
- *Accrued liabilities:* Reviewing accrued liabilities to determine whether there are any that are unusual in nature or amount, or not otherwise disclosed to the buyer.
- *Notes payable and long-term debt:* Reviewing the covenants on any debt to understand whether any language exists that could impair the transaction.
- *Sales commitments, purchase commitments, leases, and contract obligations:* Reviewing all commitments to ensure that they are as represented and that they will survive the sale or transfer.

The due diligence work can help the buyer understand the relationship the company has with its customers and vendors, and obtain a better understanding of the seller's motivation for the sale. This work is valuable to the buyer in negotiating price and terms for the purchase. In situations where the due diligence results in an uncertainty over the value of certain assets, the acquisition can be structured with part of the payment being contingent on future realization of asset values or satisfactory resolution of liabilities.

Account system review. The stability of the operations of a business leading up to and after its sale are of great importance in ensuring the success of the deal and integration of its operations. As part of the due diligence process, your CPA can review the accounting system of the target company to assure that it will generate the operating information necessary to help manage its success. Your CPA can assess the staffing level of the accounting department and determine whether the staff is adequate and appropriate for the circumstances.

Purchase price allocation.   In an asset acquisition, CPAs can also assist in allocating the purchase price among the assets purchased and in setting the opening balance sheet.

Financing

Separate from accounting issues are the issues surrounding valuation and pricing of the purchase and obtaining financing for the transaction. Accountants experienced in acquisitions often assist in obtaining financing for the acquisition in the following areas.

Valuation.   Your CPA will be able to advise on the reasonableness of the asking price or, by reviewing the valuation, establish a price based on the underlying value of the target company. There are several alternative approaches that can be employed in arriving at the value of a target company. All acceptable valuation methods consider asset valuation, compensation to owners, current and future profits, dividend-paying capacity and cash flow. In developing a valuation and price, care should be given to consider conditions as they exist before implementing any changes. You should be cautious that the price paid to the seller does not include unwanted assets that are not productive for the company, or that you are not paying the seller for the changes that you must implement after the sale.

Closely held businesses

Restating the financial statements.   The financial statements of a closely held company may not disclose the true operating results of the company. In a closely held company, transactions with related parties often distort profits. Examples of transactions that require consideration and adjustment include the following:

- *Owners' salaries:* Owners' salaries may not be comparable with nonowner managers in similar positions. Owner compensation may be higher than normal and include disguised dividends; or lower than the norm, reflecting the necessity of keeping salaries down to ensure the survival of the company.
- *Family salaries:* Other family members may be on the payroll at either artificially high or low levels, reflecting similar conditions

as in owners' salaries. Family members may receive compensation without working.

- *Rent:* Closely held businesses often operate out of facilities owned by the business owners. Rent for these facilities often must be adjusted to reflect current fair market values or expected future rent.
- *Automobiles:* Frequently, owners and other family members in closely held businesses use company-owned vehicles or receive auto allowances that could be reduced or eliminated.
- *Meals, entertainment, and travel:* Owners of closely held businesses may entertain at a combined business/social level; travel may be at a level that is more extravagant than necessary for business purposes.
- *Repairs, maintenance, and training:* In anticipation of a sale, a business owner may postpone needed repair and maintenance expenditures or employee training in order to improve the short-term financial condition of the company. These necessary ongoing costs should be added back into operations.

Corporate spin-off.   If the acquisition considered is a division of a large company, care should be given to reflect all selling, general, and administrative charges that may not be directly included in operating results, but are buried in overhead or corporate charges. The central corporate charges may be set artificially high to claim all cash flow, or low to improve operating performance of a division. Ensure that all components of selling, general, and administrative expenses are considered and deducted to arrive at true operating results.

Show results after add-back or normalization.   Adjusting operating results for the expenses necessary to normalize operations will provide a more accurate picture of the profits and cash flow potential of the company. The adjustments can then be factored into the purchase price. Adjusting the balance sheet to eliminate personal assets will ensure that the purchase price reflects the true worth of the company.

Business plan.   Your CPA can help in preparation of a business plan reflecting the assimilation of the new company and the future operating goals. The plan should include consideration of how the proposed deal will be structured, with operations reflecting normalized related party expenses, and should incorporate any changes necessary to present the future plans for the company. Finally, the business plan should clearly reflect the company's ability to generate profits and demonstrate adequate cash flow to service debt used to acquire the company.

Your CPA can offer advice on the most appropriate source of financing for a deal. Depending on the type of business, assets acquired, the potential profits and cash flow, consideration will be given to bank lines of credit, bank term notes, financing of assets by leasing, funding from a finance company, federal and state development organizations, long-term subordinated debt or equity. Experienced CPAs can help locate financing by making referrals to the appropriate financing sources and working with your investment bankers.

SUMMARY

We are back where we started. CPAs with experience in acquisitions can help in offering general business advice. Accountants can use their analytical skills to objectively review a proposed transaction and offer advice as to whether the deal should be done at all. Many times, the best strategy is to *not* act.

Frequently, when the transaction is completed, the paperwork is signed, the financing is in place, and it is time to run the newly acquired company, the advisor who remains and has the closest ongoing relationship with you is your accountant. By choosing your accountant wisely, you will effect not only the acquisition but also prospects for success of the company for years to come.

The Role of the Business Appraiser

JEFFREY D. JONES
PRESIDENT
CERTIFIED APPRAISERS, INC.

When an independent opinion is needed to determine the value of a business, business ownership interest, or the underlying assets of a business, a qualified appraiser should be hired to conduct an appraisal and prepare a written report. The focus of this chapter will be to address the concept of value and price; the scope of services that can be provided by appraisers; standards required to be followed by appraisers; and the qualifications and criteria for selecting appraisers.

THE CONCEPT OF VALUE AND PRICE

The concept of value was set forth as early as the first century B.C., when Publius Syrus wrote his Maxim 847: "Everything is worth what its purchaser will pay for it"; or, as an early British economist, Samuel

Bailey, wrote in 1825, "Value, in its ultimate sense, appears to mean the esteem in which an object is held." Thus, a small or midsized business may have a high value to its owner resulting from the efforts expended to build it, but it may have a much lower value to a potential buyer who may be more interested in return on investment than past efforts of the seller.

Economic value refers to an investment's capability of producing economic benefits for its owners or users. As a measurement, value refers to the worth of something according to some standard. The measurement or estimation of economic value is what appraising is about. Price, on the other hand, refers to the amount that is being asked for an item or that has actually been expended to acquire it. It has been said that price is what you pay, and value is what you hope to get.

In the heat of negotiations for the sale or acquisition of small and midsized businesses, the distinction between price and value often gets blurred. Hiring qualified appraisers who can properly render independent opinions of value can save many hours of frustrating negotiations between sellers and buyers. Business brokers report that less than 25 percent of all the businesses for sale ever actually sell. The primary reason for this poor result is that the sellers' expectation of price did not meet the market of buyers' perception of value.

When appraising a business, the most common standard of value is fair market value. A common definition of fair market value is found in Revenue Ruling 59–60 stated as follows:

> The price at which a property would change hands between a willing buyer and a willing seller when the former is not under any compulsion to buy and the latter is not under any compulsion to sell, both parties having reasonable knowledge of all relevant facts.

Inherent in this standard of value is the concept that the buyer is a willing generic buyer and not a specific buyer who may be influenced by synergistic or specific investment motivations not available to the generic buyer.

There are other standards of value that can be utilized, depending upon the circumstances of each assignment. Other common standards of value used to value businesses are fair value and investment value. While there is no universally accepted definition for fair value, in most states it is the statutory standard of value applicable to dissenting stockholders' rights, wherein minority shares are valued on a pro rata basis of the whole company, excluding any discounts for lack of control, marketability, or minority interest that would otherwise be considered in determining fair market value.

Investment value is usually defined as "value to a particular investor based on individual investment requirements." Many actual transactions of midsize companies are consummated based on investment value rather than fair market value due to synergistic or investment criteria of a specific buyer who is able to pay more for an investment than would the generic buyer who would not have any synergistic or unique economic advantages.

When valuing machinery and equipment, fair market value is the normal standard; however, the definition is usually further defined depending upon the circumstances under which the assets are being sold. The Machinery & Technical Specialties Committee of the American Society of Appraisers has developed the following specialized list of defined terms to describe the standard of value being used to appraise machinery and equipment.

Reproduction Cost—New is the cost of reproducing a new replica of a property on the basis of current prices with the same or closely similar materials.

Replacement Cost—New is the current cost of a similar new property having the nearest equivalent utility as the property being appraised.

Fair Market Value is the amount expressed in terms of money, as of a certain date, that may reasonably be expected for property in exchange between a willing buyer and a willing seller with equity to both, neither under any compulsion to buy or sell and both fully aware of all relevant facts. (In the valuation of personal property, this definition must be further defined based on the function and purpose of the appraisal.)

Fair Market Value in Continued Use is the estimated amount expressed in terms of money that may reasonably be expected for a property in exchange between a willing buyer and a willing seller with equity to both, neither under any compulsion to buy or sell and both fully aware of all relevant facts and including installation and assuming that the earnings support the value reported.

Fair Market Value—Installed is the estimated amount of an installed property expressed in terms of money that may reasonably be expected in exchange between a willing buyer and a willing seller with equity to both, neither under any compulsion to buy or sell and both fully aware of all relevant facts.

Fair Market Value—Removal is the estimated amount expressed in terms of money that may reasonably be expected for an item of property between a willing buyer and a willing seller with equity to both, neither under any compulsion to buy or sell and both fully aware of all relevant facts, considering removal of the property to another location.

Liquidation Value in Place is the estimated gross amount expressed in terms of money which is projected to be obtainable from a failed facility, assuming that the entire facility would be sold intact within a limited time to complete the sale.

Orderly Liquidation Value is the estimated gross amount expressed in terms of money which could be typically realized from a sale, given a reasonable period of time to find a purchaser(s), with the seller being compelled to sell on an as-is, where-is basis.

Forced Liquidation Value is the estimated gross amount expressed in terms of money which could be typically realized from a properly advertised and conducted public sale with the seller being compelled to sell with the sense of immediacy on an as-is, where-is basis.

Salvage Value is the amount expressed in terms of money that may be expected for the whole property or a component of the whole property that is retired from service for use elsewhere.

Scrap Value is defined as the amount expressed in terms of money that could be realized for the property if it were sold for its material content, not for a productive use.

Insurance Replacement Cost is the replacement cost new as defined in the insurance policy less the cost new of the items specifically excluded in the policy, if any.

Insurable Value Depreciated is the insurance replacement cost less accrued depreciation considered for insurance purposes.

Real estate appraisers use the term market value rather than fair market value. The definition of market value expands on the concept of fair market value to further clarify the characteristics under which the concept of value is being measured. A current economic definition agreed upon by agencies that regulate federal financial institutions in the United States is:

The most probable price which a property should bring in a competitive and open market under all conditions requisite to a fair sale, the buyer and seller each acting prudently and knowledgeably, and assuming the price is not affected by undue stimulus. Implicit in this definition is the consummation of a sale as of a specified date and the passing of title from seller to buyer under conditions whereby:

1. Buyer and seller are typically motivated;
2. Both parties are well informed or well advised, and acting in what they consider their best interests;
3. A reasonable time is allowed for exposure in the open market;
4. Payment is made in terms of cash in United States dollars or in terms of financial arrangements comparable thereto; and
5. The price represents the normal consideration for the property sold unaffected by special or creative financing or sales concessions granted by anyone associated with the sale.

There are three economic principles that impact value. They are known as the *principle of alternatives,* the *principle of substitution* and the *principle of future benefits.* The principle of alternatives states that in any contemplated transaction, each party has alternatives to consummating the transaction. A willing generic buyer always has the alternative of other investments, or to make no investment at all.

The principle of substitution states that the value of a thing tends to be determined by the cost of acquiring an equally desirable substitute. This principle is applicable to the market approach where an investment is valued based on comparison with selling prices of guideline investments.

The principle of future benefits states that value changes in relationship to the expectation of future benefit derived from an investment. This principle is applicable to the income approach to value, wherein the expectation of earnings is converted into a value using a capitalization rate, multiplier, or discount rate that measures the systematic risk of the market for investments as a whole, and the unsystematic risk characteristics of the industry, individual firm, and type of investment.

WHEN AN APPRAISER IS NEEDED

An appraiser should be consulted whenever an independent viewpoint is needed. Unlike an accountant or attorney, an appraiser is not an advocate for his client. Given the same information and criteria, the opinions of value should be the same regardless as to who hired the appraiser. That said, appraising is not an exact science, and seldom is it possible to measure value with exact, mathematical accuracy. Instead, the appraiser must exercise a certain amount of judgment, make choices, and then arrive at a conclusion of value.

The function and use of an appraisal are important factors that can influence the determination of value, and they should be prominently stated in the appraisal report so that the client or users can better understand the circumstances under which the appraisal was conducted.

There are many reasons that an appraisal is needed. In general, they can be grouped into the four following basic categories:

- Transaction-based.
  Asking price for a seller.
  Offering price for a buyer.
  Value of an ownership interest for a buyout or buying.
  Employment stock ownership plans.
  Going public or going private.
  Financing.
- Tax planning-based.
  Basis for inheritance taxes.
  Basis for gift taxes.
  Recapitalization/estate freeze.
  Charitable contributions.
  Allocation of value among the tangible and intangible assets.
- Litigation-based.
  Compensatory damages.
  Divorce settlement.
  Minority interest rights.

Reorganization under bankruptcy.

Expert testimony.

Appraisal review.

- Insurance-based.

For payment of taxes.

Liquidation of estate stock.

Continuity of business (key man life insurance).

Buy/sell agreements.

APPRAISAL DISCIPLINES—THERE IS A DIFFERENCE

There are many appraisal disciplines that cover a broad range of businesses, real estate, machinery and equipment, and personal properties. No one person has the knowledge or skills to appraise everything. As in so many other professions, the requirement for specialists in the appraisal field is an absolute necessity. The American Society of Appraisers is one of the largest appraisal societies with over 6,000 members. It has identified six major appraisal disciplines and established appraisal standards, ethics, qualifications, testing, and certification for each of these disciplines. Additionally, there are many other specialized appraisal societies that have established appraisal standards, ethics, qualifications, testing, and certifications for their respective appraisal disciplines. The following is a list of the most prominent appraisal societies and their disciplines. A directory of their members can be obtained by contacting their national office.

Major Appraisal Societies

Appraisal Societies	Discipline
American Association of Certified Appraisers 800 Compton Rd., #10 Cincinnati, OH 45231 800-543-2222	Real Estate
American Society of Appraisers P.O. Box 17265 Washington, D.C. 20041 800-ASA-Valu	Businesses, Real Estate, Machinery and Technical Specialties, Personal Property, Appraisal Review and Management, Gems and Jewelry
Appraiser Association of America 386 Park Ave. South, #2000 New York, NY 10016 212-889-5404	Personal Property

Appraisal Societies	Discipline
The Appraisal Institute 875 North Michigan Ave, #2400 Chicago, IL 60611 312-335-4100	Real Estate
Appraisal Institute of America, Inc. 60 East 42nd Street New York, NY 10165 212-867-9775	Fine and Decorative Arts, Personal Property, and Gems and Jewelry
Association of Machinery and Equipment Appraisers 1110 Spring Street Silver Spring, MD 20910 301-587-9335	Machinery and Equipment
Institute of Business Appraisers P.O. Box 1447 Boynton Beach, FL 33435 407-732-3202	Businesses
International Society of Appraisers Riverview Plaza Office Park 16040 Christensen Rd., #320 Seattle, WA 98188 206-241-0359	Antiques, Furniture, Decorative Arts, and Gems and Jewelry
National Association of Independent Fee Appraisers 7501 Murdock Ave. St. Louis, MO 63119 314-781-6688	Real Estate
National Association of Master Appraisers 303 West Cypress Street San Antonio, TX 78712 210-271-0781	Real Estate
National Association of Real Estate Appraisers 8383 East Evans Rd. Scottsdale, AZ 85260 602-948-8000	Real Estate

All of the appraisal disciplines have common standards and codes of ethics, but the experience and qualifications needed to conduct appraisals and the methodologies used to determine value is significantly different for each discipline.

Machinery and equipment appraisers and personal property appraisers conduct appraisals of items owned by businesses or individuals. Examples include: machinery used in offices and industrial plants; office furniture; furniture and fixtures in retail stores; inventory; restaurant equipment; medical practice equipment; tooling and personal property such as coins, stamps, antiques, vehicles, and boats. These items are sometimes valued individually and sometimes valued as a whole in an operating facility. Machinery and equipment appraisers are generally familiar with manufacturing and supply costs, age and life characteristics, and cost segregation.

Real property appraisal involves the valuation of land, improvements, and associated rights. Examples include: residential properties, commercial properties, industrial properties, agricultural properties, and special-purpose buildings. Real property appraisers must be more or less conversant with the fields of building, civil engineering, architecture, surveying, forestry, soil science, agriculture, accounting, real estate brokerage, lending, urban land economics, government real estate regulations, and real estate law. A real property appraiser also needs an understanding of the income aspects of real estate, financing, and rates of return applicable to various types of investments.

Business appraisal has to do with the value inherent in ownership in an operating entity of a commercial, industrial, or service organization pursuing an economic activity. Examples include: common stock, preferred stock, debt instruments, warrants, options, sole proprietorship businesses, partnership interests, and intangible assets. The business appraiser draws heavily on the theory and practice of corporate finance and securities analysis, in addition to the requisite understanding of economics, business management, and accounting.

The following checklist helps determine whether the appraisal assignment should be done by a business appraiser or a real estate appraiser.

Business Appraisal or Real Property Appraisal Checklist

The following checklist helps determine which discipline—business appraisal or real property appraisal—is the pertinent appraisal discipline when valuing an entity. In some cases, as indicated by the checklist, both disciplines may be required.

A Business Appraisal	A Real Property Appraisal

Is the entity to be appraised:

[ ] A commercial, industrial or service organization pursuing an economic activity other than the sole operation of real estate?	[ ] A residential or commercial property (such as a single family residence, apartment house or office building)?
[ ] An equity interest (such as a security in a corporation or partnership interest)?	[ ] An interest in real estate (such as tenant in common or joint tenancy)?

Business Appraisal or Real Property Appraisal Checklist (Continued)

A Business Appraisal	A Real Property Appraisal
[ ] A fractional or minority interest (i.e., less than 100 percent of the entity)?	[ ] A whole or partial interest in real estate?
[ ] Difficult to split up (perhaps because the owners do not have a direct claim on the assets)?	[ ] Owners have a direct claim on their real estate interest?

Does the entity to be appraised:

A Business Appraisal	A Real Property Appraisal
[ ] Derive its revenues from providing goods or services?	[ ] Derive its revenues from the use or leasing of real estate?
[ ] Primarily use assets such as machinery, equipment, employee skill and talent in providing goods or services, and depend on assets other than or in addition to real estate to generate earnings?	[ ] Use real estate as its primary asset?
[ ] Conduct an economic activity which is more important than the location of the real estate where the economic activity is being conducted?	[ ] Conduct an activity wherein the location of the real estate is a primary valuation factor?
[ ] Likely have a value that fluctuates with conditions in its industry (as opposed to fluctuations in the real estate market)?	[ ] Have a value which fluctuates primarily with the real estate market?

Does the entity have:

A Business Appraisal	A Real Property Appraisal
[ ] Intangible assets such as patents, trademarks, copyrights, franchises, licenses, customer lists, employment contracts, noncompete covenants and goodwill which the entity uses to generate earnings?	[ ] Assets that are primarily tangible real estate. Insignificant or no intangible assets?
[ ] Substantial assets that can be moved?	[ ] Real estate and real estate related assets that cannot be moved?
[ ] A variety of tangible and intangible assets which interact to produce economic activity?	[ ] Primarily tangible real estate assets that produce the economic activity in the form of lease revenue or real estate use?
[ ] Significant operating expenses such as management, labor, marketing, advertising, research and transportation?	[ ] Operating expenses that are limited to real estate oriented expenses such as property management and maintenance?

Source: Business Appraiser or Real Property Appraiser—Determining Which to Use, Reprinted with permission, American Society of Appraisers, P.O. Box 17265, Washington, D.C.

APPRAISAL STANDARDS

Only a small percentage of individuals representing themselves as appraisers have been tested and certified by a professional appraisal society, and are thereby obligated to follow ethical and practice standards.

Each of the major professional appraisal societies has developed its own ethical and practice standards required to be followed by their members for their respective appraisal disciplines. Since 1986, the Standards Subcommittee of the American Society of Appraisers has been issuing practice standards for various aspects of conducting and reporting business appraisals. In 1991, the Institute of Business Appraisers, through its Standards Committee, issued a comprehensive set of ethical and practice standards required to be followed by its members. In 1993, the American Institute of Certified Public Accountants established a Business Valuation Committee, and it is now developing appraisal standards for its membership.

In 1988, nine of the leading U.S. professional appraisal organizations formed the Appraisal Foundation to serve as an umbrella organization for the appraisal industry. This organization has promulgated the Uniform Standards of Professional Appraisal Practice (USPAP), which established the first comprehensive appraisal practice standards for all appraisal disciplines. Standards 1 through 6 relate primarily to real estate appraisals. Standards 7 and 8 apply specifically to personal property and machinery and equipment, and Standards 9 and 10 apply specifically to business appraisals.

The ethics provisions of USPAP include the following elements:

- An appraiser must not engage in conduct that is unlawful, unethical, or improper.
- Compensation cannot be contingent upon the reporting of a predetermined value or a direction in value that favors the cause of the client.
- An appraiser must protect the confidential nature of the appraiser-client relationship.
- An appraiser must prepare written records of appraisals, including oral testimony, and retain such records for a period of at least five years after preparation or at least two years after final disposition of any judicial proceeding, whichever period expires last.
- In accepting an assignment, an appraiser must have the competency to conduct the appraisal or, alternatively, disclose the lack of knowledge and/or experience to the client before accepting the assignment.

The appraisal standards cover a broad range of appraisal activity. In summary, they are as follows:

1. Understand and correctly employ those recognized methods and procedures to produce a credible appraisal.
2. Not commit a substantial error or provide misleading information.
3. Must observe the following appraisal guidelines:
   a. Adequately identify the business and/or assets.
   b. Define the purpose and intended use.
   c. Specify any limiting conditions.
   d. Specify the effective appraisal date and extraordinary assumptions.
   e. Define the value being considered (fair market value, fair value, liquidation value).
   f. Collect and analyze relevant data regarding the nature and history of the business, financial and economic conditions of the business and industry, past results, current operations and future prospects, sales of guideline companies, prices, and terms and conditions affecting past sales.
   g. Describe the extent of the appraisal process employed and consider all appropriate valuation methods and procedures, and select one or more.
   h. Consider the size of interest being appraised and elements of ownership control.
   i. Reconcile various indications of value resulting from approaches used to arrive at the value conclusion.
   j. Provide signed certification stating: statements are true and correct; appraiser's independent and unbiased analyses; opinions and conclusions; compensation is not contingent on results or use; the report is in conformity with USPAP; signature of lead appraiser; and list of those who provided significant assistance.

APPRAISER QUALIFICATIONS

Appraiser qualifications will vary depending upon the type of property being appraised. Business appraisals are typically conducted by people with strong business backgrounds. They include business brokers, finance majors, accountants, and business consultants. Real estate appraisers will often have backgrounds in real estate brokerage and/or engineering. Machinery and equipment appraisers often have engineering backgrounds, or they have worked for equipment supply companies and/or auctioneers.

The credentials and credibility of an appraiser are key factors if the value conclusions are to be believable. Every appraisal assignment has the potential of litigation, and in such an event, the appraiser with the best credentials will usually prevail in a court of law. Users of appraisals frequently make the following mistakes when hiring an appraiser:

1. Fail to check the references of the appraiser.
2. Selects the appraiser with the lowest fee rather than the best credentials.
3. Select an appraiser who is not independent, such as the personal accountant for the company or a personal friend who would not be seen as independent by other parties.
4. Select an appraiser who does not have any experience in the required appraisal discipline.
5. Select an appraiser who does not have any experience in appraising similar properties to the subject property.
6. Hire part-time appraisers who have not kept up to date on appraisal standards and methodology.
7. Fail to get an engagement letter in writing from the appraiser specifying the scope of the assignment and the proposed fee.

All appraisers should have an introductory letter and resume. Ask for these items when contacting an appraiser, and then use the following criteria to serve as a benchmark from which to compare:

Educational Background

1. Do they have at least a college degree in their appraisal discipline or related field?
2. Have they taken courses in appraisal methodology from an accredited college or professional appraisal society?
3. Have they served as an instructor for appraisal courses taught on behalf of a college or professional appraisal society?
4. Do they have their own research library of appraisal textbooks, economic research materials, trade publications, and industry-specific materials relating to their appraisal discipline?
5. Are they actively participating in continuing educational programs within their appraisal discipline?

Professional Credentials

1. Do they belong to any professional appraisal societies?
2. Are they active in their professional societies (held any offices or served on any committees)?
3. Have they achieved any professional appraisal designations? (Designations issued by the accounting, legal, or engineering profession do not require any appraisal experience or testing and should not be relied upon as appraisal credentials.)

4. To achieve their professional designations, did they have to pass a written test, obtain approval of a completed appraisal report, and/or spend any time in the profession? (Some so-called appraisal professions are more interested in dues-paying members than in setting professional standards. Ask the appraisers about the requirements to obtain their designations.)

5. Are the appraisers required to take continuing education courses to maintain their professional designation?

Experience

1. How many years of appraisal experience do they have? (Many appraisal societies require at least two years experience before an appraiser can earn any appraisal designations.)

2. What types of appraisal work have they done (transaction-based appraisals, tax-based appraisals, insurance-based appraisals and/or litigation support)?

3. What experience do they have in giving expert testimony in courts of law? (Good appraiser must not only be able to write well, they must be able to verbally communicate under pressure with the client, users of the report, attorneys, judges, and juries.)

4. What experience do they have in appraising the specific type property? (It is not necessary that the appraiser have owned or managed similar properties; however, the appraiser should at least be familiar with the type property.)

5. Do they work alone or do they have a support staff? (It is very difficult for one person to do all the aspects of an appraisal by himself and be able to do any kind of production that would economically sustain him. Having a support staff to assist in the research and prepare the report is an indication that the appraisal will be done correctly and on time.)

Personal Characteristics

1. The appraiser should have a high degree of honesty and ethics. Being a member of a professional appraisal society is one assurance of having these attributes. Checking references is another way of determining the appraiser's honesty and ethics.

2. The appraiser should have a high degree of intelligence and an analytical mind. His education level is one indication of his ability to meet this criteria.

3. The appraiser should be detail-oriented, but able to grasp the "big picture." Being a good salesperson is not enough. An appraiser must have the unique ability to communicate well, understand the scope of the assignment, have the patience to do the proper research, conduct the appraisal in an analytical manner, and prepare an error-free report.

APPRAISAL FEES

It is unethical for an appraiser to charge a fee based on a contingency or preconceived value. Most appraisers' fees are calculated based on an hourly rate for themselves and their support staff. The fee may be communicated in one of two ways to the client. Some appraisers charge by the hour and will give the client an estimate of the number of hours required to complete the assignment; however, if it takes longer than estimated, the client will be responsible for paying for the additional time. On the other hand, if the appraisal can be completed in less time, the client benefits from the lower cost. Often, the client prefers a fixed cost for the appraisal, so the appraiser will estimate his time and then propose a fixed fee for the report. Most appraisers charge an hourly rate for litigation support because it is nearly impossible to estimate the time requirement for this type of activity. It is not uncommon that an appraiser will have two different hourly rates, one for conducting the appraisal and preparing the report, and another higher rate for serving as an expert witness. In all cases, the appraiser should provide the client with an engagement letter prior to starting the assignment that specifies the purpose, use, scope of the assignment, and the proposed fee arrangement.

SUMMARY

The measurement or estimation of value, specifically economic value, is what appraising is about. When an independent opinion of value is needed, hiring a qualified appraiser to conduct an appraisal using applicable standards and then to render an independent valuation can save many hours of frustrating negotiations in the buying and selling of businesses and their underlying assets.

Appraisers measure economic value based on standards of value such as fair market value, fair value, and investment value. Factors that influence value include the function and use of the appraisal, risk characteristics of the investment, and the economic principles of alternatives, substitution, and future benefits.

Appraisers are not advocates for their clients. Given the same information and criteria, the opinions of value should be the same, regardless who hires the appraiser. Appraising is not an exact science and it is seldom possible to measure value with exact, mathematical accuracy. The appraiser must exercise judgment and make choices and then arrive at a conclusion of value based on a dispassionate analysis of the facts of each assignment.

The function and use of an appraisal generally can be grouped into transaction-based uses, tax planning-based uses, litigation-based uses, or insurance-based uses. Value will be influenced by the selected standard of value and the function and use of the appraisal.

There are many different appraisal disciplines that include business, real estate, machinery and equipment, and personal property. Appraisers specialize within these disciplines. Each of the appraisal disciplines has one or more professional appraisal societies that provide training, education, standards, and codes of ethics for their members. The Appraisal Foundation is an umbrella organization for the appraisal industry, and by way of its various committees, professional standards have been developed that most of the appraisal societies and their members follow in the course of conducting appraisals and reporting opinions of value.

The credentials and credibility of an appraiser are key factors if the value conclusions are to be believable. When hiring an appraiser, the client should verify the appraiser's educational background, professional credentials, actual experience, and personal honesty and ethics as it relates to the type of property to be appraised. Furthermore, the client should insist upon an engagement letter with the appraiser that specifies the purpose, use and scope of the assignment, and the fee arrangement. In the acquisition or sale of a business, an appraiser should be hired for the same reasons that accountants and attorneys are hired—their specialized expertise.

C H A P T E R
T W E N T Y - F O U R

The Role of the Machinery and Technical Appraiser

LESLIE H. MILES, JR.
CHIEF EXECUTIVE OFFICER
MB VALUATION SERVICES, INC.

The assets of a company are made up of many tangible and intangible properties. Buyers of a business, in many cases, do not concern themselves with the value of these assets other than for reasons that are secondary to the acquisition. The buyer of the company is first and foremost measuring the return of and on the investment. The question is, "What will this company do for me?"

Although the primary reason for acquiring a business is the return derived from that business, acquisitions have occurred for companies in order to close them, thereby taking out the competition. At other times, an intangible such as a patent, trademark, or client base may be important. For any reason other than the continuing operation of the business, value of the additional or remaining assets can become important.

Secondary reasons for measuring the value of assets before or after an acquisition can be the tax consequences. In many cases, the tax liabilities may impact the expected return in a way that was unanticipated. The obvious tax consequence is depreciation as it impacts the net return. This is usually a known amount when buying a corporation in which depreciation simply continues on books where values are already assigned. On the other hand, there are many sales in which there is a requirement for allocation of the depreciable assets. This allocation may be through an agreement of both buyer and seller, as either side could be affected. The seller is concerned about recapture on assets that have been depreciated below the new value assignment. The buyer wants to capture as much of the purchase price in depreciable assets as possible. Even if buyer and seller agree on an asset allocation, it is always possible that the IRS may challenge and effect a change.

In some states, the ad valorem tax issues become very important. Most states use mass appraisal techniques and typically request the company's original cost and date of acquisition from which a value is derived. Although states may differ, the majority of appraisers for assessment districts take the original cost and index to the current date and then apply an age/life formula that indicates a percent good. These percent good factors, in many cases, do not allow assets to fall below a certain base percentage depending upon the category of assets. There are some states that consider assets to never fall below a 30 to 40 percent residual. Once this base is reached, the number can still go up each year due to inflation built into the index applied to original cost.

One can see that the reallocation of assets may have a legal requirement for rendering this *new value* to the assessing district. This, obviously, with a higher allocation, can increase the ad valorem tax to be paid. In addition, the district's appraisal technique may not adjust for historical cost and may use the allocation date in which its percent good tables begin again.

To assist in these situations, it may be necessary to obtain the services of an independent appraiser, although it is possible to represent value with company personnel and opinions. However, in most cases, this is the same as an individual representing himself in a court of law. On the other hand, a particular appraiser may not be appropriate in specific cases. An example of this would be an appraiser not experienced in litigation areas with specific emphasis to ad valorem tax issues or IRS valuation. The user of the report should also be assured that the definition or interpretation of a value concept is appropriate. In tax cases, there is written code or law that may reference fair market value or market value or some other synonymous term. That value is interpreted many different ways and can be slanted toward a particular advocacy position by the authority and, in some cases, by the taxpayer. Thus there should be an understanding of value concepts and their uses. For the purposes of this chapter, the definitions of the following terms in Chapter 23, by the American Society of Appraisers' MTS Committee are set out for reference:

> *Note:* Unique circumstances may demand specific definitions not found in Chapter 23. Many terms are used to describe notions of value. The definitions offered are to provide the fundamental concepts. They are not the only acceptable definitions, since contracts may dictate a somewhat different notion. Therefore, these definitions may be expanded or modified as the purpose and function of the appraisal may dictate, as long as the fundamental concept is not altered.
>
> *Reproduction Cost—New.*
> *Replacement Cost—New.*
> *Fair Market Value.*
> *Fair Market Value in Continued Use.*
> *Fair Market Value—Installed.*
> *Fair Market Value—Removal.*
> *Liquidation Value in Place.*
> *Orderly Liquidation Value.*
> *Forced Liquidation Value.*
> *Salvage Value.*
> *Scrap Value.*
> *Insurance Replacement Cost.*
> *Insurable Value Depreciated.*

The definitions in Chapter 23 have been developed by the M&E Committee and accepted by the 1991 Board of Governors of the ASA and previously published in the *ASA MTS Journal.*

These definitions are set out for machinery and equipment and may differ somewhat from those used in real estate. It is obvious that most appraisals of real estate do not anticipate the removal from one location to another, as does personal property. For these reasons, there are some unique factors between properties that require some alterations in definitions.

At the time of this writing, there are 11 states that have ad valorem tax assessment on inventory. Inventory is that raw, in-process, or finished material for the manufacturing of or sale of products that are sold on a day-to-day basis. The following are some suggested definitions that may apply to inventory:

> *Forced Liquidation Value (for inventory)* is "the estimated gross amount expressed in terms of money that might be realized at a properly advertised and conducted public auction sale, orderly liquidation sale (or a combination of the two) with the seller being compelled

to sell with a sense of immediacy on an as-is, where-is basis, under present-day economic trends."

Orderly Liquidation Value (for inventory) is "the amount of gross proceeds that could be generated by a properly conducted inventory liquidation held under forced sale conditions and over a reasonably short period of time. This takes into consideration any inflationary or depreciable conditions that affect value, such as mix, quantity, type and condition of inventory, marketability, and psychological appeal. It is assumed that the buyers would be responsible for cost of removal at their own risk and expense, and that any price would be F.O.B. point of origin."

Liquidation Value in Continued Use (for inventory) is "the projected amount obtainable with the *assumption* that the entire inventory would be purchased intact as a functioning, viable adjunct to the sustained production of the finished product. The value concept considers that fair market value (cost) cannot be obtained because of forced sale conditions; reflects that the inventory would have acceptance to a buyer; and yet considers the impact of failure."

Fair Market Value (for inventory) is "the estimate of today's cost to the current owner and under that buyer's pricing structure. It discounts for any depreciated factors including all forms of obsolescence, if any, and deducts in inventory found lacking in utility."

Fair Market Value in Continued Use (for inventory) is "the price which a willing buyer would be justified in paying for the inventory in-place, and a willing seller would be warranted in accepting if each is: (1) well informed or well advised; (2) motivated by reactions of typical users; (3) free of undue stimulus; (4) financially capable of ownership and/or use; and (5) allowed a reasonable length of time to test the market." For a manufacturer's inventory, it assumes that continuation of marketable products, thereby encompassing work-in-process and support items for proprietary products.

As there is potential for some type of value requirement, an appraisal may be something that should be considered from the very beginning. For an acquisition, an appraisal could be useful for documentation and insurance, values of assets that may be excess to the needs of the company, loans in which the assets may be collateral for the purchase, a measurement of recovery in the event that the business does not work out as suggested, buy and sell agreements, purchase options on leases, and tax as previously discussed. The following are some suggestions on choosing an appraiser as adapted from an article written by Jackie L. Montalvo, published in *Dimensions of Value,* 5th Edition, Chapter 5, "Choosing an Appraiser."

When contracting an appraisal firm, there are questions that should be asked of the firm as well as directed to the staff appraisers. If an appraiser is independent, he may follow his own policies and procedures regarding appraisals, whereas the staff appraiser is obligated to follow all rules and regulations set forth by his employer. It is important to know the background of the appraiser or appraisers assigned to a project, as their expertise may be within a different industry and/or may not be to the level necessary for the project in question. This is especially true regarding machinery and equipment, where the individual's training process requires years to reach the level of what some firms term as "senior appraiser."

Being a senior appraiser, project leader, or engagement appraiser for an appraisal assignment requires a level of knowledge and experience that, until recently was gained primarily from on-the-job training, as no formal education or degree was available. Although great strides have been made in the appraisal profession regarding formal education, practical knowledge and on-the-job experience is a necessary part of appraising machinery and equipment, and is not something that can be gained solely from books. Laying the groundwork for the beginning appraiser is, as in any profession, crucial to his future success. To become a professional golfer, for example, it is necessary to begin formal training before any bad habits have been formed. Mastering the game of golf takes hours of practice everyday; if practice is not continually ongoing, the level of present capability will not be maintained or improved. Success in any field requires drive, dedication, desire, and a willingness to learn.

An individual who has the desire to become a competent machinery and equipment appraiser, like the golfer, must realize the goal cannot be quickly attained. Proper training requires that certain steps be followed in a progressive order:

1. The first step of training could be working in sales, marketing, research, or as a *market analyst* to familiarize the novice with nomenclature used within the appraisal profession regarding machinery and equipment and the related value concept meanings. Working in this area requires contact with manufacturers, competitors, dealers, and the general public for gathering required information. This exposure will enhance his communication skills, as well as broaden his knowledge of the appraisal profession. There are some firms that start with step number 2 as on-the-job training; incorporating step number 1 is preferred.

2. The next step of training would be as an *appraiser trainee,* which also involves market analyst work but includes on-the-job training, listing basic peripheral equipment such as office furniture and business machines, small hand tools (powered and manual), material handling, and miscellaneous plant furniture such as ladders, bins, baskets, and workbenches. This step will give exposure to the method of listing an appraisal whether it be by the dictation or

written method, teach how to describe an item properly, and expose the trainee to the use and general application of the various value concepts, all of which will enable him to become value-oriented.

3. When the trainee is able to accomplish listing basic peripherals, he will then progress to the level of *junior appraiser.* The junior appraiser should be able to list minor equipment such as computers, forklifts, drill presses, bench and pedestal grinders, cutoff saws, and other common equipment found in most any manufacturing plant. To accomplish this requires constant exposure to these various industries to be able to recognize and properly describe these items. The ability to properly describe equipment is an art that is learned before the capability of placing values, understanding the various value concepts and their meanings, and then applying these concepts to equipment.

4. Once value understanding is accomplished, the individual will have reached the level of *appraiser* and will begin training under the direction of a senior appraiser, describing and placing values on major equipment. At this level, the appraiser is taught to handle certain aspects of the job that allows direct communication with the client. This is very important, as communication is developed only through experience and is typically the last step in the training process before becoming a senior appraiser.

5. A *senior appraiser* has the ability to handle all aspects of a job from initial contact with a client, quoting the job, performing the appraisal, producing the bound formal report, and collecting the fee. This is not to say that a senior appraiser has total knowledge of all industries, but rather the ability to find information and the wherewithal to seek the expertise of others, when needed. It takes approximately five years from the initial step of market analyst to become a senior appraiser in the machinery and equipment profession.

Although these levels of expertise have been labeled market analyst, appraiser trainee, junior appraiser, appraiser, and senior appraiser, they are merely terms and may vary with each company; however, the order of training defined under each level should be followed to obtain the top goal of this profession.

It is possible for an appraiser to be limited in his ability due to his area of expertise; for this reason it is important to know, when looking at an appraiser's qualifications, if he is disciplined in a specialized area. An individual who has been practicing the profession of appraising for 20 years and specializing in an industry such as medical equipment may require assistance to properly perform an appraisal in industries such as metal equipment, wood equipment, plastic equipment, chemical equipment, food processing equipment, and paper mills, as his knowledge may not relate to those industries.

To remain current within the appraisal profession, an appraiser should continue his education, as well as educate the user of his reports (the client). This can be done by attending, giving, and participating in seminars, which allow both parties the opportunity to clarify any past problems or confusion. Individualized seminars could also be made available by the appraiser to provide a method of contact with the client on a more personal basis. Newsletters, quarterly and/or yearly publications are other ways of providing client education, and can be used as educational tools for individual and group in-house training sessions. Communication through education stimulates new ideas, which in turn could generate procedural alterations to better meet the client's needs.

There are many appraisal firms, with more being formed every day; this is also true of appraisal societies. Becoming a member of these societies gives an appraiser the ability and opportunity to achieve senior certification and/or designation in the appraisal profession; however, credentials do not necessarily make a qualified appraiser.

The MAI (Member Appraisal Institute) designation relates to fair market value of real estate and, at this time, does not encompass the appraisal of machinery and equipment. This well-known designation, which typically takes years to obtain, adds a high degree of credibility and professionalism to the appraiser due to the stringent experience, testing, and educational requirements. The American Society of Appraisers has similar requirements, and was the first multidisciplinary society in which senior members may be multiple- or single-disciplined using the senior designation ASA after their name. Some of the basic eligibility requirements for this designation are:

A college degree or equivalent;
Five years appraisal experience;
Personal investigation;
Passing oral and written tests;
Meeting attendance requirements; and
Recertification every five years.

The American Society of Appraisers, as well as other societies, requires recertification, sometimes by a point system, in an attempt to assure continuing education. This can be accomplished by meeting attendance, educational participation, authorship, and service requirements within the various segments of the organization or its chapters. For an individual to be a member of the Association of Machinery and Equipment Appraisers (AMEA), he is required to be employed by a firm that has been a member of the Machinery Dealers National Association (MDNA) for a minimum of five years. Comparatively, AMEA is a relatively new organization that refers to machinery and equipment as its only discipline; it is now a testing and recertification society. Nevertheless, the AMEA is a well-respected organization.

Having more than one appraisal designation may indicate that the appraiser is a professional who wishes to emphasize his professionalism by the use of designations and/or memberships in the appraisal societies. Designations and memberships provide educational opportunities through courses and publications, lend credibility in areas such as court testimony, presentations before peers, and appraisal reports. However, the mere use of designations does not automatically confer equal competence to all appraisers who hold these credentials. It is possible to obtain an excellent appraisal from an appraiser who is not designated, but extremely knowledgeable under the concept of value applied to the equipment, inventory, or real estate being appraised. It is also possible to have an appraiser with the most prestigious credentials obtainable provide an appraisal report that would be considered improper by many societies and individual appraisers, just as everyone with a driver's license is not necessarily a good driver, and most, in all probability, are not capable of driving in the Indianapolis 500. There are varying degrees of capability in obtaining any type of license just as there are differences in appraisers, regardless of age, experience, or designations.

It is also possible to have appraisers at different levels of capability within a very credible appraisal firm, and there may be an even greater disparity between appraisers within the same valuation society. Naturally, the societies do their best to have appraisers maintain consistency, value accuracy and fiduciary responsibility, but they cannot monitor the formal report, which, in most instances, is held in confidence. Therefore, it should not be assumed that a designated appraiser is going to practice the methods and standards of valuation for which the society stands. There are many organizations that issue credentials, which, in lieu of testing requirements, have stringent experience requirements, but the validity of those requirements are not checked. This does not mean that such organizations are not worthy of membership, but that the basic knowledge of the existing members might be questioned (if this laxness in attitude were known).

Organizations, memberships, and even *experience* do not make a good appraiser, just as a real estate broker, engaged in the sale of real estate, is not automatically a good appraiser. However, there is no question that a real estate broker selling real estate has an advantage when appraising real property, if he has the ability to relate to that sales experience. The machinery dealer or auctioneer has certain advantages in conducting appraisals of equipment if there is no conflict of interest. Individuals who are members of societies have an advantage in valuation work if their memberships are upheld by continuing education and active participation in the organizations to which they belong. Designations are good to have and do add credibility to the individual appraiser, but the experience, knowledge, professionalism, and how they are utilized and applied, are the distinguishing features of a good appraiser.

It is possible for an appraiser to have knowledge within a specific area but be limited in his capability due to his lack of knowledge of the various value concepts and their use. For example, an appraiser whose only involvement in writing appraisals has been for acquisitions and insurance purposes could conceivably have a difficult time making a value judgment under any of the failure concepts; therefore, it is important to know the appraiser's knowledge and experience level in this area.

An appraisal should reflect a value that could be recommended as a proper price in light of all prevailing conditions. The formal value analysis should be provided by a reputable appraiser unaffected by prejudice or bias. He should be able to understand and consider the use and volatility of all value concepts, enabling him to handle all aspects of his job. "Volatility," as used in this paragraph, refers to the likelihood of a later test or happening "in fact" at or close to the indicator.

Most appraisal societies and organizations have written codes of ethics that are provided to govern each individual appraiser's conduct and practice. An appraiser that is a member of these organizations should adhere to the letter and spirit of those codes through his standard appraisal practice, and should maintain membership of only those societies that allow him to conform, without conflict, to each respective society's ethics, as well as his own personal and professional beliefs.

A client should be confident that the appraisal firm that he retains is one of high integrity and credibility; further, he should expect that any errors or omissions made in the report, discovered after payment has been made, will be corrected as long as there is proper justification supporting those changes. It is becoming more commonplace for a client to review the assigned values and justification in order to see that all information is included and considered before the final report is issued. This procedure helps avoid time delays and later revisions due to some oversight or mistake by the client, typist, and/or the appraiser in charge.

When considering an appraisal firm, there are several areas that should be evaluated. One area with regard to an appraiser or appraisal firm would be background and acceptance in the marketplace. When looking at areas such as financial restructuring, acquisitions, and/or leveraged buyouts (LBOs), the acceptance of an appraisal firm is very important. A client using an asset-based lender will most likely shop around for the best interest rate and best structured payback he can get; this would require the acceptance of his appraisal report by many lenders. It is known throughout the appraisal profession that there are "in-house" lists of acceptable appraisal firms, a practice followed by many lending institutions. A lender's client could have had a recent appraisal study from one that would not be acceptable by the lender; this would, therefore, require another appraisal by one of the accepted appraisal firms on that particular lender's list. The greater the appraiser's acceptance in the marketplace for use in an asset-based loan, the more palatable the recommendation for that valuation firm.

With regard to financing, the appraisal process is one of the final steps. When contracting an appraisal firm, it is important to understand typical time *requirements* for any given project; this generally depends upon the scope of the work that is to be accomplished. If, for example, real estate and machinery and equipment are combined in one report, having separate departments in the appraisal firm could enable work within the various areas (real estate and machinery and equipment) to be done simultaneously, so that the culmination of each area will meet the time requirement for production of the formal report. It is difficult to discuss exact "on-site" timing as there are too many variables, such as multiple locations, number of items to be listed, unanticipated requirements, or density including cancellations or delays, travel time, number of values to be applied, asset tagging, or other types of requests.

It may not be necessary to contract with different companies to perform appraisals within the different disciplines of valuation concepts. It behooves any appraisal firm to be well rounded in its capabilities. Some, therefore, may be able to perform all, or a portion of, any of the areas mentioned here and accomplish them at the same time. Departmentalization staffed with multidiscipline certified and designated appraisers would enable an appraisal of a company's assets in total to be made through one company rather than many. This can avoid overlaps between disciplines, and provides consistency in the understanding of concepts. There are three major categories (numbers 1, 2, and 3 of the following six disciplines listed here) that make up business assets other than intangibles, cash, or receivables:

1. *Machinery and equipment,* sometimes referred to as personalty or fixed assets, is typically described as items used for product manufacture rather than items considered as a part of real estate or available for day-to-day sale. This would include such items as machine tools, office furniture and business machines, vehicles, plant furniture, and material-handling equipment.

2. For *real property,* which could be commercial, industrial, unimproved, rural, or residential property, it is necessary to determine whether other items should be considered as part of the real estate and improvements or equipment. Bridge cranes or wall-mounted water fountains might be considered equipment for purchase allocation, insurance, or in a few cases, remarketing, under a removal concept.

3. *Inventory,* which in the past was valued by an assumption of residual percentage applied to cost, can now be sample-tested using computer software that breaks down products into the various mixes in order to derive a measurement that might apply to the overall inventory. This new concept provides more comfort in the inventory assets heretofore not held. The new procedures are:

   Inventory mix as observed;

   "Causes and effects" measured;

Stocking and record-keeping scrutinized;

Turns and obsolescence queried; and

Sampling of the overall inventory made to complete the analysis.

When inventory is being valued as described, the appraiser becomes familiar with the printed inventory supplied while on-site and then can appreciate inventory quality, understand the descriptions, recognize any proprietary materials or parts, observe differences in record-keeping as it relates to raw, in-process, finished inventory, and what is considered in each of these areas; the appraiser can understand how cost is applied to the inventory schedules, including units of measure. This specially developed software is set up to allow measurements of inventory in any form without reinspection so that judgments can be made as changes take place in the client's inventory mix. This approach to measuring inventory is required more often due to the more detailed inspection of the furnished inventory that may be utilized for current and/or future advance rates or other monetary considerations.

4. *Business valuations* are typically requested when a client is selling a company, and are sometimes necessary to measure the viability of the business. In making a purchase (allocation), value is placed on the machinery and equipment, real estate, and inventory. Additional value considerations are made for the business over and above physical assets if the company is considered as profitable and/or having future potential. There are some cases when the "goodwill value" of a business, if properly analyzed, indicates an amount at or less than the assets to be allocated. Business valuations are required more frequently so that other decisions might be influenced. If there is a requirement of an adjustment in the business for improvement, or if the company is extremely profitable with a good future, this may be reflected in the "business valuation"; business brokers, purchasers, and asset-based lenders are becoming more aware of this type of measurement.

5. *Software appraisals* can be difficult to analyze due to the various methods of measurement. The worth of software is the return on an investment that might be projected by its sale and/or use. Two specific methods of measurements are income, and cost of replacement (adjusted); income is typically used to establish fair market value and reproduction cost for fair market value in-use. Remarketing of software is very difficult to anticipate, thus valuations are used more to determine market potential, use viability, and allocation for a purchase.

6. Many areas of a business are considered *intangible*. Some examples are: trade name, customer lists, trained personnel, patents, recipes, some types of software, strategic location, product lines, and management. In most cases, intangibles are incorporated within the

business valuation but can be broken out where sufficient information can be discovered or is supplied; this could allow a proper measurement to establish value. The capability of recognizing intangibles and their contributory factors is an important element in the selection of an appraisal firm by those who use these types of value studies.

There are additional services that can be offered by an appraisal firm that might benefit a client when choosing an appraisal firm. "Extras" may include updates, revisions, asset tracking, inventory auditing, market studies, special reports, and computer information transfer.

There are general questions to ask of appraisers or appraisal firms in order to help determine their understanding of areas directly related to the project. The individual doing the investigation should understand that not all the recommended questions are appropriate in all cases and/or may have been answered in previous queries or be common knowledge to the industry. Some questions may be used to "get" comfortable with the individual or simply measure consistency of responses. The following questions to ask an appraisal firm are offered in random order, and not necessarily the most suitable for a given interview.

1. How long have you been in business?
2. How do you define all concepts of value for machinery and equipment, real estate, and/or inventory?
3. Does your company sell equipment, real estate, and/or inventory?
   Brokerage?
   Auction?
   Entire companies?
   Orderly liquidation?
   Sales from your own warehouse?
4. How many employees do you have?
5. How many appraisers do you have? Do you have qualification sheets for all of your appraisers?
6. Does the signing appraiser of the report have to be on-site?
   How long?
   Are there assistants?
   Can an assistant be left on-site to complete the work?
7. How large is your research library; what does it generally contain?
8. Do you have an asset database for equipment and real estate?
   How many items?
   Where do you get the information?
   How is the information kept up to date?

What categories are used to store the information; how easy is it to retrieve?

9. Is your company prepared to testify on any appraisal it performs and at what cost?

10. Are your appraisers designated by any societies?
    Which ones?
    Are the designations obtained from testing (passing examinations)?
    Are the designations for a specific discipline, such as machinery and equipment, real estate, fine arts, gems and jewelry?

The following questions would be asked of an individual appraiser (independent fee appraiser) in addition to the preceding:

1. Are you designated by any societies, and did you have to pass examinations, be tested, and/or attend classes?

2. How long have you been an appraiser?

3. Would you personally be the signer of the formal report?

4. Do you have any specialization in which you know more than any other area, such as woodworking, plastics, other?

5. Estimate the number of appraisals for which you have been totally responsible.

6. Have you ever testified in court?
   What value concepts?
   What type of assets?
   Representing debtor, creditor, or both?
   Are you willing to testify on any appraisal you conduct and at what cost?

7. What is your background in general; would you send a qualification sheet?

8. Do you have any support staff?

9. Have you ever written articles; if so, have you been published? Where?

10. If the appraisal project involves a particular industry, ask the following:
    Could you speak generally about the industry and the usual types of equipment you would find there other than the standard items you find in most industries?
    What is the general economic condition of that industry?

When conducting the interview, there are certain responses you should expect from an appraiser or firm that is knowledgeable. The following are considered to be appropriate responses; if not given, a sufficient explanation supporting the individual's interpretation should be offered. The responses are numbered to correspond to the questions preceding:

1. The firm should be in business long enough to have the experience necessary to conduct the job in question. This time measurement could be used for other reflections such as:

How successful and established the company is.

The individuals who are to conduct the work have been associated in a value-oriented business long enough to allow a confidence level not normally associated with a company in business for a short time.

Whether too little experience for the amount of monetary consideration or overall scope of the project is evident.

2. Values should be defined differently for equipment, real estate, and inventory due to the variations associated with those assets. Real estate cannot be removed, whereas equipment moves from place to place. Inventory may be dependent upon whether the appraisal is being done for a manufacturer's inventory, distributor's inventory, wholesale inventory or retail inventory, and so on.

3. The response to selling equipment should either be yes or no, without any vague representations. The majority of appraisers who sell assets have a license to do so and are able to provide names of companies they have sold that can be checked. It does not necessarily matter whether the appraiser has sold equipment in the past and could be a matter of lender preference, but the forthrightness of the response or, conversely, the defensive posture taken by the individual being interviewed could have meaning to the investigation.

4. The number of employees could indicate a general maturity of the company no matter how long the company has been in business. It would reflect on the amount of work being conducted in order to support that employee base. The employee base should include only those salaried and paid directly by the appraisal firm, not subcontractors or part-time employees.

5. The number of appraisers is different from the number of employees, and may depend upon the definition of the word appraiser. An appraiser is the individual who assigns values and conducts the on-site listing, as opposed to the support staff, such as typists, accountants, and so on. Regarding support staff, there are typically three support people to each appraiser. It is always advisable to obtain qualification sheets for all appraisers who could be assigned to any project. If it is known which appraiser is going to be assigned to the project, it would be a matter of referencing his qualification sheet as a reminder of who that individual is. It is prudent to keep a master file on the company, as well as individual subfiles on each appraiser, so that their reports may be analyzed at a later date. As stated earlier, it is possible for one appraiser to be more qualified than another within the same firm or as measured by the interviewer who achieves a comfort level with that specific individual. If one appraiser is more respected than another by a particular client, this would enable the company to continue doing business with this client even if another appraiser is in disfavor with the client. Any company should allow any appraiser to handle jobs for which he is requested.

6. The signer of the report should have viewed the assets to which values were assigned. Items of significant value should be directly appraised by the individual responsible for the project—the senior appraiser—and, therefore, enough time should be allowed so that appraiser can complete that portion of the study. It is not necessary for the signer of the report to be the individual who lists all items; assistants or junior appraisers (appraiser trainees) can list standard types of equipment such as office furniture, plant furniture and fixtures, and so on, although the senior appraiser is still responsible. Assuming that all major equipment has been observed by the appraiser and the appraiser is comfortable with signing the final report, not having listed all items at the facility, there certainly should be no objection to having support personnel complete the itemization process.

7. The size of a library may be difficult to describe, but could be stated in number of books; square footage; dollars spent or allotted each year; or types of storage, books, tabloids, computer database, and other. The interviewer should look for the quality of the materials a library contains. There should be basic research material for all types of appraisal work, whether it be inventory, real estate, and/or machinery and equipment. Machinery and equipment and inventory should have sales data and asking prices for all categories to be appraised. If your interview is general in nature, the categories of referenced material may limit the appraiser to only those respective segments of industry. At the very least, machinery and equipment appraisers should have such reference material as the *Green Guide,* serial number reference books, books supplied by services that monitor auctions, information personally gained from prior investigations and auction attendance, and possibly information obtained from others through trade agreements. Most real estate appraisers should have the *Marshall & Swift* and/or *R.S. Means* reference books, and many reports of sales gathered on an ongoing basis or as a result of past appraisal studies. A real estate reference library should be investigated for location and dated comparables.

8. The previous question regarding what a library contains could answer any questions regarding a research database. However, the database may not be brought up, so it may be necessary to ask specifically about it. In any event, the database must be interpreted, and specific questions can give some reference as to its quality. Obviously, without an on-site inspection to view the appraiser's facilities and procedures, it is impossible to know if the responses are accurate. It is advisable, therefore, at the first opportunity, to make a spot inspection after an interview in order to qualify the responses. The quantity of items in a database can be estimated, and should be in thousands, but could be more limited if the appraiser has a narrower scope of practice such as oil field equipment. Again, the number of items may not be as important as the dating of those comparables or the quality. Expect quick responses to questions regarding how the information is gained; when a library is kept current, it should be easy to detail where the information is coming from. There should be at least four good sources from which information continues to be gathered, and possibly others in which comparables are obtained on an "as-needed" basis.

Certainly, the use of other databases is acceptable, but then the reference library must be evaluated with no less scrutiny than that of the individual or company being interviewed. Answers can go from one extreme to another and still be acceptable, and the answer may be obvious from previous questions. However, the general gathering of information is a different response than one that addresses the procedural method by which it is being maintained for easy retrieval. The retrieval method may be through the use of categories, or in computer terminology, "database structure." When asking for information on a specific piece of equipment, the response of how that information can be found could clarify whether the database is being used properly or the research is being stored in a manner acceptable for retrievable.

9. Any appraiser should be willing to support the indicated results, and, therefore, willing to testify. Even though an individual or company may not be expert in testimony, they should be willing to testify when required.

Cost for testimony is separate from appraisal fees, and is typically much more expensive on a daily rate because testimony does not allow the appraiser to work on other jobs, which are, in the long term, more profitable. An example of this would be an appraisal that cost $25,000 formulated by a standard acceptable day rate charge, whereas testimony, considering only two days, could cost $2,000 and may be three to four times the day rate charged for the original appraisal.

Due to the scheduling of the testimony, it is possible that the appraiser may have had to turn down other jobs that would have had long-term benefits, including that of serving a client who gives the appraiser other business. The appraiser would be unable to utilize office staff (usually considered billable) and, therefore, must be supported out of the testimony fee. In response to the question, it is necessary to understand the difference between willingness to testify and the cost inherent in testimony.

10. It is not necessary for all appraisers to be designated by any society, but it is certainly a way of measuring the effort of the individual that is directed toward continuing his education and professionalism; that he strives to maintain his standing within the appraisal profession rather than treating it as a sideline to some other business. Societies have different membership requirements; the American Society of Appraisers and the American Institute of Real Estate Appraisers require a broad education, specific discipline testing, and recertification. This may hold true of many other societies, which will strengthen the credibility of the certification. In contrast, some designations are simply obtained by filling out an application and sending in an annual fee. This does not mean, however, that the application does not have specific requirements that must be met and possibly investigated before the certification is issued. Several such societies publish a wealth of information each year that is extremely valuable in the appraisal profession and, therefore, contributes to the profession. These various societies may impose later educational and testing requirements and possibly even recertification which, again, would strengthen the designations' credibility. It is necessary to understand the requirements of the various societies and their designations rather than simply the number of designations. If the appraisal foundation guidelines are accepted for state licensing, *all* appraisers may someday be required to be licensed and recertified even if not a member of the society.

The responses to questions posed to an individual appraiser should generally be similar to those given by a firm. However, there are additional questions that could be asked of an independent fee appraiser. The response numbers correspond to the questions:

1. Society requirements for designations assigned to an individual appraiser can typically be outlined by the member who is active or designated within that society. Generally, the same type of response should be expected as indicated in company response number 10.

2. Time is associated with experience and experience should be associated with accuracy. Unfortunately, this is not always the case, as appraisers can become complacent and not adapt to new technology or ideas. But it stands to reason that the greater the experience, if associated with continuing education, the better the appraiser, and potentially a more credible witness. There are many good appraisers with limited experience, as there are those with a vast amount of participation in conducting appraisals or sales. The best of all worlds would be an appraiser who was associated with more experienced individuals and, thereby, gained knowledge over a shorter period of time than the more experienced person who had as his guide only trial and error. It should be ascertained whether the less experienced appraiser has gained knowledge and is continuing to improve upon his skills as an appraiser with time. It is possible that the less experienced appraiser could be a better choice than the more experienced appraiser by virtue of his being innovative and having a greater desire for interest to being the best within his profession.

3. If the appraiser being interviewed is the one who signs the report, this is an indication of status or position within the firm. If someone else has this responsibility, more than likely the individual being interviewed is a "union appraiser" or is subject to review by a supervisor who should possibly also be interviewed.

4. Specialization has good and bad points that should be addressed. If an individual has specialized expertise, that person may be the best for specific jobs, but not all jobs. Experience can be diversified between many industries, but not all; therefore, expertise imposes limits on the type of assignments given to such a specialist. A better explanation of this factor can be read in "Liquidation Value" in the American Society of Appraiser's *Valuation* Monograph, December 1977.

5. The exact number of appraisals performed by any individual might be difficult to provide, but certainly an estimate of the number of reports per year is possible. Most active appraisers would have accomplished at least 30 or more per year and, in some cases, depending upon support staff and type of studies, could have performed in excess of 100. Obviously, with only 365 days in a year, it would be difficult to explain an individual appraiser performing 1,200 appraisals over a three-year period. However, it may indicate that a particular senior appraiser was responsible for the conduct of appraisals accomplished by others. The wording of a question must be specific and the answer properly interpreted. There is a difference between how many appraisals an individual was responsible for as opposed to how many he actually performed. A "junior appraiser" may not have performed any of the appraisals for which he was responsible, because he did not have the level of experience required.

6. Testifying in court has many facets that should be analyzed. If judicial appraisal support is ever anticipated, no matter how unlikely, the testimony question can be of utmost importance. An individual who can explain replacement cost could be boxed in on questions associated with market, and vice versa. It may even be difficult for an appraiser with experience in one type of industry or field to testify on another field with special emphasis to the differences between real estate, inventory, and machinery and equipment. If an appraiser *typically* represents a creditor, a sharp debtor attorney could imply that the appraiser is an *advocate* and, therefore, his testimony would be considered biased. Again, ascertain that the appraiser is willing to testify and/or support the values that are indicated in the studies for which he is responsible.

7. All appraisers should have a qualification sheet; some may be more in-depth than required. In any event, the background of an appraiser *is* as important as for an employee applying for a job that requires experience.

8. An individual appraiser may or may not have support staff, and could use subcontractors. If there is no support staff and an assignment is possible for a large job with restrictive time requirements, it may be necessary to determine who the subcontractors would be, as when an appraiser has a reputation for accomplishing excellent work and the interviewer wants to give this appraiser a larger assignment. However, there are some appraisers who don't want to tackle large jobs; therefore, the support staff will be a moot point. In any event, the number of personnel can give some insight as to the scope of project that can be directed to an appraiser.

9. Many appraisers have written articles, books, or have been contributing writers to various publications. If they have been published, it would be advisable to read and analyze any articles, especially those accepted outside the individual's own company. However, *any* writing will give insight as to the individual's character and professionalism or experience. If nothing more, it shows the appraiser's interest in his profession, and could be one more attribute for measurement.

10. An appraiser should be able to generally explain the types of equipment in the industry that may be the subject of an assignment. That said, appraisers are value-oriented and, therefore, should not be required to speak technically. However, if an appraiser can speak generally on the types of equipment that might be found within a subject industry, it stands to reason that he has accomplished this type of work in the past. The appraiser should also have a general opinion, routinely updated, to the past economics or current trends within that industry.

These questions and answers are not considered criteria for analyzing an appraiser's qualifications or credentials. The idea is to stimulate thinking on organizational techniques for choosing an appraiser.

Appraisers should be willing to submit to such an interview without being offended, as long as there is an understanding between both parties that the interviewer does not wish to be totally educated on how to be an appraiser. Finally, remember there is nothing wrong with the answer of "I don't know" as long as it is honest and followed by, "but I will find out."

A most important question in using an appraiser for tax litigation is his experience in that area. Knowing what, how, and when to say something can affect the decision by a judge, jury, or assessment board. Of equal importance is the interpretation of the proper concept. Most tax codes and law only reference or accept fair market value as the criterion for tax cases.

Analyze the three fair market value concepts defined earlier. Fair Market Value of anything can be in use or as installed to be used for purpose or to be removed. The concept of Fair Market Value—Removal is somewhat confusing, but was written in an attempt to indicate that there is a value without consideration of installation. If one is to do an appraisal of assets, it is either to be as if installed with consideration for installation or without consideration of installation. It is this area where interpretation of fair market value becomes confusing.

Fair Market Value Installed and Fair Market Value in Continued Use also have differences and the values can be different. Fair Market Value Installed considers an asset based upon market sales when available, plus an additional value for the installation. Fair Market Value in Continued Use considers the equipment as part of all other equipment, including its installation and as contributing to the operation. The difference between installed and in continued use is most easily understood in the development of value from the cost approach, which takes replacement cost as of the current date and deducts for physical deterioration to arrive at an answer. From that depreciated replacement from physical deterioration is a deduction for the functional or technological difference of the replacement to the subject. The idea is to adjust the current replacement to the subject in dollars. The physical deterioration and functional obsolescence factors can be referred to as *betterment adjustments*. The functional difference is also referred to as *excess operating expense*. After the deduction for physical deterioration and functional obsolescence, there is an economic obsolescence factor that must be considered.

Fair Market Value in Continued Use may consider the economics of an industry, to adjust for economics in an industry in which one must compete. If the industry is affected by some downturn that can be measured, that is an industry-specific economic obsolescence factor to use. An example of an adjustment could be a measurement of capacity. If an industry typically operates at 80 percent of capacity and is currently operating at 60 percent, there is mathematically a 25 percent economic obsolescence penalty. On the other hand, if the industry is doing well, there may be no economic obsolescence factor applied. There are times when a positive economic factor could be shown in an acquisition, but this is very seldom applied in computing value; rather it is used for an analysis of a sale.

In computing Fair Market Value Installed, the difference is the economic application as referred to earlier. If an item sells for a number less than the removal of the betterment (physical deterioration and functional obsolescence), the obsolescence factor is specific to the item and applied individually to the equipment it appropriately represents. Fair Market Value in Continued Use considers the operation as a whole, in which all items connectively are used to contribute to a profit. In that particular instance, the owner or buyer does not care what the equipment sells for in the used market, but rather what the assets would be worth if they made up one machine, which we could refer to as the plant. It is for that reason that this approach tends to be most appropriate for allocation of a purchase price. The buyer does not consider each piece of equipment's value, because the purchase is for the plant of equipment in which all assets are already a part of the facility. The following is an example of the cost approach calculations to arrive at value.

Replacement cost	$10,000
Physical deterioration	−2,000
Replacement less Physical	8,000
functional obsolescence	−1,600
Replacement less Physical and functional	6,400
economic obsolescence	−2,400
Value derived	$ 4,000

When a purchaser buys a plant of assets without consideration of the product line or the operation, but rather for the equipment installed to be used for whatever purpose the new buyer wishes, the buyer does consider what each piece of equipment is worth, plus the depreciated installation. Obviously, if the item-specific and industry-specific economic obsolescence factors are the same, the answer would be the same. If the value is fair market value without consideration to installation, the cost approach again explains depreciation theory, but the starting point is replacement cost new without the addition of installation.

Many argue that ad valorem tax should be assessed on fair market value of items as they exchange in the marketplace. With some exceptions, there is a great deal of protest based upon this point alone. The tax assessors in values derived from using mass appraisal techniques may incorporate installation and shipping. In many cases, the taxpayer and/or assessor considers the arrived values unreasonable to the market, and appraisers are hired to represent either side. Typically, the assessors will ask that fair market value be interpreted as installed, and in some cases in use, whereas the taxpayer wants the value to be based upon fair market value without consideration of installation. Although this is subject to interpretation, abuses still abound on both sides. There have been instances in which tax assessors will not realistically look at condition of equipment for true depreciation, and in some cases use Replacement Cost New as being the same as value. On the other hand, taxpayers have brought in appraisal reports at Liquidation Value or some forced sale element in which the representation for all equipment is the same as fair market value. Although there are cases in which these positions may be true, the red flags will immediately appear, which can usually be resolved before an assessment board or in the settlement of a lawsuit. Theoretically, the taxpayer's position is that the equipment is what is being assessed for taxation, not the installation. It has been theorized that installation, for consideration of equipment value, can be an intangible.

When used equipment is sold, it is the movable equipment that historically retains its value, whereas that which is lost when an installed piece of equipment is removed has no anticipated value. Why then are installation, shipping, and tax included for value in use? As long as the equipment is installed, continues to operate, and contributes to an operation, there is a value. However, that value is contributory to its operation where it is located and, therefore, is affected by other factors that enable it to yield a return on investment. These factors could be assemblage, specific engineering, product line, and location due to supply. Installation can include that which is referred to as hard and soft costs. There are also physical installation costs, as well as others that cannot be observed. These costs can be lost after removal and could contain the following:

Physical (Can Be Observed)	Nonphysical (Can No Longer Be Observed)
Wiring	Labor
Foundation	Transportation
Support structure	Permits
Proprietary adaptations	Insurance
Process plumbing	Engineering
Electronic or mechanical interfacing	Energy
between equipment	Training
	Run-in tweaking
	Handling

For both columns, there is value to the operation through the installation; however, value for all of this is lost upon removal. In some cases, shipping can be value to its current location. For example, foreign machines that require transportation from one country to the United States would include a duty tax in the pricing. Consequently, the price in the United States is the replacement cost by which values can be derived at its location. However, if equipment is removed, the balance of those items just listed that describe costs would have no meaning or contribution to the sales price on the used market.

Installation costs can only be valuable to the current user at an amount equal to the historical cost. Even then, that value is applicable to its continued operation as associated with all other equipment considered part of the process. Due to this, installation is a value to the business or to anyone who wishes to use the equipment where it is located. Fair Market Value in Continued Use provides contribution and, therefore, is directly tied to the specific business. Only in that context is installation, to an ongoing operation, part of the equipment value. In other words, as an ongoing operation, installation has value and is subject to depreciation along with the equipment it serves. Consequently, Fair Market Value in Continued Use is proper for allocation as it becomes part of the equipment in the operation; the allocation is the equipment's value contribution to the business.

If the equipment is being measured for fair market value as a piece of equipment for purposes such as remarketing and ad valorem tax, installation can then be considered an intangible. It may be that one facility requires a piece of equipment to be elevated, whereas another facility requires this same piece of equipment to be placed in a pit below grade. In each case, the cost of installation is increased. Consequently, these installations would not be considered standard as they were engineered to meet specific manufacturing requirements of each business. Even the way a machine is wired, plumbed, or positioned can cause differences in installation costs for the same type of equipment at different facilities. Therefore, installation is part of the business and considered contributory in nature.

Let's say an individual, while walking through a plant, asks an appraiser, "What is that air compressor worth?" Assuming a standard 5-hp compressor, the appraiser knows this item is exchanged in the marketplace for approximately $600. Therefore, the response should be approximately $600. The typical assumption for this question is that it is always directed to the item without consideration for taxes, freight, installation, and other related costs. In other words, as stated in the pamphlet titled *Texas Property Tax—1993,* "The market approach is most often used and simply asks, 'What are properties similar to this property selling for?' The obvious alteration to this question can be 'at this location.'" The answer would relate to what an item exchanges for in a particular market; or, when unknown, what a piece of equipment should exchange for in that particular market. If the question had been asked, "What does a piece of equipment like that cost today?" the answer given would most likely relate to a new price, because the word "cost" was used rather than "worth." Obviously, a question is more easily understood when it is more decisive. For instance, the words "cost new" could be used instead of using the word "cost."

When measuring fair market value, it is typically understood that installation becomes an intangible, or zero, as installation is contributory and can differ from one facility to another. Items associated with installation lost in exchange are intangible when considering the value of equipment on a piece-by-piece basis. This may not be true of an operation since all of the component pieces make up the manufacturing process.

If equipment is taxed, there must be a basis from which to assess value; for state sales tax, it is price paid. Obviously, price and value may or may not be the same. If tax is based on value, there must be a definitive way of establishing that value. Most understand there are three approaches to value: the market approach, cost approach, and income approach.

As it relates to most equipment, the market and cost approaches are predominantly used and, where possible, the market approach is preferred to derive the economic obsolescence factor. However, for most major equipment, the cost approach is utilized since those market sales are not always found, especially under different value concepts.

The income approach is very seldom used, as it is extremely difficult to establish an item's contribution to a profit that can lead to the recapture of investment. Assume that a piece of equipment produces a certain amount of capacity that sells for an amount of money having a 15 percent margin. To establish the contribution of that machine, all burdens such as space, labor, sales, original engineering, marketing, client base, support, and name would have to be deducted to derive a value for that piece of equipment. Obviously, the larger the facility with its additional contributions from other equipment, the more complicated the contribution measurement becomes. Carrying this further, equipment in different facilities may have different income capabilities; therefore, the standard must be identified. In addition, equipment of different manufacturers, different costs, different ages and conditions may have the same income considerations, yet could indicate an inappropriate value as applied to the specific item.

There have been examples where the income approach could be calculated in a way that a value greater than historical cost is indicated. One would only purchase a piece of equipment that is not only going to recapture its investment, but is going to provide a profit as well. Assuming this to be correct, other than the calculation for risk in developing a discount rate, any piece of equipment *should* contribute more than its cost. If a piece of equipment does not contribute more than its cost can justify, it must be assumed there was a miscalculation by management, which often occurs.

In instances where market sales are inappropriate or are not found, the cost approach can be extremely beneficial in calculating a *reasonable* value. Under general appraisal theory, this approach begins with replacement cost in like kind and utility, and deducts for all betterment; that is, age of the subject and functional differences. Economic obsolescence, which still needs to be calculated at this point, is the most difficult to obtain and support, at which point, as previously stated, the market approach can be used.

When using the cost approach, physical deterioration can be calculated by using either age/life, direct dollar, or the 0–100 percent estimating method. Functional obsolescence can be determined by measuring differences in capacity, efficiency, energy use, or through assistance from the manufacturer who upgraded the machine, a figure that is usually converted to a percentage that is used as a sales tool for marketing the newer model. At this point, economic obsolescence remains and *must* be determined! Most often, this is arbitrarily assigned through experience. Some appraisers merely say they have considered all forms of obsolescence, and use one percentage without quantifying each depreciation factor individually; this is referred to as *accrued depreciation*. There is more credibility when this can be broken down and demonstrated. To demonstrate an economic obsolescence factor, the result must be reasonable for the equipment when there are no used market sales available.

Most users of appraisal reports understand the word intangible to mean that which cannot be seen, smelled, or touched. It is inaccurate to use the word intangible for something that can be observed such as foundations and wiring. However, an appraiser understands that there are exceptions, such as software on a physical disk or that which can be printed out; recipes that convert into a product, which can be smelled, observed, and sometimes tasted. Some of the structure or accessories lost in exchange are valued only as part of an installation and are no different from the computer disk containing software. The result does not change whether installation is considered as an intangible under the fair market value concept or simply a zero value. In some cases, it is understood that equipment has less value in the marketplace if it has been adapted than in its original standard configuration. However, it could be argued that fair market value, "willing buyer and willing seller," should consider the value as if there is a willing buyer for that piece of equipment in that configuration and, therefore, ask, "What is the value as it is without that type of deduction?" Consequently, for ad valorem tax to be equitable, items that have no value on a removal basis may have to be considered. An example of this would be a concrete tank built on the premises, which, upon removal, would be destroyed. It may be better to say the concrete tank has value as a tank, without considering installation or removal. This would indicate a reasonable value that can be measured, and meets most tax codes without an argument ensuing about removal or installation. It simply answers the question, "What is the equipment worth where it is?" That means, whether the equipment is to be moved or not, no deduction is taken for removal and no addition for installation is applied.

There are times when owners of businesses wish to sell the equipment rather than the business and may elect some form of liquidation. In remarketing of equipment, it is wise to hire someone reliable for giving experienced advice in a remarketing attempt. This assistance may be in the form of advice on how to sell and who to use to accomplish the sale. There may be some requirement for refinancing as an incentive to making the sale. An appraisal firm can be requested to act as a go-between agent for a lender or seller, but certainly it could be a consultant. The appraisal firm may wish to act as a consultant with regard to liquidator's selection, style of brochure or advertising, timing, and possibly even the setup and conduct of the sale. Naturally, the appraisal firm should have experience in these areas and, if selected, be given proper compensation for acting in that capacity. An appraisal firm can also act as a broker of the business at a later date due to marketplace exposure in conducting the appraisals. However, in most cases, business brokers are used for this purpose, or the owner is approached by other interests.

There are no exacts for realistic recovery, but measurements can be taken of what might happen at a given time based upon history. It could be anticipated that value changes for equipment would continue if they occurred within a particular industry. Anticipated change should be weighted in a protected way in order to avoid optimism that would create an unrealistic forecast. Anticipated effects as observed in the past are: condition, mix, psychological appeal, location, and obsolescence. There are others that might not be anticipated, such as from improper advertising, theft, strikes, threats of violence, poor weather conditions, and any other acts of nature.

It may be possible to obtain or create some sort of insurance that solidifies or protest a valuation for liquidation. There are many areas that may be used for this protection:

- A guarantee with the standard statements of limitations or restrictions associated with those statements.
- An insurance policy that has the same effect as a guarantee, but is written as a policy submitted by an insurance company.
- Certificates of Deposit, bank letters of guarantee, repurchase agreements by manufacturers, and puts.

Use caution with the three protective measures just noted. Every repurchase agreement by a manufacturer, as good as it may sound, may be from a company that is financially incapable of honoring that agreement. In inventories, a vendor's repurchase agreement may be an offset of their receivables or the establishment of a credit balance. A guaranteed appraisal is not used for forecast, but rather as a value at the date of inspection; it is unlike the guarantee of an auctioneer, because an auction company expects the assets to be sold immediately at auction, which is the reason the guarantee is made.

If an owner wishes to conduct his own sales, the following steps are suggested:

1. Obtain advice from those experienced in conducting such sales.
2. For a large group of assets, consider selling them item by item in an order that does not destroy the credibility of a sale's acceptance (easy-to-sell items sold toward the end of a sale, rather than at the beginning).
3. Use proper marketing techniques with expenditures that will bring an awareness of the potential buying clientele for asset availability.
4. Select advertising without overkill and place it in such media as tabloids, trade journal publications, and newspapers, or other public media; send direct mail brochures to previous customers or to those on purchased mailing lists.
5. Have a proper indication of fair market value (asking price guide) under the current economic conditions in which the sale is being made.

6. Have an orderly liquidation value opinion to use as a basis for the actual sale, assuming negotiations would take place.

7. Use your appraiser as a sounding board in the beginning and as the sale progresses so that alternatives are not destroyed by depletion of good assets or bad sales.

If it appears that all assets can be sold as a business, it is possible to use the same type of marketing strategy as discussed for the item-by-item liquidation, so that the initial notifications are made to customers, competitors, and suppliers in the hope that they or others may wish to capture that market share. In order to sell the assets as a business, it is usually necessary to have the real estate or a transferable lease with all improvements and inventory as a part of the package. In all cases, it should be a requirement that one or more appraisals be made as protection against a later attack based upon the premise of not having conducted a commercially reasonable sale. An appraisal should be accomplished even if there are agreements or indicators that make everyone involved comfortable that the sale being held is proper and just. If it can be demonstrated to potential purchasers that the company can be profitable with the right management and that the business is there, a marketing approach using an in-place concept may be appropriate. This may be a good time to do a replacement cost study, to be used as part of a marketing technique, to show a prospective client that the discounted fair market value for which the assets are being offered can be compared to that which it would take to replace such a facility. This would then show a Fair Market Value in Continued Use concept as indicating a desired price, whereas there would be an understanding that the Liquidation Value in Place is the guideline for what *may* happen after all negotiations.

A second type of marketing, as mentioned earlier, is the use of a professional liquidator who is familiar with proper marketing and sales techniques and who typically works on a percentage of the gross sale. An owner of a company may prefer this type of remarketing method, assuming that the commission charged and projected expenses are in line. It is recommended that there be an agreement on a proper fee with a maximum limit on expenses. There are many variations of this type of fee and expense structure, but all have their advantages and disadvantages. A maximum expense limit could result in a poor marketing strategy due to the liquidator not wishing to spend more than budgeted; it may have been miscalculated in the first place. A good liquidator would absorb additional needed expenses in his fee in order to perform a proper job; a good auctioneer would wish to maintain his credibility, reputation, and customer acceptance. Additional advertising may mean additional gross revenue and thereby an increased fee, assuming that fee is based upon a percentage of gross sale. Flat-rate fees (no percentage) are not recommended due to the lack of incentive for the sales personnel. However, this may be acceptable where there is a guaranteed minimum below which there would be no fee or, at least, a scaled down version of the fee. It is recommended that a liquidator work on some form of percentage of gross sale due to the incentive nature of this approach.

Liquidators may give guarantees, but with additional percentage points applied to the fee for that exposure. A business owner may be willing to pay additional percentage points in order to have some comfort base. It should be understood that all types of assets do not allow a company to make guarantees. Some conditions exist either due to equipment type or economics that cannot allow the guarantee method because of a potential volatile recovery. There should be an investigation in which the seller could then derive a measure of comfort from the liquidator who has done a proper marketing analysis. A good liquidator would, through his analysis, be prepared to set an expense limit requesting some flexibility by the client that allows an expense adjustment with client approval. It is possible for expenses to be monitored on a weekly basis by a report from the liquidator. This would allow a client to see that the original accepted guidelines are being performed as indicated before things can go too far in a different direction. Of course, there are always unknowns, and it is possible to have conflicting dates eliminate potential purchasers from the sale. Dates should be checked by all parties in order to avoid, if at all possible, a conflicting situation within that industry that would affect attendance of potential purchasers. If you have total confidence in your liquidator, a fee without guarantee could be the most acceptable method.

Another consideration for a professional liquidator might be to offer fees that could be applied on a scaled basis with the higher percentages toward a greater gross; there have been cases where the opposite fee structure would be more palatable, but these are unusual.

In analyzing different methods of sale, note that the higher gross indicator is not necessarily the best net result. When the time comes for liquidation, it is the fiduciary responsibility of an experienced liquidator to advise which type of sale may provide the best net results. This type of advice may not be known at the initiation of an appraisal and is usually impossible to anticipate due to altered conditions that may exist in the future.

There are many good national auction firms that know how to properly advertise market assets. With all things equal, there would, in all probability, be very little difference between the sale recovery produced by one auctioneer to another. If the assets are of the type that historically produces an excellent draw (buyer attendance), in all probability, the sale will be excellent regardless of the national company holding the sale. However, the liquidator can make a difference if all things are not equal. An example of this would be the difference in operations between some of these sales companies. If an auctioneer can combine orderly liquidation as a protective measure for portions of the equipment not readily sold at auction, the net results could be higher than for a straight auction sale. On the other hand, a sale could be unsuccessful if a sales company were to use sales techniques inconsistent with those commonly used, and/or if they were required to alter certain proven standard techniques. Poor sales techniques could encompass the following:

- Improper amount of time for advertising exposure.
- Too many days to hold the sale.
- Improper or nonstandard set-up techniques (allotting), including:
  Selling equipment in an order that depresses sales.
  Moving the crowd without thought to flow.
  Improper cleanup.
  Lack of movement or demonstration of equipment when required.
- A poorly displayed brochure.
- Other cost-cutting requirements that may be imposed.

Guaranteed auctions are becoming more the standard approach in the competitive auctioneer market. But be aware that the guaranteed auction is not always what it may appear to be on the surface. In order to help explain guaranteed auctions, the following example is used: A group of assets are expected to have an auction sale recovery of $500,000±. In addition, we assume expenses are expected to be at or around $25,000. (The numbers are totally hypothetical, and any substitutions would allow an analysis similar to these.) Auctioneers have become very creative in making guarantees that may seem reasonable or fair, but sometimes have differences that need to be totally understood before making a decision. Three examples using these figures will be demonstrated, each having a guarantee of $350,000.

A. *Gross* sale guarantee	$350,000
Expenses	25,000
Fee 10% of $500,000	50,000
Net to client on sale of $500,000	$425,000
B. Guarantee—*Net* to client	$350,000
Expenses come out of next	25,000
Auctioneer receives fee of next (10% of $375,000)	37,500
All above $412,500 allows 75% to seller and 25% to auctioneer (seller $65,625 and auctioneer $21,875); Net to client on sale of $500,000	$415,625
C. Guarantee—*Net* to client	$350,000
50% split all above $350,000, and auctioneer takes care of expenses (Auctioneer $75,000 and Client $75,000) Net to client on sale of $500,000	$425,000

If the expected sale and/or actual sale were to be altered, a different analysis might take place, as follows:

Gross sale of $550,000	Scenario A	$470,000
	Scenario B	$453,125
	Scenario C	$450,000
Gross sale of $600,000	Scenario A	$515,000
	Scenario B	$490,625
	Scenario C	$475,000
Gross sale of $400,000	Scenario A	$340,000
	Scenario B	$350,000
	Scenario C	$375,000

At a gross sale of $350,000, A continues to decrease to no less than $290,000, whereas B and C stay the same. Below $350,000, A's net is constant at no less than $290,000, which is the effective net guarantee; the auctioneer's guarantee was in reality a *gross* of $350,000. As the auctioneer is asked to increase the gamble, there is the possibility of less net to the seller and a higher possible fee to the auctioneer.

It is possible that an owner of a company may wish to sell the entire group of assets to someone who is willing to pay $400,000. Let us assume the auctioneer pays an additional $10,000 in interest, insurance, security, and utilities, yet assumes no rent—which is typical for this type of transaction. The owner of the company has the use of the money immediately, and the auctioneer makes $65,000 if recovery is assumed at $500,000. In all of these examples, there are potential variables. With a constant recovery of $500,000 and expenses of $25,000, the analysis is easy. It is the gamble that causes variations in fee payments to the auctioneer and the potential increase or decrease in net recovery to the owner. In most cases, the client who wishes to share more of the gamble with the auctioneer will give up dollars to pay for the increased exposure to the sales agency. The numbers used are not necessarily ones that might be used in the final analysis, but are included in the examples to create a better understanding of this negotiation process. The numbers are considered reasonable if all things are equal.

Another method of security or assurance is known as the *sliding scale fee*. In this example, there is no guarantee, but there is possible incentive for the auctioneer to work harder in obtaining higher sales results. The following could be used for comparisons:

A. A sale with no guarantee and a 5% fee plus expenses.
   Net to client after expenses: $450,000.

B. Incentive Style: Sliding Scale—Ascending
   Auctioneer's fee based upon: 5% of the first $300,000, 7.5% next $100,000, 10% next $100,000, and above.
   Net to client after expenses: $442,500.

C. Protective Style: Sliding Scale—Descending

Auctioneer's fee based upon: 10% first $300,000, 7.5% next $100,000, 5% next $100,000, 3% above.

Net to client after expenses: $432,500.

In analyzing the sliding scales (B and C), there will be a continuing decrease in the net recovery as compared to a straight commission auction sale as in A. However, many clients believe that the ascending sliding scale is an incentive that will cause a salesperson to work harder at obtaining the highest recovery possible. If there is some strong question as to obtaining the $500,000, the incentive style may be elected, if the sliding scale fee were used. In example C, the decreasing sliding scale is considered as a protective style when there is a strong possibility that the amount of recovery has a probability of being greater than $500,000 for the proposed sale. In example C, there eventually could be an increase in the net recovery for the client as compared to B; carried to a mathematical extreme, the recovery could be higher than A, but is highly unlikely. Sliding scales have become very popular and are sometimes coupled with guarantees, no payment of fees below a certain amount, or the other limitless combinations that come out of the liquidator's creativity within the bidding process.

SUMMARY

Clearly, there is much more to the assets of a company than initially might have been considered. Those who have been purchasing businesses over the years have been faced with these problems and have their own methods as to how to handle them. However, for those just beginning, perhaps this information will be helpful. And remember, regardless of the valuation requirement, it is essential to read the contract or law. If there is a purchase option at the end of a lease, determine a value before exercising that option. Remember, there are various interpretations of value, and the slant of that interpretation is typically influenced by those who have the most to gain.

PART FIVE

THE DEAL ITSELF

CHAPTER TWENTY-FIVE

Deal Structure: It Can Be More Important Than the Price

RUSSELL ROBB
O'CONOR, WRIGHT, WYMAN, INC.

I have been in the M&A business for the past 10 years, and nothing has fascinated me more than structuring deals. In fact, most of my peers, whether they are business brokers, intermediaries, or investment bankers believe that the deal structure is more relevant than the price. Proper structuring of the transaction is usually the difference between doing the deal or not doing the deal.

Most owners start out wanting all cash when selling their business, but the figure that appears to be fairly accurate is that only one out of three transactions is for all cash at closing. To corroborate this, I refer to the *Mergerstat Review* of a few years ago and published by Merrill Lynch. Of the nearly 2,000 reported merger and acquisition transactions that they tracked with a minimum value over $1 million, only 34 percent of these deals were done for cash alone.

There is an axiom that the seller sets the price but the buyer sets the terms. What is evident is that if the seller demands all cash in the transaction, he probably will receive a lower price for the company. Buyers are often capable of paying all cash at closing, but are afraid they will lose all their leverage if the business does not turn out to be what was represented. Terms are perhaps more important when buying small companies that do not have audited financial statements, and particularly if the sale is a "stock" transaction in which the buyer assumes all the assets and liabilities on the balance sheet. Even though an "asset" purchase is a safer method of acquisition for the buyer, the use of terms in the structure is a safeguard for any improprieties and/or oversights by the seller.

ASSET OR STOCK PURCHASE

Deals often fail to close even when the buyers/sellers perceive they have successfully reached an agreement in principle. While answering the question why deals "crater" is not part of this chapter, it should be realized that the subsequent interpretation of the deal structure is a major reason that deals fail. Hence, it is most important that the ramifications of the structure are understood by both parties early in the negotiation.

As a general rule, sellers prefer to sell stock and buyers prefer to acquire assets. The sellers' motivation is to minimize taxes and maximize after-tax profits. The buyers' motivation is to be able to "step up" the value of the assets acquired to increase the ability to borrow more from a bank and to have a higher base for greater depreciation, which in turn shelters forthcoming earnings from taxes. The buyer also wants to avoid any contingent liabilities in the transaction.

There is a big difference for a C corporation being sold depending on whether the transaction is an asset or stock sale. The difference is that an asset sale would trigger a double taxation, that is, once to the corporation and second to the stockholders. The buyer, on the other hand, generally does not want to buy the selling company's stock and inherit unknown liabilities. This set of terms is part of the deal structure and is a major item to clarify in writing, because it can make a material difference in what the buyer offers for a price and what the seller accepts.

ALL CASH VERSUS TERMS

The other critical deal-breaker connected to structuring is the concept of net present value. For example, if an appraiser, or in fact, if the buyer and seller agree that the value of the business is worth $5 million, that value must be stated in terms of cash or cash equivalency, regardless of terms of the sale. Clearly, a $5 million cash purchase price is worth more than the same monetary offer that is structured to include non-compete, consulting and earnout agreements, none of which bear interest and all of which are paid over time.

One might initially think that structuring the deal for something other than all cash at closing is merely for the benefit of the buyer. Not so! From a seller's perspective, accepting terms as part of the transaction allows him the benefit of the installment sales tax provision; that is, taxes are paid over numerous years.

The installment sale is a sale or exchange for a promissory note or other debt instrument of the buyer. The gain on the sale is recognized, pro rata, whenever principal payments on the note are received. It may be guaranteed by a third party and may even be secured by a "stand by" letter of credit.

Additionally, the seller may want to sell, yet want to participate on the upside of the business going forward. Such participation is possible either by selling less than 100 percent of the company and/or participating in an earnout for part of the purchase price. Furthermore, the seller might like to phase out of the business over time, and either stay on as president or take a lesser role as chairman, or become an outside consultant to the business. Structuring deals is only limited to one's imagination.

Andre Laus is principal of the Bristol Group, a Providence, Rhode Island-based firm specializing in corporate improvement. Laus has been an acquirer of many companies. His advice in structuring deals is as follows:

- *Be flexible with the real estate component of the business.* Most buyers would rather rent the plant and invest their money in growing the business. Real estate usually does not make money for the operating company, and many times it is difficult to recover its full value within a multiple of EBIT.
- *Do not be afraid of seller's notes to the buyer.* It is unusual where a founder, temporarily remaining in place, is not desirable. Additionally, the best deal for buyers is one in which seller paper can be used as subordinated debt. Consequently, as long as former owners are owed money, then they have a right to view themselves as quasi-partners, and I would suggest that the insightful buyer will consider structuring a share of future earnings improvement to the former owner's benefit . . . as long as he's in place.

Service companies require the most careful attention to structuring, because they comprise 70 percent of all businesses compared to 20 percent for manufacturers. Service companies are driven by conducting business through personal relationships. Often if the key person leaves the company to join a competitor, the business goes with that person. According to Jim Tonra of McLaughlin & Tonra of Wellesley, Massachusetts:

A buyer can expect to pay up to 50 percent of the price at closing and the balance in the future. Sometimes, when the risk of retention of customers is high or very concentrated in few accounts, the buyers expect the seller to assume some risk in the form of a holdback. The risk assumed usually diminishes to zero after the first year. It is customary for these transactions to be in the form of asset purchases. The buyer acquires the fixed assets, inventory, and customer base, and leaves the seller with the cash, accounts receivable, and payables. The seller should be prepared to provide a three- to five-year note, often with a balloon payment at the end or at predetermined intervals.

EARNOUTS

It is no revelation that buyers want to buy companies based on today's earnings and today's book value. On the other hand, sellers want to sell their company based on tomorrow's expected earnings. According to James W. Bradley, co-author of *Acquisition and Corporate Development:*

> The earnout is a contingent purchase, which allows some deals to go through that would otherwise be impossible. Sometimes the seller's price is such that the transaction can only be justified by the buyer at levels of future earnings considerably above what the buyer can expect with any degree of certainty. Here an earnout may allow the deal to be consummated. If a seller is willing to accept an earnout arrangement, a more aggressive pricing strategy can usually be formulated. The objective of the earnout is to quantify uncertainty. One should recognize that the seller must be satisfied with the initial down payment as compensation for the company. Many feel that earnout payments, if and when they come, are gravy.

An exception to using earnouts as a portion of the deal structure—for example, 10–50 percent of the purchase price, the CML Group, Inc. (NYSE) with sales of $800 million has consummated transactions that are 100 percent earnouts. Of the 18 earnouts completed by CML, 16 were negotiated with no down payment to 20 percent of the compensation at closing. While most acquirers use earnouts as a bonus arrangement in structuring transactions, CML uses earnouts as the deal in its entirety or near entirety. The true value of the company, therefore, is determined by the earnout as opposed to an up-front valuation, and the seller is expected to share in some of the risks as well as the rewards. As EBIT multiples are pushed upward in a hot M&A market, the use of earnouts becomes more relevant.

POOLING OF INTEREST ACCOUNTING

Another method of overcoming the price barrier between the buyer and seller is to structure the deal as a *pooling*. There are various conditions for a transaction to be treated as a pooling under the rules of GAAP; however, I will not elaborate on those issues in this chapter.

Let us suppose the value of the acquiring company is $8 million, and the selling company's value is $2 million. If we combine the two companies in a pooling, they are worth $10 million, of which the seller would own 20 percent of the new entity.

The biggest advantage for the seller in a pooling is the fact that it is a tax-free event, or more accurately stated, a tax-deferred event. Upon selling the shares of the new entity, the seller pays a tax based on the value on the old basis. Since capital gains tax is a major after-tax consideration in most transactions, a pooling is a viable alternative to the seller. By enacting a pooling with a public company, the seller overcomes the lack of liquidity inherent with private companies. In a pooling, there is no reevaluation of asset values nor assignment of value to goodwill. For the buyer, the advantage is that the transaction combines the income of the selling company for the entire year, no matter when during the year the transaction takes place.

RECAPITALIZATION

Recapitalization, known as a "recap," is when the company borrows funds using corporate assets as collateral and then redeems stock from its founders. The founders retain ownership until the new management team is able to pay off the debt. Therefore, the retiring founders receive cash upon retirement, and the new management earns its ownership eventually, once the debt is paid down.

In this situation, it is necessary for the company to have sufficient assets and income to support leveraging the company to its maximum level in order to distribute the proceeds to the equity holders. A recapitalization is a valid way for a son to buy his father's business as long as the transaction does not severely impair the company's capital.

ESOP

Employee stock ownership plans (ESOPs) usually require a minimum of 100 employees, a certain level of corporate profitability, and at least 30 percent of the company's ownership in the hands of the employees. In an ESOP buy-out plan, the company borrows cash from an outside lender to take out the owner on a tax-free basis. The lender is repaid over time, out of the employees' contribution to the plan. If the plan works properly, the owner relinquishes his control to the employees, and successfully transfers ownership to the employees. If the company fails during the transition, then the owner loses the unpaid balance.

EXAMPLES OF DEAL STRUCTURE

A common structure in acquiring a manufacturing company for a $3 million price would be as follows:

Buyer's cash	$1M
Bank's cash (secured by company's assets)	1M
Seller's financing	1M
TOTAL	$3M

The seller's financing can be one or a combination of note, noncompete agreement, consulting agreement, or an earnout arrangement. The noncompete and consulting agreements are traditionally noninterest-bearing instruments and nonsecured, while the earnout is contingent on the company's performance. The seller is usually very concerned how the note will be secured by the buyer. The buyer will want the seller's note subordinated to the bank note. On the other hand, the seller will want the buyer to offer solid collateral secured by personal guarantees, preferably "joint and several," as well as backed by first lien on tangible assets. From the buyer's perspective, seller's notes are important to:

- Justify a desired return on equity.
- Ensure debt is lower cost of capital than equity.
- Entice the seller to cooperate in the transition of the business.
- Provide leverage if it is necessary to enforce the terms of the representations and warranties.

Many times the structure of the deal is based on what the banks demand for debt coverage and leverage ratios, and on the other hand, what the investors demand for return on equity. This situation is cited in Examples A and B by Edmund Sears of Benchmark Consulting Group, Inc. in Boston, Massachusetts.

During a recession and an ensuing credit crunch, it becomes more difficult for buyers to secure acquisition financing. As a result, deals have to get done with less leverage and more equity, further lowering the price so that the buyer can get the same return on equity. A company might have sold for six times the earnings before interest and taxes (6 × EBIT) and financed with 2:1 ratio of debt/equity, yielding an 18 percent return on equity (ROE) for the buyer, as shown in Example A. During a recession, financing may be possible only at a 1:1 debt/equity ratio. In order for the buyer to achieve the 18 percent ROE deemed appropriate for this investment, the price has to fall to $12.5 million, or 5 × EBIT, as illustrated in Example B.

Example A (in Thousands)

EBIT	$ 2,500	$2,500
EBIT Multiplier	6	
Purchase Price	15,000	
Financing Debt	10,000 × 10% interest	(1,000)
Equity	5,000	
Pretax Profit		1,500
Taxes (40%)		600
Net Profit		$ 900
Return on Equity		900/5,000 = 18%

Example B (in Thousands)

EBIT	$ 2,500	$2,500
EBIT Multiplier	5	
Purchase Price	12,500	
Financing Debt	6,250 × 10% interest	(625)
Equity	6,250	
Pretax Profit		1,875
Taxes (40%)		(759)
Net Profit		$1,125
Return on Equity		1,125/6,250 = 18%

In the preceding situation, the covenants of the bank and the demands of the equity investors dictated not only the structure of the deal, but also determined the maximum acceptable price!

The availability of institutional financing for any type of business can change dramatically due to changes in the economy and market conditions. Seller financing may be the only way to sell the business at a full price when outside financing is not readily available. Seller financing is a popular means of structuring the deal and is used in half the completed transactions.

SUMMARY

For Buyers

A simple method to remember for structuring deals is *the rule of one-third:* After an equity investment of one-third the purchase price, the cash flow must provide the CEO/owner's salary, a return on investment, plus enough money to service the debt. As a buyer, it is important that the deal structure allows his acquisition objectives to be consistent with his financial capacity. The buyer should not overleverage himself in consummating the deal, or should not shortchange his working capital requirements in the new entity based on the necessary capital equipment and information systems going forward.

For Sellers

Deal structure is very important not only for completing a transaction, but to increase the viability of the company's future. Often, owners who are able to sell for mostly cash drain the buyer of most of his financial resources, leaving the new owner with little or no extra cash for necessary improvements or to overcome ensuing shortfalls. In such a case, the buyer may not be able to meet his remaining obligations to the seller. As a seller, it is very important to consider early the worst case scenario you will accept for a deal structure. For example, a minimum expectation might be a price that would cover all your debts, all your capital gains taxes, and all expenses related to the sale.

Most buyers or sellers would be well advised to receive a second and third opinion on an impending deal structure from their entrusted advisors in the transaction such as an intermediary, corporate appraiser, transaction attorney, and/or accountant. Very few deals are totally alike so it is vital to utilize professional and experienced counsel.

CHAPTER TWENTY-SIX

The Blue Pill: Creative Financing Strategies for Business Acquisitions

JOHN W. SLATER, JR.
MANAGING PARTNER
ASSET SERVICES, L.P.

Fred Smith, founder of Federal Express, is reputed to have flown to Las Vegas at least once during the company's early days, and as a result was able to meet the company's payroll after a successful evening at the tables. While clearly creative, this financing technique cannot be recommended for most companies. Business owners have very simple criteria for seeking business acquisition financing. They want to finance the entire purchase with third-party debt at a low interest rate and without giving up any equity in their business or in the businesses being acquired. If forced to give up equity, they want the opportunity to buy the stock back in the event the acquisition goes well. "Creative" financing techniques are invented to help business owners approximate this desired goal. From time to time, the investment community will seize on a particularly appealing approach and sell it aggressively as the answer for a wide range of business financing needs. An experienced if somewhat cynical investment banker once referred to this as "selling them the blue pills."

There is no one "creative" financing technique that works in every situation or that works consistently over time. In fact, time is normally the enemy of any particular financing technique, as the markets respond quickly to good ideas and prices adjust to the situation. Rather than focusing on specific techniques currently in vogue, but that will likely be unusable by the time they are published, this chapter focuses on the key variables that drive the availability and usefulness of various financing techniques. The goal is to give the reader the tools to evaluate his or her current situation in the context of history and to seek out the best financing alternatives available at a particular time to meet a particular need.

FINANCE 101: DEBT AND EQUITY

They have many names, but the two basic tools of finance are debt and equity. Debt is a promise to pay money on a specific schedule with a specific return to the lender. Lenders expect to be repaid, and, while different lenders will accept and expect compensation for dramatically different levels of risk, no lender will knowingly risk loss of its principal from failure of the borrower. If the lender does take such a risk, it has made an equity investment. For this reason lenders typically require collateral such as real estate mortgages, equipment liens, or a pledge of financial assets such as accounts receivable, notes receivable, and so on. In addition, most lenders will be quite restrictive in underwriting their loans to assure that the borrower is creditworthy.

An equity investor on the other hand incurs a risk of loss in the event the enterprise in which he or she is investing fails. The equity investor does so in hope of a large return on investment in the event of success. Sometimes, the difference between debt and equity becomes blurred (as in the case of convertible subordinated debentures or loans with equity purchase warrants), but to understand finance, it is critical to retain the perspective that there is a basic difference between debt and equity. Other factors that affect the analysis include whether the particular financial instrument calls for a current return to the investor and whether the owner of the instrument has rights to be involved in the management of the business enterprise. Debt entails a current return to the investor, but equity returns are normally deferred (often for many years,) while the business builds up its financial reserves, funds growth, and repays debt. Finally, equity holders normally have some right to control the management of the business through voting of stock or even negotiate the right for minority investors to take control of the business in the event it fails to perform in an agreed manner.

For reference, the names of various financial instruments with their typical characterizations as either debt or equity are set forth here. Notwithstanding, it is helpful to focus on the basic differences just described when looking at any particular instrument.

Debt	Equity
Bank loans	Common Stock
Bonds	Preferred Stock
Mortgage loans	In-the-money convertibles debentures
Factoring arrangements	Partnership interests
Repurchase agreements	REIT certificates
Out-of-the-money convertibles debentures	

SKIP THE ECONOMICS LESSON, I WANT THE MONEY

"I don't understand bankers: I'm good for the money; why won't they just lend it to me?" If readers haven't felt this way one time or another, they almost certainly have not tried to obtain a loan. A banker has been defined as someone who lends you an umbrella when the sun is shining, and takes it away when it begins to rain. From the bankers' perspective, this is perfectly reasonable. They borrowed the umbrella from their depositors and will be required to return it to them whether or not their loans are repaid.

Bankers are bound by the financial markets, which in turn are surprisingly consistent in the demands they make for a return on investment capital. Over long periods of time, different types of financial instruments carrying various levels of risk demand returns, which approximate the following:

Instrument	Yield/Return Inflation Rate Plus
Treasury Bills, Money Market, CDs	0%–0.5%
Risk-Free Long-Term Bonds (i.e. U.S. Treasury)	2–3%
Long-Term Investment Grade Corporates	2.5–3.5%
Junk Bonds	6–10%
Common Stock of Established Public Companies	9.3%
Common Stock of Speculative and Small Capital Public Companies	14.5%
Equity in Private Companies	25–30%

The mechanism by which the returns are achieved varies dramatically. Debt instruments must be paid on a regular basis (monthly, quarterly, and so on), and normally, principal must be amortized in addition to payment of interest. Holders of common equity on the other hand may go for many years without receipt of the first dividend and still receive a satisfactory return through market appreciation, public offerings, or other. To a great extent, the art of finance entails matching the needs of a particular situation to the market's desire for the levels of return anticipated at different levels of risk. "Creative" financing entails finding pockets of opportunity where the market misunderstands the level of risk in a particular situation or for some other reason underprices a particular type of capital. In doing so, the market enables the owner of equity in a business enterprise to obtain a greater return than he or she would otherwise be entitled to, taking into account the inherent risks in the business. In a world where information moves at the speed of light, such imbalances rapidly correct themselves.

THE LBO MARKET

Depending on the observer's point of view, the leveraged buyouts of the 1980s came about either as the result of financial genius or from greed run rampant. Of course, to some extent, both genius and avarice played a part in the LBO boom. Far more important, however, was the congruence of a number of factors that radically but temporarily, changed the availability and pricing of debt and equity.

The LBO grew out of a technique known as "bootstrap financing." As early as the 1960s, but particularly following the recession and stock market collapse in 1973 past 1974, wily financiers had been able to acquire businesses at prices sufficiently low in relation to their asset values so that most if not all of the acquisition price could be financed with asset-based debt. This technique was made possible as a result of the "financing" supplied most businesses by their trade creditors. Often, 30–40 percent of the capital structure of a manufacturing or distribution firm is made up of liabilities to its suppliers and other vendors. This is typically unsecured debt, even though the trade creditor has supplied the business with valuable goods and services that are held as inventory or converted into receivables upon resale, and thereby are available for pledge to third-party asset-based lenders. A true bootstrap acquisition requires a very low price in relation to the seller's marketable assets and is only feasible in times of extreme market distress, as sometimes occurs following recessions or after periods of high inflation when increasing inventory values are not fully reflected in corporate balance sheets.

The 1980's LBO boom followed an extended depression in stock prices that began in the early 1970s and, on an inflation-adjusted basis, continued through the summer of 1982. In this period, public companies traded at significant discounts from the values of the underlying businesses that they owned. Acquirers, even after paying significant premiums in contested takeovers, still found that the acquired business had adequate cash flow to pay high levels of debt service. At the same time, a new form of debt financing, junk bonds, became available to fund these acquisitions. For a time, the financial markets were willing to fund 100 percent or more of the acquisition price of public company purchases through the public sale of high-interest rate debt. In truth, many of these junk bonds were actually equity; and in fact, the underwriters often received significant equity stakes, typically warrants, in the issuing companies in exchange for underwriting the debt. The purchasers of the bonds received a comparatively high rate of interest, but in many cases were not rewarded for the full extent of the risk they took on. This was made possible in part by government regulations that encouraged savings and loan associations to invest in corporate securities. The party came to a halt when market values rose to a level where the deals were no longer workable, and defaults began to occur. Nonetheless, for a brief moment in history, the relative prices of debt and equity moved dramatically from their normal ratios, and financiers who had the understanding, the contacts, and the nerve to take advantage of the situation leveraged their knowledge into ownership and control of significant corporate assets.

AND THE WHEEL KEEPS ON TURNING

The specifics vary with time, thus it is unlikely that the leveraged buyout boom will be replayed in the exact manner witnessed in the 1980s. But it can be predicted with the highest level of confidence that similar opportunities will continue to present themselves to intelligent financiers in the future, probably including some of the readers of this book. The certainty that the opportunities for creative financing will continue to present themselves to quick-witted financiers and businesspeople is derived from the frequency that such opportunities have arisen in the past. The three examples that follow demonstrate the regularity with which opportunities for creative financing are presented, and illuminate some of the factors that may result in creating such opportunities in the future.

Tax Shelters

Over the years, tax incentives have frequently provided the opportunity for financing business ventures without requiring equity investment. Two specific tax shelter techniques helped fund a significant amount of business expansion during the 1960s, 1970s, and 1980s. These were industrial revenue bonds and tax shelter syndications.

Industrial revenue bonds were first made available to industry in the 1930s to encourage plant relocations to the South. Such bonds used the tax exemption available to states and municipalities to provide low-interest "municipal" financing to private borrowers. Ultimately, such financing was made available throughout the United States before being subjected to strict limitations in the 1980s to prevent loss of significant federal revenue. Due to the nature of the process by which many of these bonds were underwritten for sale to individual purchasers by investment bankers, industrial revenue bonds frequently provided 100 percent financing of project costs, and in some cases even financed soft costs, which were only tangentially related to the hard costs of plant expansion. Aggressive borrowers were often able to obtain leverage far in excess of that which could have been obtained from banks or other traditional lenders.

Tax shelter syndications took advantage of the fact that newly purchased business equipment, and to a lesser extent real estate, often threw off tax benefits that significantly exceeded those that could be utilized by the businesses acquiring the assets. Smart financiers took advantage of this situation to create real estate and equipment limited partnerships, which often provided companies with 100 percent financing for their business needs on a lease basis while still providing a good return to third-party investors and healthy fees to the syndicator. As with the industrial revenue bonds, tax shelter syndications were severely limited in the 1980s and are no longer a major factor in business financing.

Government Guarantees

Over the years, federal and local government guarantees have been used by business to arrange debt financing in excess of that which would be acceptable to their traditional lending source such as banks. Examples of such programs include Small Business Administration loans, Economic Development Administration loans, Farmers Home Administration loans, and others. The basic effect of these programs has been to shift to favored private businesses the benefits of the strong credit ratings of governmental guarantors. This has had the effect in most cases of providing those businesses that took advantage of the programs with lower interest rates and, usually, less stringent underwriting and higher advance rates. Many programs of this type continue to be available either at the federal or the state level, with the Small Business Administration loan guarantee being the best-known example.

Distributor Financing

Over the years, many firms have effectively financed their activities through arrangements with distributors of their products or services. Common examples of such arrangements are the franchise programs by which many of the leading retail chain establishments in America have been able to quickly establish a national presence. McDonald's and Holiday Inns are among the best known. Franchisees invested billions of dollars to build and equip restaurants and motels, from which the franchiser then earned substantial franchise fees based on revenues generated. To accomplish the same result with internally generated financing would have required the owners of the companies to conduct massive equity offerings, which would have ultimately diluted the founders to very small ownership positions in their firms. Using the franchise technique, they were able to develop very strong cash flows and ultimately to finance significant development without having to give up excessive amounts of equity ownership.

Other firms have reversed the process, generating substantial capital for growth by selling off existing corporate assets while maintaining revenue streams from franchise agreements and management fees. Sometimes, companies own operating assets that investors value more highly than does the company that owns the assets, in which case, substantial financing can be obtained through sale of the assets to third parties while retaining their use through lease agreements, management agreements, royalty agreements, and so on. This has frequently been the situation with real estate assets such as hotels, office buildings, shopping centers, and the like.

During the 1970s and early 1980s, large holdings of natural resources, particularly oil and gas reserves and timberland, were conveyed to master limited partnerships, which traded in the public markets based upon a multiple of the cash flow from the assets, which typically was far higher than the multiple at which the same cash flow was being valued in the public equity markets. In the limited partnership context, investors tended to ignore standard accounting measures, such as reported profit and loss, and focused on the cash flows from the assets. As a result of these asset sales, substantial value was created that was frequently used to buy in the stock of existing shareholders, concentrating ownership in the control groups or providing funds for making acquisitions. LBO financiers saw an opportunity and began making acquisitions of asset rich companies, arranging financing after the fact by spinning off the "undervalued" assets.

THAT WAS THEN, BUT WHAT DO I DO NOW?

As this chapter is being written (in early 1996) equity prices are at an all-time high. For the past several years, the most "creative" form of financing has often been a public stock offering. In the acquisition context, financiers who have the financial wherewithal to "bridge" an acquisition to a public offering have frequently been able to arrange what is in effect 100 percent acquisition financing. One of the earliest and best-known examples of this technique was the acquisition in the early 1980s of Gibson Greeting Cards by a group controlled by William Simon, former United States Secretary of the Treasury. Mr. Simon and his associates acquired

Gibson in a leveraged buyout, investing only approximately $1 million of their own funds, with the balance obtained through loans. Within 18 months, a booming stock market enabled the acquirers to take the company public again at a price that valued their equity stake at approximately $70 million. In subsequent years, financiers have frequently invested in private companies with the expectation of a rapid public offering. In such cases, the financiers structure a major portion of their investment as debt or preferred equity. At the time of the public offering, the debt and preferred equity portion of the original investment is repaid from offering proceeds and the investors retain a significant ownership interest with very little capital investment.

Sometimes, acquisitions utilize several of the techniques. During the 1980s, Malone & Hyde, a major regional grocery distributor, was taken private in a leveraged buyout transaction. Following the LBO, one of the company's subsidiaries, the now well-known Autozone chain of retail auto parts stores, began to grow rapidly and needed additional capital. To assist in meeting Autozone's financing needs and to permit management to focus its energies on Autozone's growth, the grocery distribution business was sold to a major national distributor, Fleming Companies. The financiers were able to recoup a significant amount of their original investment and continued to retain a major ownership stake in Autozone. Ultimately, Autozone was taken public and has been spectacularly successful as a retailer and as an investment for management and for the financiers who backed the management team.

For buyers who do not have the advantage of a public "currency," a technique that frequently works well is the earnout or contingent purchase price. Let's assume, for example, that Buyer A wants to purchase Business Y with profits of $1 million per year. Buyer A has evaluated the business and concluded that, based on its past performance, Business Y is worth $6 million. Seller N, who owns 100 percent of Business Y, agrees with A's valuation of the past, but believes that the business will grow 50 percent over the next three years and is therefore actually worth $9 million. To bridge the gap, A can offer N $6 million and its closing, plus an earnout in the event profits exceed $1 million. In the simplest example, the parties might split all profits over $1 million annually for a period of five years. Thus the buyer obtains not only inexpensive financing from the seller, but the seller's commitment to work hard for five years to assure that the business will succeed.

THE FUTURE

Successful financiers throughout history have used "creative" financing techniques to enable them to grow or acquire companies with significantly greater capital then they had personally available. The robber barons of the nineteenth century used government land grants and stock manipulation to develop and acquire the great railroads that crisscross America. Bill Gates used a contract with IBM to fund the development of MS-DOS and ultimately Windows to obtain a stranglehold on the software industry. Similar opportunities exist today and will continue to present themselves in the future. Bright entrepreneurs and financiers will seek out market anomalies to fund the growth of their businesses while retaining the maximum equity ownership feasible. They will use some of the techniques of the past and techniques not yet dreamed of.

C H A P T E R
T W E N T Y - S E V E N

Stock versus Asset Sales: Pros and Cons for Buyer and Seller

DARRELL L. FOUTS
COLORADO BUSINESS CONSULTANTS, INC.

When first considering the sale of their company, most owners and their financial advisors cry out "stock sale." Most buyers and their financial advisors insist an asset sale[1] is the only logical method of acquisition. This is usually assumed without understanding the pros and cons of such a sale and how they may impact final price and terms of the transaction.

Buyers and sellers both tend to look at immediate tax issues and disregard the many other considerations necessary to facilitate a successful sale. In addition to tax issues, buyer and seller must evaluate the impact of a stock or asset sale on the continued life of the business to be transferred. This decision will be influenced by the tangible, intangible, and/or contingent assets and liabilities that may or may not be transferred, the representations and warrantees the seller can tolerate, the interests of various stockholders, and, finally, price and terms.

To fully appreciate how each of these issues may affect the type of sale best suited for a particular company, it is necessary to first look at each issue separately and then discuss how they interact.

The central theme when selling a company is to transfer it successfully to the new owner; that is, assuming it is a profitable, healthy company, and should remain so after the sale. Sales volume should remain intact. Supply sources should continue in place, and employees should continue at their jobs without significant changes. These conditions are to be expected by the purchaser unless specific understandings are in place that the transfer will cause certain changes or disruptions in the business and the purchase price has been adjusted accordingly.

Therefore, even if some of the motivations are in place to support an asset sale, it may be imperative to transfer the company by means of a stock sale in order to sustain the business's operational integrity. Examples of such a situation are many, but a few key ones are:

- Major contracts with customers that could be terminated and/or renegotiated due to an asset sale.
- Single-source or major supplier contracts at favorable prices and terms that may be canceled or subject to adjustment under an asset sale.
- Acceptable union contracts or employee agreements that would require renegotiation.
- Favorable tax treatment that would be lost, such as unemployment and workers' compensation rates.
- Licenses and/or permits that are essential to the business but cannot be transferred.

Even one of these situations may have enough importance to override a buyer's interest in an asset sale. Should this be the case, it is incumbent on the seller (who will normally have a preferred tax treatment) to accommodate the buyer in other areas, such as price, terms, representations, and/or warrantees.

An additional number of important issues must be addressed if a buyer is to accept a stock sale. First, all stockholders must agree to the sale, or the buyer will be left to deal with potential minority stockholder problems. Second, the buyer must insist on a more in-depth inspection of the legal, tax, and accounting records of the company than is necessary under an asset sale. Under a stock sale, the buyer acquires and is responsible for the entire legal entity of the company, so it is very important to ascertain if the company has any ongoing, historic, or contingent tax and/or legal issues that may have a negative impact on the buyer. These may be such things as current litigation, current or past employee problems, product warranties, IRS disputes, underfunded retirement plans, and so on. And, while it may be possible to estimate the cost of some identified problems such as those listed, it is almost impossible to estimate the future cost of contingent liabilities that may or may not be identified by time of transfer.

Under a stock sale, all assets and liabilities of the company, tangible, intangible, and contingent transfer to the buyer. Under an asset sale, only those assets and liabilities of the company, tangible and intangible, which are identified and agreed to, will be transferred to the buyer. All others remain with the selling corporation.

Thus, we come to the next major issue of a stock versus asset sale, namely the representations and warrantees of the seller as agreed to in the buy/sell contract. There are many pages of reps and warrants in any asset purchase agreement, but there are many additional ones in a stock purchase agreement. Most reps and warrants by the seller are to protect the buyer from potential misstatements of the seller, which cannot readily be verified either as to accuracy or impact on the value of the business.

In the case of a stock sale, there is potential for many more unforeseen and/or unidentified contingent liabilities that will be automatically assumed by the buyer. Since these would be additional unknowns, the seller must represent that there are no such unknowns; if something does show up after the sale, and within the time frame of the warrants, (usually one to five years), the seller must agree to protect the buyer from any costs and other implications associated with these problems—that is, the seller must warrant against and indemnify for such happenings. Under no circumstance, should a buyer agree to purchase stock unless these extra representations and warrantees are in the purchase agreement.

Many companies, due to contractual or tax problems, cannot feasibly be sold except by transfer of stock. Knowledgeable buyers can often acquire these quality companies, not otherwise available under an asset sale, by agreeing to a stock sale. If properly handled, a stock sale can be beneficial to both buyer and seller.

If an asset sale will not have a negative impact on the continuing business operation, then this form of transfer is *usually more appropriate* even though it creates more tax problems for the seller.

The asset sale is easier to accomplish. There are generally fewer unknown risks and, if the business transition is not a problem, there are many benefits to both buyer and seller. Since the parties can be more selective about which assets and liabilities are to be transferred, fewer representations and warrants are required from the seller. Liabilities not specifically assumed by the buyer remain with the seller. These generally include all contingent liabilities such as taxes and litigation, and may include unwanted contracts and employee agreements. Thus, the buyer acquires a cleaner company, unencumbered by undesired problems and commitments. Because of this, the buyer is usually more amenable to the transaction and is willing to pay a higher price with fewer terms.

With the asset sale, the buyer also has more flexibility in how the new company is set up. Any type of existing business or newly formed business entity may acquire the assets. The new owner may agree to hire all or part of the old workforce; may honor, cancel, or renegotiate any or all of the contracts held by the old company; may establish a new and different tax base; and may formulate entirely new employment policies.

Should this sound like the ultimate situation, be advised that there are a significant number of negative or potential problem areas in an asset sale usually not evident in a stock sale.

Maintaining major customers and suppliers once their contracts are invalidated by the sale is a real problem. Even if they stay with the new company, they usually want to renegotiate price, terms, and conditions. The suppliers often require new credit information and switch from open account to COD status until the new company can establish an acceptable credit rating. Customers worry about the stability of the new company and sometimes look for alternate sources of supply. Unions often attempt to sweeten their contract with the new company, especially if the company must have a unionized workforce.

Finally, the tax issues for buyers and sellers always have a major impact on how the sale is structured. This is first in the minds of both parties as well as their advisors, but it is important to remember that tax issues should not drive the sale. The other issues, collectively discussed, are more important to the success of the sale. Regardless of the method of transfer, the tax issues can be mitigated and adjusted to provide fair treatment to both parties. If not, a sale probably will not take place.

In a stock sale, the tax situation favors the seller as he or she is transferring personal property held over six months, and therefore receives capital gains treatment. Usually, this rate will allow for lower total taxes than if the gain were taxed at ordinary income tax rates. The buyer then owns the stock at the total purchase price and can only get tax credit for the purchase when the stock is sold. Also, the acquired company must continue under its existing tax position, and no additional deductions can be accomplished due to the sale. This situation can be mitigated by identifying what portion of the total value of the stock could and should be allocated to personal service agreements between the company and the seller; that is, consulting and noncompetition agreements. The portion assigned to these would be taxed as ordinary income to the seller, but could be expensed against future income by the company. This would increase the tax burden to the seller, give some relief to the buyer, and still allow for a stock sale. There are numerous other procedures that should be considered, such as tax-deferred exchanges of stock and various stock redemption options. The goal is to minimize the tax burden to both buyer and seller or at least make it more equitable to facilitate the sale. If it is impossible to reduce the tax burden of the buyer, it is usually necessary to adjust the price and/or terms to induce the buyer to consummate the transaction.

In the case of an asset sale, there is usually more flexibility in how the tax burden can be shared between the buyer and seller. The main goal is to allocate the purchase price as accurately as possible and still provide the seller with capital gain treatment where possible, and the buyer with values that can be expensed as quickly as practical against future income. Remember that the amount applied to goodwill is now considered capital gain to the seller and can be expensed over 15 years by the buyer.

All of the issues discussed in this chapter should be carefully reviewed prior to deciding whether a stock or asset sale best meets the needs of a particular transaction. The buyer should be supported by a knowledgeable transaction attorney and a CPA familiar with tax issues and due diligence in the transfer of a business. The seller should have an advisory group composed of a transaction attorney familiar with this type of sale, the company's current CPA, an estate planner, and a business broker knowledgeable in the sale of a company of the size and type involved. If the principals and their advisors carefully review all of the issues, a successful transfer should be the result.

ASSET SALE

Seller

Pros	Cons
Easier to obtain approval from buyer and his or her attorney.	May result in higher taxes.
Fewer reps and warrants.	Higher potential for business disruption.
Easier to retain selected assets and liabilities.	
Can sell without 100% stockholder approval.	

Buyer

Pros	Cons
Better tax position for new company.	Usually higher price and fewer terms.
Protected from undisclosed and contingent liabilities.	Higher potential for problems at transfer (customers and suppliers).
Can be more selective of assets and liabilities to be acquired and assumed.	Loss of company tax positions.
Can select new business entity.	

Buyer

Pros	Cons
Can selectively rehire employees.	
Can selectively continue company contracts and commitments.	

STOCK SALE

Seller

Pros	Cons
Usually lower taxes.	Must offer better price and terms.
Can better maintain integrity of business transfer.	More personal liability for reps and warrants (remains responsible for contingent liabilities by contract).
	Possible restrictions on net worth until warranties expire.
	Harder to find buyer.
	Usually need 100% stockholder approval.

Buyer

Pros	Cons
Better transition of the business.	Less tax shelter or deferred tax shelter.
Better price and/or terms.	More potential for undisclosed liabilities and other problems.
May be the only way to acquire.	
Keep company's preferred tax positions.	Possibility that seller will not/cannot back warranties.

NOTE

1. Asset sale refers to the sale of an operating business in total by transfer of substantially or all tangible and intangible assets and the assumption of any, all, or none of the liabilities. The company common stock is not transferred.

C H A P T E R
T W E N T Y - E I G H T

Due Diligence Process for Buyers: Discovering the Truth

LAWRENCE E. STIRTZ
CHAIRMAN
STIRTZ BERNARDS BOYDEN SURDEL & LARTER

Buyers will always be given an opportunity to conduct an examination of the business being considered. This examination is called *due diligence*. There are endless lists (one is provided at the end of this chapter) and outlines describing this process in great detail. To complete each step in these lists, however, would stretch the resources of the most well-financed buyer, so it is helpful to develop an understanding of the purpose and objective of the due diligence process so that each step provides information that will improve the final decision.

To further our understanding, a definition is in order. A trip to the dictionary tells us that one meaning of "due" is "appropriate." Similarly, a definition of "diligence" is, "earnest and persistent application to an undertaking." Another definition whose source I cannot cite is, "a critical examination of the facts"; or we could return to our title, "discovering the truth." If we use the foregoing to design a statement of purpose and objective, it might read, "an appropriate examination of the facts to discover the truth." This may be as close as we will come to clarity and should suffice for our purposes.

In addition to a working definition, you, the buyer, will need common sense and intuition. These will go far to tell you when you have enough "truth" and should get on with your decision. To proceed with the examination, you will need to answer an initial question: "What is it that I think I am buying?" A group of assets: equipment that does something special, products that are in demand, know-how, location, systems, inventory, design skills, engineering capabilities, market domination, productive capabilities—the list is endless; however, it is necessary to know what the thing or things are that create the value in the business that is being considered for purchase.

Estimates of value should be made of all the assets and liabilities of the business; and if the principal value drivers can be identified, the examination will be more focused.

Now that you know what to do, how do you do it and how do you know you have the right answers? To take the last question first, in my experience, you won't know that your answer is correct; this is where intuition helps. A method of deciding what is important is to ask the right questions about the business based on its characteristics. If you as the buyer are considering a retail business, your questions might be about what attracts the customers and leads them to make a purchase. Is it what is sold? Is it where it is sold? Is it how it is sold? Is it the price it is sold for? If other stores are selling less of the same item(s) using the same methods and prices than the business under review, then you might conclude it is location. If this is the case, then the examination should include determining future availability of the location, planned development or other change in the area, and the like. You might discover that pricing and sales systems are also different from those used by other similar businesses. The examination should then be expanded to verify profit margins and the ability to buy product at similar prices in the future or to maintain a similar expense structure (to assure continued profitability). You would further be interested in retaining employees or the ease of training new ones (sales system maintenance); a further inquiry might be to determine how likely it is that a competitor could copy the systems or meet pricing, and thus estimate how long you could maintain your competitive advantage.

The process is the same for all businesses: determine the nature of the business and look at the key areas, including productive capabilities, product development, systems, marketing strategies, sales methods, market dominance, and expense structure, to decide which one(s) create a competitive advantage for the business. The next step is to find the best way to verify the existence and the probable duration of the competitive advantage.

When you know "what you think you are buying," the "truth" questions can be asked: "Do the facts support that you are getting what you think you are buying? Do they indicate a value that supports the purchase price?" To help determine whether the facts support your initial conclusions, there are several "tools" available, which have been used by auditors for years and are not difficult to master. They are also integrated; that is, more than one probably will be used in any given step.

It might be useful here to explain what an auditor does, which is in part, "to examine enough reliable evidentiary material to form an opinion regarding an assertion made by a third party." This is not an exact definition, but it will suffice. The point that is useful, in the buyer's context, is the assertion that there is a business that has a value. We must form an opinion regarding that. A gratuitous comment: Auditors are required to be independent of the asserting party and totally objective about the outcome. This attitude will serve well in the due diligence process. In other words, let the evidence take you where it will.

- *Examination:* This means look at things, but don't stop there; interpret them. What does the document mean in its context? What can be examined? Office space, factory space, inventory, financial statements, tax returns, invoices that prove payments, authorizations, forecasts, ownership documents, traffic counts, market surveys, patents, legal opinions, people, and more. The idea is to look at whatever you can think of to support the preliminary conclusions or disprove them.

- *Interview:* Talk to people—employees, vendors, customers, competitors, folks in the community, bankers, whoever will talk to you. Make a list of things to ask, and keep asking the same questions of different people with different perspectives, then cross-check the answers. Finally, interpret the information.

- *Confirmation:* Ask third parties to confirm facts to you in writing or orally. Accounts receivable balances, accounts payable balances, union contracts, vendor contracts, bank balances, average purchases or sales over a period of time, equipment repairs, on-time delivery statistics, market share information, services provided by consultants, accountants, attorneys, and reports thereon—whatever seems relevant. This is different from examination in that others are asked to verify something about their relationship with the business under examination or something they know about it directly, not through representatives of the seller.

- *Verification:* All of the tools listed may be used in this process. An example is to prove that the total of accounts receivable on the financial statement is correct. This may be done by understanding the system and testing it, as well as confirming balances with customers, or examining shipping documents. If a revenue stream is to be verified, documentation is required regarding backlogs, customer retention order intervals and amounts, new customers acquired over some period and old customers lost over the same period, trade and market information regarding future demand and product life. The idea is to do enough to feel that the amount or fact is verified.

- *Testing:* Every business has systems. They control financial matters, production, sales, marketing, legal, and more. Understanding these systems enables you to examine documents and other information to determine whether the systems are doing what they are intended to do; for example, in the case of financial systems, are they safeguarding the assets? Do they result in all transactions being recorded properly on the company's books and records? If they do, then you can place more reliance on the financial statements as presented. Do they prevent product liabilities; do they prevent environmental violations?

- *Computations/analysis:* Use information independently obtained to calculate certain amounts to prove that information given to the buyer is correct. Knowing space, employees, and equipment available, how much product could reasonably be produced is an example. Others are determining reasonableness of sales or forecasts from trade market information and company share, and supporting assumptions of forecasts by interviewing sales or marketing employees or customers. The list is as long as the imagination.

- *Public records:* Some ownership of property and amounts owed by businesses are a matter of public record; therefore it is easy to examine them to determine who the owners are or to whom money is owed.

The preceding tools, applied with common sense and intuition to the factors identified as those that do the most to generate the value in the business, can give you, the prospective buyer, the "truth" you are looking for.

You must now turn your attention to the purchase price or valuation of the business. You have verified that all the assets exist and the seller has title subject to acceptable liabilities. The physical assets are easy; accounts receivable are collectible and worth face amount, or slow and worth something less. Inventory is salable and valued at book value or adjusted; equipment and real estate can be appraised. All of these are then added together and a total is arrived at. Something is still missing, though, and that is goodwill, or as described previously, the "competitive advantage." Through the examination described, the existence and probable duration of this advantage should have been determined. To arrive at an opinion of total value for the business, it will be necessary to estimate a present value of the future cash flows created by this intangible and add it to the other values. Valuation is dealt with elsewhere and will not be discussed further here.

Detailed Checklist Buyer's Due Diligence Investigation

	Sufficient Information	Decision Information Ranking 1-Low 5-High
Company Background		
Company name and address for parent and subsidiaries.	_____	_____
Country, state, and dates of incorporation.	_____	_____
History of name changes.	_____	_____
Significant events since incorporation—capital reconstructions, etc.	_____	_____
Changes in controlling ownership.	_____	_____
Extent of holdings in subsidiaries.	_____	_____
Dates of subsidiaries' acquisitions.	_____	_____
Names and addresses of company auditors, legal counsel, and other professional advisors.	_____	_____
Trading activity description by company and major area of activity.	_____	_____
Number of persons employed by company and major area of activity.	_____	_____
Details of authorized and issued share capital, and classes of shares.	_____	_____
Analysis of voting powers of various classes of shares.	_____	_____
History of share issues.	_____	_____
Listing of major shareholdings.	_____	_____
Share performance statistics (if available).	_____	_____
Total market capitalization.	_____	_____
Investment ratings and history.	_____	_____
Details of properties owned or leased.	_____	_____
Environmental/assessment for each property owned or leased.	_____	_____
Details of lease agreements.	_____	_____
Management and Personnel		
Organization of function and line management responsibilities.	_____	_____
Frequency and composition of board and other management committee meetings.	_____	_____

Pages 368–378 comprise a due diligence checklist presented with the permission of Joseph Myss, its author. It is broad, and therefore should be tailored to the individual needs of the user.

Detailed Checklist Buyer's Due Diligence Investigation (Continued)

	Sufficient Information	Decision Information Ranking 1-Low 5-High
Review of minutes of such committees.	_____	_____
Names and responsibilities of directors and other senior employees.	_____	_____
Ages, remuneration, length of service, and positions held by directors and senior employees.	_____	_____
Nationality, location, qualifications and shareholdings of directors and senior employees.	_____	_____
Listings of directorship held in other companies.	_____	_____
Existence of service agreements.	_____	_____
Pension and deferred compensation plans.	_____	_____
Life insurance coverage and other benefits received by directors and senior employees.	_____	_____
Experience of management.	_____	_____
Leadership abilities.	_____	_____
Analysis of unused management potential.	_____	_____
Analysis of key position backup.	_____	_____
Analysis of management weaknesses.	_____	_____
Assessment of additional management requirements.	_____	_____
Existence of management development planning.	_____	_____
Recruitment procedures.	_____	_____
In-house/external training programs.	_____	_____
Bonus and incentive plans.	_____	_____
Company dependence on skilled labor.	_____	_____
Sources of labor.	_____	_____
Competitor demands on local labor pools.	_____	_____
Methods and levels of pay.	_____	_____
Union involvement/contracts.	_____	_____
Pension plans/life insurance coverage.	_____	_____
Benefit programs—company housing, automobiles, personal loans, medical benefits.	_____	_____
Vacation entitlements.	_____	_____
Working conditions, and date and results of last OSHA review.	_____	_____

(Continued)

Detailed Checklist Buyer's Due Diligence Investigation (Continued)

	Sufficient Information	Decision Information Ranking 1-Low 5-High
Accident frequency rate.	_____	_____
Employee turnover statistics.	_____	_____
Key employee loss history.	_____	_____
Strike record.	_____	_____
Assessment of employee morale.	_____	_____
Status and evaluation of employee grievances and suits.	_____	_____
Assessment of management promotion of initiative and ingenuity in employees.	_____	_____
Profit-sharing programs.	_____	_____
Wage/salary review policies.	_____	_____
Production and Purchasing		
Location, size, and condition of plants and other major facilities.	_____	_____
Description of machinery and equipment and productive techniques.	_____	_____
Details of power sources.	_____	_____
Current productive capacity usage.	_____	_____
Unused capacity analysis.	_____	_____
Organization and division of manufacturing responsibility.	_____	_____
Shift and overtime working.	_____	_____
Production planning programs.	_____	_____
Material-handling techniques.	_____	_____
Work-in-process controls.	_____	_____
Subcontractor utilization.	_____	_____
Licensing agreements.	_____	_____
Assessment of senior production employees.	_____	_____
Technical competence of skilled labor.	_____	_____
Analysis of costing system.	_____	_____
Review of trends and fluctuations in labor and material usage, efficiency, and yield.	_____	_____
History of scrapping and rejections.	_____	_____
Idle time analysis.	_____	_____

Detailed Checklist Buyer's Due Diligence Investigation (Continued)

	Sufficient Information	Decision Information Ranking 1-Low 5-High
Absenteeism history.	_____	_____
Delivery timing history.	_____	_____
Review of overhead cost elements and comparisons with prior years.	_____	_____
Comparison of production costs with production cost data for the industry (if available).	_____	_____
Analysis of requirements for additional capital investment in productive facilities.	_____	_____
Review of new product plans and production status.	_____	_____
Review of products nearing end of useful life.	_____	_____
Analysis of technological obsolescence.	_____	_____
Description of purchasing function.	_____	_____
Review of coordination with production and quality control departments.	_____	_____
Listing of major and critical raw materials; availability analysis and price forecast.	_____	_____
Review of future purchasing requirements and underlying assumptions.	_____	_____
Existence of program to standardize material and supply items.	_____	_____
Sources and terms of raw material supply, together with alternative sources of supply.	_____	_____
Nature and extent of competitive bidding procedures.	_____	_____
Warehousing facilities.	_____	_____
Inventory holding requirements.	_____	_____
Analysis of reliance on imports.	_____	_____
Existence of monopoly suppliers.	_____	_____
Analysis of potential changes in purchasing requirements due to technological or product changes.	_____	_____

Marketing and Sales

Description and sales history of all products/product lines.	_____	_____
Trademarks held.	_____	_____

(Continued)

Detailed Checklist Buyer's Due Diligence Investigation (Continued)

	Sufficient Information	Decision Information Ranking 1-Low 5-High
Patents/registered designs held.	_____	_____
Sales statistics in quantity and value for all products/product lines.	_____	_____
Seasonal sales patterns and history of pattern shifts.	_____	_____
Product mix flexibility.	_____	_____
Inventory holding requirements in quantity and value by product and product line.	_____	_____
Total market size by product.	_____	_____
Market share by product.	_____	_____
Domestic/export penetration.	_____	_____
Major customers.	_____	_____
Distribution methods.	_____	_____
Licensing agreements.	_____	_____
In-house transportation facilities.	_____	_____
Warehousing/storage facilities.	_____	_____
Pricing policies.	_____	_____
Credit agreements.	_____	_____
Intercompany sales statistics.	_____	_____
Export sales restrictions.	_____	_____
Government contracts.	_____	_____
Long-term contracts.	_____	_____
Delivery record.	_____	_____
After-sales service requirements.	_____	_____
Warranty guarantee provisions.	_____	_____
Competitor product analysis.	_____	_____
Competitor market share by product and product line.	_____	_____
Competitor marketing policy.	_____	_____
Analysis of international competition.	_____	_____
Advertising expenditures by product and product line.	_____	_____
Media usage analysis.	_____	_____
New product backup.	_____	_____

Detailed Checklist Buyer's Due Diligence Investigation (Continued)

	Sufficient Information	Decision Information Ranking 1-Low 5-High
Trend analysis of forecast market growth.	_____	_____
Analysis of industry ability to meet current/future demand.	_____	_____
Consideration of likely changes in government policy.	_____	_____
Review of sales organization.	_____	_____
Details of active advertising and promotion campaigns.	_____	_____
Salespeople's incentive plans.	_____	_____
Customer contact strength.	_____	_____
Market expansion analysis.	_____	_____
Loss leader retention program.	_____	_____
Market research program.	_____	_____
Market penetration by geographical area.	_____	_____
Comparison of historical sales forecasts with actual results.	_____	_____
Sales cancellation and returns policy.	_____	_____
Order processing systems and costs.	_____	_____
Order backlog status.	_____	_____
Accounting Records		
Description of accounting records.	_____	_____
Description of equipment used to maintain accounting records.	_____	_____
Assessment of reliability of records.	_____	_____
Adequacy of accounting equipment.	_____	_____
Listing of EDP hardware together with age, condition, and lease terms, if any.	_____	_____
Company plans for EDP hardware requirements (short- and long-term).	_____	_____
Compatibility with accounting systems of acquiring company.	_____	_____
Existence of accounting manuals.	_____	_____
Level of integration of costing records with financial records.	_____	_____
Details of cost accounting system.	_____	_____

(Continued)

Detailed Checklist Buyer's Due Diligence Investigation (Continued)

	Sufficient Information	Decision Information Ranking 1-Low 5-High
Assessment of reliability of costing system.	_____	_____
Description of budgeting system.	_____	_____
Analysis of effectiveness of action taken on budget variances.	_____	_____
Assessment of budgetary control techniques.	_____	_____
Comparison of forecasting history with actual results history.	_____	_____
Assessment of reliability and accuracy of forecasting system for both profit forecasts and cash flow.	_____	_____
Summary of management information reporting flows.	_____	_____
Assessment of accuracy and usefulness of management information.	_____	_____
Timeliness of management information.	_____	_____
Operating Results		
Listing, explanation, and comments on significant accounting policies.	_____	_____
History of changes in accounting policies.	_____	_____
Sales, gross profit, net profit for last 5–10 years.	_____	_____
Ratio analysis of gross and net profits for last 5–10 years by product and product line.	_____	_____
Comparison of ratios with industry results and statistics.	_____	_____
Description and analysis of main elements of overhead and significant fluctuations.	_____	_____
Analysis of significant elements of other income and expense.	_____	_____
Existence and explanation for extraordinary items and prior year adjustments in last 5 years.	_____	_____
Trend and detailed ratio analysis by product and product line for all major elements of expense.	_____	_____
Quantity and value of key operating results to discount inflationary effects.	_____	_____
Analysis and discounting of effects of foreign exchange fluctuations on net profits.	_____	_____

Detailed Checklist Buyer's Due Diligence Investigation (Continued)

	Sufficient Information	Decision Information Ranking 1-Low 5-High
Description and history of tax status, current and deferred.	_____	_____
Analysis of effects of different financing structures on net profits.	_____	_____
Description of any profits subject to controls over remittance.	_____	_____
Assessment of past earnings as a true indicator of future maintainable earnings.	_____	_____

Balance Sheet Review

Fixed Assets

Description of fixed assets by category.	_____	_____
Validation of title to assets.	_____	_____
Basis of valuation by category.	_____	_____
Assessment of inflationary effects.	_____	_____
Cost of replacement.	_____	_____
Depreciation rates utilized and assessment of adequacy.	_____	_____
Minimum capitalization value.	_____	_____
Basis for capitalizing assets of own manufacture.	_____	_____
Treatment of tooling costs.	_____	_____
Useful life assessment criteria.	_____	_____
Treatment of profit/loss on disposal of assets.	_____	_____
Method of accounting for investment tax credit.	_____	_____

Receivables

Point at which product is regarded as sold.	_____	_____
Basis of taking profit/loss on long-term contracts.	_____	_____
Basis of treatment of deferred installment sales.	_____	_____
Basis for providing for doubtful accounts receivable.	_____	_____
Basis for providing for after-sales service/maintenance.	_____	_____
Credit control procedures.	_____	_____
Discounts allowed.	_____	_____

(Continued)

Detailed Checklist Buyer's Due Diligence Investigation (Continued)

	Sufficient Information	Decision Information Ranking 1-Low 5-High
Ratios of return and allowances to sales.	_____	_____
History of bad debts.	_____	_____
System of aging analysis.	_____	_____
Existence and method of debt factoring.	_____	_____
Ratio analysis of receivables.	_____	_____
Number of customers.	_____	_____
Names of large customers.	_____	_____
Details of any unusual payment arrangements.	_____	_____
Inventory		
Basis of valuation.	_____	_____
Definition of cost/market value.	_____	_____
Basis of overhead inclusion.	_____	_____
Basis and adequacy of provision for slow-moving and obsolete inventories.	_____	_____
Analysis of intercompany profits in inventories.	_____	_____
Treatment of variances in standard costing systems.	_____	_____
Treatment of profit on long-term contracts and provision for losses on such contracts.	_____	_____
Frequency and adequacy of physical counts.	_____	_____
Accuracy and quality of inventory records.	_____	_____
Analysis of inventory security and insurance coverage.	_____	_____
Ratio analysis of inventories.	_____	_____
Investments		
Basis of valuation for quoted and unquoted investments.	_____	_____
History of results of investment policy.	_____	_____
Analysis of liquidity of portfolio.	_____	_____
Assessment of results of idle-cash management.	_____	_____
Current Liabilities		
Credit taken (listed by major vendor).	_____	_____
Discounts received.	_____	_____
Settlement delay history.	_____	_____

Detailed Checklist Buyer's Due Diligence Investigation (Continued)

	Sufficient Information	Decision Information Ranking 1-Low 5-High
Assessment of adequacy of provisions for outstanding liabilities.	_____	_____
Assessment or provision for guarantees and warranties.	_____	_____
Analysis of contingency provisions.	_____	_____
Listing and assessment of pending litigation.	_____	_____
Assessment of actuarial deficiencies in pension plans.	_____	_____
Treatment of unfunded pension commitments.	_____	_____
Policy with respect to vacation accruals.	_____	_____
Analysis of provision for current and deferred taxation liabilities.	_____	_____
Dates and results of federal, state, and local tax audits.	_____	_____
Existence of major taxation issues not yet resolved.	_____	_____
Adequacy of tax planning.	_____	_____
Adequate provision for interest and/or dividends payable.	_____	_____
General		
Assessment of adequacy of insurance coverage.	_____	_____
Assessment of potential for conversion of nonproductive assets into cash for working capital purposes.	_____	_____
Existence of short- and long-term borrowing facilities and unused lines of credit.	_____	_____
Consolidation policies and accounting treatment of associated companies.	_____	_____
Treatment of intangible assets.	_____	_____
Policy on deferral of advertising and/or promotional costs.	_____	_____
Existence and details of stock options.	_____	_____
Existence and details of capital commitments.	_____	_____
Repayment terms of short- and long-term debt.	_____	_____

(Continued)

Detailed Checklist Buyer's Due Diligence Investigation (Continued)

	Sufficient Information	Decision Information Ranking 1-Low 5-High
Forecasts		
Analysis of accuracy of company's forecasts in the past.	_____	_____
Assessment of validity of assumptions used in forecasts.	_____	_____
Consistency of accounting policies with previously published results.	_____	_____
Accuracy of calculations underlying forecasts.	_____	_____
Listing of main factors liable to upset forecasts.	_____	_____
Assessment of effects on forecasts of the acquisition/merger itself:		
• Preservation of combined market share.	_____	_____
• Implementation problems.	_____	_____
• Maintenance of personal contacts.	_____	_____
• Timing of receipt of anticipated benefits.	_____	_____
Comparison of budgets and forecasts with management financials to date.	_____	_____
Discounting of forecasts for inflation.	_____	_____
Analysis of effect on forecasts of changes in key assumptions.	_____	_____
Assessment of adequacy of contingency provisions.	_____	_____
Statement of range in relation to profit forecasts.	_____	_____
Accuracy of tie-in of operating forecasting to cash flow projections.	_____	_____
Analysis of relationships of company forecasts to overall industry forecasts.	_____	_____

CHAPTER TWENTY-NINE

Buying Midsized Manufacturing Businesses: An Example

STALLWORTH M. LARSON
PRESIDENT
CORPORATE GROWTH SERVICES

WHY BUY A BUSINESS?

To provide some initial focus we might ask, why would anyone buy a business in the first place? The simple, rational answer by all accounts would be to create wealth. This correctly suggests that buying an existing business is, at least in some cases, preferable to starting one in the same field. Certainly, owning a business, whether through acquisition or creation, is not the only way to generate wealth. Other fields of endeavor have yielded greater and smaller fortunes over time. We can distinguish also between active and passive investment. Stock market investing, which implies less control and noninvolvement in day-to-day operations, has also produced significant wealth.

On the other hand, there are many who, by virtue of their personality or perceived opportunities, prefer to pursue wealth and, not incidentally, happiness, by working for someone else. Needless to say, this eliminates a raft of prerequisites and problems for them. They do not have to worry about having or raising capital, meeting payrolls, being the locus of where the buck stops, and so on.

Then again, for whatever the reasons, throughout the ages, a percentage of people are simply not in touch with, or interested in, creating wealth, or indeed in working, period. These are the choices then: Do not work and survive on society's handouts, work for someone else, or work for yourself. And if you choose to work for yourself, what will be your field of endeavor?

Here we assume you have, at least preliminarily, decided it will be manufacturing, and that you will enter this field by buying an existing business instead of starting one. We also assume we are dealing with buying midsized manufacturing businesses to own and operate. Presumably, you would choose this route to wealth over others because it offers you a sufficient prospect of superior returns relative to your individual alternatives with an acceptable level of risk and an agreeable lifestyle.

WHAT IS A MANUFACTURING BUSINESS?

Manufacturing businesses come in virtually as many varieties as there are tangible products consumed in an economy. Nevertheless, some common threads bind all manufacturers. Fundamentally, a manufacturer purchases raw materials from outside suppliers, and transforms or consumes them in a physical process of creating a different product. As a consequence, value is added to the utilized factors of production, and the resultant product is worth more in the market than the sum of the costs incurred in the manufacturing process; or at least it better be, or the manufacturer will not be in business long.

This then is the purpose of a manufacturer: to fill a need in the market at a cost below what the market is willing to pay. As intimated, the needs of the market are manifold and dynamic. The variety of needs at any given time is figuratively infinite, and over time constantly changing, with additions previously beyond the market's ken and deletions that might have seemed inconceivable before. Computers and the proverbial buggy whip come to mind.

Nevertheless, manufacturers can be variously categorized by what they do and how they do it. On the market need/customer side, we can distinguish fundamentally between manufacturers of industrial and consumer products. Within each of these categories, we can divide between hard goods like machinery and equipment for industrial customers and automobiles or appliances for consumers, and soft goods such as chemicals for industry and food products or apparel for consumers.

Still on the product level, we can separate manufacturers by whether their products are custom-made, such as a job shop would produce for an industrial customer or a custom cabinet shop for a single buyer; standard-like fasteners for industry or BBs for a BB gun; or, finally, proprietary items such as Pentium chips for industry or a branded toiletry item for consumers.

Bridging somewhat these product categorizations, we can also distinguish between final and intermediate products. If you take the view that a consumer by definition is only in a position to purchase final products, then you can say that intermediate products are by definition industrial, since another manufacturer uses them to produce a final product, which in turn, depending upon the category, could be either an industrial or a consumer product.

Manufacturers can also be separated by the nature of their production process. Fully integrated manufacturers start with raw materials that they fabricate into, say, parts, and then assemble into finished products. There are also partially integrated manufacturers such as manufacturers of components. As a further distinction, there are manufacturers that utilize continuous processes like many chemical producers and others that employ a batch and/or workstation procedure. Generally speaking, the former will be more automated with a resultant higher capital cost and investment. Finally, bridging both the product and production distinctions, we can separate generally between high-tech, low-tech and no-tech products and production.

WHY BUY A MANUFACTURING BUSINESS?

You *could* buy a service business after all! The talents or strengths and weaknesses of any population are almost as varied as their physical appearances and personalities. Some people are better suited to be shopkeepers and sell products others have made, and others to make those products. Regardless of which field, manufacturing or service businesses in general offer the best prospective investment returns; nevertheless, the shopkeeper will probably fail as a manufacturer (and vice versa), making an investment in a manufacturer a potential disaster.

Beyond this obvious point, arguments can be made that manufacturing in general provides greater upside potential in wealth creation, including the wealth received by the jobs created, than service businesses. The prime line of reasoning here has to do with leverage, both operational and financial. Essentially, through automation, it is easier to achieve operating leverage in a manufacturing business than in a service one. Operating leverage refers to positive marginal output within particular limits of marginal factors of production consumed. The simplest way to think of this might be machine time. The number of hours a machine is operated, with necessary repair and maintenance time factored in or possibly postponed or not accomplished, can dramatically affect the profitability of an enterprise and particularly the return achieved on the capital investment in the machine. Since service businesses in general are more labor-intensive and less subject to automation, they do not yield comparable gains in marginal output.

As sales expand, a larger contribution margin to fixed costs is achieved. This flows more cash to the bottom line, which can fund further growth yet. Distributors add no value to the products they sell beyond the service value they offer, and this is worth less in the market than a manufacturer's value added. Consequently, the distributor's or service business's dynamic between its variable and fixed costs as it grows is not as powerful a generator of marginal profits.

Further, the marketing and sales geographical range of a distributor or service business is often less than a manufacturer's. Manufacturers generally have more possible growth avenues than distributors or service businesses. They can often integrate vertically and/or horizontally and adjust and expand their product offerings again over a greater range of possibilities than other types of businesses. Finally, midsized manufacturers by definition may offer a better platform for growth than even large ones, in that they are starting from a lower base.

Just as the power of financial leverage can go wrong and hurt a business badly, so can operating leverage. The fun quickly goes out of a business when it falls below its break-even point. Of course, all types of businesses have their break-even points. However, given the greater number of factors involved in a manufacturing business, the greater complexity of its operations, there are more things that can go wrong. Also, whereas a midsized manufacturer may more easily achieve a higher growth rate than a large one, it is in turn, almost by definition, less established and so subject to greater risks.

Financial leverage, of course, is the financing of increasing sales with higher portions of relatively less costly debt funds instead of equity. This is achievable because the cost of debt funds is lower than for equity, for two reasons. First, the cost of debt is tax deductible; and second, with a fixed return and seniority in liquidation, debt has less downside risk than equity. Thus, if the enterprise is creditworthy, debt financing can be obtained less expensively than equity. The result is that, with increased profits and the fixed cost of the debt portion of the capital structure, a greater percentage of the profits flow to the equity holders. Negative, or reverse, financial leverage is, of course, when profits dwindle and the debtholders must be paid their due to keep the doors open, leaving instead a disproportionately lower percentage and possibly zero for the equityholders.

Since most midsized company debt is secured, and manufacturing businesses with their plant and equipment have more assets to offer as security, debt financing is typically more available and less expensive for a manufacturer than for a service business in this size category. This again makes financial leverage, and a greater return on equity investment and so wealth creation, more achievable for the owner of a midsized manufacturer.

AMATEURS NEED (SHOULD) NOT APPLY

As rude as this may sound, it is sound advice. Any business is a complex entity, but a manufacturer is even more so. There are a thousand and more details to be identified, tracked, mastered, and dealt with.

On-the-job training has its merits, especially if someone else is paying for your education. However, if you are paying for it yourself, it can be the most expensive education you will every buy, and dwarf what you pay for your children's college tuitions. Therefore, if you do not want the deck really stacked against you, do your homework before you buy. Once you do buy, learning the business, coping with its constant changes, let alone running it, will not leave you any time for learning your ABCs, assuming you also want to keep your head above water.

On top of all this, there is another, even more important set of challenges to be dealt with. It is called competition. The strength of our free market system derives from the efficient allocation of our society's scarce resources. These include capital, raw materials, labor, time, and so on, as well as market demand, and they go to the most effective users of them. In simple terms, this means survival of the fittest.

Creative destruction is a related concept, and competition is the device that accomplishes this vital process. Therefore, whereas competition in an open and free market is society's best economic friend, it most likely will not seem like yours if you have just bought a midsized manufacturing business. There really is no place to run and no place to hide. To survive, you must succeed.

To improve your chances of success (and survival), choose carefully the competitive environment you enter. Just as the weekend duffer is best advised not to go head-to-head with world-class golfers for big, or indeed any, bucks, if you have no experience in manufacturing, you would be courting disaster to buy a midsized manufacturing business. As ignorant and unsophisticated as the selling owner of that proverbial mundane manufacturer may seem, if you are new to his business, it is certain that he knows more about his business and market than you do. More important, unless he is the sales and profit leader in his market—and maybe even if he is—in all likelihood, he has competitors who know even more about the business than he does and whose objectives include eating at least some, if not all, of his, soon to be your, lunch.

The point is, although we all need a first job at least once in our lives, amateurs do not make good buyers of midsized manufacturing businesses. Industry-specific experience, or better yet, current involvement, makes for the best buyer.

The successful owner of a midsized manufacturer is a leader. Running a manufacturing business requires the skills of inspiration, organization, foresightedness, and steadfastness. Wishy-washy people should not apply either. There is a tremendous amount that needs to be done, people to be motivated and enabled to accomplish their best, factors of production to be arranged, markets to be developed. All along the way, there are many risks to be avoided, and more important, many risks to be taken. Whereas leadership is more important than brilliance, intelligence is a prerequisite for success. With so much to be done, energy levels are also very important.

WHAT TYPE OF MANUFACTURING BUSINESS
SHOULD YOU BUY?

As discussed, manufacturers come in a vast variety. So, of course, do potential mates. The key is to find the one of each best suited to your background, personality, and abilities. If you want to find a nice mundane manufacturer with a good cash flow, in truth you probably really do not know what you want. This makes it unlikely you will ever find either what you want, or indeed what makes sense for you.

The choice of the kind of manufacturing business you should buy is best answered with reference to the question of which field will maximize your chances of success, given your own scarce resources including your innate abilities, your experience, and the capital you can mobilize. Clearly, you should not enter a technical field unless you have up-to-date technical talents. Otherwise, you would be playing catch-up, at least at first, with your new competitors. Worse yet, if you enter a field employing a rapidly developing knowledge and experience base, you may be so busy catching up with your competitors that by the time you do they will have moved well ahead; thus, you never do catch up.

Technically based fields are not the only hyperdynamic ones. Fashion, for example, is a moving target, which presumably requires a special eye and quick reflexes to exploit. Unless you have such an eye and are equipped with such reflexes, it is hard to imagine how you will successfully compete against those who do.

Also, as mentioned, some manufacturing businesses are more capital-intensive than others. Manufacturing processes that require expensive equipment and/or need to be large-scale for efficient operation would not be good for the buyer on a limited budget.

In considering various types of manufacturing businesses you might enter, try to determine and understand the key factors to success in the various fields you study. All companies in any given industrial segment deal with essentially the same realities of the economics, technology, and competitive situations of their field. An industry's economics are determined by its capital investment requirements and the costs of its factors of production. The technology will most likely be established, but still may be either fast or slow to change on its inevitable path to innovation and evolution.

In other words, regardless of the stages of development of the various participants in any given industrial segment, the segment itself is in one of the three stages of growth, maturity, or decline. Each of these stages presents a different set of competitive challenges and opportunities. Even today, presumably, there are still profitable manufacturers of buggy whips.

You will need to understand these aspects in order to properly evaluate your profit potential and risk profile in any given field. Assuming what would seem obvious, that you would not buy a business to preserve its status quo, you need to appraise how you will add value and so achieve the return on your investment that you seek.

Value is added through increased profits, or as explained later, increased free cash flow. These can be increased only through increased sales or reduced costs or, if you are really good, both. In any case, to judge how you might increase sales, you need to study the industry because growing sales can only be achieved by gaining market share from your competitors, by causing the size of the market you serve to increase by benefiting from its increase as a result of other factors. Increasing a business's advertising budget might get more market share, at least temporarily, and new product introductions or enhanced distribution could expand market demand. Bear in mind, however, no move goes unnoticed in a free market.

Speaking of free markets, this is another key aspect you will need to analyze. Not all industries and not all businesses in any given industry enjoy, in effect, 100 percent free markets. Indeed, any business with a labor union, particularly if it is in a jurisdiction without a right to work law, does not enjoy a free market vis-à-vis its labor supply and costs. Similarly, a manufacturer dependent upon a sole supplier for any factor of its production does not enjoy the protection of a competitive market for its cost of such supply. A major customer may be reflective of a less than free market for the manufacturer's output, as well as an important risk area.

WHICH MANUFACTURING BUSINESS SHOULD YOU BUY?

Once you analyze your relative competitive strengths and weaknesses, and narrow—or better yet, select the best field for you—the question of which business in that field to buy depends in the first instance on which businesses in it are for sale or can be induced to sell. The answer to this lies in the most crucial analysis of all as to which alternative offers the greatest return on investment prospect. This analysis must focus on what the business in your—not the previous or some other owner's—hands will likely produce in profit. The task then is to determine how much you can afford to pay for the business and still experience the minimum return on the investment you require to justify making it. Finally, you have to negotiate with the seller to purchase the business for this target price or less.

In evaluating a manufacturing business to buy, you need to look at three elements. The first and most fundamental is the franchise of the business. This means the market the business serves and its competitive position in serving it. The quality and value of a manufacturing business's franchise is a function of both of these aspects. If the market need is small in sales size, transitory like a fad item, or fading like buggy whips, it will, of course, be worth less. On the next level, if the competitive situation in serving the market need is severe either in terms of the number of competitors, the presence of an 800-pound gorilla of a competitor who has a big, oppressing, and low-price umbrella, or entails such low barriers to entry that the garage shop operators will forever forestall the joys of proper pricing, you probably should look for another business.

As to barriers to entry, they are generally lower in distribution and services businesses than in the manufacturing sector. Also, as mentioned, a business's franchise is weakened if it is only dependent on one or a small number of customers or suppliers. In either case, the business's leverage in the market it serves is diminished.

If there is a basic franchise to the business, the next question is as to the adequacy of the business's productive capacity to produce its current, and an increasing level of, sales. If the business has last decade's machinery and equipment, and the competition has upgraded, you need to factor into your analysis the required investment to get up to speed. Equipment is usually key to a manufacturing business; and modern, or indeed, the latest available equipment, is very often a requirement for success vis-à-vis the competition. Depending upon the nature of the product(s) manufactured, necessary equipment can range from hand tools to massive machines. This might figuratively describe the range from light manufacturers to heavy. In addition to fabricating equipment that might shape, extrude, coat, and even alter the physical properties of raw materials, manufacturers also utilize material-handling equipment, which in some cases can be both highly sophisticated and very expensive.

Finally, if the franchise is there and the capacity is there, you need to confirm that the basic systems to make the whole thing work are there or that you can put them in place soon enough. These systems include most importantly the people involved or that need to be involved. They also include basic sales, manufacturing, financial, and management information infrastructure and procedures.

In this investment analysis, location is even more important vis-à-vis a business's economics than your lifestyle preferences. Generally speaking, the economics of manufacturing determine good and bad locations.

For example, labor availability is important in terms of the quantity, quality, and cost of labor inputs in the manufacturing process. Some of the pertinent questions relative to labor availability include whether there is an adequate supply of labor to fill the normal turnover and growth needs of the business. Does this labor supply presently have, or does it have the potential to develop, the necessary skills to carry out the manufacturing process? Is the location such that a labor union is involved in the business or likely to become involved in the future; and if so, is the labor union in question a net plus or negative for the business?

Raw materials' availability is important in terms of not only the number of suppliers possible and the quality of their products, but also the transportation economics of getting the materials from the suppliers to the manufacturer. Power cost is often a significant factor and can vary materially from one location to another. Availability of adequate professional services also varies from location to location.

The transportation economics of getting a manufacturer's output to wherever its customers want them is also important. For example, how far away from the manufacturer's location does its output have to be moved, and what is the time and the cost required for this? Specific questions here include access to major truck (for example, interstate highway) routes, availability of rail siding, and proximity to air or water transport facilities.

The political climate of a location can also be very important. For one thing, it impacts the cost structure of a manufacturer in terms of tax rates. This climate also affects the general conduct of the business in terms of the community's receptivity or antipathy toward it. Life is either made easier or more difficult for the business by the attitude toward it, and business in general, that flows from the local political situation.

Environmental questions are very important with respect to a manufacturer's operations and location. You need to evaluate the materials used in the manufacturing process, the end products sold, and the disposal of the waste materials that result. In terms of the manufacturer's location, perhaps first and foremost is the question of whether it can pass an environmental inspection. Other environmental questions are also important. For example, is the business located in an area of poor air quality, which impacts its permitted emissions levels and therefore the output, or the cost, of its operations? Could the manufacturer's operations, or perhaps more likely the expansion of its operations, be constrained by any regulations like the Endangered Species Act? And not to be overlooked are the simple and straightforward quality-of-life issues. Is the business located in a clean and orderly modern industrial park, or is it in a long since abandoned, rundown, and crime-ridden part of town? Such considerations materially affect how people feel about working, let alone their performance, in one location versus another. Also not to be overlooked are access to suitable housing and recreational options.

HOW DO YOU FIND A MANUFACTURING
BUSINESS TO BUY?

As mentioned earlier, the first step in finding a manufacturing business to buy is to figure out what kind makes sense for you. Only you can really determine this. However, outside advice can be helpful. You can learn from the experiences of people who have done what you are trying to do. Also, of course, people on the inside of manufacturing businesses like those you might think appropriate can give you a feel for what your life on the inside might be like. Intermediaries, accountants, and attorneys who have seen and worked with others who have tried to buy, and bought, businesses can give you valuable insights, perhaps most particularly from those situations that did not work out.

The process of searching for a business to buy and dealing with the opportunities that are presented to you will either confirm your initial decisions about what would make sense for you or cause your ideas to evolve. In either case, as you go forward, you will most likely be more sure of your direction. Thus, although you should not start that journey of a thousand miles without a destination in mind and a plan for how to get there, you do need to take the first step.

In doing so, you have a basic choice of ways to proceed. You can conduct the process by yourself, or you can enlist the help of intermediaries. Intermediaries expect to be paid for their services. However, it is most likely that the cost of their services will be more than offset by the value they add to your effort and, most important, to your result. Intermediaries will give you exposure to more of the market you wish to explore, and they will enable you to leverage your time in the acquisition search process. People who are involved with the process on a regular and professional basis are more efficient and effective in carrying it out.

Just as there is a so-called hidden job market for job hunters, there is also a hidden acquisition market. Selling a business is a delicate matter. It involves crucial negotiations over value and deal structure, and entails serious business risks. As such, seller prospects need to be careful in approaching the market. They need to minimize the risks of foolishly losing negotiating position or prematurely breaching confidentiality. The latter can result in damaging rumor material for competitors' salespeople, concerned vendors, and antsy employees. As such, many prospective sellers are cautious in responding to strangers' inquiries about whether they would like to sell their business. In a psychological sense, an intermediary is less of a stranger, even if not previously known. An intermediary is recognized as a professional who subscribes to the ethical practices of the profession and provides a buffer with respect to confidentiality.

Consequently, if an intermediary asks any given group of business owners if they would be interested in the possibility of selling their business, he is most likely to get a higher and more positive response rate than a prospective buyer approaching directly. However, credibility has to be achieved to get this higher response rate. The intermediary does this not only by presenting himself as a professional but also by communicating, and so endorsing, the buyer prospect's financial and business credentials to undertake discussions.

When an intermediary is engaged by a seller, his job is to identify and develop the interest of as many qualified buyer prospects as possible. Through this work he strengthens the negotiating position of his seller clients, and helps them achieve a higher value for their business. On the other hand, when an intermediary represents a buyer's interest, his mission is to identify sellers that meet his client's acquisition criteria and bring the parties together as soon as his client determines that a prospect fits his search criteria. He does this from information the intermediary gathers on the seller. In this way, the intermediary hopes to initiate negotiations for his client before the seller develops alternate buyer prospects or works his way up the learning curve about the process.

There is a considerable amount of work and time involved in effectively buying a business. The obvious goals in the process are to find the best business to buy and to acquire it for the lowest price and best terms possible. Finding the best business to buy is a function of the thoroughness and effectiveness of the search effort. The lowest price is often a function of the number of acquisition options or choices the buyer has. This again is a product of a thorough and effective search program. The best terms are usually obtained by those with the most experience in such transactions and the most developed negotiating skills.

For this reason, and the labor required to successfully conduct the process itself, you will probably be better off engaging an intermediary. Through his working relationships in the market, plus the seller prospects he can identify and contact, an intermediary can give you maximum, controlled, and confidential access to the full market of potential acquisition prospects meeting your criteria. An intermediary can also support you during the negotiation and deal-structuring stages, as well as assist in the due diligence and closing phases. The criteria for the selection of an intermediary to engage should include that the intermediary's market reach match the geographical scope of your possible interest.

Although most intermediaries will work with buyer clients on a nonexclusive basis, it is often important for them to have a de facto exclusive engagement. For one thing, it is generally less prospective for an intermediary to function in a situation where he is, in effect, in a competitive position vis-à-vis his client. On the other hand, if other intermediaries are involved, there is no way for any one of them to control the quality of the effort, let alone the confidentiality. Also, since any intermediary's chances of earning a contingent fee on the project are so much less, the overall quantity of effort is probably less too.

Another reason to use just one intermediary is that if your acquisition criteria are relatively narrow, you will do better if you control the approaches to seller prospects. It could work against your interests if a

number of intermediaries take your criteria and approach the marketplace. In this situation, the owners of businesses you might be interested
in could get an inflated view of the demand factor for their businesses,
and thus be more difficult to come to attractive terms with.

As mentioned, if an intermediary is involved in a transaction, there
will be an intermediary fee. However, it is theoretically immaterial
whether the seller or the buyer pays the fee since, in essence, it comes
out of the money the buyer pays to the seller. However, in practical
terms, seller prospects are likely to be more responsive if they are informed on first contact that the buyer is paying the fee.

Note, though, that you should be cautious about two-fee transactions.
That is, if the seller is represented by an intermediary and you by one as
well, unless they agree to share one fee, any two-fee deal you propose
will be competitively disadvantaged to other buyer prospects whose
deals only involve one fee.

HOW DO YOU BUY THE BUSINESS?

Successfully buying a business involves more than just finance and negotiation. There is a very strong human side to the process and the
event. This is particularly the case when a founder entrepreneur is selling. It is true in every psychological and emotional sense that in such
situations the seller is selling "his baby." Not only does he most likely
feel a loyalty to his employees, customers, and suppliers, and not wish to
do any of them harm, but also he is confronting divesting himself of a
part of his very identity.

In this regard, it is extremely important for the buyer to approach the
seller in the first instance as if he were also a seller. The buyer thus
needs to be a seller of his own good character, ability, and worthiness to
buy the seller's business. Unless the buyer establishes positive personal
chemistry with the seller, it will be very difficult to put together and
close a successful deal. If the chemistry does not start out positively, it
is difficult to later make it so.

What the seller wishes is multifold. Certainly, he wants to be paid in
full without difficulty at least the full market value of his business, if
not more. He also wants his stewardship of the business, and indeed his
life, validated through a successful sale to a worthy and appreciative
buyer. And, yes, in many cases he wants to secure his immortality
through the continuation of the business more or less as it had been after
the sale. Of course, these emotions do not all run with the same force
through every seller, and indeed there are sellers who evidence none of
them. Nevertheless, the buyer who does not factor in the likelihood of
their existence, at least below the surface, makes his task more difficult.

Unhappy as it may be for some buyers, many businesses are sold
without asking prices. From a seller's perspective an asking price is

nothing more than a ceiling on his pricing potential. An asking price expressed as a range is effectively the same thing with a second, lower number included presumably because the seller is not brave enough to give a single point asking price or, more important, no asking price. Certainly, to a buyer, an asking price is welcome; it makes the job easier. He knows where the ceiling is, and can devote all of his energy to working down from there. However, buyers should not shy away from sellers just because there is no asking price.

If a buyer is not competent enough to figure out what the seller's business is worth to him, he probably should not risk becoming a buyer. Furthermore, if a buyer is not disposed to working out a win-win solution with the seller, or if he is a low-baller hoping to find some desperate fool of a seller, he is in danger of wasting his time at least and buying into an unhappy seller at worst.

Most buyers are properly concerned about wasting their time. As such, an asking price provides many of them with a comfort level to two of their key questions: whether the seller is "for real" and whether he is realistic. These are appropriate questions because many a person, principal, and intermediary have wasted their time with sellers who were not. There will always be purported sellers whose real agenda may be to flatter their egos by having petitioners declare how brilliant or rich they are. Similarly, there will always be sellers who, regardless of strong advice let alone need to sell their business, are simply not in touch, and do not want to be brought into touch with the reality of the market value of their business. There are also sellers who have consciously or subconsciously decided to exercise their ultimate owner's perquisite and never fire themselves.

In lieu of an asking price, there are other ways to get a fix on the answers to these key questions. Polite probing as to why the seller wants to sell, and discerning evaluation of the response along with inquiry as to how the seller is inclined to approach the valuation question usually works. If polite probing does not lead to a sufficient level of comfort on the points, it is probably worthwhile to conduct deeper, more pointed probing.

If the seller is represented by an intermediary, it is probably a good sign, because an experienced professional is guiding the seller. More important, the intermediary has to answer the same two key questions, plus a third before he can afford to allocate the scarce resource of his time to representing the seller. The intermediary is almost certainly working, at least in significant part, on a contingent fee basis—no sale, no payday for the intermediary.

The intermediary's third key question is whether the business is salable. There are those that are not. Be aware that not all intermediaries have the same level of experience and judgment. There will always be intermediaries who engage in wishful thinking, usually because they do not have enough other work. So do not be bashful about evaluating the caliber of the intermediary as a reflection of the quality of the

opportunity. If the intermediary has been paid a significant upfront retainer or commitment fee by the seller, that can be a good indication
that you have a real seller. If the intermediary does not have an exclusive engagement from the seller, you should wonder about the intermediary's caliber as well as the seller's commitment to the project.

Let us assume you have made it this far; that is, you have decided that
you want to buy a midsized manufacturing business; you have determined the kind of manufacturer you should buy, and you have found the
manufacturing business for you and established the necessary personal
rapport with the seller. Now all you have to do is figure out how much
you can afford to pay for it and still look forward to a return on your
capital and time, which will enable you to create the wealth you are
seeking. Next you have to persuade the seller to sell his business to you
for no more than this amount. Then you have to structure the transaction, presumably to maximize the mutual benefits of yourself and the
seller; that is, purchase price and protection. Finally, you need confirm
your investment decision through due diligence and have the transaction
documented and closed.

In negotiating transaction prices, buyers are often told by sellers
about all of the cost savings the business will experience after closing as
a result of the elimination of redundancies. Sellers also tout all of the increased sales that will result from synergies that will be achieved and so
the consequent higher profits the buyer will enjoy. Sellers will even tell
buyers that they will do better in the business because of their higher
energy levels and/or willingness to make incremental investments in it.
The point of all these comments is, of course, to entreat the buyer to pay
the seller a higher price. But the seller does not get paid for what the
buyer brings to the party; rather, buyers pay for the demonstrable, documented cash flow-generating capacity of the business in the seller's
hands at the time of the closing.

In other words, for the purposes of valuation, you should look at any
business as a cash-generating machine. The value of the business is a
function of how much cash it generates, the risks associated with the
generation of this cash, the cost of the investment funds used to acquire
it, and their liquidity after investment is made. Cash flow is variously defined, but the simplest way to think of it is as the excess cash that is
available from the operation of the business that is yours to use as you
wish. You might choose to deploy this free cash flow either in incremental investment to preserve, or more hopefully grow, the business; or as
savings, investment, or expenditure outside of it for whatever other objectives you may have, including your personal comfort and pleasure.

This cash flow for your discretionary use is of course what is left from
every dollar earned from the sales of the manufacturer's products after
paying all of the costs of producing those items, and paying for the organization that accomplishes those sales, including—if you are working in
the business—the market value of your labor contribution. Cash flow

also factors paying the costs of any third-party-provided funds used to acquire the business, such as bank loans; and after paying the taxes due on the profits; and otherwise. Repayment of the principal of any borrowing from your discretionary cash flow is, in effect, deployment of it as incremental equity investment in the business.

Also note that growth of the business requires working capital financing, which in most cases must come ultimately from the cash flow the business produces. In a very real sense, rather than being discretionary incremental investment in the business, this is essential for the preservation of the business, recognizing again the Darwinian reality; namely, in this case, that any business that does not grow will fade in the face of the growth of its competitors.

Since this chapter is not about valuation, which is amply covered elsewhere, suffice it to say here that a number of valuation models are available, and each has its supporters. For your purposes, simpler may be better lest you misallocate time to analysis of this point, which might in turn lead to paralysis instead of action. No matter how sophisticated the approach, valuation exercises all entail assumptions, which, of course, renders their results a function of the quality of the assumptions.

Nevertheless, as background, the key components of the valuation of a business are the stream of earnings in the form of discretionary, or free, cash flow produced by it; the terminal value of the business for you—that is, when you sell, liquidate or otherwise exit from it; and the minimum rate of return you require to justify your investment. With these three variables, you can solve for the fourth, namely what initial investment will yield the required rate of return. However, the results need to be further massaged to factor in the risks of the investment.

What Are the Risks?

These risks fall essentially into three categories: in the operation of the business, external, and in the exit process. The risks in the first category are seemingly endless, which is why amateurs should not apply, or at least should be scared off before they buy if they are paying attention. Every aspect of the business constitutes a risk area—they don't need be enumerated to make the point. Market demand for your product can change up or down for many different reasons, including changes in the market's needs, changes made by your competitors, or changes made by yourself. Accidents happen, to your employees, to your customers—sometimes while using your products—and to others. Some of these people may look to your business, or worse to you, for recompense. In short, the stream of cash flow you look forward to from your new business, your new cash machine, is subject to innumerable vicissitudes.

External risks include all the usual suspects: war, pestilence, and your friendly government, or better said, governments. Fortunately, war does not break out at any moment. There are usually storm clouds visible in advance. You would probably not choose such a time to launch into your new midsized manufacturing investment—unless, of course, you were in some war material manufacturing business. Pestilence, on the other hand, certainly in such forms as earthquakes and hurricanes, can indeed occur at any moment and cannot be seen coming within the time frames of most investment decision processes.

Your friends and "servants" in public office and their regulatory sidekicks might represent the most dangerous external risk of all. They look like you, sound like you, but sometimes they absolutely do not act as you would want them to, and you and your investment could be hurt in the process. Politics draw into your orderly world of investment analysis the ultimate wild card. Politicians can change the rules of the game while you are playing, meaning *after* you have put up your money. They can also effectively take you out of the game, or even call the game off before it's over, forcing you to leave significant amounts of your money on the table for someone else to scoop up after you leave. Consider the impact on your carefully crafted investment analysis of an increase in the capital gains tax after you make your investment. Changes in environmental laws and regulations have also had major impacts on business profits.

Exiting is hardly a sure, let alone predictable, factor at the time of your investment. It is impossible to project the likely results of your exit with any precision. Certainly, you cannot intelligently guess what the condition of the economy will be when you want, or worse need, to exit. This condition will inevitably affect the liquidity of your investment at the time, and so its value realization potential. Still, you can make judgments at the outset about the likely sources and magnitude of interest in your business when you want to exit it. But do not fall into the trap of assuming that just because you are smart enough to buy the business that there will be another smart person available when you want to sell it. This is the "greater fool" theory.

Financial Matters

As in privately owned businesses of all kinds, the financial statements of small manufacturers do not necessarily reflect reality, nor even the accountants' prescribed rendition of reality. It is said that private businesses are the greatest tax shelters of all. Therefore, adjustments need to be made to a seller's financial statements for analysis. Typical items to be alert for are nonoperational expenses, including of course, excess owner's salary and perquisites, which are really a return on his own capital invested in the business; unaccounted for cash sales; over- or undervalued inventory, which impacts cost of goods sold; expensed costs that should have been capitalized; and extraordinary, nonrecurring expenses.

In calculating free cash flow, be alert to any seasonal working capital financing needs of the business. Many manufacturers' sales follow a seasonal pattern. Producers of Christmas decorations are an obvious example. Needless to say, these manufacturers have a specific seasonal sales pattern that peaks months before Christmas when shipments are made to distributors and retailers. In the months leading up to this sales peak, the manufacturer builds inventory in preparation for shipment. In the months following, accounts receivable balloon. Since the company's vendors are not typically in a position, let alone interested, to finance this buildup, the manufacturer must have available either bank lines of credit or surplus cash from previous operation's cash flow to do so.

Moreover, bankers do not typically like to carry all of the burden. Therefore, even if credit lines are available, it is most likely that they are supported by a healthy contribution from the equityholders, again hopefully in the form of a portion of previously generated cash flow. In this respect, cash flow allocated to this need is not free. Consequently, an analysis of a firm's free cash flow-generating capacity, based only upon fiscal year-end statement dates, would likely overlook this point if the fiscal year-end was not at the high point in the seasonal cycle. Visualize how different the Christmas decoration manufacturer's balance sheet would look on June 30 versus December 31.

In looking forward, a buyer also must consider any additional capital expenditure requirements to grow the business, as well as the financing needs for any resultant working capital increases. It might be argued that these are uses of free cash flow, again in the form of incremental equity investment in the business, since it is the owner's decision whether to grow his business, and that the value of such incremental investments will be realized in increased future free cash flow and an enhanced terminal value. On the other hand, as mentioned before, the reality of the business marketplace is more likely that any owner who fails to invest in the future growth of his business will lose out to his competitors. If you take the latter view, free cash flow is what is left after these expenditures as well.

Since the financing decisions and tax rates for a business are in large part specific to an individual owner, the cash flow-generating capacity of a business is usually discussed on a debt-free, before-tax basis in order to establish a common denominator, so to speak. For information presentation purposes, adjusted earnings before depreciation, interest and taxes (EBDIT) is most often used as a proxy for the cash-generating capacity of a manufacturer. The adjustments again relate to nonoperational and nonrecurring costs. EBDIT is sometimes written as earnings before interest and taxes, plus depreciation (EBIT-D) and even EBIT-DA (depreciation and amortization).

In any case, we are now down to the question of what the value is of the particular cash-generating capacity of a given midsized manufacturer. As in all purchases, the buyer's perceptions of the risk inherent in that cash flow, the liquidity prospects of his investment, the growth potential in his hands, and the level of his felt need to buy enter into the equation. Some buyers have a greater need to buy than others. Whatever the makeup of the buyer, often participants in the markets for small manufacturing businesses talk about multiples of earnings, or really, again, cash-generating capacity. The multiple, whatever it may be, is an expression (put simply, the reciprocal) of the risk-adjusted rate of return requirement of the buyer. The multiples most often heard in the small manufacturer arena range from four to six times EBDIT. The more mundane the business, the lower the multiple discussed; and the more exciting (higher value added, leading edge, and so on), the higher. Mediocre and marginal small manufacturers get offers below a multiple of four, and sexy ones over six. By contrast, distributors that add little value in carrying out their business sell for multiples plus or minus three.

At this point, we should mention a not uncommon cry heard from sellers about all their wonderful equipment, dies, patents, brand names, and so on. However, to their disappointment, these wonderful things, along with all the other assets and liabilities involved in their business, are worth, all together, precisely what the free cash flow-generating capacity produced by their particular conglomeration of assets and liabilities is worth. Buyers need not pay sellers twice for the same thing. You may also hear sellers protest that they paid some large amount for a particular piece of equipment. What they paid for it is again separate from, and indeed immaterial to, the free cash flow-generating capacity of the business and its particular contribution to it.

This is not to say that a business may not have assets that are in excess of those needed to efficiently conduct its business. However, in this case, it is unlikely that you as a buyer will ascribe significant additional value to them since you intend to be as efficient as you can be in your investing. A buyer may pay some extra amount for, say, excess inventory or equipment, but generally it is better for the seller to work these off in operations leading up to a sale, or to sell them separately to whatever market for them may exist (the used equipment market for example) before a sale of the business.

As mentioned, the assets and working liabilities of the business make up a conglomeration that together produce the free cash flow you are buying. Therefore, other than deal-structuring issues, the valuation of the business assumes you acquire 100 percent of the business assets and working liabilities. The term "working liabilities" is meant to denote accounts payable and accrued expenses. Other liabilities are capital in nature, whether they be long-term debt used in the acquisition or otherwise in its capital structure, or short-term working capital loans borrowed from a bank or otherwise.

In the conglomeration of assets and liabilities you are acquiring, receivables and payables are often considered deal-structuring items. Many transactions leave either or both of these in the hands of the seller for collection and payment respectively. This is not in the buyer's best interests, however, on an operational level. The buyer needs to have control over these accounts, and more important, the relationships behind them.

The receivables are due from what are now the buyer's customers and the seller's former customers. The payables are due to the buyer's ongoing vendors and the seller's former vendors. These relationships are fundamentally different. The buyer's interests would not be well served if the seller hounded his customers for payment of the receivables. This might happen, since, regrettable as it may be, there are people who become less inclined to pay their bills if they are owed to someone upon whom they are no longer dependent for future favors. Similarly, the seller is no longer dependent upon his former vendors for future shipments. Thus, in a certain percentage of the cases, his inclination to pay these bills in full, let alone on time, diminishes. Meanwhile, the future shipments from these vendors are now for the buyer.

There are ways for the buyer to control the preclosing receivables and payables short of acquiring them. If, for structuring reasons, it is agreed that the seller keep either or both of the receivables or the payables, the buyer can collect the receivables through the business for the seller and pay them over as received. Payables can be paid by an escrow agent either from checks presented by the seller at the closing or from cash deposited with an escrow agent to be paid out as the payables come due.

Valuation implies a cash price. But in addition are a terms price and an earnout price. A terms price implies seller financing. Sellers are inclined to provide financing because it increases the liquidity of their business. This is because there are more prospective buyers who have enough cash for a down payment than there are those who can afford an all-cash transaction. Since prices are set by supply and demand factors, the more demand the seller can generate for his business by making it affordable to more prospective buyers, the higher the price he should be able to get. A seller-financed price for a business theoretically should exceed its cash price for other reasons, too. This is because the seller-provided terms result in a delay in the receipt of the seller's value, which needs to be addressed with respect to the time value of money, and an increase in the risk that the seller will not be paid all of his value. For accepting such a risk, the seller theoretically should be rewarded with a higher price. However, in truth, the benefit he gained from the increased liquidity for his business might in the final negotiation and analysis offset these other factors.

An earnout price entails still more risk for a seller. Generally speaking, this is where the seller agrees to make some portion of the purchase price a function of the results of the business after closing. In essence, the seller has now shifted a portion of his previous equity investment in his own business into an equity investment in the buyer's business. Clearly, this is an even riskier proposition for the seller than seller financing. As such, his expected price with an earnout should exceed the price he could get without it.

Earnouts inevitably include upside limits for the seller on his potential reward from the future results of the business. These limits are typically denominated in terms of the percentage of the future results to be paid to the seller and the length of time that the earnout runs. In return for accepting the upper limit, which again would have to result in a total purchase price higher than he could get in a seller-financed sale, it is not unreasonable for the seller to expect some downside limit which, in return for the chance to do better than he otherwise could, would be set somewhat lower.

SUMMARY

Before you buy a business, you should consider that as good as the business is, as good as the deal is, and as good as you are, it might not work out. One or more of the innumerable risks may, in the end, "get" you. Or, hard as it may be to admit, your initial judgments on how good the business deal was could have been flawed. Worse yet, maybe you prove to be not that good a manufacturer after all. You should give the possibility of failure some consideration.

One of the great features of our economic, social, and legal systems is that failure need not be terminal. This is a key ingredient in the vitality, strength, and progress of our economy and society. Great and small attempts and experiments are made possible, and thus encouraged, because it need not be the end of the world for those trying and experimenting if they do not succeed. They are free to try again, provided they have done at least some planning ahead.

Think about what it would take to start again, and make sure that you maintain enough of these elements in case you need them, including capital and your character. Neither invest all of your capital nor risk your character if you get into difficulty. Keep some powder dry for another day and know when, and be ready, to walk away with your head held high if the time comes. Another key ingredient in your contingency plans for dealing with failure is your support system. Assuming you have a fulfilling personal life, your investment and its survival are not more important, and you will need this all-important support in place for your comeback.

If you find yourself intimidated by these considerations, perhaps you should allow for yourself to be put off by them. On the other hand, if you have come this far, in all likelihood, you are the type of person for whom the path to wealth and happiness lies in working for yourself. Therefore, if after all of your introspection and analysis, you conclude that you are capable and competent to both buy and successfully operate a midsized manufacturing business, do it. The world is full of might-have-beens. Very few of them create wealth. Those who do have carefully scanned the horizon, decided their destination, and taken the first step. And our society, in addition to their own lives, is much the richer for it.

CHAPTER THIRTY

ESOPs: Pros and Cons

JOHN D. MENKE
MENKE AND ASSOCIATES, INC.

NEW ADVANTAGES UNDER THE
1984 AND 1986 TAX LAWS

The Tax Reform Act of 1986 signed into law by President Reagan on October 22, 1986, ratified and expanded the dramatic tax benefits afforded employee stock ownership plans (ESOPs) under the 1984 Tax Reform Act. As a result, an owner who sells part or all of his stock to an ESOP can obtain a number of significant tax benefits that are not otherwise available under a conventional sale or merger. The following describes these tax benefits and the other pros and cons of a sale of stock of an ESOP.

Tax-Free Rollover

The most dramatic provision of the 1984 and 1986 laws is the tax-free rollover provision contained in new Internal Revenue Code § 1042. Under this provision, a taxpayer may defer paying any federal income taxes on the sale of closely held stock to an ESOP, provided that he reinvests the proceeds in qualified replacement securities within 12 months of the date of sale.

In order to qualify for this deferral, the shareholder must sell closely held domestic company stock that he has held for three or more years. Stock that the shareholder originally acquired as section 83 stock, as restricted stock, as bargain stock, or as stock under a stock option plan or as a distribution from a qualified plan, does not qualify for this deferral. Second, after the transaction is complete, the ESOP must own at least 30 percent of the total value of all outstanding company stock (other than preferred stock). For purposes of this rule, any stock options are treated as though the optioned stock is already outstanding. Third, the employer company must file a consent to the tax-free rollover transaction. Last, the funds must be reinvested in qualified replacement securities within the period beginning three months before the sale and ending 12 months after the sale.

Qualified replacement securities refers to any securities issued by a domestic corporation that did not, in the year preceding purchase by the taxpayer, have passive investment income (rents, royalties, dividends, interest, and so on) in excess of 25 percent of the gross receipts of such corporation. Accordingly, the proceeds may be reinvested in either corporate stocks or in corporate bonds of either publicly traded or privately held corporations. On the other hand, the proceeds may not be reinvested in government securities or in mutual funds.

The ESOP is required to hold the securities that it has purchased for at least three years after the acquisition date. If the ESOP disposes of part or all of these securities (other than by means of a normal distribution to a terminated or retired participant), the company will be liable for a 10 percent penalty tax.

The seller must carry over his basis from the old securities to the new securities. Thus, if the seller subsequently sells the replacement securities, he will then incur an income tax based upon the difference between the fair market value of the securities at the time of sale and his original basis.

Some of the ways in which the new tax-free rollover provision may be especially useful to corporate owners are described in the following subsections.

Alternative to Sale

Under the 1984 and 1986 ESOP provisions, purchase of an owner's stock by an ESOP will almost always be more beneficial to the owner than a sale or merger. For example, in the case of a sale to a third party, the seller will incur an income tax, lose control, usually lose his salary and fringe benefits, and usually will not be able to keep any retained equity. In comparison, there will be no federal income tax (and usually no state income tax) to the seller if he sells stock to an ESOP under the tax-free rollover provisions of the 1984 act. In addition, the seller can keep control, continue to receive his salary and fringe benefits, and keep as much or as little of the stock as he desires. Of course, the seller will be subsequently taxed if he later sells the replacement securities. However, in most cases, it will be advisable for the seller to defer the tax.

By taking advantage of the tax-free rollover provision, for example, a shareholder can sell $1 million worth of his closely held stock to an ESOP and subsequently acquire $1 million worth of corporate stocks and bonds. By electing the tax-free rollover provision, he would save $280,000 or more in federal income taxes, making him eligible to receive dividends and interest on $1 million worth of securities rather than on only $720,000 worth of securities. Further, if the shareholder holds these securities until his death, he will escape the income tax altogether. One caveat should be mentioned with respect to the purchase of corporate bonds. A bond is deemed to be sold or exchanged when it matures. Thus, if a bond matures prior to the owner's death, the income tax will then be incurred. Accordingly, any shareholder who purchases corporate bonds as replacement securities should be careful to purchase long-term bonds.

Investment Diversification

Previously, the only way an owner of a closely held company could achieve investment diversification without incurring an immediate income tax was to engage in a tax-free merger with a public company. In order to qualify for a tax-free merger, however, an owner must transfer 80 percent or more of his stock in exchange for public company stock. In effect, the owner *has* to give up control. Moreover, he still has no investment diversification.

Under the ESOP rollover provision, these problems are avoided. In order to get tax-free treatment, the ESOP need only acquire 30 percent ownership, and the replacement securities can be fully diversified.

The ESOP rollover provision also solves the problem of the locked-in shareholder. Under present law, if a shareholder holds his stock until death, the stock will receive a step-up in basis in his estate, and the income tax will be avoided. If, on the other hand, the shareholder sells part or all of his stock, prior to his death, he will incur both an income tax and an estate tax. As a consequence, many shareholders have been locked into their existing investments. Now, with the tax-free rollover provision, these shareholders can sell part or all of their closely held stock and purchase marketable securities without incurring any federal income taxes.

Charitable Contributions

The tax-free rollover provision may also make it much easier for the owner of a closely held corporation to make charitable contributions. Under the private foundation laws, the owner of a closely held business is generally prohibited from contributing closely held stock directly to a private foundation. However, under the new tax-free rollover provision, this problem can be avoided. The taxpayer may sell his closely held securities to the ESOP and reinvest the proceeds tax-free in publicly held securities. He can then transfer the publicly held securities to a charity or to a private foundation without violating the rules regarding the acquisition and holding of employer securities.

CAPITAL GAINS

An ESOP can also be used to lock in the capital gains tax rate. If, for example, a shareholder wishes to sell less than 30 percent of his stock, or wishes to invest the proceeds in other than qualified replacement securities, he may sell part or all of his stock to the ESOP and elect capital gains treatment. As a result, he will be taxed at the 28 percent rate, even if he retains significant stock ownership. This is in contrast to a partial stock redemption, which is usually taxed at ordinary income tax rates.

INTEREST EXCLUSION

In order for the ESOP to acquire a 30 percent ownership interest and qualify for a tax-free rollover transaction, it will be necessary in many cases for the ESOP to obtain a bank loan. In order to facilitate such loans, the 1984 Tax Reform Act granted a special interest exclusion for ESOP loans. Under code § 133, a bank, a savings and loan association, an insurance company, or a mutual fund may exclude from gross income 50 percent of the interest received on any loan used to acquire employer securities by an ESOP, provided that the ESOP acquires and retains more than 50 percent of the outstanding stock, and provided that voting rights on the stock that is purchased with the loan proceeds are passed through to plan participants. The 50 percent interest exclusion is lost, however, if the ESOP's ownership interest drops below 50 percent during the period of the loan repayment.

If the lender is in a tax-paying position, the tax savings on the interest income should enable the lender to make the loan at a below market rate of interest. Under this provision, the typical interest rate on most ESOP loans has been 85 percent of prime. If the ESOP does not acquire more than 50 percent of the outstanding stock, or if the voting rights are not passed through, the ESOP will have to pay the normal rate of interest rather than the discounted rate (prime rather than 85 percent of prime).

To date, most ESOP loans have been used primarily as a means of facilitating a tax-free rollover transaction. But an ESOP loan can also be used to acquire newly issued stock from the company, to finance a taxable transaction, or to finance a leveraged buyout transaction in which an ESOP acquires part or all of the stock of the acquired company.

DIVIDEND DEDUCTION

The 1984 Tax Reform Act amended § 404 of the Internal Revenue Code to provide for the deductibility of cash dividends paid to an ESOP, provided that the dividends are passed through in cash to plan participants within 90 days of the end of the tax year. In the alternative, the dividends may be paid directly to the participants without first being paid to the plan.

The purpose of the dividend pass-through provision is to provide greater employee incentives by enabling the participants to realize current income from the plan. In many cases, the payment of a cash dividend has had a dramatic effect on employee motivation and incentive. The dividend deduction applies to either common stock dividends or to dividends on convertible preferred stock.

Participants are fully taxable on these payments, and are not eligible for the $100 exclusion of dividend income. The dividend is deductible to the corporation in the taxable year in which the dividend is distributed to the participants. The dividend is deductible, however, only with respect to shares that have been allocated to plan participants.

The 1986 Tax Reform Act further amended § 404 to provide for the deductibility of dividends used to make payments on an ESOP loan. The deduction is allowed in the taxable year of the corporation in which the dividend is used to make loan payments. The dividend is deductible, however, only on the stock that is purchased with the loan proceeds.

This provision is particularly useful in cases where a contribution of 25 percent of eligible payroll (the maximum allowed under § 404(a)(9) of the code) is not sufficient to repay the annual principal payment to the lender. In such cases, the solution may be to pay a deductible dividend, and use the dividend to make up the difference between the contribution amount and the required principal payment. The dividend must, however, be "reasonable."

One disadvantage of both types of dividend payments is that a dividend must be paid to all holders of the same class of stock. Thus, if the founder still holds 70 percent of the outstanding stock, only the portion of the dividend that is paid to the ESOP will be deductible. Similarly, if the ESOP holds stock that was not purchased with the proceeds of a loan, only the dividends paid on the stock bought with loan proceeds will be deductible. A solution to this problem is to recapitalize the corporation so that the ESOP purchases a separate class of dividend-paying stock.

MECHANICS OF TAX-FREE ROLLOVER TRANSACTIONS

Election of tax-free rollover treatment is optional for the seller. The seller may, if he wishes, elect to be taxed on part or all of the proceeds. Assume, for example, that the ESOP purchases 30 percent of the outstanding stock from shareholder A for $1 million, and that shareholder A desires to invest $600,000 in stocks and bonds and $400,000 in real estate. In this case (assuming his basis in the stock is zero), $400,000 of the gain will be taxable, and the remaining $600,000 will be tax-free.

By the same token, it is not necessary for the ESOP to acquire 30 percent ownership if the seller does not desire tax-free rollover treatment. If the seller is willing to pay the tax, he may sell any amount of stock to the ESOP, whether more or less than 30 percent. To the extent that any sale of stock to an ESOP does not qualify for tax-free rollover treatment, the seller will be taxed at favorable capital gains rates. This is a distinct advantage as compared to a partial stock redemption, which is usually taxed as a dividend. Dividend distributions are taxed as ordinary income to the shareholder and as a nondeductible distribution of profits by the company.

In certain instances, a shareholder may wish to take advantage of tax-free rollover treatment, but may not own the requisite 30 percent, or may not want to sell 30 percent by himself. In such cases, it is permissible to aggregate sales from two or more sellers so that the ESOP acquires the requisite 30 percent ownership. Any aggregated sales, however, must occur simultaneously in order to qualify. If, for example, shareholder A sells a 20 percent interest on January 1, and shareholder B sells a 10 percent interest on January 2, shareholder B will be eligible for tax-free rollover, but shareholder A will not.

If shareholder B does not wish to sell any shares, shareholder A could still qualify for tax-free rollover treatment by selling a 20 percent interest and by having the ESOP simultaneously purchase enough treasury stock or newly issued stock to result in 30 percent ownership of outstanding shares by the ESOP. It should also be noted that once the ESOP acquires 30 percent ownership, any subsequent sale of stock to the ESOP will automatically qualify for tax-free rollover treatment.

In order to elect tax-free rollover treatment, a seller must attach a Statement of Election and an Employer Consent form to his personal income tax return. The seller must also execute and have notarized a Statement of Purchase form within 30 days of the purchase of each replacement security. To the extent he has purchased replacement securities prior to filing his personal income tax return for the prior year, he must also attach these Statement of Purchase forms to his income tax returns. To the extent he has not purchased replacement securities by the time of filing of his income tax return, he must attach such Statement of Purchase forms to his next year's income tax return.

A seller may buy and sell securities during the 12-month election period. However, once a seller uses part or all of the sale proceeds to purchase "replacement securities," he cannot later change his mind and designate other securities as the replacement securities.

One additional requirement of the tax-free rollover provision is the requirement that none of the stock acquired by the ESOP in a rollover transaction may be allocated to the seller (or his family) or to anyone who owns (together with his family) more than 25 percent of the outstanding stock of the company. For purposes of this rule, the seller's family includes his spouse, brothers, sisters, ancestors, and lineal descendants. In the case of a 25 percent or more shareholder, the family includes only his spouse, and his children, grandchildren, and parents. Any stock allocated to a participant's account under the ESOP is also counted in determining whether such individual is a 25 percent or more shareholder.

If a seller elects tax-free rollover treatment with respect to part or all of the sale proceeds, then he and his family are not counted as part of the eligible payroll, and are not eligible to receive allocations under the ESOP. By the same token, if a shareholder and his family own 25 percent or more of the outstanding stock at the time of the transaction, or subsequently become a 25 percent or more shareholder (by virtue of his participation in the ESOP or otherwise), then he and his family are no longer eligible to receive allocations under the ESOP. There is an exception, however, for lineal descendants of the seller. Under this exception, the lineal descendants as a group may receive allocations of up to 5 percent of the stock purchased from the seller.

Note that any loss of plan benefits by the seller, or by a 25 percent or more shareholder, or by any related parties can be "made up" simply by adopting a supplementary executive retirement plan (SERP) for the affected parties. Under a SERP, each year the company simply sets aside a number of shares equal to the number of shares the affected individual would have gotten under the ESOP. The company then distributes the cash value of these shares to the affected individual at the same time and in the same manner as he would have otherwise received under the ESOP.

MECHANICS OF ESOP LOAN TRANSACTIONS

Under prior law, it was necessary for the lender to lend directly to the plan. The loan would then be guaranteed and/or collateralized by the company. This type of loan structure frequently complicated the loan documentation. Under the 1984 amendments, this structure is no longer necessary. Under code § 133, the lender may now simply make the loan directly to the company, and the lender will still qualify for the 50 percent interest exclusion, provided that the company loans the money on "substantially similar" terms to the ESOP, and provided that the ESOP uses the money to acquire voting common stock or voting preferred stock of the company. The advantage of this approach is that the lender can use the standard form of loan agreements and collateral agreements that he would use in the case of any corporate loan. In order for the ESOP's loan from the company to be "substantially similar" to the bank's loan to the company, the interest rates must be identical, and the ESOP's loan must be repaid (or forgiven) at least as rapidly as the company's loan is repaid.

It is not always necessary to use an outside lender. If, for example, the company has accumulated funds under a profit-sharing plan, these funds may be rolled over into an ESOP (subject to fiduciary considerations) and used to purchase company stock. In addition, if the company has excess funds, the company may itself be the lender. The company, however, does not qualify for the 50 percent interest exclusion under code § 133. By using one or more of these sources of internal cash, the company may be able to reduce or eliminate the necessity for borrowing from an outside lender.

CASH FLOW INCREASES

As indicated in the following chart, a company can reduce its corporate income taxes and increase its cash flow and net worth simply by issuing treasury stock or newly issued stock to an ESOP in any amount up to 15 percent of eligible annual payroll. Using this approach, a company may drastically reduce or even eliminate its corporate tax liability. The cash flow impact can be dramatic. If the contribution to the ESOP is made in lieu of cash contributions to a profit-sharing plan, the cash flow savings are even more dramatic. Of course, the owners must consider that these contributions of stock will result in some dilution of their ownership interest.

USING AN ESOP TO INCREASE CASH FLOW

Assumptions

Qualified payroll = $2,000,000
Pretax earnings = $500,000
Profit-Sharing Contributions = $300,000 cash
ESOP Contributions = $300,000 of newly issued company stock

Computation—One Year Only

	No Plan	With Profit Sharing	With ESOP
Pretax Earnings	$500,000	$500,000	$500,000
Contribution (15% × $2,000,000)	-0-	300,000	300,000
Adjusted Pretax Earnings	500,000	200,000	200,000
Federal and State Taxes (44%)	220,000	88,000	88,000
After-Tax Earnings	280,000	112,000	112,000
Add-Back Noncash Contribution	-0-	-0-	300,000
Cash Flow and Net Worth Increase	$280,000	$112,000	$412,000

An ESOP can also be used to generate cash flow savings if the company is contemplating a stock redemption. Stock redemptions are nondeductible, but by using an ESOP instead, the stock repurchase can be made with deductible dollars. Moreover, as shown by the following chart, if the ESOP replaces a profit-sharing plan, the cash contributions that would have been made to the profit-sharing plan can be made to the ESOP instead, thereby enabling the plan to purchase the stock without any additional cash flow expense to the company whatsoever.

A STOCK REDEMPTION MAY BE SEVERAL TIMES AS COSTLY AS AN ESOP PURCHASE

Assumptions

Profit-sharing contributions—$100,000 cash—invested in stock market
ESOP contributions—$100,000 cash—used to purchase company stock
Stock redemption—$100,000 per year

Computation—One Year Only

	No Plan	With Profit Sharing	With ESOP
Pretax Earnings	$300,000	$300,000	$300,000
Contribution	-0-	100,000	100,000
Adjusted Pretax Earnings	300,000	200,000	200,000
Federal and State Taxes (44%)	132,000	88,000	88,000
After-Tax Earnings	168,000	112,000	112,000
Stock Redemption	100,000	100,000	-0-
Cash Flow	$ 68,000	$ 12,000	$112,000

MAXIMIZING EMPLOYEE INCENTIVES

From an employee standpoint, the ESOP is almost always a better incentive plan than is a profit-sharing plan. The philosophy of a profit-sharing plan is that if the company make a profit, a portion of this profit will be shared with the employees, and the employees will thereby have an incentive to maximize company profits. In theory, this sounds workable; in practice, it is not. In practice, most companies report that little or no employee incentive or motivation is generated as a result of profit-sharing contributions. The difficulty is that profit-sharing plans are not tangible, and there is no direct link between employee productivity and employee benefits under such a plan.

An ESOP is frequently superior to a profit-sharing plan in the following respects:

- The ESOP creates a direct link between employee benefits and employee productivity. As a consequence, the ESOP is frequently a better employee incentive plan.
- In most cases, employees are not interested in stock market investments, but are interested in owning stock of their own company.
- In many cases, the company's own stock is a much better investment than is the stock market, since smaller firms frequently can maintain a better growth rate than larger firms.

Ideally, the ESOP can provide a better employee incentive plan, a better investment result for the employees, and simultaneously provide a market for the shareholders of the company.

Replacement of Profit-Sharing Plans

Replacement of a profit-sharing plan may be accomplished in either of two ways. One approach is to "amend and restate" the profit-sharing plan as an employee stock ownership plan. If a profit-sharing plan is amended and restated as an ESOP, part or all of the prior funds may be used to purchase employer stock. However, in order to eliminate any risk of fiduciary liability, we strongly recommend that prior profit-sharing funds *not* be used to purchase employer stock, since these funds remain subject to the requirement that they earn a "fair rate of return." A second approach is simply to "replace" the profit-sharing plan with an ESOP. Under this approach, the profit-sharing plan remains as a separate "frozen" plan. The disadvantage of this approach is that the frozen plan must still meet the participation requirements of § 410(a) of the code each year.

Disadvantages

The principal disadvantages and possible problem areas that should be evaluated in considering an ESOP are as follows:

- *Dilution.* If the ESOP is used to finance the company's growth, the cash flow benefits must be weighed against the rate of dilution.
- *Fiduciary liability.* The plan committee members who administer the plan are deemed to be fiduciaries, and thus can be held liable if they knowingly participate in improper transactions. In general, the fiduciary liability under an ESOP is less than under a profit-sharing plan, since the ESOP is primarily invested in employer stock. Under a profit-sharing plan, the fiduciary has a wide range of choice of investments. The fiduciary must, therefore, diversify the investments, and all investments must meet the fair rate of return requirement. An ESOP, on the other hand, is exempt from the

diversification and fair rate of return requirements, since the ESOP is designed to invest in employer stock.

- *Minority shareholders.* The ESOP, in effect, creates an additional shareholder, which is essentially in the same position as a minority shareholder. Thus, the major shareholders can be held liable if they engage in activities that are detrimental to minority shareholders. On the other hand, an ESOP participant does not stand in any preferred status to other minority shareholders.

- *Disclosure.* During their participation in the ESOP, plan participants are *not* entitled to receive annual reports or attend annual shareholder meetings. Upon distribution, however, the employee becomes entitled to receive annual reports and attend shareholder meetings, if he holds the stock rather than selling it back to the ESOP.

- *Valuation.* The stock must be valued annually in order to establish its worth for purposes of purchasing the stock, allocating the stock, and distributing the stock. If the valuation is prepared by a qualified third party, the valuation should be immune from subsequent adjustment. If, however, the stock is overvalued, the consequence depends upon whether the stock was contributed or purchased. If the stock was contributed by the company at an excessive valuation price, the penalty would be a reduction of the deduction that the company had taken for the contribution. If the stock was purchased by the ESOP, the deduction would not be affected, but the seller would be required to pay back the excess purchase price. In addition, under ERISA, the seller is subjected to a 5 percent penalty tax for each year that the stock was overvalued.

- *Liquidity.* If the value of the stock appreciates substantially, the ESOP and/or the company may not have sufficient funds to repurchase stock, upon employees' retirement. In most cases, very little liquidity will be needed in the first five years of the plan, since the employees who terminate in the early years are only partially vested. After the first five years, the ESOP will normally need to keep approximately one-third of the fund in liquid investments (in order to provide liquidity for retiring employees). However, if the stock appreciates dramatically, the liquidity needs will increase correspondingly.

- *Stock performance.* If the value of the company does not increase, the employees may feel that the ESOP is less attractive than a profit-sharing plan. In an extreme case, if the company fails, the employees will lose their benefits to the extent that the ESOP is not diversified in other investments.

- *Pro rata offers.* Any offers to purchase stock on behalf of an ESOP must be made on a pro rata basis to all shareholders. Thus, unless the remaining shareholders agree otherwise, a retiring shareholder, for example, cannot sell his stock without offering other shareholders the opportunity to also sell stock on a pro rata basis. This is the same requirement that applies to corporate stock redemptions.

DESIGNING THE PLAN

An ESOP is a plan qualified by the Internal Revenue Service as an equity-based deferred compensation plan. As such, it is in the same family as profit-sharing plans and stock bonus plans. An ESOP, however, differs from a profit-sharing plan in that it is required to invest primarily in employer securities, while a profit-sharing plan is usually prohibited from investing primarily in employer securities. An ESOP also differs from profit-sharing plans and from stock bonus plans in that an ESOP is permitted and authorized to engage in leveraged purchases of company stock. As a consequence, an ESOP requires different accounting procedures and a different method of allocating stocks and other investments among the employees than other types of plans. For this reason, the plan should be designed by an ESOP specialist in order to avoid IRS difficulties.

If the ESOP is not leveraged, the code allows the company to make tax-deductible contributions of up to 15 percent of eligible payroll. Contributions can be made in any amounts up to 25 percent of payroll if the company has unused contribution carryovers, or if the plan is combined with a money purchase pension plan that provides for a fixed annual contribution of 10 percent of annual payroll. If the ESOP is leveraged (either directly or indirectly), the company is allowed to make tax-deductible contributions of up to 25 percent of eligible payroll to the extent necessary to make principal payments on a loan, assuming that the company does not also contribute to another employee benefit plan. If the company makes a full 25 percent contribution to an ESOP, it would be precluded from making any contributions to another defined contribution plan such as a profit-sharing or 401(k) plan. It should be specifically noted, however, that the interest on any ESOP loan is deductible over and above the 25 percent limit on contributions to pay principal, provided that not more than one-third of the contribution is allocated to the highly compensated employees.

The 25 percent special contribution limit is only applicable to the extent that the contribution is used to pay loan principal on or before the due date for filing the corporate tax return, including extensions. It is not necessary that the loan be obtained, or that the stock be purchased prior to year-end. However, it is necessary that the first principal payment be made prior to the filing of the corporate tax return.

The ESOP, like a profit-sharing plan, must cover all nonunion employees who are at least age 21 and have one year of service. An ESOP may either include or exclude union employees. In practical effect, share ownership under the plan is usually proportionate to the relative salaries of the participants in the plan.

Under the 1986 act, employer contributions must vest under one or the other of the following vesting schedules:

Year 1—0	Year 1—0
Year 2—0	Year 2—0
Year 3—20	Year 3—0
Year 4—40	Year 4—40
Year 5—60	Year 5—100
Year 6—80	
Year 7—100	

An employee is entitled to commence receiving his plan benefit once he has incurred a five-year break in service. Such distribution may, at the option of the company, be paid in a lump sum or in five equal annual installments. Except in the case of death or retirement, if the plan has incurred a loan, distribution need not commence until the loan has been repaid in full.

If the distribution is in a lump sum, it may be rolled over into an IRA. If the distribution is in company stock, and the stock is "put" to the plan in exchange for a promissory note (payable in five equal annual installments of principal), the note can be rolled over into an IRA. If, however, the stock is sold in exchange for a note, the company must post "adequate security" for the note.

Once a participant reaches age 55, he may elect to diversify up to 25 percent of his plan benefit. Once he reaches age 60, he may elect to diversify an additional 25 percent of his plan benefit. The plan must offer at least three investment options. In the alternative, the plan may simply distribute the requisite amount, and the participant may then roll over this amount into an IRA. If the participant has not attained age 59½ and does not roll over his distribution into an IRA, he will be subject to a 10 percent penalty tax in addition to ordinary income taxation.

Distributions from the plan are normally made in cash, unless the participant specifically requests that the distribution be made in stock. Under certain circumstances, the option to take the distribution in stock may be eliminated entirely. If the participant has received the distribution in stock, he must be given a "put" option to the company and to the trust (which guarantees the marketability of the stock for a period of up to 15 months) and a "right of first refusal" (which prohibits him from selling the stock or gifting the stock to any third party).

The plan is administered by a committee established by the directors of the company. *Unless the company elects to qualify the loan for the 50 percent interest exclusion under code § 133, all voting rights are normally exercised by the committee.* However, employees are allowed to vote on any matters involving liquidation, dissolution, recapitalization, merger, or sale of all the assets of the corporation. Thus, voting control of the ESOP may be maintained by the initial shareholders, even after they no longer own 51 percent or more of the company stock. That is, if the original shareholders control the committee, they will be able to control not only the stock they still own, but also the stock owned by the ESOP. As long as the shareholders are careful in appointing the committee members, there need never be a loss of voting control.

SUMMARY

As a result of the 1984 and the 1986 Acts, ESOPs are more attractive than ever. Although they are not for everyone, for those companies that qualify, ESOPs can provide greater financial benefits, both for the owners and for the employees, than most other alternatives.

CHAPTER
THIRTY-ONE

Strategies for Acquiring Troubled Businesses

DENNIS J. WHITE
PARTNER
SULLIVAN AND WORCESTER

GAYLE P. EHRLICH
PARTNER
SULLIVAN AND WORCESTER

Troubled businesses can often present unique acquisition opportunities, with attractive pricing and terms. They can also involve a very different set of challenges, pitfalls, and ground rules from typical mergers and acquisitions.

Without detailed preparation, even experienced M&A practitioners risk unwelcome surprises in the process of buying a troubled business. Such surprises can include the unintended assumption of seller liabilities, the purchase of assets burdened with liens, and the loss of a deal despite a signed purchase and sale agreement. In addition, the timetable for completion of such an acquisition is usually unpredictable at the outset because it is largely driven by the cooperation of the target company and the demands of its creditors and customers.

A prospective purchaser has a number of alternative routes in pursuing the purchase of a troubled business. Some lead inevitably into a bankruptcy courtroom; in other cases, bankruptcy proceedings can be avoided. Whichever route is selected, however, the purchaser must have a basic understanding of where it is headed and the advantages and disadvantages of each alternative in a given deal.

In strategizing about the best approach, the purchaser of a troubled business should consider a number of objectives and their relative importance under the circumstances of the acquisition:

- The value of preserving the goodwill of the target, as well as the means of minimizing the disruption to its business and customers.
- The interim stopgap measures that should be implemented to preserve the quality of operations and to close the deal quickly, if preserving goodwill is important.
- The effect of the passage of time on the value of the target business. Certain deals should be locked up at an early stage to avoid competition from rival bidders; and in other circumstances, it may be advantageous to allow the severity of the financial troubles to fully materialize in order to gain additional leverage over the target.
- The target's assets should be sold free of existing liens, claims, and encumbrances to the extent possible.
- The target's liabilities and disputes with its creditors should be avoided or at least minimized, to the extent possible.

Usually, not all these objectives can be achieved, and the purchaser must make difficult trade-offs in formulating the most realistic strategy. Nevertheless, bargains are available to the buyer who can act quickly and decisively.

BUYING A BUSINESS OUT OF BANKRUPTCY

Businesses in Chapter 11 are often prime targets for acquisition. Because of the protection afforded creditors under the Bankruptcy Code, a company is potentially put "into play" the moment a Chapter 11 petition is filed. Under the Code, when a company enters bankruptcy, it becomes a new legal entity, a debtor that is operated in the first instance for the benefit of its creditors, and only secondarily to preserve the long-term value for its stockholders. Usually, existing management is allowed to continue to operate the business; hence the term "debtor in possession."

However, in certain cases, the court will appoint a neutral party, a trustee, to run the business.

A Chapter 11 case culminates in a plan of reorganization, which provides the terms and conditions of treatment for a creditor's claims and a shareholder's interests. In order to be approved, a plan must generally observe the relative priorities for different classes of interests as set forth in the Bankruptcy Code. Under the Code, the stockholders of a debtor corporation are not entitled to retain their equity interest unless unsecured creditors receive payment in full over time, or a consensual plan of reorganization is agreed to by creditors. Secured creditors are entitled to recover their claim only to the extent the value of the underlying collateral in which they hold a perfected lien supports the claim; if there is a shortfall in collateral coverage, the deficiency is treated as an unsecured claim. The priorities for treatment provided in the Bankruptcy Code are a springboard for negotiating a consensual arrangement under a plan of reorganization. The parties are free to agree to receive alternative treatment, and quite often do.

Valuation is a pivotal issue in bankruptcy proceedings. The various creditor and shareholder groups typically assign and endeavor to persuade each other and the bankruptcy court of widely disparate values for the debtor's business in order to promote their own self-interests. For example, secured creditors interested in a quick liquidation of the debtor's assets to satisfy the debtor's collateralized debt will often urge a liquidation methodology for valuation purposes. Depending on the debt structure and value of the assets, junior secured and unsecured creditors may join the senior secured creditors in an effort at promoting a quick, albeit reduced, return rather than bearing the risks of payment over time. Equityholders will almost always urge a going-concern valuation projected over a 5- to 10-year period. The particular valuation methodology utilized will greatly influence the ultimate sales price. Valuation litigation is expensive and time-consuming. Direct negotiations with the various creditor and equity groups can help reduce litigation costs and provide a sponsor for a purchase offer in the event the debtor is unreceptive.

A bankruptcy court sale must be noticed and approved in a public forum. The process is overseen by a bankruptcy judge whose charge is to maintain a somewhat level playing field for all interested purchasers in order to assure the receipt of at least fair value and prompt competitive bidding. The bankruptcy court approves the successful offer based on a variety of criteria, including the best interests of the creditors and stockholders, the community's interest in maintaining employment for its residents, and the tax revenue of a going-concern enterprise. If a sale will yield sufficient proceeds for distribution to unsecured creditors, the recommendation of the unsecured creditors committee will weigh heavily with the judge. Unsecured creditors will usually be interested in receiving the greatest and highest return, but they may also desire to assure the continued existence of a customer.

Perhaps the most significant benefit to a purchaser in buying assets out of bankruptcy is that the assets can often be acquired free and clear of all liens and claims, which instead attach to the sale proceeds. The bankruptcy court will typically issue an order authorizing the sale and making findings of fact, including a finding that the assets are sold free and clear of all liens and claims, and that the purchaser has acted in good faith. As a practical matter, the ability to appeal such an order by the court successfully is limited.

It is virtually impossible to "lock up" a deal in bankruptcy court before the judge's final order. The court will usually provide for a competitive bidding process culminating in an auction, notice of which will be widely published in the trade and business press, as well as sent directly to likely prospects. Alternatively, the bankruptcy court may hear expert testimony as to the assets' value, and hear evidence of efforts to generate competing offers. A prospective purchaser can spend a significant amount of time and money in due diligence, exploration of terms, even in negotiation and execution of a purchase and sale agreement, only to have the court not approve the sale. Certain precautions may minimize lost expenses, such as including in the purchase agreement a minimum over-bid threshold, expense reimbursement covenants, and similar terms. However, such terms are subject to court approval, and consequently there can be no assurance against becoming an out-of-pocket stalking horse offeror.

Procedurally, an acquisition of a Chapter 11 debtor's business through a bankruptcy sale can be made in two ways: either upon motion to the court or through confirmation of a Chapter 11 reorganization plan. The motion route is quicker, being achievable in as little as 30 to 45 days. The bankruptcy court, however, is not likely to be receptive to a quick sale of a substantial portion of a debtor's business, unless it is convinced the business is a wasting asset (the inventory will spoil, the customers will go elsewhere, and the like). If the sale involves substantially all the assets of the debtor, then in most instances it will be approved as part of a plan of reorganization, which usually takes significantly longer. One way to speed plan approval is for the target to file the plan at the very commencement of the case with preapproval by the creditors. Such a prepackaged plan, if fair, will usually be welcomed by the bankruptcy judge.

A purchase through a plan of reorganization can be accomplished either consensually with debtor's management or through competing plans proposed by the various interested parties such as a secured creditor, bondholders or unsecured creditors committee. Generally, the debtor's management has the exclusive right to propose a plan of reorganization for the first 120 days, subject to a court-approved extension. Only a debtor, creditor, or stockholder may propose a plan. In order to gain standing to propose a plan, an interested purchaser may sometimes buy existing creditors' claims.

BUYING ASSETS OUTSIDE OF BANKRUPTCY

An asset acquisition outside of bankruptcy may be accomplished in three ways:

From an assignee or trustee after an assignment for the benefit of creditors;

From the troubled company directly;

Through a foreclosure sale conducted by a secured lender.

In an assignment for the benefit of creditors, an assignee (some neutral party) takes title to the assets for the benefit of all creditors, then liquidates the assets and pays the creditors in the order of their priority. The acquiror is therefore purchasing the assets from the assignee, who works for the creditors, not the troubled company. In a negotiated purchase from a troubled company or an assignee, however, the purchaser does not receive any relief from creditors' security interests or other liens. The assets remain subject to any existing liens unless releases are negotiated with individual secured creditors, with the result that there is a continuing risk of an involuntary bankruptcy filing by creditors. Certain bankruptcy safeguards can be included within the terms and conditions of an acquisition from an assignee or target company. For example, the purchase can be conditioned upon receipt of releases from the same number of creditors representing the same dollar amount of claims necessary to confirm a plan of reorganization in a Chapter 11 proceeding (a majority in number and two-thirds in amount by class).

Purchasers may also require that a certain portion of the purchase price be placed in escrow pending the passage of time, or the occurrence of certain events, or both. Provided that the funds do not pass through the assignee's or target company's hands and the escrow expressly provides that the funds are an asset of the purchaser, then the escrow arrangement should successfully protect the purchaser from a preference challenge in the event a bankruptcy case is filed within 90 days following distribution of the funds from escrow (90 days is the preference look-back period for noninsiders). Likewise, a purchaser could hold back a portion of the purchase price or have the target post a letter of credit. The target may correctly claim that the funds are immediately necessary in order to stave off creditors and trigger an involuntary bankruptcy proceeding. If the sale cannot be accomplished at a satisfactory price and comfort level outside of bankruptcy, then it may be advisable to proceed with a bankruptcy court sale.

In completing a purchase of a substantial portion of a troubled company's assets outside the ordinary course whose principal business involves the sale or rental of merchandise from stock, it is necessary to comply with the Bulk Sales Act as provided under Article 6 of the Uniform Commercial Code (*UCC*); otherwise, the transfer is ineffective as to the target's creditors. There are exceptions to the Bulk Sales Act, which include sales pursuant to judicial proceedings, assignments for the benefit of all creditors, and transfers to a new business assuming the debt of the target. The requirements for complying with the Bulk Sales Act are procedural in nature and should be scrutinized before proceeding, particularly since the act varies somewhat from jurisdiction to jurisdiction. In general terms, the bulk sales law requires notice of the sale to all creditors of the target 10 days prior to the transfer. Those creditors receiving notice have a period of six months from receipt of notice in which to commence legal proceedings.

Alternatively, the assets of a troubled company, including its stock, can be acquired through a foreclosure sale conducted by a senior secured creditor under Article 9 of the UCC. Here the acquiror is able to purchase assets free and clear of all subordinated liens. A UCC foreclosure sale of personal property can be accomplished in a private sale context with as little as 10 days notice to a nonconsenting troubled company and junior secured creditors, or earlier, if the troubled company and junior secured creditors consent. Even a public UCC foreclosure sale can be accomplished in as little as a few weeks.

A purchase through a foreclosure sale is only possible where there is a cooperative secured creditor who has a senior or validly perfected lien in the debtor's assets. Secured creditors may be hesitant to proceed with a foreclosure sale structured to allow a previously negotiated transaction to proceed. It is important that the foreclosure sale be conducted in a commercially reasonable manner and that there be current appraisals that justify the value. There is no means of preventing the troubled company from filing a petition under the Bankruptcy Code prior to sale. Likewise, there is a continuing risk that the company will subsequently be placed in an involuntary bankruptcy proceeding and the sale challenged as a fraudulent transfer—that is, a transfer for less than fair value. The statute of limitations for fraudulent transfer challenges can be six years or longer. Under these circumstances, the preferable alternatives may be negotiating individual consents from other creditors or a bankruptcy filing.

Whichever approach is followed, it is usually difficult, if not impossible, to obtain meaningful representations and warranties with respect to the purchased assets since there is usually no financially responsible party to stand behind them. Because of this, due diligence is critical in connection with the acquisition of a troubled company. However, the time limitations and operating difficulties that often plague troubled companies make due diligence particularly difficult.

Antitrust laws are operative in acquisitions of troubled businesses both in and out of bankruptcy. The Bankruptcy Code provides for an accelerated review period of 10 days under the notification statutes. There is no similar accelerated period for the review of acquisitions of troubled businesses outside of a bankruptcy case.

Certain liabilities of the target company, whether the acquisition is completed inside or outside of a bankruptcy proceeding, may prove unavoidable regardless of how the acquisition is structured. For example, if the buyer continues a product line, it may become liable for past product liability exposure under the successor company doctrine. Similarly, if the buyer operates in the same premises, it may, depending on the circumstances, become liable for existing, but undiscovered environmental problems that later surface. Successor liability resulting from ERISA or the tax laws may also be unavoidable.

The attractive sale prices and unique opportunities associated with buying troubled businesses are indeed appealing. The returns involved in several high-profile turnaround acquisitions have been impressive. Such rewards, however, are only available to those who are willing to risk an up-front investment of time and money and who are well tutored or advised in the intricacies of the process.

CHAPTER
THIRTY-TWO

Managing the
Business—and Yourself

JAMES J. BLAHA
PRINCIPAL
BAC, INC.

Peter Drucker in *MANAGEMENT—Tasks*Responsibilities*Practices* wrote "Management . . . is a discipline, or at least is capable of becoming one. It is not just common sense. It is not just codified experience. It is at least potentially an organized body of knowledge."

The focus of this chapter is on knowing and managing yourself, your business, and current disciplines of management fundamentals. It is directed at the intermediary and M&A firms, but will be meaningful to buyers, sellers, and other professionals associated with M&A.

TIME MANAGEMENT

One of the biggest challenges in M&A work is how to spend your time. Since much of our work is contingent upon success fees, this is probably the most important decision you make each day. Managing yourself is the hardest part of time management.

Time is a human concept. Time was once dictated by nature; the worker got up when the sun did, and worked until the task was finished, not until a clock told him to stop. Then Ben Franklin admonished "Time is money" and we never got over it. Today, the pace is speeding up. We expect eyeglasses in an hour and food that can be microwaved. Even 15 years ago, when we received a letter, we could reflect on a response. Now when our faxes and e-mail arrive, we are expected to react immediately!

Time management programs are a lot like diet books. We start with great expectations, but falter along the way. In the college class I teach on time management, I see students exit with newfound confidence that they *can* take charge of their workload. Then, when they face the first crisis with a high-pressure deadline, they revert to their old habits. They come back to class and tell me that they have failed.

We are all too hard on ourselves. Psychologists tell us it takes at least two to three months to break a habit. If you are missing deadlines in the office, and you find yourself trying to jam too much into the weekend, understanding time management can pay off in a big way.

I am not going to list tips on time management—all of which you can find elsewhere. However, I work with a lot of company presidents and CEOs, and observe how successful people handle responsibilities. Consequently, I have come to the conclusion that *attitude* is far more important than *technique*.

The most effective managers rarely appear to be harried or rushed. They may be intense and highly focused, but their pace is not dictated by the clock. Their desks may be neat or appear to be chaotic. Successful people know *where the company is going and how it is going to get there*. All their work is directed toward that goal. They know what to react to, what to delegate, and what to ignore.

That doesn't mean that they don't put in 15-hour-days when there is a push or crisis, but they space that work with periods for gaining perspective. At my office, executives often close their doors after lunch and take a 20-minute break. Those 20 minutes can cancel out the "never-was-a-good-idea-after-3:00" syndrome. But my students protest, "That's fine for someone at a top level. I march to someone else's drum. I've got work that I must accomplish according to someone else's timetable."

Here's where attitude comes in. You are still in charge of your head. Try to take a brief break, take a couple of deep breaths, or vary your pace in some fashion. Those few minutes will energize you to do the job more effectively and efficiently. Try it.

LEADERSHIP/PEOPLE SKILLS

Managers do things right while leaders do the right things. Previously, I cited the successful person's philosophy of knowing where the company is going and how it is going to get there. This is where management really proves itself. You must influence others to support these goals. The ability to hire/fire/promote is a powerful weapon but in itself will not assure quality performance.

Much is written about leadership skills. *Employee empowerment* is considered one of the most effective tactics used today. It gives individuals responsibility at a fairly low level. The often-cited example of Ford allowing any worker on the Taurus assembly line to shut it down propelled its quality control to the top of the ratings.

But sharing power has to be carefully planned. Start with smaller responsibilities, build on that success, and move forward. Resist the temptation to find fault. When mistakes are made, correct what is necessary, focusing on the problem, not the person. There is little initiative in an office in which an employee risks being humiliated over an error.

Your staff's success enhances your own productivity. The goal should be to hire good people, give them the training and tools they need, and then get out of their way. We spend more time with our co-workers and colleagues than we do with our own families. We need to convey our sincere caring, particularly when they are experiencing personal problems, without invading their privacy or creating an unprofessional relationship. A thoughtful inquiry on the health of an aged parent or on a child's schooling can mean a lot.

"People sense" is a must in our business. Some of the best opportunities in M&A today lie with the privately held companies in which entrepreneurs who built them are ready to sell. They probably started their companies in the garage or basement, sweated making the payroll, coped with competition and government regulations, and now have to give up their "babies." It's much like marrying off children.

My company, BAC, was handling such a company in Kansas on an exclusive basis. It was highly profitable, with an exciting new patented product just coming on the market. The strategic buyers we had carefully screened were salivating over it. The owner felt he lacked the energy or resources to give it the marketing push it deserved.

The town was so small that the presence of strangers lunching with the company president in the local restaurant would have provoked too much speculation, so whenever a potential buyer visited, the president's wife graciously provided an elaborate luncheon in her home. The meal reflected a great deal of time and work.

Several companies competed aggressively, and ultimately, their final offers were very close. The turning point came when one of the potential buyers sent the seller's wife a thoughtful thank-you note for the luncheon, and commented on her hobby of quilt-making. As soon as the note arrived, the seller called to tell us. The deal tilted toward this buyer and was signed a few months later. The act of writing a note to his wife told the seller more about the successful buyer's philosophy than any brochure possibly could. It suggested the quality of his future relationship with employees and the town. We keep in touch with our sellers and are happy to report that the "marriage" has been a very profitable and compatible one for all concerned.

Another example did not have such a satisfying ending: A very high-powered husband-and-wife team, both of whom had come out of large investment banking firms, decided to buy companies. They had been married very recently. They were planning to visit a business we were handling on an exclusive basis. The seller inherited the company and proceeded to run it into the ground, due in part to his drinking problem., His self-esteem was at an all-time low, and we explained to the potential buyers that a great deal of sensitivity was needed.

The woman demanded scornfully, "What has sensitivity got to do with business?" We looked at her and realized that there was no point to try to answer her question. The dynamic duo later cornered the seller, browbeat, and humiliated him, and were later surprised when he refused their offer. Maybe they were successful in investment banking but they were real amateurs in M&A.

CREATIVITY

Creativity was once the province of ad agencies and R&D centers. Today, many people are working harder, not to get ahead but just to keep up. Problems are complex and that's-the-way-we've-always-done-it won't cut it. Allow your foolish side to come out. Be a hunter or a revolutionary. The difference between the mentality of a corporate person versus an entrepreneur is that the latter says "Ready, fire, aim!" Don't be afraid to at least flirt with an idea and later discard it.

In M&A work, recasting book value, cash flow, sales and margins, and checking out appraisals and environmental audits are still the meat-and-potatoes of our work. We can't do a deal without these facts, but we often need to bring new perspectives to the table to close the deal.

We needed all the creativity we could muster in the sale of a California division of a major company. The deal was at an impasse; three key people had tried to buy the company but were prohibited by company policy. They were bitter, the buyer was concerned and the seller saw his sale slipping away. If these three men left, it would be a serious loss to the company.

A "hostage agreement" was the answer. The seller agreed that the management team was a major asset. In a confidential clause, we put a price on the heads of each of the three key people, stipulating that if any jumped ship during the first year, the sum would be deducted from the purchase price. (The contract included a payout over a three-year period.) We identified the problem and then tried to consider all the possible solutions. All three stayed, but it is unlikely the deal would have been signed without this agreement.

Creative people draw up drafts with broad general ideas and avoid getting bogged down in minor details. When you agree on the concept, you polish only the ideas that are going to be used. There's no need to "gift wrap the garbage"; that is, allocate more time to a job than it is worth.

Workaholics are seldom creative. Every office has marathon work periods when a project must be completed, but if you find yourself constantly working weekends and taking work home at night, back off. Workaholics tend to be perfectionists and go stale on problem-solving. Don't lose your perspective.

CRISIS MANAGEMENT

Creativity comes to the fore most significantly during *crisis management*. Few businesses today escape serious challenges. When it's announced that the government is investigating your buyer, your seller's biggest customer just went into Chapter 11, or the media is reporting an incomplete and inaccurate story of your client's business practices, you have a crisis.

Restructuring and downsizing are among the more visible crises management situations today. Turnaround operations are considered a special case of crisis management. Contingency planning is a basic requirement for an M&A firm.

The problem-solving fundamentals that we learned long ago still apply here:

1. Define the problem.
2. Look for creative options.
3. Choose one.
4. Develop a plan of action and implement it.
5. Evaluate the results.

Resist panic. Don't waste time on blame—there's probably enough of it to go around already. Your group will look to you for emotional support. Be positive but don't minimize the problem. Avoid what-if disaster thinking. Beware of the quick-fix solution.

Our first point in this chapter dealt with *attitude* that enables you to focus on company goals, not day-to-day operations. Next we pointed up *creativity* to help solve problems and make better use of time. If you can bring these two principles to *crisis management,* you have a good chance of working your way out of it. Remember, Murphy's Law is a law.

NEGOTIATIONS

We all negotiate every day: You and your spouse discuss if you are going to the ball game or ballet; you point out the benefits of the software that you like and the pitfalls of the other package under consideration; management teams strive to agree on goals for the coming year.

It is important to distinguish between *collaborative* and *competitive* approaches to negotiation. The former aims at gaining one's fair share without sacrificing the rights of the other side (win/win). The competitive approach emphasizes win/lose, and maximizes gains for one's own side, even if deceit, trickery, and manipulation are involved. The question of ethics comes strongly into play.

In M&A work, whether you are representing the buyer or seller, you have to keep switching hats to tune in to their viewpoints. As each issue comes up, both the buyer and seller are saying "What's in it for me?"

At BAC, we say "We represent the deal." You can bargain for either the buyer or seller, but if either decides to pick up his or her marbles and go home, it's all over. It's important to keep the deal as a goal and do whatever is necessary to keep moving toward it.

Students say "But when do you quit? At what point do you decide to walk away from the deal?" This is when M&A becomes an art. We've seen companies chase a deal when it made no business sense at all. The acquisition became nothing but a "tar baby" to the new buyer.

But we also remember a buyer who hung in, negotiating on a specialized machine business in the 1980s. He and the seller had agreed on $7 million as the price, and the date was set for closing. At the last minute, the buyer's financing source backed out. The seller was furious and refused any extension without another $1 million added to the purchase price and $250,000 in earnest money. If the deal fell through, the buyer would forfeit the deposit. The buyer suffered a number of sleepless nights but did complete the transaction.

In 1995, the buyer and his partner shared a dividend of $12 million. (Yes, we said $12 million!) The buyer took a calculated risk and it paid off.

Tension and stress are inevitable when there is a lot of money on the table. Abraham Lincoln often used humor to defuse a situation when he sensed his cabinet was locking itself into rigid positions. He would tell a story, clear the air, everyone would relax a bit, and then go back to the subject.

When BAC handled the sale of a paper company, the buyer wanted to compromise our fee. After a good deal of conversation that went nowhere, we agreed on a telephone conference on Tuesday at 10:00 A.M. before resorting to litigation. Feelings were running high on both sides.

At the appointed time, we explained very soberly that we had four requirements. Our first demand was "two gross of yellow-ruled pads."

There was silence at the other end for a moment, and the buyer responded very seriously, "You're listing these in order of importance, of course."

"Of course," we assured him.

He burst into laughter, and we continued and reached an agreement. But the little bit of humor took the hard edge off the tension.

It's been our experience that deals fall apart more over minor points than major one. Separate the people from the problem. We were well into due diligence on a company when one of the buyer's young CPAs pointed out that the owner's Mercedes was on the books, and therefore was part of the deal.

The seller flushed. "The hell it is. That's my car!" He folded his arms.

We quickly intervened and acknowledged that, as part of the deal, it had been agreed earlier that the car remained with the seller.

The young CPA was correct in his balance sheet debits and credits but inexperienced in negotiations. A multimillion dollar deal almost died over a $50,000 item.

The buyer and seller must work together after the deal is closed, at least for a transitional period. Experienced buyers understand this and avoid letting negotiations slide into explosive confrontations. A Connecticut corporation told us that after reaching an agreement with the seller, their acquisition team adds a bonus, such as a seat on the board. It sets the tone for future relations.

CAREER SELF-SABOTAGE

Career self-sabotage is often overlooked in the self-help books on business. We see it manifest in a blowup with the boss, or when people become so tense they cannot effectively present their work. If you disagree, a well-reasoned presentation that focuses on the issue will usually get a good hearing. In contrast, a confrontational attack on a superior marks an employee as a hothead who cannot, or will not, control his or her behavior. The employee has put the supervisor in the position of losing face if the employee's idea is accepted.

Harry and Joe, two brokers in a midwestern M&A firm, continually failed to follow company procedures. After repeated warnings, both were terminated the same day. Joe stormed out of his boss's office, slammed doors, dumped the contents of his desk into boxes with much huffing and puffing, and stomped out.

Harry quietly asked if he might use his office for a few days longer to tie up some loose ends, cordially shook hands when he finally did leave, and maintained contact with his old boss. The inevitable time came when both had to submit their previous employer as a reference. Which one got the better recommendation?

This kind of a loser life script reinforces feelings of failure. The self-defeating personality swings between self-blame and blaming others for problems. If someone else caused all the difficulties, the loser avoids responsibility for them, but even more important, feels helpless to solve or change the situation. When people no longer feel they are in control of their lives, their frustration mounts. *Failure to accept responsibility for yourself is a significant contributor to career self-sabotage.*

This vicious cycle can be changed. Office problems are usually life problems, and this pattern is probably repeated in the employee's personal relationships. While most of us are smart enough not to tell off our boss or a client, negative patterns impact our job performance from time to time. We all have been known to shoot ourselves in the foot. Remember that the intermediary's role is to keep the buyer and seller from shooting themselves in the foot as well, and hence kill the deal.

If you aren't satisfied with your performance, try to analyze the situation. Mentally rewrite the script. How else could you have handled it? If you had acted differently, what would likely have been the response? Plenty of self-help books are available on self-esteem and positive self-image. Know yourself. Learn to be your own best friend.

BUSINESS ETHICS

Is the term "business ethics" an oxymoron? The legal versus the ethical, the letter versus the spirit of the law, the action versus the consequences ("I didn't inhale") . . . the controversy rages on.

In M&A, fees are substantial. The intermediary is privy to much confidential information. When hundreds of thousands of dollars are at stake, it's easy to say, "I didn't make the rules, I just play by them."

We aren't going to get into a philosophical discussion of ethics, but rather consider the pragmatic aspects of running a business. Perhaps the test developed by the Center for Business Ethics at Bentley College in Waltham, Massachusetts, puts it in perspective:

Is it right?
Is it fair?
Who gets hurt?
Would you be comfortable if the details of the decision were made public?
Would you tell your child or young relative to do it?
How does it smell?

At the risk of sounding simplistic, BAC's 28 years in the M&A field has taught us that the maxim "Honesty is the best policy" still stands. Honesty is just good business.

Good businesspeople don't have to relax their standards to be successful. A very wealthy retainer client who had previously bought one company through us was meeting a prospective seller at lunch. The financials on the company for sale looked good, and our client was very interested. In an expansive mood, the seller bragged that he had an "inside track" with his customers, implying that there were under-the-table payoffs.

From a practical standpoint, the meeting was all over. We made a graceful exit, and on the drive back, our client never referred to it. He didn't have to. We had worked with him long enough to know that he would not become involved in a shady deal at any price. If the seller was devious in one area, he was probably covering up other irregularities as well.

Our client knew it could be very expensive to be unethical. A company is usually a reflection of its management. When employees see materials for the boss's new swimming pool charged to plant maintenance, or fudging on insurance claims, they see these practices as a license to cut corners too.

Employees have both the time and opportunity to figure out how to get around the system. It can range from major embezzlement to padding expense accounts. This kind of moral decay can happen anywhere, but is far more prevalent in a climate in which questionable business practices are the norm.

The business community is incredibly small. News travels through the network very fast. Most of our work comes through referrals. Any short-term gain in cutting corners is going to be offset by the longer-term reputation that will stick. Ideally, market forces will compel a firm and individuals to behave ethically.

ENTREPRENEURS/INTRAPRENEURS

From a dollars-and-sense standpoint, statistics tell us that the greatest gains in productivity are coming from small companies, not the Fortune 500, long the backbone of our economy. The old "economies of scale" don't hold true any longer. To survive in the '90s and beyond, we have to address the problem of individual creativity and productivity within a business.

Many large companies are creating small businesses within their corporate structure, or "intrapreneuring." They allow selected employees to innovate new products, and run their section as a stand-alone operation without traditional constraints. Obviously, the project must be compatible with the corporate culture. General Motors is not likely to authorize an entrepreneurial effort in the greeting card business. But these entrepreneurial zones are allowed to operate independently, and yes, even to fail. It differs from the typical inventor who usually engineers the product, whereby the entrepreneur handles the creation of the product as well as the marketing/distribution.

Many plays and books have been written about the frustration of the corporate culture and the pressure for conformity. We read constantly about executives who chuck it all and buy the fishing boat in the Caribbean or pursue other dreams.

To leave the corporate cocoon with its security and benefits to run your own business is not easy. Yet a corporate executive whom BAC helped to buy his own printing firm reported, "I haven't had this much fun since my first job out of college. For me, it was the right decision."

Downsizing and reengineering brings us a new breed of entrepreneur. We see talented executives accustomed to bottom-line responsibility for major divisions who find themselves without a ship. Many have difficulty finding jobs in their former salary range. Others are no longer interested in working as an employee. They are ready to run their own show, and thus ask BAC to find a company for them to buy/run.

BAC's Business Partner Program grew out of this need. It enables a qualified individual to become President/COO of a profitable business with a significant equity position. BAC matches Business Partners with a company appropriate for their backgrounds. The businesses, primarily in manufacturing and distribution, have real growth potential. The Business Partner runs the day-to-day operation with BAC participating only at the board level.

A transaction under this program in 1994 was a divestiture of a big board corporation that makes special carbide-grooving tools. The Business Partner and BAC have just closed a second deal with an Indiana company whose products complement and can be distributed with those of the first company. Each company will operate as a stand-alone, retaining its name and key management. The marketing synergy and purchasing economies will be a real boost to both businesses. We plan to continue adding strategic acquisitions.

Another Business Partner company was purchased from an elderly man ready for retirement. It manufactures precision screw machine products. Our business partner is presently negotiating for two more companies whose specialized equipment would enhance the capacity of his present shop.

These completed transactions have been highly successful, with the new entrepreneurs increasing profits and enjoying their new roles. They have the fun of running their own shows but have the backup of BAC and its contacts if support is needed.

Running a small company can be more difficult than managing a larger firm. The new COOs must wear many hats. They must cope with serious problems without the resources of a large corporation. Helpful business tools such as sophisticated marketing studies are unaffordable. Therefore, we usually encourage potential business partners to look for larger businesses than outlined in their original acquisition criteria. Currently, most banks are willing to work with us.

Corporate cultures change and the Business Partner Program appears to be one whose time has come. No one predicted that the tradition that saw our fathers join a firm and retire 40 years later would vanish. What will the millennium bring in the world of M&A? None of us knows, but we know change will continue and we will have to change, too, to keep up.

Much of our approach to management follows the Socratic method, the art of asking the simple and devastating question: "What exactly are you trying to do?" and more important, "Why?"

Knowing and managing yourself is still the basic ingredient of success. We are very optimistic about the future, and believe that the opportunities for the individual who is prepared are unlimited. Whether you are the buyer, seller, intermediary, or other related professional in an M&A transaction, the tools will change but the philosophy from the song in *Casablanca* will stand: "The fundamental things of life apply as time goes by."

EPILOGUE: This article evolved from a college class I teach at Northwood University on Contemporary Applied Management. Later, I condensed the material to a one-day seminar on management and M&A, currently a one-day educational course as part of the Certified Business Intermediary certification (CBI). This CBI program is sponsored by International Business Broker Association (IBBA) and the M&A Source.

Index